"This book is a must read for anyone preparing for pastoral ministry or currently in ministry. Highly readable, it seeks to reclaim a pastoral identity that is rooted in the divine action of a ministering God. Building on the work of Charles Taylor, Root first lays out the historical evolution of the current hollowing out of pastoral identity through an excellent exploration of six pastors from Augustine to Rick Warren. Then, turning to Foucault, Jenson, and Old Testament texts, Root boldly asserts the identity of God as one who ministers to his people. Root encourages pastors to reclaim an identity based on their participation in God's acts of ministry. It is in these very acts of ministry that a window is opened to the transcendent and ministering God in a secular age."

—**Annette Brownlee**, Wycliffe College, University of Toronto

"In a world longing for enchantment but too cynical to accept it, pastors can understandably feel irrelevant and confused. In *The Pastor in a Secular Age*, Andrew Root provides a helpful overview of how our world became so disenchanted and what it might look like to attend to God in a world that has forgotten how to do so. As a spiritual director, I continually encounter people who are longing to sacralize their lives and who desperately need help learning to find God in the events and emptiness of life. Root harks back to the holy event of God's presence and asks us to consider the power of a ministry that can both sit in the silence of emptiness and point to the sacred in wonder."

—**Danielle Shroyer**, spiritual director and author

"Andrew Root's *The Pastor in a Secular Age* is an inspiring read and a wonderful resource for ministers and others who care about the role of the church and the vocation of ministry today. As institutional churches and denominations in the West continue a steady decline of social influence, ministers face a crisis of identity. This work situates and explains that feeling of crisis, and articulates a powerful vision for recapturing a sense of ministry as the conduit of God's presence, of divine action, in the world. Drawing from his in-depth understanding of Charles Taylor's philosophical insight, and utilizing case studies of pastors from history and the present, Root offers a compelling portrait of a fresh and invigorating way to approach the vocation of ministry. This is a timely and significant resource for churches, seminaries, and pastors, a vision for ministering in the immanent frame."

—**Kyle Roberts**, United Theological Seminary of the Twin Cities

# the
# pastor
# in a secular age

Ministry in a Secular Age previous titles:

*Faith Formation in a Secular Age: Responding to the Church's Obsession with Youthfulness*

# the
# pastor
# in a secular age

Ministry to People Who No Longer Need a God

MINISTRY IN A SECULAR AGE,
VOLUME TWO

# Andrew Root

**Baker Academic**

*a division of Baker Publishing Group*
Grand Rapids, Michigan

© 2019 by Andrew Root

Published by Baker Academic
a division of Baker Publishing Group
PO Box 6287, Grand Rapids, MI 49516-6287
www.bakeracademic.com

Printed in the United States of America

Library of Congress Cataloging-in-Publication Data
Names: Root, Andrew, 1974– author.
Title: The pastor in a secular age : ministry to people who no longer need a God / Andrew Root.
Description: Grand Rapids : Baker Publishing Group, 2019. | Series: Ministry in a secular age ; VOLUME 2 | Includes index.
Identifiers: LCCN 2018043311 | ISBN 9780801098475 (pbk. : alk. paper)
Subjects: LCSH: Pastoral theology. | Non-church-affiliated people. | Christianity and culture. | Christianity—21st century.
Classification: LCC BV4011.3 .R659 2019 | DDC 253—dc23
LC record available at https://lccn.loc.gov/2018043311

ISBN: 978-1-5409-6208-9 (casebound)

In keeping with biblical principles of creation stewardship, Baker Publishing Group advocates the responsible use of our natural resources. As a member of the Green Press Initiative, our company uses recycled paper when possible. The text paper of this book is composed in part of post-consumer waste.

19  20  21  22  23  24  25        7  6  5  4  3  2  1

green press
INITIATIVE

To Mike King,
the best example I know of a leader who seeks
the action of the living God in and through ministry,
with gratitude for your friendship, support, and encouragement

# contents

**Part 2:   The God Who Is a Ministering Pastor**

# preface

The summer before my senior year in high school, I saw *Terminator 2* at least twenty times. You know the movie: the one when bad-guy Arnold Schwarzenegger becomes good-guy cyborg, now reprogrammed not to kill John Connor but to protect him. Yet, to say I *saw* the movie isn't really right. Rather, it was on in the background, running on a huge screen, while I hung out with my friends. That summer, like 1950s teenagers transported to the early 1990s, we hung out at the drive-in movie theater. My friends smoked cigarettes and drank warm beer while I tried, with epic failure, to find a summer romance. I'd never seen the original *Terminator*, but that had no impact on my following and enjoying *T2*. When I finally did watch the original, I had a much better grasp on the narrative that made *T2* run; but watching *T1* before *T2* didn't seem necessary, even with the gaps filled in.

This book you're holding is volume 2. Braving hubris, I'd say it is a little bit like the early *Terminator* franchise. No, there are no "I'll be backs" or liquefying robots. But it does continue with a story about our changed world, about the rupture with which we in the church have not yet wrestled enough. This volume particularly explores how our secular age has impacted the identity and practice of the pastor. It does this, like the movies, by playing with history and time.

Yet, most importantly for this preface and most like the *Terminator* movies, you don't need to have read volume 1 (*Faith Formation in a Secular Age*) to find your way through volume 2. This book you're holding can stand alone. And if you're a busy pastor, my advice would be to read this book first before moving backward, like I did in the early '90s with the *Terminator* franchise, to volume 1.

That said, this book does continue the task laid out in volume 1. That task was both a descriptive and constructive one. Like volume 1, this book delves headlong into a discussion with Charles Taylor's *A Secular Age*. This time I show how the secular age challenges and shifts the identity and practice of pastors. If you're looking just for a dialogue with Taylor, then part 1 may be as far as you need to go. If you're coming to this book looking for theological discussion, then all the storytelling, historical examples, and philosophical genealogy may be worth skipping. In the end, however, I think these parts work best together, though like volume 1, the descriptive focus in part 1 of this volume will make part 2 feel a little like a different book. But in my mind this is necessary, for the story I sketch in part 1 is to show why distinct theological assertions about divine action are difficult, forcing me to take up this challenge in part 2.

So in part 1 of this book, I tell this story, like Taylor, by using history. I'll offer you the tale of six different pastors, stretching from the fourth to the twenty-first century. Before going any further I need to be clear on why I'm using the story of *these* pastors and not others. I'm using them because they have been the elites. By elite I do *not* mean the best, brightest, or even most important. I think all six are flawed. By elite I mean they have directly impacted our imagination (our imaginary). Their works and ideas have shifted the ways many of us conceive of a pastor. I draw on them *not* because they are the best pastors, or even most representative (they are not), but because in their lives they moved us closer and closer to our now secular age, adding to what I call below a pastoral malaise. Using them this way, I ask you to read them as archetypes. They all, in their own way, are exaggerations that tell us something about how pastoral identity has changed.

As I've said, the point of this story is to show that this pastoral malaise has its center in our struggle to speak of divine action. It therefore wrestles with how this age radically changes the conditions of belief for the people the pastor serves. If I've done my job well in part 1, you'll feel slightly overwhelmed, wondering what the point of being a pastor can be in a secular age. But that leads me to say something else clearly before going any further: I believe that pastors have deep significance. These may be hard times for pastors, but God still speaks through and uses pastors. And this is so because God is still faithfully acting in the world, and the pastor is central to the events of God's arriving.

After doing the descriptive work in part 1, I'll turn to the constructive, offering a theological vision that places ministry as the central shape of divine action itself. After reading part 1, some of you will want me to offer my own model for the seventh type of pastor. Many of you will wonder, "What comes after Rick Warren?" This is an important question that I hope to answer in another project. But that couldn't be my aim in this book. Rather, because part 1 asserts that the pastoral malaise revolves around the loss of a theological vision for divine action that has impacted pastoral practice, part 2 needs to face this challenge and provide this vision. Therefore, part 2 moves from history to a biblical theology that draws specifically from Old Testament texts and the work of Robert W. Jenson. My task in part 2 is to offer a theological contribution that claims that God's being is revealed as ministry. We share in God's being as a fellowship of action—through receiving and giving ministry. It is through ministry that we encounter the being of God. I began moving in this theological direction in volume 1, wrestling with Pauline texts. Here I push it much deeper, making these points through Old Testament texts and pushing the edges of and adding to Jenson's thought.

As you read part 2 you'll notice that I've used masculine pronouns for God. I wish I didn't have to do this. But for the sake of the flow and clarity of writing I stuck with it throughout. To compensate, I've tried to use feminine pronouns for the pastor as much as possible. I've done this not only to balance my pronoun use but more so because I deeply believe in the pastoral vocation of women.

No one has helped me more with this book than the Reverend Kara Root. In many ways her experience, practice, and insights fuel this project. I've been more than blessed to have her as partner both in life and in idea construction. There are many others who read and offered feedback on this volume. As with volume 1, pastors Jon Wasson and Wes Ellis brought great insights, reading closely and asking very helpful questions. Here in these pages I continue a conversation with Father Chris Ryan. Father Ryan's handle on Taylor has helped me much, keeping me from Protestant mistakes. Two of the best theologians Luther Seminary has to offer, Amy Marga and Lois Malcolm, offered very helpful feedback throughout. Pastor and Old Testament scholar Karl Jacobson was kind enough to wrestle with part 2, checking my use of Old Testament texts. Talented up-and-coming theologian Justin Nickel was in dialogue with me around the thought of Robert W. Jenson. Bob Hosack and his team (most especially Eric Salo) at Baker were again, as usual, wonderful to work with, suffering through my propensity to over-footnote. Finally, I want to offer my deep thanks to Pastor David Wood. David has become an important friend and dialogue partner over the last six years. Few people I've known have been as involved in supporting pastors than David. His insight and encouragement were essential.

Andrew Root
Martin Luther King Jr. Day 2018

# introduction

Both stories stuck with me. I couldn't shake them. Neither were actually experiences that happened to me, but when I heard them, something moved me. I wasn't learning something new, but like all great stories, they were showing me something I'd sensed (in this case even written about) come into sharper view.

## The First Story

It was just an ordinary Sunday at our small church, our sanctuary sparsely filled with the usual fifty or so people. Yet we had a great privilege this ordinary Sunday that most small churches rarely get: a well-known guest preacher was with us. In the middle of his sermon he told this story, which seemed to make the room, and my imagination, glow hot.

The preacher explained that he knew a man born in a small midwestern town not long after the turn of the twentieth century. This man came into the world with great struggle and wore the marks on his body; he suffered significant deformity. On seeing him, his mother and father rejected him, refusing to nurse or even love him. But this cursed baby was nonetheless the couple's responsibility, so they hired a young girl, an immigrant from the old country, to do what they imagined was the terrible task of caring for the cursed child. Lonely and feeling lost in a new world, this young girl embraced this baby who was so rudely met by this world.

For the next five years the young girl, nearly a child herself, raised the baby, showering him with love, looking in his eyes, and touching with tenderness all the supposedly monstrous traits he bore, whispering to him that she saw him, that he was a beautiful person, and that she loved what others said was broken about him. Since first picking him up, she sang to him, dozens of times each day, the same refrain. As he grew, so did their connection. But tragically, as the early twentieth century produced more cold institutions for the sick, it soon made more financial sense to institutionalize the child than to pay the girl to care for him. As if losing her own child, the girl grieved. Holding the now five-year-old to her chest, she sang her refrain for the last time. Remembering all the times of caring for him, of sharing in the wonders of his person, she said goodbye.

The child grew into a boy and then into a young man in the harsh institutional obsession of early twentieth-century asylums, suffering under the assumption that because his face bore a supposed deformity so too did his mind. At some point, he was told the name of this girl who had loved him. And while the memories of her embrace all but disappeared, buried under days past and suffering endured, he soon could remember only her name; the pressure of being a castoff had pulverized all else.

When his eighteenth birthday came around, he had a plan. No longer could they keep him in the asylum; he was now of age to take his destiny into his own hands. So he checked himself out and walked up the tallest hill he could find, carrying in his pocket the pills he'd been saving up to finally end his misery. As he sat atop the hill, working up the final nerve to swallow the pills and end his hell, he reminded himself that he was unwanted and unlovable. "Why, God?" he shouted like Job. "Why have you hated me so much? Never have you cared! I'll do you the favor and end your disgust of me by ending my misery!"

As the echo of his shouted words died away, he took the pills into his hand and readied himself to throw them into the back of his throat, but suddenly he was stopped, interrupted by singing. Someone was behind him. He stood to find who it was, the voice so clear and near. He heard this person singing, "God's mercy is wide, God's love is deep, and you, dear child, are loved." Wiping the angry tears from his face, his imminent dreadful ending interrupted by this song, he searched for the voice. He saw no one, but he heard it again: "God's mercy is wide, God's love is deep, and you, dear child, are loved." Though the voice was so clear, he realized he was alone on that hill. But hearing it again, he discovered he was anything but alone. Putting the pills back in his pocket, he walked down the mountain like Moses with a revelation. God had seen him and had spoken.

Still broken, but moved to discover what this voice could mean, the boy became a pastor. Over the next five decades, he would lead hundreds into their own contemplative moments of hearing the voice of God. But still, into his seventies he could make no sense of the singing voice that beckoned him back from death into life.

As his life shifted into retirement and his later years, he again prepared himself for death, but this time with deep appreciation for the blessings of life. By chance, he got word that the name he had carried so near his soul, the young girl who had been his only experience of love for nearly the first two decades of his life, was still alive. He had never tried to reconnect with her—after all, he could remember almost nothing about her, and yet he carried her name near his heart like a sacred charm.

So his wife contacted her, making arrangements for her to come and visit. He wasn't sure this was wise; again, he remembered nothing about her. As she arrived, now in her late eighties, she was a stranger—until her eyes met his. The warmth of her face communicated something surpassing time and space; it was as if looking in her eyes awakened parts of him that he'd been accessing but only at a submerged level. Seeing her brought them to the surface, and, as if he were five again, he felt the immediacy of her care, her joy, and her person next to his.

As they sat together and reminisced, she held his hand and told him she had never felt more important, more called into something beyond herself, than to care for him as an infant, to embrace and share in his life. His memories of years of torture were now being washed away by the confession of her love for him. And then, still holding his hand, with her other hand she grabbed his elbow and said, "Do you remember what I used to sing to you?" He shook his head. Quietly, with her beautiful, aged voice, she sang, "God's mercy is wide, God's love is deep, and you, dear child, are loved."

A shiver went through him, as deep as his soul, perhaps as deep as the mystery of being itself, as his mind raced him back to that hilltop when he was eighteen. It was her song that had come to him then, as clear and audible as if she had been standing there singing it to him. The speaking God had come to him singing. He had asked God why he was unloved, and God responded. With those pills of death soaking in the perspiration of his hand, it was through her song, the tender music of a scared, lonely girl who had loved him through the beginning of his life, that God spoke. It was her song that God used to move him from death into new life.

The guest preacher made some important points, but my mind was now elsewhere. I wanted to know: What was this? It appeared to me that this woman's care for this small boy was so profound that it created an event of God's speaking. It was so deeply connected to the movement of resurrection (and exodus) that it reached into death with new possibility. As I thought about what she did for him, about how I would describe it, I could only call it *ministry*. She ministered to this baby, loving him, caring for him, and sharing in his personhood. And her ministry to him seemed to play a song of resurrection, a song he couldn't shake even years later when his being faced the ultimate act of confirmed worthiness. As he faced his demise, the marks of ministry pressed on his spirit, opening him to the beckoning of the Holy Spirit. The young woman's care for the boy was indeed ministry, because it embraced death by sharing in personhood and, through this, brought forth transformation. Is it possible that ministry is this profound? Is it possible that resurrection itself sings a song of ministry and that we too are called to sing, like a frightened immigrant girl and a frail old woman? I asked myself, sitting in our little church, How seemingly weak, but nevertheless shockingly powerful, is ministry?

Ministry is too often seen as some function or professional action done by clergy; just as a clerk files papers or a programmer writes code, so a pastor ministers. It is the name of the core function of a profession. And as such, it is just a generic description of some *human* action. But this story opened my eyes to something deeper. It asserted that ministry is the very event that unveils *God's* action in the world. This is not because it is the rubbing of some bottle that brings God forth like a genie, but rather because God is a minister, constantly and continually acting in the world to minister new life out of death. God calls human ministers to echo God's own personhood by sharing in the personhood of others as ministers.

This story opened my eyes to see ministry as a spiritual force that stretches deeper than is often imagined, something that needs no ordination credentials or license. This story seemed to show that ministry is, of course, something pastors do, but it is also something much more than that. This woman was no *ordained* pastor, and yet her ministry to this unwanted child was the vehicle that God used to bring forth transformation. And having experienced this ministry, the boy walked down the mountain to become a pastor, spending his life helping others see and experience the song of resurrection, called ministry, using weakness to create a force stronger than a hundred nuclear bombs.

## The Second Story

As she placed the book in my hands, she refused to let it go. I held one side, and she held the other, as if our mutual grip swore an oath, and my friend Nancy Lee said with a look of intensity, "You'd better read this!" I promised I would, and promptly placed it on a stack of another fifteen books that needed reading. A few months later, on a beautiful late-summer day, I finally picked it up. Sitting on my porch, as kids on bikes and parents pushing baby strollers passed by, I read it cover to cover, sobbing my way through the last hundred pages, now clear why the book jacket read "#1 *New York Times* Bestseller." The book was *When Breath Becomes Air*, the beautifully written memoir of a neurosurgeon. It tells the story of an awakening.

Paul Kalanithi was a brilliant young man, educated at Stanford and Yale, who excelled in his training. As a scientific practitioner, he had been told and had fully embraced that patients are problems and that the surgeon's job is to eradicate the problem in the best way possible. The patient is not a person but a tumor causing seizures. The goal is to solve the riddle of seizures, keeping the patient alive, never contemplating the life and connections that this person inhabits. But just when Kalanithi was on the brink of being a successful surgeon, he became a patient, struck tragically with brain cancer.

Kalanithi now saw things differently; he was forced to look at disease and illness not from the level of the problem-solving surgeon but from that of the living, yearning, sick *person*. He could no longer see the patient as a movie set, where the doctor plays out the drama of fighting the disease, the surgeon Luke Skywalker and the cancer Darth Vader, crossing light sabers as the unfortunate patient passively hosts the battle in her body. Kalanithi came to realize that what he most longed for as a patient was not the sharp expertise of the surgeon but the ministry of the surgeon's person. Kalanithi recognized that the only way to truly heal someone is to create the space for them to share their story, to give your person to them, accompanying them in their journey of sickness that too often leads to death. Kalanithi's job now, as surgeon-patient, was to be a pastor who creates space for the ministry that shares deeply in personhood, inviting the sharing of stories as much as the articulation of diagnoses and procedures. "Had I been more religious in my youth, I might have become a pastor, for it was the pastoral role I'd sought." It was the pastoral role he discovered through his illness and transformation. He sums this all up in this beautiful story of his pastoral role as pastoral physician:

> A thirty-five-year-old sat in her ICU bed, a sheen of terror on her face. She had been shopping for her sister's birthday when she'd had a seizure. A scan showed that a benign brain tumor was pressing on her right frontal lobe. . . . But I could see that the idea of brain surgery terrified her, more than most. She was lonesome and in a strange place, having been swept out of the familiar hubbub of a shopping mall and into the alien beeps and alarms and antiseptic smells of an ICU. She would likely refuse surgery if I launched into a detached spiel detailing all the risks and possible complications. I could do so, document her refusal in the chart, consider my duty discharged, and move on to the next task. Instead, with her permission, I gathered her family with her, and together we calmly talked through the options. As we talked, I could see the enormousness of the choice she faced dwindle into a difficult but understandable decision.

*I had met her in a space where she was a person, instead of a problem to be solved.* She chose surgery. The operation went smoothly. She went home two days later, and never seized again.[1]

I was shocked by the direct description that Kalanithi gave to his awakening, to this new way of being a doctor; he called it *pastoral*. He was transformed by seeing himself as a pastor. He recognized it in his weakness, like Paul in 2 Corinthians, now that his cancer had knocked him to the floor. He could hear the soft song of ministry playing in the universe, a hum of resurrection that had the power to transform even death into life through the sharing of personhood. It had the ability that pure scientific know-how didn't: to provide new possibility.

Kalanithi was transformed into a pastoral physician, finding his destiny. But this book wouldn't end happily ever after. Rather, the cancer in Kalanithi's body soon overtook him, making it impossible for him to continue his work. The pastoral physician who was transformed by cancer was now being overcome by it. As Kalanithi's only child came into the world, profoundly ministering to his frail person with her own, he would leave it. Writing her a letter that she'd read years later, when he was but a foggy memory transfused into her consciousness by the stories of others, he conveyed to her the deepest expressions of gratitude, reminding her to never think of her life as meaningless. Her very existence gave a dying man the deepest joy of shared personhood; her life was a ministry to him, her being the gift a dying man so desperately needed.

I was now sobbing loud enough for dog walkers on the sidewalk to wonder if I was OK. As I moved into our kitchen, I found my wife, Kara, working away at her computer, preparing something for the evening's presbytery meeting, while multitasking to complete the other duties expected of her as pastor of Lake Nokomis Presbyterian Church. My eyes swollen and my mind reverberating at that warm, low frequency that happens when you've been engulfed in something beautiful, I said, "You've got to read this book. It's wonderful, so moving. And what's amazing is that the author has an awakening through having cancer that transforms him into a pastoral physician, freeing him to minister to people by being with them."

Listening, but distracted by her ever-long to-do list, Kara shot back, "Cool. I'm glad a surgeon gets to be pastoral, because I'm not sure anyone cares if a pastor is."

Kara's snarky response was born not only from a pending presbytery meeting and too many things to do as the day was coming to a close but more so from her recent return from leading worship and spiritual direction at a pastors'

---

1. Paul Kalanithi, *When Breath Becomes Air* (New York: Random House, 2016), 90 (emphasis added).

conference. She explained that so many pastors felt buried under institutional demands that they rarely had time or energy for ministry. And many weren't even sure what to expect or hope for as an outcome of their action. Some had dreams of doubling or quadrupling their church's size, and others fantasized about being a popular blogger or author, but few had a real sense of what it would even look like for God to act. After all, in our secular age, divine action often seems unbelievable. The roads that once seemed to connect us directly to the divine appear either closed or uncomfortably bumpy. The pastor can feel like an odd person, living an embarrassingly outdated vocation. At its worst, it can feel like being a full-time employee of the Renaissance Festival, playing a part from an old world that people at times (e.g., Christmas and Easter) appreciate but most often find unnecessary. And, as Kara discovered, even those who find it necessary seem more concerned with institutional structures (and the anxiety of their failing) than with an experience with God. The pastor either becomes the guardian and custodian of declining religion or needs to reinvent himself or herself as a religious entrepreneur, connecting busy, disinterested people with the programs and products of a church.

What is the purpose of being a pastor if it isn't to build the next megachurch or be the next Rob Bell (or better, be the next Rob Bell by building the next megachurch)? Other than these ambitious (and often unrealistic) longings, there seemed little other purpose driving the practice and identity of pastors, in her humble opinion. The days of managing sacred things and leading revered communities, where people constructed their most primary meaning, were all but gone. And who really had time to think much about all this anyway? Pastors, she explained, live with a sneaking suspicion that all they're good for is managing religious stuff that no one really values.

*But, they do!* I thought. Kalanithi's book is a *New York Times* bestseller, and the story of the child, the girl, and the song points to something profound that we're all longing for: a sense that there is something binding our experience and the universe itself together. Or maybe Kara was right: for sixteen straight years, nurses, and not clergy, have topped the Gallup poll of the most trusted professions in America. Eighty-two percent of people said that nurses were trustworthy. Only 42 percent trusted clergy or pastors. Police officers, grade school teachers, and pharmacists all ranked higher in trust, honesty, and ethics than pastors.[2] It is safe to assume that so few Americans trust pastors

2. Megan Brenan, "Nurses Keep Healthy Lead as Most Honest, Ethical Profession," Gallup, December 26, 2017, https://news.gallup.com/poll/224639/nurses-keep-healthy-lead-honest -ethical-profession.aspx.

"While pastors are as important as ever in Christ's kingdom, in a society undergoing spiritual reconstruction they seem less significant. In the past, a career in ministry might have appealed

because of self-inflicted wounds brought about by scandal and moral failure. But I also think there is another layer to this decline that affects pastors more directly. Perhaps these numbers are low because in the end many people aren't sure what pastors are good for, other than guilting people to come to church and drop a twenty in the offering plate.[3]

So pastors don't rank near the top, but why are nurses so high? Nurses of course do a lot, but they often assist more than lead, lacking (at least in perception) the technical knowledge and extensive training of physicians. But nurses rank number one because, while the surgeon needs an awakening (like Kalanithi) to see you as a person, nurses recognize that you need the ministry of another (a place to share your fears, to be comforted and known) as much as you need your blood pressure taken or your bandage changed. Nurses are the most trusted because nurses do ministry.[4]

This Gallup poll, in a nutshell, points to what this book will seek to explore. We live in a time—call it a secular age—when society has devalued the pastor and yet we nevertheless yearn for ministry. Just look at Pope Francis: he has won over the world, and particularly religiously cynical Western Europeans as well as North American Protestants, because he has chosen to be a minister. He holds nearly the same views as his predecessor, but he is beloved far beyond Benedict because he chooses to move in the world not as a theologian or cleric but as a humble minister, as a nurse who washes feet and hears stories. He refuses to live in an ornate villa; he will live only in a humble flat because he sees himself not as a head of state but as a minister, living not separate from but with people.

This book will sketch a story. Gleaning from the work of Charles Taylor, it will tell how the dawning of our secular age in the West has hollowed out the vocation of the pastor, making core commitments to divine action questionable at best. Unlike Communist China post-revolution, our secular age has

---

to any leader who sought recognition and respect. Today, however, Christian ministers are as likely to be ignored and insulted as they are to be admired and revered. It's not a job for the thin-skinned or the weak of heart." David Kinnaman in Barna Report, *The State of Pastors: How Today's Faith Leaders Are Navigating Life and Leadership in an Age of Complexity* (Ventura, CA: Barna Group, 2017), 155.

3. *The State of Pastors* report reveals this loss of esteem in a secular age: "Half of all working Americans say church work is 'much more' (28%) or 'a little more' (22%) important than their career choice. One in five says a pastoral vocation is of equal importance with their career (20%), and one in six believes their own vocation is more important than a Christian minister's (18%). Exceptionally inclined to believe their career is more important than pastoring are Millennials (31%) and those who are religiously unaffiliated ('nones,' 47%)." Barna Report, *State of Pastors*, 130.

4. The nurse may also more directly than the pastor stand between life and death, providing practices with consequence (take these pills or stop eating these foods or else damnation will be upon you—in the form of a catheter and hospital bed).

not forcefully eliminated the pastor, but it has slowly erased the transcendent referent that would make the pastor ultimately needed. The pastor is like the manager of a video rental or VCR repair store. Few people are upset they exist, and many are nostalgic about their past importance, but all of their training and know-how is needed only in the rarest of cases, such as when you find your dusty wedding video from 1991 in an old box only to discover the reels on the VHS are stuck. Yet not long ago we simply couldn't get on with life without a pastor. We needed a pastor to assist us in our most important events and experiences, to help protect us from evil and lead us into grace. But this has become obsolete. As our secular age has made divine action unbelievable, the pastor has become a warm, kitschy relic of a passing age, someone people like having around but aren't sure why.

Part 1 tells this story, delving into the history of our secular age and its impact on the pastor, and using Charles Taylor's ideas and other historical examples to articulate the challenges the pastor faces. Using Taylor as my baseline, I'll present a genealogy of pastoral identity. I'll show how Taylor's larger philosophical thesis is connected with the evolving identity of the pastor. To explore this I'll draw from the stories of six pastors—Augustine, Thomas Becket, Jonathan Edwards, Henry Ward Beecher, Harry Emerson Fosdick, and Rick Warren. Each of these men were significant representatives of the role and identity of a pastor in their era. For good or ill, they all reacted to—and even produced—essential elements that would lead to our secular age. They are archetypes, generalizations that reveal something true about the time and culture. In part 1, we are trying to tell the story from the center, where white males were the shapers of the cultural pastoral identity. Part 2 becomes more constructive, drawing from the genius of those on the margins. Here women and people of color will take center stage.

Chapter 9 will serve as a bridge or coda that will prepare us to make a more distinctly theological leap in part 2. This coda will explore Michel Foucault's lectures on pastoral power. Playing some of the same notes as part 1, it will further show why being a pastor is such a challenge in a secular age. But also playing new notes, it will prepare us to explore the depth of God's shepherding nature, spotting how ministry is central to God's own being.

Pushing these ideas further, part 2 seeks to free ministry from being seen as only a professional function and moves into seeing ministry as the very way of imagining divine action in our secular age. It picks up a major thread from volume 1 in this series and describes more deeply the shape and nature of what the boy experienced with the young woman, what Kalanithi discovered, and what nurses do: this thing called ministry. In volume 1, seeking to define what faith is, we named this reality through the experience of the apostle

Paul with Ananias. Here we'll explore more deeply what ministry might be, particularly at the level of God's action, with the goal to articulate ways for pastors to reclaim the identity and meaning of their calling. Ministry is a robust theological category that brings divine action into human experience, helping us recognize God's presence, even in a secular age.

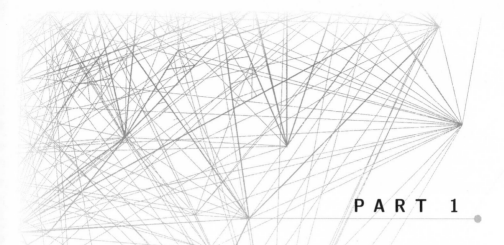

# welcome
# to the pastoral
# malaise

# 1

## a historical map of the pastor
## in our secular age

"I'm not sure what I'm doing," he said. I'd never met him before, but I'd talked with hundreds of hims (and hers) after speaking at pastors' conferences. The air of fragile confidence was familiar, this sense of being lost in the house you grew up in. "I've been a pastor for fifteen years, and most days I have no idea what I'm doing," he continued.[1]

I could only pause and allow the silence to invite him to say more. "I mean, I know what I'm doing, maybe all too well. I have no trouble filling my days

1. Kevin Vanhoozer gives some context to this pastor's feelings: "Uncertainty about what pastors are good for is not good for a minister's soul. If the metaphor by which you minister is 'helping profession,' then you had better be prepared to say what kind of help you have to give. But this was precisely the problem. What do pastors have to say and do that other people in the helping professions—psychologists, psychiatrists, social workers, and so forth—are not already doing, and often doing better? Today there are many 'experts' in a variety of helping professions who are offering solutions and strategies for coping with diverse personal problems. Mental and social health services offer up a smorgasbord of theories and therapies for what ails us." Kevin Vanhoozer and Owen Strachan, *The Pastor as Public Theologian: Reclaiming a Lost Vision* (Grand Rapids: Baker Academic, 2015), 9. Todd Wilson and Gerald Heistand add, "You may know that pastors these days are going through something of an identity crisis. By and large, they don't know who they are or what they're supposed to be doing. Behind the benign pastoral smiles and inspiring sermons and multi-million dollar building campaigns and ever-expanding ministry footprints, there lurks in the hearts and minds of many pastors confusion as to what a pastor is and what a pastor does. In the words of Princeton Seminary president Craig Barnes, the hardest thing about being a pastor today is simply 'confusion about what it means to be the pastor.'" *Becoming a Pastor Theologian: New Possibilities for Church Leadership* (Downers Grove, IL: IVP Academic, 2016), 1.

and doing the things that make me a good pastor. I actually think I am a good, even faithful, pastor."

There was the confidence. When it came to being a pastoral professional, he had it. These had been fifteen years of success. Of course he had stories of failures and mistakes, but like all good professionals, he had learned from them. So in a sense, he had a very good idea of what he was doing and was successful at it.

But then the confidence cracked. "Yet I have this sick feeling, this kind of dull unease in my stomach, that something is wrong. I'm not sure of its origins or why it's there, but it's just this discomfort, like I'm missing something."

"Like something is slipping through your fingers," I said.[2]

"Yes," he returned, "but in a way that gives me a nauseous feeling."[3]

## Welcome to the Malaise

Canada is known for snow, hockey pucks, and Tim Horton's coffee. Not surprisingly, the Great White North is less well known for hosting the Massey

2. "Being a pastor is hard enough as it is: the *New York Times* reported in 2010 that 50 percent of pastors feel unable to meet the needs of the job, with 90 percent saying they feel unqualified or poorly prepared for ministry." Kevin Vanhoozer, "The Pastor Theologian as Public Theologian," in Wilson and Heistand, *Becoming a Pastor Theologian*, 40. Sondra Wheeler adds more texture to this: "The greatest risk of ministry isn't burnout, though the burdens and isolation of the role can be dangerous and corrosive. Neither is it moral failure in itself, although we have in recent years seen shocking evidence of how widespread and destructive such failures are. The greatest risk is the one that is behind and beneath both exhaustion and much pastoral misconduct. It is cynicism: loss of faith in the meaningfulness and efficacy of the work that ministers do." *The Minister as Moral Theologian: Ethical Dimensions of Pastoral Leadership* (Grand Rapids: Baker Academic, 2017), 124.

3. I understand that it is a debate on whether the pastoral vocation is in decline. The pastor I was speaking to seemed to be intuitively and existentially echoing E. Brooks Holifield (*God's Ambassadors: A History of the Christian Clergy in America* [Grand Rapids: Eerdmans, 2007], 348), who says,

> And what about the seeming decline of the profession? More than a few scholarly accounts of ministry have affirmed or implied the narrative of decline. It has become common to say that in the twenty-first century the clergy exercise leadership over a smaller number of domains than they did in previous centuries. They no longer help write the laws of the state, as they did in seventeenth-century New England. They no longer constitute, as they did until the late eighteenth century, the intellectual class of the culture. They seldom lead, as they had in antebellum America, the largest humanitarian and philanthropic institutions, or edit the culture's leading journals. They rarely become the presidents and trustees, as they once had, of the elite colleges and universities. They have lost exclusive "jurisdiction over personal problems" as a result of competition from psychiatrists and social workers. Clergy typically receive lower salaries than most other professionals. And with 25 percent of Americans now graduating from a college or university, ministers are, in most communities, no longer the most highly educated persons. In more than one cultural realm, the ministry has indeed lost authority. And if this is what decline means, the argument is convincing.

Lectures on politics, culture, and philosophy. Yet these lectures are famous, not only being aired on the CBC (Canadian Broadcast Channel) but also boasting past presenters like Noam Chomsky and Martin Luther King Jr. In 1991, Charles Taylor, the Montreal philosopher whom we met in the first volume of this series, delivered his lectures, called "The Malaise of Modernity." Taylor articulated something in these lectures that he would continue to explore years later in his book *A Secular Age*, in which he investigates the way that our late modern world strikes us with a general feeling of discomfort, a kind of uneasiness. Taylor describes this as a malaise, a kind of nagging illness, the source of which can't be identified. He explains that this low-grade cultural stomachache may have its origin in at least three things: "(1) the sense of the fragility of meaning, [and the] search for an over-arching significance; (2) a felt flatness of our attempts to solemnize the crucial moments of passage in our lives; and (3) the utter emptiness of the ordinary."[4]

It's no wonder that the pastor I met above felt a dull sense of unease, a vocational nauseousness, like he didn't know what he was doing. If this cultural malaise has indeed arrived, then it is no surprise that the pastor would feel like patient zero. In *A Secular Age*, Taylor calls this unease "the malaise of immanence."[5] It is as though living in a world free of transcendence, enchantment, and an organization around divine action has given us a freedom that leaves us with a discomfort we can't pinpoint, a dull boredom we can't shake. As I discussed in volume 1, we have arrived in a secular age not because people no longer see it as necessary to go to church (and are willing to mark "none" on a survey) but rather because the very idea that there could be a personal God who orders and acts in the cosmos has become unbelievable (or at least contested). Or we could say that we now live in a world where it is quite easy to forget, deny, or simply not care that there is a transcendent dimension to reality. Taylor's point is that the price paid for this freedom is an uneasy boredom, an ailment of felt flatness.

If ministry were only about getting people to join the institutional church, then the pastor could hone her professional skills and battle for market share. And many denominations and seminaries have settled for this understanding of the pastor. But what caused the pastor I was talking with to have a stomachache and overall feeling of malaise was the unexpressed realization that

4. Charles Taylor, *A Secular Age* (Cambridge, MA: Belknap Press, 2007), 309.
5. Taylor adds, "A crucial feature of the malaise of immanence is the sense that all these answers are fragile, or uncertain; that a moment may come, where we no longer feel that our chosen path is compelling, or cannot justify it to ourselves or others. . . . The fragility that I am talking about concerns the significance of it all; the path is still open, possible, supported by circumstances, the doubt concerns its worth." *Secular Age*, 308.

the very God he preached had become unnecessary. And in turn this led him to feel somewhere deep enough beyond words that in this shrouded void *he was not needed at all.*

He was standing in the line of an old vocational tradition, of course, but he nevertheless felt like he was on new ground. Pastors like Augustine of Hippo, Thomas Becket, and Jonathan Edwards never dealt with the fragility of meaning, the flatness of our moments of passage, and the emptiness of the ordinary. It would be as hard for them to understand the feeling of malaise as it would a smartphone. They ministered in a world where haunting meaning spilled out of every corner in omens and revelations. And not only were baptisms, weddings, and festivals embedded in the thick cosmic drama of worship and absolution (so much so that Becket had to remind King Henry that he too must obey), but the passage from life to death was short and sudden. This was anything but flat, and the ordinary was filled to overflowing. For Augustine and Becket, anything ordinary existed in a chain of being that played its part in sacred reality. For Edwards, ordinariness, particularly of raising children, held such cosmic weight that his primary pastoral task (particularly from the pulpit) was to push his congregants to live upright ordinary lives in order to raise children well enough to keep them from hell. For Edwards's Calvinist Puritanism, ordinary life was the stage where heaven and hell collided.

Not so much for this pastor. He was living in a different time, quite literally. We'll discuss this time transformation more below. But to illustrate, for Augustine, Becket, and, in his own way, Edwards, time wasn't frozen in a linear progression as we now assume. Certain moments cast meaning over all of ordinary life by shifting time. The people to whom Augustine, Becket, and Edwards ministered had a shared imagination (a "social imaginary" as Taylor calls it)[6] that led them to assume that Good Friday in the year 435, 1138, or 1752 was closer to the original day of the crucifixion than a mid-summer evening in 433, 1130, or 1750. Or to say it more directly, they would say that a "holy day"—say, Good Friday 2018—is closer to the crucifixion than an "ordinary day"—say, July 10, 2015.[7]

6. "The social imaginary, as Taylor conceives it, 'is not a set of ideas' but rather 'what enables, through making sense of, the practices of a society.'" Michael Warner, Jonathan VanAntwerpen, and Craig Calhoun, eds., *Varieties of Secularism in a Secular Age* (Cambridge, MA: Harvard University Press, 2010), 19.

7. Taylor says, "The Church, in its liturgical year, remembers and re-enacts what happened in *illo tempore* when Christ was on earth. Which is why this year's Good Friday can be closer to the Crucifixion than last year's mid-summer day. And the Crucifixion itself, since Christ's action/passion here participates in God's eternity, is closer to all times than they in secular terms are to each other." *Secular Age*, 58.

The meaning of the crucifixion is so heavy that it bends time, giving us passage into living and participating in the crucifixion's cosmic significance, and transforming our empty ordinary days into a haunting, sacred experience. It was the pastor's job to stand on the boundary of these times, helping people make sense of the flood of meaning as the pastor moved people back and forth between ordinary and sacred time. The ordinary was preparation for the coming extraordinary passage into sacred time. There was no need to find meaning, because all of reality was pocked with time-traveling wormholes, and it was the pastor's job, particularly in Becket's time, to drive people in and out of these time-bending events.

But this time jumping was wearying. Just as an astronaut prepares for zero gravity, it was assumed that no one could jump time without training. The level of constant preparation in the ordinary time for the passages into the extraordinary time was a burden. And it seemed to just keep ramping up—the number of prayers, the need to touch relics, the fasting, and so much more. Nevertheless, it was the pastor's job to, in love, keep prodding and pushing the people to prepare, because one time jump or another was around the corner; celebration of the Eucharist, Good Friday, Pentecost, or some other wormhole was soon to be on the horizon. And if we weren't ready, the meaningfulness was so heavy that it would rip our souls into pieces. And we were all in this together, so if you decided not to pray, or even secretly dabbled in witchcraft, we all could be obliterated when we hit the zero gravity of sacred time—Good Friday was as frightening as it was celebratory.

The pastor had to live under this constant burden while avoiding the temptations to which many succumbed. The pastor had to balance the utter power of driving the vessel (called the church) that not only organized, almost in full, people's lives but also moved people in and out of these wormholes of salvation.

The world of the pastor I was talking with at the conference couldn't be more different. But this radical difference didn't come through a coup d'état. It was not a direct and immediate overthrow that led the open wormholes one day to suddenly be paved over the next. Rather, getting us to this secular age, in which time is frozen in linear progression and ordinary life is freed from the pressure of cosmic significance, has taken many years and many more small changes that have slowly but surely shrunk the once gaping wormholes.

## More on the Malaise

It is not that meaning, rites of passages, and the significance of the ordinary have been annihilated; it is just that they have been hollowed out, repurposed for ends other than experiencing the divine. This is why it feels like a malaise. Slowly but surely in the West the transcendent dimension to life became optional in no small part because people (particularly a growing elite) became sick of pastoral prodding. They wanted their ordinary lives to be less haunted, less directly connected to divine consequence.

But this wanting to be free from the sacred monopoly that the pastor or priest possessed had its origin not in doubt but in belief, not in apathy but in the passion to follow God. Seeking to be even *more* faithful to God, soon people wrestled the keys to the vehicle of salvation from the hands of corrupt priests, who were reformed to no longer drive buses of salvation but teach individuals to drive for themselves. The Protestant Reformation made each person responsible for his or her own being before a Holy God. All were taught to read the Bible for themselves, given the keys to drive their own faith. And where they would maneuver was no longer into the haunting wormholes where time was bent but around the common neighborhood of their ordinary lives.[8]

With pietistic desire to give everyone direct access to the vehicle of salvation, the bold line between the sacred and secular became much thinner. This was not because everything was now secular (as we today assume it to be) but because everything was *sacred*. Even diaper changing and cow milking, as Luther would say, were transformed into tasks done before God. Previously, the ordinary duties were done outside the sacred and, at best, could be seen only as preparation for the coming horizon of the wormhole. But after the Reformation, these common tasks were not just preparatory but the actual location of divine encounter. The Reformation was a reform of our daily practices as much as our theology.[9]

Everything now held cosmic consequence.[10] The pastor's job was no longer to stand on the precipice between sacred and secular time, moving in and out of the sacred. Now the pastor was to mount the pulpit steps and preach the

8. James K. A. Smith provides a nice summary of Taylor here: "At its heart, Reform becomes 'a drive to make over the whole society to higher standards' (p. 63) rooted in the conviction that 'God is sanctifying us everywhere' (p. 79). Together these commitments begin to propel a kind of perfectionism about society that wouldn't have been imagined earlier." *How (Not) to Be Secular* (Grand Rapids: Eerdmans, 2014), 37.

9. Paul Bernier supports this when he says, "This stratification of the church into realms of sacred and profane, into 'agents' and 'those acted upon' had been established by centuries of legal precedent and theological justification. Until the Protestants came along, those desiring reform did not question the validity of the lay-clergy dichotomy; they simply sought to lead the ordained to a better fulfillment of their vocational ideal." *Ministry in the Church: A Historical and Pastoral Approach* (Eugene, OR: Wipf & Stock, 1992), 162.

10. Taylor adds, "And . . . it is clear that the Reformation was driven by the spirit of Reform in an even more uncompromising mode. One of its principal talking points from the very beginning was the refusal to accept special vocations and counsels of perfection. There were

Word, directing the hearer to repent and remember that all time and therefore all tasks are sacred. Because the event of salvation was released from its isolation in sacred time, all time, be it spent nursing babies or plowing fields, bore the responsibility of the sacred. All believers were now priests, because all parts of life witnessed to salvation.[11] These ordinary tasks now held even more cosmic significance, though stripped down like a 1980s punk band. All the magic and much of the pomp that reminded people of the difference between sacred and secular time was done away with (for example, shifting from a fresco-filled church in Italy to a Puritan Congregational Prayer House in New England: one is built to remind you that you have left the profane and moved into a sacred space; the other is empty and plain to remind you that God comes into the ordinary—like this simple, white room—making all space sacred).

After the Reformation, meaning, rites of passage, and the ordinary were no longer organized around a bold sacred and secular divide, as they were for Augustine and Becket. Now everything was sacred. For Edwards, meaning was everywhere and the weight of salvation carried out in the ordinary actions of work, marriage, and child-rearing. In Edwards's Puritan Calvinism, every minute and every task were to reshape the created realm, releasing it from the hold of evil to reflect the holy. The pastor needed to be as involved in civic matters as in ecclesial ones because all of ordinary life had divine consequence, and it was through a polite, disciplined society that life would reflect the divine.

If there was a line between forces, it was no longer dividing sacred from secular time but now dividing order from disorder, God from the devil. The devil sought to push ordinary life toward chaos; it was our corporate vocation to double down on the ordinary, taking disciplined action to free it from the devil's control. It was every Christian's job to create a dependable world out of our ordinary lives that reflected heaven and freed people from hell. Witches needed to be burned not because people had gone totally mad (though maybe a little) but because the devil was always at work, and most directly in our shared ordinary lives—in the behavior of our children. If evil was allowed a foothold in our civic space, the whole society would

---

not to be any more ordinary Christians and super-Christians. The renunciative vocations were abolished. All Christians alike were to be totally dedicated." *Secular Age*, 77.

11. "And one of the driving forces of the Protestant Reformation, as central almost as the doctrine of salvation by faith, was the idea that this total commitment must no longer be considered the duty only of an elite which embraced 'counsels of perfection,' but was demanded of all Christians indiscriminately. This was the ground for the reformers' vigorous rejection of all the supposedly special vocations of monasticism." Charles Taylor, *Sources of the Self: The Making of Modern Identity* (Cambridge, MA: Harvard University Press, 1989), 185.

become demonic and our salvation would be lost. It seems counterintuitive to us now, but Salem's witches needed to be burned so our ordinary lives would be a place of flourishing (that is, of safety, security, justice, and a prosperous and positive life). Because all of ordinary life was sacred, there could be no risk of giving the devil a foothold, particularly in our homes, schools, and meetinghouses. We needed to keep the devil in the forest, out of our shared social space of order, and keep him in a literal but also metaphorical space of chaos, dark magic, and frightening mystery. We needed to keep the devil in the forest and keep the forest from overtaking the village through our diligent discipline and order of our ordinary lives. For a pastor like Edwards, the only way for human beings to flourish was to repent of sin, find discipline, and therefore be free from hell. But this freeing from hell had the concrete manifestation of creating a society where people's ordinary lives led to human flourishing most directly in order, decorum, and politeness. Puritan Calvinism created dependable structures to order our ordinary lives, so that the world became a place where human beings could flourish.[12]

### The Chaplain Pastors

For pastors in the nineteenth and early twentieth centuries, like Henry Ward Beecher and Harry Emerson Fosdick, a huge piece of pastoral identity was to work for human flourishing by being deeply involved in civic matters. Beecher used his pulpit to fight against slavery, becoming close friends with Abraham Lincoln. Fosdick spoke against war and addiction, becoming a staple in early twentieth-century New York cultural life, with John D. Rockefeller Jr. always by his side.

Like Edwards, both Beecher and Fosdick saw the pastor as fighting for human flourishing. But, unlike Edwards, both Beecher and Fosdick took direct steps to shake off the rigid Puritan Calvinism that feared devils and hell around every ordinary corner. Both followed Edwards in contending that in these ordinary spaces we worked out our salvation. But unlike Edwards they no longer thought the devil was in the forest. The titans of industry who built churches, like Beecher's Plymouth Congregational Church in Brooklyn and

12. Ruth Abbey points in the direction we'll be headed in the chapters that follow: "One of the distinctive features of the modern western outlook is that humans no longer see ourselves as ensconced in, and in important ways defined by, some larger cosmic order. People no longer see ourselves as being part of a world of forms, nor situated in the hierarchy of God's creation above the animals but just below the angels, nor as belonging to a great chain of being." *Charles Taylor* (Princeton, NJ: Princeton University Press, 2000), 81.

Fosdick's Riverside Church in Manhattan's Morningside Heights,[13] had helped disenchant the forest, running iron rails through it and piercing its crust for oil.

Pastors in Beecher's and Fosdick's times, however, were insulated from a malaise and loss of pastoral identity because they were the producers of and also protectors of human flourishing. Things had changed from Edwards's time, when the clergy were by far the most educated men of the colonies, who not only could read and govern but also provide the knowledge of salvation. In Edwards's day the pastor had a monopoly on importance. This was no longer the case for Beecher and Fosdick; the world that those like Edwards helped build allowed for education to move far beyond church matters, and a dependable world allowed the institution building and economic stability that could produce a Rockefeller.

But while the world had changed, pastors like Beecher and Fosdick were still essential. As the nineteenth century unfolded, things gradually flipped; where the Reformation had said that there was no divide between the sacred and secular because *everything* (particularly our ordinary lives) was sacred, things shifted, like a negative of an old photo, to the opposite. People began to assume that because there was no divide between the sacred and secular, and ordinary life was important, maybe everything was just secular. After all, the devil had been cast out of the forest, and the world disenchanted through technology, science, and medicine. So maybe ordinary lives were just secular and the world was mostly free from sacred haunting. As industrialization took hold, we needed pastors to check our secular excesses and to encourage us to live upright lives, particularly now that most of us were living in new urban centers, where temptation was ripe. We needed pastoral exhortation not to keep us from hell (as Edwards would believe) but to allow us to flourish, *as an end in itself*. For Edwards, flourishing was a sign that we were a society bent toward salvation, reflecting heaven. In Fosdick's time, human flourishing could become its own end, cut loose from any sacred purpose. Yet we needed pastors to remind us to avoid that which turned us personally from flourishing (things like drinking and gambling that attack the affirmation of ordinary life) and to call titans of industry to remember their responsibility to keep the world a dependable place where machines helped humans flourish and not flounder. The pastor felt no malaise because he was the chaplain of the dawning secular age, adding religious moralism to the system that had turned our ordinary lives into something fully secular. In a world that had become

13. The wealthy businessman Henry Bowen not only funded most of the church but also worked hard to recruit Beecher as pastor. Rockefeller did the same with Riverside Church and Fosdick.

fully secular, the pastor became the manifestation of our conscience (our better gods), holding an important and meaningful place.[14]

Yet, though the pastor held this seemingly important place, he was no longer the lynchpin of our cultural life. Now that ordinary life was no longer sacred, but only secular, it wouldn't be long until the chaplain position was extraneous. As the twentieth century dawned, the world the pastor inhabited could be imagined for only and exclusively human flourishing, period. We could get human flourishing without needing God at all (a thought that would make Edwards turn over in his grave). It seemed ever possible that we could get to human flourishing and continue to create a dependable world without any real longing for sacred time or need to be protected from the devil. It was assumed that we no longer even needed pastoral chaplains to keep us on the right track.

Soon enough, some pastors, at least intuitively, agreed, turning to the new sciences such as psychology to do their pastoral work and to the new methods of text criticism to read their Bibles. After all, the pastor's job was not to take people into sacred time or uphold the sacredness of ordinary life but to help people flourish, and it appeared that the new secular disciplines of psychology and sociology were much more helpful in this vein. Now that ordinary life was just secular, hyper-pragmatism entered pastoral practice. Who needed those theological ideas? Our job was to help people flourish—to be society's conscience—not to move them into an immaterial, counterintuitive reality. (This pragmatism has never left the American pastoral imagination, because our pastoral imaginary is tightly wound around the social imaginary of the secular age—even in the most conservative evangelicalism).

Now, an immanent frame enclosed our lives in *entirely* natural (as opposed to supernatural) ways of being.[15] The immanent frame was being used to define

14. This is in contrast to the numbers around the trust of nurses we discussed in the introduction and shows that the pastor was still the chapel of our secular age at this time. Holifield says, "Various rating scales placed the ministry among the most desirable and respected occupations. In a national poll in 1947 that asked people to rank the 'prestige' of eighty-eight occupations, ministry ranked thirteenth. . . . A 1958 survey ranked them seventh, and a poll of college students that year placed them fourth among eight professions judged according to their 'usefulness to society.' Some ministers worried about their 'reduced importance' in American culture, but the public seemed to hold them in high esteem." *God's Ambassadors*, 236.

15. Taylor explains the immanent frame: "The sense of the immanent frame is that of living in impersonal orders, cosmic, social, and ethical orders which can be fully explained in their own terms and don't need to be conceived as dependent on anything outside, on the 'supernatural' or the 'transcendent.' This frame can be lived as 'closed' but also as 'open' to a beyond, and the tension between these two spins runs through the multiplying gamut of mutually cross-pressured positions that I call the nova." Charles Taylor, afterword to Warner, VanAntwerpen, and Calhoun, *Varieties of Secularism*, 307.

as completely secular not only our ordinary lives but also the pastoral task. George Albert Coe, a teacher of Fosdick's at Union Seminary, could assert that the goal of Christian education was not the transcendent (sacred) reality of the kingdom of God but the democracy of God: an immanent bound space of human flourishing that had no need for a transcendent referent.[16] The Bible was taken apart, like one of the engines of Ford's motorcars, and the immanent cultural background and source material of the text was examined, shaking out its transcendent quality, leaving many to question whether it still possessed the sacred power to drive us to salvation or whether it was just a book.

When pastor Karl Barth in a working-class village in Switzerland mounted his pulpit steps in 1914, on the eve of World War I, armed with the best of German theological education, he became dizzy with despair, overcome with a stomachache not unlike the pastor I met at the conference. As he cleared his throat to preach and caught the eyes of the tired faces of his congregation, fatigued from their work in the mines and overwhelmed by the duties of their ordinary lives, he realized he had nothing to say. Like the pastor I met, he had no idea what he was doing. The Bible had no more meaning, the passages of congregants' lives flattened by industrialization, their ordinary experience now completely immanent and secular. And Europe itself was about to be shaken to its core by war.

Barth had essentially followed the lead of Beecher and Fosdick, seeing himself as the chaplain of the modern world enclosed in an immanent frame. Human flourishing could be achieved in a fully secular way.[17] It was the pastor's job to support human flourishing by reminding society of its moral commitments. Barth believed with his professors that the pastor's job was to participate in the progress of human flourishing,[18] which needed no sense of divine action or a sacred reality. But when these same professors' names appeared on the front page of the newspaper, signing the Kaiser's declaration of war, this young pastor realized that being a chaplain of a secular society who willingly gave up the preaching of God's judgment, sin, and salvation

16. See George Albert Coe, *A Social Theory of Religious Education* (New York: Charles Scribner's Sons, 1927).

17. Abbey adds, "In tracing this mission in the domestic realm and depicting the increasing imposition of order on society, Taylor goes where thinkers like Max Weber, Norbert Elias, Michel Foucault and Albert Hirschman have gone before. Eventually religious belief came to be associated with morality and morality in turn became associated with conduct, so it is not hard to see how what began as a religious mission gradually occluded God and the transcendent and came to concern itself entirely with human behaviour." *Charles Taylor*, 206.

18. Friedrich Schleiermacher justified theology in the university by asserting that it is a professional vocation needed within society. Just as a good society needs lawyers and doctors, so it needs pastors. *Brief Outline of Theology as a Field of Study* (Lewiston, NY: Edwin Mellen, 1990).

could not lead to the human flourishing it promised. He'd been duped; deconstructing his Bible and being the chaplain of a secular society led not to human flourishing but to the hellscape of France's trenches. And so Barth had to start all over, seeking a way to speak of the coming of a transcendent God into the immanent frame of modern life.

Barth's strategy was to find within biblical language itself a way to speak of God's breaking into a modern world framed by immanence. Yet, back across the pond in America, another tactic was chosen to deal with this new unease: full-on battle. Angrily bound in the immanent frame, a group of pastors and professors decided that the only way to deal with a secular age was to destroy it. Returning to the fundamentals—to the sources (the Bible and creeds) before the immanent frame challenged them—they set their sights on those pastors who conceded to being chaplains of the secular age and who saw their task as furthering human flourishing. (A major issue that conservatives even today have yet to solve is how, in opposing the reductions of the immanent frame, they can avoid the perception of being against justice and mercy and can support all humans flourishing.) Fosdick's pastoral ministry would be ground zero of this battle. He'd be painted as a modernist and kicked out of the pulpit of his Presbyterian church, taking arrow after arrow from fundamentalists.

The battle appeared to come to a head in 1925, when fundamentalists threw all their weight behind the trial of John Thomas Scopes, accusing him of teaching evolution in his Tennessee classroom. The fundamentalists had a secret weapon—William Jennings Bryan, the three-time presidential candidate—as prosecutor. No one could argue that Bryan was a backwoods hick, someone disconnected from the organizing of our ordinary lives. Bryan showed a need to move back from the secular presumptions of our lives and to remind us that it is in educating children that we work out our salvation, taking us back toward Edwards's day.

Sure enough, Bryan won the battle, but the fundamentalists lost the war, appearing backward and rigid. They'd miscalculated how little people were willing to return to Edwards's time, to deal again with pastoral prodding and the haunting of divine consequence in each moment of their ordinary lives. The fundamentalists underestimated what an exciting freedom the secular age was; our ordinary lives were now assumed to be completely our own. We were free to do with our lives what we wanted—new forms of leisure in the 1920s and expression in the 1960s were before us. It was too thrilling to pass up—but only if we could find ways to deal with the uneasy feeling that this freedom of living without divine consequence also flatted our experiences. The need to cope with this feeling gave us all the more reason to delve headlong into the leisure of the 1920s and consumer consumption and sex of the late 1960s.

## Mid-Century Transition

Between the 1920s and 1960s, Fosdick remained a significant figure, unscathed by the fundamentalist battles now that the fundamentalists had retreated and become separatists. If they couldn't move the whole culture back to a time when ordinary life bore sacred significance, then they could surely do it in small communities, chasing the devil back into the woods and preparing, through the rigid disciplining of their ordinary lives, for the coming apocalypse.[19]

When Fosdick was put on the cover of *Time* in 1930, it showed that indeed the pastor had a significant place in the modern world. The pastor as the conscience of our secular, ordinary lives was not only important but also esteemed—his contribution to human flourishing was essential. By the time Fosdick retired in 1946, this was unquestioned. The 1950s would further solidify the pastor's necessity. Our secular economy and government needed religion to bolster its claims for human flourishing over atheist communism. Though both American capitalism and Soviet communism were fully secular, ours was on the high ground because it allowed for the *freedom* of religion. "Freedom" became a loaded moral phrase that spoke to both secularists and the religious. Our secular age may have led to intense conflict, yet we could all agree on the importance of freedom (as long as we didn't ask too many questions about what freedom was for or what it looked like). In the 1950s, against the heat of the Cold War, the esteem of the pastor seemed to be gaining, hitting heights it hadn't seen in decades, as again the ordinary lives of citizens became essential (never mind that this had more to do with geopolitical victory than with salvation).

Yet when Fosdick died in October 1969, the importance and esteem of the pastor was about to come under an attack it couldn't anticipate. As the South was set ablaze by racial conflict and the new media of television awakened the North to the evil of our national apartheid, pastors cut from the cloth of Fosdick boarded buses, outnumbered only by college students. The pastor was the conscience of our secular ordinary lives, working and speaking for human flourishing; there was no place he was needed more than in the South. Not only were African Americans in the South *not* flourishing, but the racists were attacking their ordinary lives, bombing churches, and keeping them from diner counters, bus seats, and drinking fountains. Pastor Martin Luther King Jr. may have understood American Protestantism better than anyone. By staging resistance at the center of ordinary life (again on buses and at diners), he revealed an overwhelming lack of flourishing. White mainline pastors

19. I'm referring here to the arrival of premillennialism.

couldn't but act, calling on President Kennedy (and Johnson) in Washington to do the same.

Participation in the civil rights movement would be the last and best victory for the Fosdick-type pastor. In many ways, it would be the very summit, the high point on the line graph, which signaled both the peak and simultaneously the decline of the pastor's influence—and this drop in importance and trust of the Fosdick-type pastor would be steep. As the late 1960s dawned and a new age of authenticity took root (which we discussed at length in volume 1), the large youth culture decided that it could not trust the leaders of the societal structures to work for human flourishing. As the blood of eighteen-year-olds filled rivers in Vietnam, those in power, whether in Alabama or Washington, were painted as fascists, seeking their own power over human flourishing. The whole system was labeled corrupt, and, to their surprise, so too were the chaplains of the secular age. Organized (particularly Protestant mainline, Fosdick-like) religion was seen as a pawn for the powerful, corrupt in its own right. White mainline pastors, of course, pointed to their work for racial equality, holding up the battle scars they'd earned during their march to Selma. But it was too late; even those pastors who fully embraced the new ideologies, following, for example, the death of God theology,[20] were painted as disconnected and backward.[21]

In the new movement that the baby-boomer generation would create, the past would be jettisoned and disestablished with the hope of creating a new society of *free* love—where human flourishing was not coldly institutional but romantically warm, where ordinary life was from top to bottom completely about freedom, casting off all old conventions. The counterculture provided a new spirituality that promised the freedom of love, sex, and excitement. It became a new spirituality of authenticity, where all were free to find their own path to fulfillment by defining for themselves what it meant to be human.

20. For example, this was a radical take on how Christianity could engage a dawning secularization. A small group of theologians sought ways of being Christian and church without, oddly, the necessity of God, or at least classic theism. For discussion of this period and its broader shape, see Kenneth L. Woodward, *Getting Religion: Faith, Culture, and Politics from the Age of Eisenhower to the Ascent of Trump* (New York: Convergent, 2017). See particularly chapters 6 and 7.

21. "National opinion polls showed ministers had fallen in 'public esteem and confidence.' A 1967 Lou Harris poll showed that only 45 percent of the public expressed 'confidence in the clergy,' as opposed to the 74 percent who felt good about physicians or the 62 percent who spoke well of educators. Critics now spoke of 'the pretensions of the white Anglo-Saxon Protestant establishment,' announcing that 'its past supremacy' was 'everywhere threatened and tumbled' and that seminarians were 'generally busy extricating themselves from its shameful tentacles.' The rhetoric was hyperbolic, but everyone recognized that something was changing." Holifield, *God's Ambassadors*, 237.

Not only was the devil no longer in the woods, but the sources of meaning, the importance of rites of passage, and the shape of ordinary life were up to you and you alone.

The age of authenticity was, in no small measure, a new way of engaging the immanent frame of the secular age without overthrowing it and returning to Edwards's or Becket's days. The world itself was presumed to be only natural and material; there was nothing in the world that was more than this. As we saw in volume 1, though, this didn't mean that there wasn't a searching for the spiritual (hippie use of psychedelics and Eastern religious practices provided a spirituality, but it was a spirituality with no need for a personal god, and was therefore bound within the immanent frame).

The bohemianism of late 1960s counterculture revealed that few people could stand this immanent framing of human life. Yet, unable (and unwilling) to overthrow the immanent frame, people sought to discover new spiritual realities within themselves. People conceded, in different measure, that the world was only natural and material, but they also believed that you could create your own spiritual meaning for yourself. The age of authenticity makes the way of being human and therefore the order of an ordinary life (or even what is "ordinary") multivalent. It became a new spirituality to be unique and *not* conform ("ordinary" is now assumed to be as vast as the number of people).[22] It was in this environment that the New Age movement would begin, seeking paranormal, experiential spirituality. In Edwards's day everyone needed to conform to keep the devil in the woods, and in Beecher's and Fosdick's days democratic conformity could produce human flourishing. A new expressive individualism now dawned, which asserted that your *own* individual ordinary life was your highest good—you needed to attend to *your own* flourishing first.[23]

The 1980s would be called the "me decade," for not only had the hippie countercultural zealots become yuppies (or bobos, as we called them in volume 1), enjoying the excesses of consumer society, but also because human flourishing in ordinary life became an enclosed individual project. The pursuits of flourishing had shifted from keeping the devil in the woods, to keeping the machines of urban America moral, to *me* being happy, flourishing in my own individual life project. An example of the shift: as much as Fosdick supported a liberal theological position, he spoke strongly against divorce.

---

22. Of course, this could never actually be true. We couldn't have a society if truly everyone could define what is ordinary, normal, or expected. But we live deeply with this commitment, though we can never truly get there.

23. This played out across gender lines as well. In many ways this was the message of the hugely impactful *Feminist Mystique* (New York: Norton, 1963) written by Betty Friedan in 1963.

As the chaplain of the secular age, pushing for societal human flourishing, he couldn't see how completely free choice of sexual partners was good for society. For Fosdick, your individual project must be subordinate to societal flourishing. Yet, just downtown, a pastor in a church in the shadow of Wall Street would herald the power of positive thinking, challenging Fosdick as New York's greatest preacher. Each Sunday, Norman Vincent Peale filled his church by giving his people (and the hundreds of thousands listening on the radio) the tools of self-help, providing ways of flourishing in your individual life project as your ultimate end.

The pastor now needed to remake himself or herself as a guru or sage, able to assist people in the pursuits of their individual flourishing. Those pastors (particularly in the mainline churches) who didn't take on the guru identity, holding to the clerical conventions of Fosdick (or even Edwards), were left behind. They were seen as relics of a past world where we naively trusted the establishment and believed we needed pastors to be our conscience. As flourishing shifted from societal to individual, people were free to find all sorts of ways to experience something spiritual inside the immanent frame. Taylor has called this "the nova effect," meaning that all sorts of third ways between cold immanence and organized religion exploded. These unique third ways provided people with overarching meaning, significance to their rites of passage, and direction in their ordinary lives. It became a new spirituality to exercise, follow a band, hike, make money, party, swing, or get your kids into Yale.[24] Up against the immanent frame, all these new options, this nova effect, infused purpose into individualized flourishing. Organized religion and its pastors seemed too stale and too boring to help.

### Reinvention

And so some pastors reinvented themselves free of the conventions of organized religion, no longer chaplains of a secular age (and no longer mainline liberal). The churches that these mainly evangelical pastors built were void of religious symbols, looking more like malls than cathedrals, fitting more the shape of people's ordinary lives of shopping and entertainment than the invitation into sacred space (we were now as far away from Augustine and Becket as we can be). These new churches in suburban America were the height

---

24. Taylor explains: "So the need for meaning can be met by a recovery of transcendence, but we can also try to define the 'one thing needful' in purely immanent terms, say, in the project of creating a new world of justice and prosperity. And similarly, without appeal to religion, we can seek to give resonance to the everyday, to nature and the things around us, by calling on our own depth sense." *Secular Age*, 310.

of secular: no time-bending gravity permeated their walls. They looked more like Johnson & Johnson headquarters than the Duomo. But these buildings played an important part in the recasting of the pastor. Now that the nova effect had hit and spirituality had taken on a multiplicity of options, the pastor needed to make himself (there were few if any women leading these churches) into an entrepreneur and his building a concrete representation of the product he was offering.[25] The cultural environment was perfect for this shift in pastoral identity; the spiritual markets were unregulated, the hegemony of established religion was done, mainline Protestant America was over, and yet the age of authenticity and its nova effect moved people to seek spirituality. The monopolies were broken up, and yet there was spiritual demand. In this perfect environment for the entrepreneur, the model of the pastor shifted from Harry Emerson Fosdick to Rick Warren, who started Saddleback in 1980.

Warren was uninterested in being the chaplain of a secular age, reminding people of their better gods. Born and raised in California, bathed in the air of authenticity and (intuitively but) sharply aware of the nova effect, he formed a church that could speak to those searching, and in turn provided what many of these new spiritualities couldn't. Warren knew that all these third ways that people were using to create individualized flourishing promised them purpose by giving them an overarching meaning, ritualizing the passages of time, and directing their ordinary lives. And yet these new options were often either too loose and undefined or too tight and domineering to provide what people needed, leaving them in a malaise, as Taylor called it. In his California upbringing, Warren had seen both the too open and the too closed; he watched classmates follow bands and embrace nature, and he rubbed shoulders with members of Jim Jones's People's Temple, which relocated to Warren's Northern California community. Exercise or hiking could take you pretty far, directing your interests and activities and giving you some meaning, but they ultimately could not provide you with enough of a life-directing purpose to overcome your malaise. Warren could sense that the freedom of the age of authenticity couldn't fulfill its promise of purpose. And so inside the nova effect he created a "purpose-driven church" and provided his people a "purpose-driven life." This attention to purpose would have the ability to direct people's ordinary lives by speaking to their individual pursuit of flourishing.

25. Woodward explains: "Evangelical religion is essentially an entrepreneurial religion. This is not a theological definition, nor is it how most Evangelicals today would understand themselves. But it is, I would argue, a definition that captures Evangelicalism's distinguishing feature." *Getting Religion*, 129.

Within twenty-five years, Warren's church attendance ballooned to over twenty thousand people on 120 acres in Orange County. Warren called it Saddleback Community Church, deliberately avoiding denominational signals in its name (Warren believed that signaling that this was a Southern Baptist church would turn off seekers of individualized flourishing). Warren's building, and his own style, represented an openness, even a partnership, in helping individuals find their own purpose by allowing Jesus to help each person flourish and overcome the malaise that the age of authenticity seemed to leave in the wake of its individualized freedom. Yet Warren did not do this by speaking against individualized human flourishing or the age of authenticity. Instead, he doubled down and wagered that Jesus was just the individualized spirituality that could actually fulfill its promise. The results seemed to speak for themselves.

Soon enough Warren would create a network for other pastors, helping them take on the purpose-driven entrepreneurial pastoral identity he had honed. Warren gave purpose to scores of pastors who had felt lost after the Fosdick-type identity no longer worked. In the early 2000s, Warren would mobilize these purpose-driven entrepreneurial pastors, launching a new initiative for laypeople called "40 Days of Purpose." Its core resource would be a book called *The Purpose Driven Life*. Showing how directly Warren had his finger on the pulse of the pursuit of individualized flourishing, it was outsold in the first decade of the new millennium by only J. K. Rowling's Harry Potter series and Dan Brown's *Da Vinci Code*.

Warren found a way to revitalize the image of the pastor next to the individualized pursuits of flourishing.[26] The pastor as entrepreneur provided a direct way to be in the age of authenticity, offering the option of Jesus in the midst of the nova effect. But this understanding of the pastor had an inherent problem that leads us back to the pastor I was talking with at the conference, the one with a nauseous, uneasy feeling of what to do.

What made Warren's perspective both genius and problematic is that he offered Jesus at the level of the nova effect. Jesus was another third option amongst the thousands of others. Of course Warren was not shy in claiming that Jesus was *the best* option, a third way that could actually deliver in providing purpose and individual flourishing. But once Jesus was a choice in the new market of spirituality, a silent concession to the immanent frame—that it should be treated as reality—would be confirmed.

The immanent frame, remember, is a natural order that asserts that our lives should be considered primarily natural. It tempts us to block out any

---

26. Warren would have an awakening after his bestseller, moving him to give himself completely to human flourishing beyond the individual—fighting AIDS in Africa, for example.

overarching sense of transcendence and of God's speaking and holds that there is no difference between sacred and secular (allowing the secular to swallow the sacred).[27] The entrepreneurial pastor's building was the clearest sign that this was indeed a spirituality acquiesced to the immanent frame. There was no sense of a sacred time or space; the church building was as secular and utilitarian as any office complex. Rather than an invitation to enter into a sacred reality, it presented a place to find the resources to personally flourish (including childcare assistance, counseling centers, support groups, exercise classes, and coffee shops).

Ironically, this would make the building essential, for it was the place that held the material resources and programs individuals needed to flourish.[28] And the bigger, the better (twenty thousand people allowing for 120 acres—Warren seemed to always talk about them together, because in the end the number of people wasn't as important as the number of acres, but the number of people allowed for the number of acres), because the larger the campus, the more resources it could provide you as you sought your own flourishing. The more resources, the more you were engaged; and the more you were engaged, the more viable this spirituality was within the nova effect. It could provide meaning, shape your passages through time, and help your ordinary life be one of individually experienced flourishing. As Mark Chaves has shown, churches in America are polarized in the sense of size; small churches are getting smaller and big churches bigger,[29] because the bigger they are, the more resources they offer to tend to your malaise by giving outlets for individual flourishing. This yielding to the immanent frame affirmed that transcendence (divine action) was difficult to imagine.

## Back to the Beginning

And this difficulty in imagining divine action is exactly why the pastor I was talking with at the conference had no idea what to do. He had done a faithful job as a pastor, but he had a deep sense that he was supposed to be accomplishing something else, building something bigger, that he just couldn't. And if he couldn't, he had nothing else to offer in the immanent frame. He

27. There are ways of finding transcendence and divine action in the immanent frame, and a major goal of this project is to show how.

28. "'It's an instrument, not a monument,' Warren said of the building's decidedly utilitarian appearance." Jeffery L. Sheler, *Prophet of Purpose: The Life of Rick Warren* (New York: Doubleday, 2009), 166.

29. See Mark Chaves, *American Religion: Contemporary Trends* (Princeton, NJ: Princeton University Press, 2011).

had grown his church, but not to the level of Warren, not even close to being a one-stop shop for all your individualized flourishing. And this meant that there was no way to block the competing pitches of other spiritualities in the nova.[30] He knew that many of his people found more meaning in all sorts of other spiritualities (vacations, their child's sport, yoga, celebrity, buying), which led him to be inherently frustrated with his people's supposed lack of commitment.[31] He found himself bouncing back and forth from blaming them to blaming himself, always feeling either guilty that he couldn't be a better entrepreneur and grow a bigger church or frustrated that they couldn't really just commit. He explained that he tried for a while to recover a Fosdick-type pastoral stance, fronting social justice and marching for human rights; and while in itself this was good and right, it couldn't provide pastoral identity. He knew he was no longer seen as the conscience of the culture. The full-blown secular age had only skepticism for a chaplain (especially after the Religious Right). He even tried returning to an Edwards-like picture of the pastor, recommitting to doctrine and focusing on a strong, direct preaching of the Word. But the more he did that, the more people expressed frustration, conceding that he was intellectual but sorrowfully disconnected.

So he stood next to me stuck, feeling a depressing malaise laced with a hot, frustrated insecurity. From this uncomfortable place he found the crux of his issue; looking me in the eyes he said, "Ultimately, I guess, I don't know what to do, because I don't know how to talk about God in a way that people sense and recognize. I'm not even sure if that's possible anymore."

He felt like this shifting landscape had left him, as pastor, with an inability to discuss divine action. Our secular age had slowly erased the dividing line between sacred and secular, freeing our ordinary lives from divine consequence

---

30. This shows why the pastor feels like this: "The larger the church, the more frequently its pastor feels energized by ministry, and the more likely it is for the pastor to report an increased passion for ministry during their tenure at the church. Once again these findings indicate that growth trajectory is a factor in some pastors' positive feelings about themselves and about ministry." Barna Report, *The State of Pastors: How Today's Faith Leaders Are Navigating Life and Leadership in an Age of Complexity* (Ventura, CA: Barna Group, 2017), 24.

31. We can see this frustration in the finding of the Barna Group's *State of Pastors* (100, 149) report:

> Even the most energizing, rewarding job has its downsides—and when pastors generally report higher levels of satisfaction than US adults overall, the job of pastoring is no exception. Given an opportunity to identify the one or two biggest downsides of their job, the top five frustrations reported by pastors are:
> 1. Lack of commitment among laypeople (35%)
> 2. Low level of spiritual maturity among churchgoers (27%)
> 3. Financial and/or administrative duties (19%)
> 4. Church politics (18%)
> 5. Implementing change in the church (16%)

and making us immune to pastoral prodding (if we want pastors at all, it is to look for their advice and support as we seek our own *individual* flourishing). Now squarely in the immanent frame and unable to create a church that could provide every resource for individualized flourishing as an ultimate (winning) option in the nova effect, he felt completely disempowered to talk about God at all. And yet to face this reality directly would only turn his pastoral malaise into a full-blown depression, riding on a wave of shame. Inside this cycle it's no wonder he had no idea what to do.

While our secular age seems to stymie pastors, surgeons like Kalanithi are awakening to the pastoral task as central and transformational. The invitation to share in the depth of human experience, to enter into the reality of death, seems to bring an overwhelming sense of transcendence within the most im-manent of occupations. So even in this pastoral malaise, there is hope.

To discover how we can talk about God (divine action) in our secular age, we must dig deeper into how much the role of the pastor has changed. We must get as clear as we can on how our societal shifts have impacted us— how they have erased the line between sacred and secular, tired us of pastoral prodding, and vacated our ordinary lives of any divine consequences. To dig into these transitions, I'll continue with the strategy I began above, using particular historical figures as representatives of these shifts. You'll notice that I used as paradigmatic Augustine of Hippo, Thomas Becket, Jonathan Edwards, Henry Ward Beecher, Harry Emerson Fosdick, and Rick Warren. I'll continue to use them as ideal types, as pastors impacted by and impacting the unfolding of our Western conception of the pastor in a secular age. (For the most part we'll follow these figures historically, though I've made the choice to start with Thomas Becket before discussing Augustine to be able to first discuss disenchantment before moving on to the self.)

As I mentioned at the end of the introduction and need to say more boldly now, these figures are only *representative types* (Max Weber labeled these "ideal types," not in the sense of "best" but as "representative archetypes"; these types reveal "certain elements common to most cases of the given phenomena"[32]). So I don't mean to put these figures on a pedestal as the *best* pastors; they are simply representative of pastoral identity in key times in our evolving secular age. Living at crucial historical moments in the unfolding of our secular age, they best illustrate what Charles Taylor is describing. I recognize that many (particularly women and people of color, like Dorothy Day and Martin Luther King Jr.) are missing from this list. There were many

---

32. For more, see Weber's *The Protestant Ethic and the Spirit of Capitalism* (New York: Charles Scribner's Sons, 1958).

people doing important work from the margins, and I will tell some of their stories in part 2, particularly as they relate to those encountering divine action as ministry (King's story will be central to chapter 11). But I use this list as *types* because I'm exploring how the pastor has confronted and changed our Western social imaginary. These are big pastoral figures doing work at transitional times and are representative of who was shaping and typifying the broader cultural understanding of pastor. Following Taylor, I'll explore how our social imaginary can be revealed from examining the elites.

Of course, to put it that way opens me up to critique by admission. There are pastors like John Calvin, Martin Luther, William Wilberforce, Billy Sunday, Billy Graham, and Rob Bell who have obviously been deeply influential but whom I don't use as ideal types. This is because I sought key historical figures who for an overwhelming amount of their lives were congregational pastors (or directly engaged with faith communities as bishop). Calvin's and Luther's places in history are more as Reformers, Wilberforce as social reformer, Graham and Sunday as evangelists, and Bell as author and speaker.

It now is time for us to dig deeper into how the historical unfolding of our secular age has impacted the pastor, teasing out in more detail what we've mapped above, exploring how and why divine action has become opaque and what this has meant for the pastor.

# 2

## the lifting fog of enchantment

*Thomas Becket and pastoring in a disenchanted age*

It would be in demand for a hundred years after it was spilled. Like other blood, it was wet and red, but unlike other blood, it was magical. If you could get your hands on a vial, it could cure disease and turn famine to fortune. But if Thomas Becket's blood was too hard to come by, then a visit to his shrine or a touch of his bones could go a long way toward changing your luck. When Thomas Becket was murdered, he was fast-tracked into sainthood. The relics of all saints held enchanted power to the people of the Middle Ages. But those of martyred saints were particularly potent; with this blood you could imagine all sorts of magical possibilities. And the story of Thomas's martyrdom itself was enough to send a chill down your spine that you were sure was produced by some spiritual force.

Yet when Thomas was born (1119) and coming of age, sainthood or martyrdom seemed far from possible. Thomas's father was either a small landowner or a low-ranking knight. But he had enough privilege to get his boy educated. How far Thomas could go wasn't certain; young Thomas stammered terribly. By the time he was twenty and sent to Paris for study, Thomas had the stammering under control, beating it back by speaking slowly and quietly. Yet his time in Paris was interrupted when his beloved mother died. Her loss meant the end of Thomas's education, forcing employment as a clerk. Speaking slowly and quietly served Thomas well, making him a good listener and trusted counsel. Soon Thomas found himself climbing the ranks of the house of Theobald of Bec. The assent gave Thomas a taste of the finer things of life, like fancy clothes, long hunts, and good meals.

Theobald of Bec was himself climbing a ladder, becoming the archbishop of Canterbury. But Thomas had little interest in church affairs. Perhaps recognizing this, Theobald recommended Thomas to the young new king, Henry II, for the position of chancellor. Where Thomas was reserved, Henry was boisterous and impulsive, young and wild, and soon became close with Thomas. King Henry was impious, with a temper that ran hot, and he sought control and was willing to break any oath to achieve it. As chancellor, Thomas's job was to collect money from Henry's landowners, making sure the king's coffers were full, while adding a little to his own. Thomas enjoyed luxuries as much as Henry but struggled with the king's lack of devotion, so Thomas prayed often, even beating himself with a whip for his own sins. Thomas's own attention to the supernatural led him to use his funds to buy a coffin full of relics and hire a soothsayer to help him determine if and when to attack Wales.

### When the Blood Spills

Henry found it cumbersome to deal with bishops and had little patience for any Roman restrictions on his power. So when Theobald of Bec died, Henry worked to place his trusted Thomas in his place, making his chancellor the new archbishop of Canterbury and therefore winning control of the church and its pastors.[1] Thomas certainly was a pious medieval man, but he was no theology student or son of a cleric. Thomas even lacked a strong handle on Latin, yet now he was archbishop.

To Henry's great surprise, when Thomas Becket took the sacred oath, which bestowed on him the ordination right, he was changed; he became a new being. A reality that was outside Thomas and that Henry could not control had overtaken Thomas, and Thomas had to obey it. Giving up the chancellorship, Thomas devoted himself completely to the call. And to Henry's shock, he vowed to protect the sacred anointed priests even more than his predecessor and his lord king.

A medieval king's job was to uphold a divine order. He was to rule his domain as God ruled the universe (as a reflection of God's rule). Thomas couldn't help but call Henry a tyrant, for Henry opposed God's anointed and

---

1. When I say *pastor* here, I really mean priest. I'm aware that there is a significant distinction between the imagination of a pastor and a priest. I'll wrestle with this in the next chapter. Here, however, I artificially equate them for the sake of the reader identifying with my point of disenchantment.

refused to concede to the chain of being—that the king is the most essential but nevertheless still a servant of God. Thomas opposed his once friend at every turn, calling Henry to confess. Bishops who would do Henry's bidding, breaking church law, were one by one excommunicated by Thomas. It was his job to stand for the church over the state, most particularly if the state refused God's law.

When three excommunicated bishops reported Thomas's actions to the king, Henry went red with rage and shouted to his court, "Who among you will rid me of this priest?" Historian Simon Schama argues that more likely Henry said, "What miserable drones and traitors have I nourished and brought up in my household, who let their lord be treated with such shameful contempt by a low-born cleric?"[2] Four knights, hearing these words, took them as a command and set out to find Thomas. Arriving at the Cathedral of Canterbury, they hid their weapons and tried to convince Thomas to join them and return to Henry. But Thomas refused.

For the knights to do what was needed next, they'd need extreme amounts of drink and hubris. They retrieved their weapons and found Thomas at vespers. The monks chanting in the candlelight would become the backdrop and soundtrack of Thomas's murder. The four knights raced to Thomas as he approached the stairs to the crypt and the center of holy worship. According to an eyewitness named Edward Grim, one of the knights jumped forward and landed a blow to Thomas's head. Then another struck, forcing Thomas to his knees. Grim reports that Thomas, on his knees, uttered, "For the name of Jesus and the protection of the Church, I am ready to embrace death."[3] Then a third knight hurled such a devastating blow that Grim says it brought with it the white of Thomas's brain, flooding the floor with a deep puddle of blood and body.

The knights, fleeing to collect their reward from Henry, left the monks to prepare Thomas for burial and collect his blood, which had soaked deeply into the floor, stained as a reminder of his ultimate pastoral sacrifice. When word of his death reached Rome, Thomas was quickly made a saint.[4] And soon his blood began to appear as a relic, believed to hold powerful magic, able to protect and heal. In 1220, fifty years after his death, Thomas's remains were moved into a shrine, allowing more people access to the powerful bones of the saint, for his pastoral action had potent power.

2. Simon Schama, *History of Britain* (New York: Miramax, 2000), 142.

3. Edward Grim, in *Vita S. Thomae, Cantuariensis Archepiscopi et Martyris*, in James Robertson, ed., *Materials for the Life of Thomas Becket*, vol. 2 (London: Rolls Series, 1875–85).

4. At the time of Thomas (twelfth century), England was fully and completely part of the Roman Catholic Church. It wasn't until the sixteenth century that King Henry VIII would lead England into a break with Rome and create the Anglican Church.

Thomas would be beloved as the protector of pastors; as a fighter for order speaking truth to power, forcing a corrupt king to recognize the enchanted importance of priests living at the speed of heaven; and as a protector of those living at the speed of earth, helping them find salvation. The people loved Thomas because he defended the power of the pastor to drive the people into the time-bending wormhole of salvation, and now his blood and bones could protect and direct. If King Henry II undercut the significance of the pastor, the people would be left hauntingly naked to face an enchanted world of demons, spirits, and spells without the powerful intervention of the pastor. Now in his death, people found Thomas's pastoral protection by possessing his blood or touching the stone or gold plates of his shrine. And this would last until another King Henry some four hundred years later would destroy Thomas's shrine as an act of reform. Unlike Henry II, Henry VIII would have the advantage of the people's changed perception that priests (and even Rome itself) were corrupt, needing pious reform. Henry VIII could use this for his own gain, smashing the shrines and stripping the altars, keeping the people from seeking a new Thomas to oppose him. The fog of enchantment was still present, but maybe not as thick, allowing the people to feel more control in their ordinary lives. And while Henry VIII may have had only power on his mind, these reforms would bring forth a golden age under his daughter, Elizabeth I.

### Dissing Enchantment

It is undeniable that we also live in a golden age, though unlike past golden ages under monarchs like Elizabeth I, ours is not the golden age of commerce, philosophy, religion, or architecture. Rather, ours is a golden age of television. Not only do we have HD streaming services like Netflix, Amazon Prime, and Hulu, but more so, the quality of the shows themselves has never been higher. The binge-worthy series are too many to watch.

In the fall of 2016 Netflix released an original show that soon became a big hit: *The Crown*. Season 1 is the story of the early reign of the other Queen Elizabeth (Elizabeth II). Using flashbacks, the show takes us to the 1930s, when Elizabeth's father, George, was made king after his older brother, Edward, abdicated the throne to marry a thrice-divorced American socialite, putting the young Elizabeth in line to rule. The season is set mostly in the 1950s, after George dies and Elizabeth becomes queen in a new world of television, celebrity, and the decline of British imperialism. Elizabeth finds herself in a position she would not have chosen, reminded again and again that she represents something much bigger than herself, which is nevertheless now in doubt. Each decision she makes must protect the crown after her uncle nearly destroyed it by choosing self-fulfillment over duty and worshiping romance over the eternal call to rule. Elizabeth is standing on a precarious fault line, caught between the ancient realm of royalty and the postwar globalizing world of jet planes.

This tenuous balance is seen no more strikingly than in her 1953 coronation. The liturgy of the ceremony is as ancient as Thomas Becket but for the first time could be beamed across the globe and into people's living rooms thanks to television cameras. The cross-pressured juxtaposition is seen no more vividly than when it comes time for the new queen to receive the anointing. As the oil marks her and the same ancient words are declared over her as were spoken over the first Elizabeth, the protectors of the royal tradition tell Elizabeth II that she is *ontologically* transformed. No longer is she Elizabeth Windsor. Now she is Elizabeth Regina, a new being. No longer an ordinary, shy girl, now she is God's representative. As the golden canopy is brought forth to shield the audience from this holy act (for their own protection), the cameras cut away. This moment is too revered, maybe too enchanted, for profane viewing. Though most viewers doubt that there is *really* anything holy happening behind that curtain, they *hope* there is and are happy for the cameras to turn away.

In the Netflix show, Uncle Edward, the formerly abdicated king, is watching the telecast in Paris. He is surrounded not only by the wife he chose instead of the crown but also by a room full of French and American onlookers. He becomes de facto commentator, a kind of Vin Scully, providing play-by-play to the confused room of citizens living in societies that long ago threw off the ancient regime of kings and queens.

As the television they are watching goes still, cameras averted from the holy act, an American in the room asks, "Where did she go?"

Edward, becoming more reflective, responds in his elitist British accent, "We now come to the anointing. The single most holy, most solemn, most sacred moment of the entire service."

The same American returns, "Then how come we don't get to see it?"

"Because we are mortals," Edward responds, now taken to a place where reverence and melancholy connect. He stares deeply into the still television as if it were an icon. Lifting his voice, now in full play-by-play mode, Edward says, "Oil and oaths, orbs and scepters, symbol upon symbol, an unfathomable web of arcane mystery and liturgy, blurring so many lines no clergyman or historian or lawyer could ever untangle any of it."

The American interlocutor rebuts, "It's crazy!"

"On the contrary, it is perfectly sane," Edward responds quickly, taking his eyes from the frozen television to the room. "Who wants transparency when you can have magic? Who wants prose when you can have poetry? Pull away the veil and what are you left with? An ordinary young woman with modest ability and little imagination. But wrap her up like this, and anoint her with oil, and hey, presto, what do you have? A goddess."

## The Cross-Pressure of Enchantment

"Magic and mortals." "Arcane mysteries and goddesses." These are concepts that feel so very far and yet somehow near to us. Elizabeth's 1953 coronation was an event caught between times. It was, as Charles Taylor would describe, an occurrence of *cross-pressure*. We live in a time when magic is left to movies and goddesses to models with sex appeal. We live in a *dis*enchanted time, when it is assumed that science has explained (or soon will) every arcane mystery,[5] and modest, unimaginative girls are only and finally that. And yet we have this sense of something we can't remember; we have this feeling that maybe life isn't as flat as we assume. Maybe ordinary girls can indeed, presto, be transformed by words and oil.

But who could admit that? This is the pressure of being crossed up; we doubt what we long for. We doubt that what we long for is sensible. Almost all of us yearn for poetry instead of prose, for mystery over cold transparency, and yet we feel the need to face the facts. We live in the twenty-first century. Still, at times our experience becomes so full, so oddly interconnected, that we doubt that we should doubt. We feel drawn to question the presumption that arcane mystery and the magic of interconnection is an illusion.

Oil is only oil. A girl is only a girl. Her DNA is related to an ape, not a god. There is nothing outside that can change something into something else, we assume. However, those filling the cathedrals of Becket's time were soaked in a completely different overarching meaning system, bound in the acceptance of arcane mysteries and ontological transformations. The pastor's job was to give order and protection from the constant flood of enchantment. It was a world drowning with meaning because it was a world soaked in divine action.

5. Taylor is leaning on Max Weber in making this argument about disenchantment. Brad Gregory offers us a nice overview of Weber and where his conception of disenchantment fits: "According to Weber, 'intellectualist rationalization through science and scientifically oriented technology' means that 'fundamentally no mysterious incalculable powers are present that come into play, but rather that one can—in principle—master all things by calculation. This implies the disenchantment of the world.'" *The Unintended Reformation: How a Religious Revolution Secularized Society* (Cambridge, MA: Belknap Press, 2012), 26.

Even today, in nearly every Christian tradition, the pastor stands before the people each week, offering in one way or another a web of arcane mysteries and liturgies, and asserts that things are more than can be seen. Holding simple bread and wine, the pastor claims that it becomes something more. Dripping water on bodies or dipping full bodies in water, the pastor claims that there is something more mysterious, even transformational, happening. And *some* people are kind enough to concur, wishing their children to be baptized and finding some personal meaning in communion. But like Elizabeth's coronation, we often feel caught between times, pressured on both sides. People are willing to have children baptized but are pretty sure that tap water has no power (or force) to bring life out of death. Willing to happily take the bread and wine, hearing the words "This body broken for you," they also know that it is store bought.

## Pastoring in Disenchantment

The pastor I met at the conference at the beginning of chapter 1 might as well have said, "I'm not sure what I'm doing, because I don't know how to talk about, or even embody, God's action in a disenchanted time." He was struck with a malaise, which as we saw in the previous chapter has its first symptom in the loss of a sense of overarching meaning.[6] The meaning that's been washed away (or at least radically eroded) is a clear vision of divine action, a sure sense that God indeed causes things in our world and directs our lives. It is *not* that the pastor no longer believes this. It just feels more and more like he is speaking a foreign language that few people, himself included, use in their day-to-day lives.

In an enchanted world, divine action was like confetti after a parade—it hung everywhere and on everything. Divine action was a language everyone, always and everywhere, spoke. Now it feels like people speak enough to remember a few words here and there but not enough to create the necessary

---

6. George Levine gives us some more on disenchantment and Weber:
   Weber contends that meaning drains out of the world precisely as we come to believe that "if one wished one could learn" virtually anything; "there are no mysterious incalculable forces." . . . Disenchantment, Weber insists, consistently affirms that without magic, without God, without teleology, enchantment is purged from the world, and, with it, the world's meaning and the world's value. In the "intellectualization of the world," Weber says, "scientific progress is a fraction, the most important fraction." Weber's narrative of disenchantment leaves only these options: either a value-laden world infused with transcendental meaning, or an amoral world from which all value is drained as it is subjected to scientific investigation. (*Darwin Loves You: Natural Selection and the Re-Enchantment of the World* [Princeton, NJ: Princeton University Press, 2006], 2, 23–24)

syntax for a *meaningful* conversation. When disenchantment sets in, the visions and words for divine action become much harder to spot and articulate.

At one level, the pastor I met would admit (as should we) that it's nice to live beyond an enchanted world. There is a real freedom in not being haunted by ghosts and chased by demons. It's (seemingly) beneficial to be able to cleanly categorize all odd, destructive, and antisocial behavior, for example, as mental illness. The immanent framing of the mental health industry wins us a leisure that our ancestors never could have imagined, as do fire trucks, pesticides, and State Farm Insurance (as we'll see below). The downpour of demons is over. The clouds have broken, and we can finally relax and let our hair down. Because we now assume that devils and omens don't exist, we have nothing more to fear but fear itself (a psychological condition called paranoia, which is a fear with no material source and therefore is fear for no reason).

Because fear is only (and finally) a psychological or medical condition, it is only in our minds. We assume fear is just a little chemical toxin in the brain with no real *thingness* to it at all. Disconnected from enchantment, fear becomes, at least for some, a pursued emotion, a welcome sensation used for entertainment. The downpour of demons is so over that we pay sixteen dollars to be frightened in cinemas, or line up to be startled in Halloween haunted houses. The horror movie becomes a recovery of a lost experience, or better, a lost worldview. We enter the theater to slide again into an enchanted world. Even for just ninety minutes, the clash of good and evil is redrawn by the magical, and the flat lives of young suburbanites are flooded with paranormal meaning.[7]

Our ancestors would have found this form of entertainment shocking. They didn't need movies; they lived in an enchanted world where demons lurked. Every day their lives were filled with frightening meaning. For instance, it is reported of one young Englishman that "for five or six years, he went to sleep with his hands clasped in a praying position, so that if the devils came for him they would find him prepared. By day he saw devils in trees and bushes. . . . The battle with Satan and his hierarchy of demons was thus a literal reality for

7. Charles Taylor discusses some reasons that going to horror movies or dabbling in pagan and occult practices may reemerge in a disenchanted world: "The decline of the world-view underlying magic was the obverse of the rise of the new sense of freedom and self-possession. From the viewpoint of this new sense of self, the world of magic seems to entail a thralldom, an imprisoning of the self in uncanny external forces, even a ravishing or loss of self. It threatens a possession which is the very opposite of self-possession. For our contemporaries who are very secure in the modern identity or even feel imprisoned within it, playing with the occult can provide a pleasant frisson for the contented, or perhaps even seem to offer a way of escape for those who feel oppressed by disenchantment." *Sources of the Self: The Making of Modern Identity* (Cambridge, MA: Harvard University Press, 1989), 192.

most devout Englishmen."[8] They would run to sacred places, like Thomas's tomb or the local cathedral, to escape and warm themselves with liturgy, prayer, and sacraments. These sacred places and practices offered respite from the terrors. We do the opposite and pay to enter spaces to be terrorized. In this disenchanted time, this act may be a way of fortifying our imaginations and reminding ourselves that demons and devils don't exist.

Because there is no enchanted realm and the deluge of demons has stopped, unlike our ancestors we can take long holidays from prayer, liturgy, and confession. We get to those practices when we feel like it and are seemingly no worse for the wear. We can return to spirituality or religion when we *feel* like it. These practices and holy festivals are no longer essential to our way of life, because our way of life has worked to free us from demons (and magic). And we should welcome this change; it was a harsh life for those in Becket's day. Yet removing the centuries-old paint of enchantment has taken with it the patina of an overachieving meaning system of divine action. And while all of us live with this, I believe that the pastor feels it acutely.

Standing in a similar place as Edward, the cross-pressured pastor still believes that prayer and confession matter (even that demons still exist) but is not sure what the central practices of petition and forgiveness accomplish. Without enchantment the use of these practices holds nearly the same weight as eating kale or doing yoga. They are undoubtedly good for you but not essential to everyone's day-to-day life and in no way necessary to shape your ordinary existence. Just as you can live a productive life without yoga, so you can be perfectly healthy without confession. Eating kale can benefit your blood pressure, and so can prayer (scientific studies show[9]).

But does prayer or confession protect us from evil and possession by demonic forces? Most (moderate and mainline) pastors would stumble at the question itself. Pastors in this age are left to justify these practices at the level of personal interest and benefit. Pastors are cross-pressured in a new way. If they refuse to concede these practices completely to individualized flourishing and self-help, they still want them to have some bigger historical significance. Yet even when these pastors refuse to see prayer as self-help (and scoff at books like *The Prayer of Jabez*), they are lost with how else to claim the importance of the practices of faith. Prayer is not the same as eating kale, but nevertheless the pastor cannot affirm that this is an enchanted realm. He is forced to conceive of these practices as he wishes not to. Caught here, the pastor often is left with frustration that the people can't just commit to come

---

8. Keith Thomas, *Religion and the Decline of Magic* (New York: Penguin, 1991), 562.

9. Zoe Blarowski, "7 Proven Health Benefits of Prayer," Care2, March 28, 2018, https://www.care2.com/greenliving/7-proven-health-benefits-of-prayer.html.

to church and practice their faith. At the same time, his people inherited an immanent frame that hollows out the meaning of liturgy, prayer, and confession, making divine action opaque. The affirmation of this disenchanted world wins us many gains but in turn strips away a meaning system that made divine action as obvious and formative in people's lives as market capitalism is today.

The pastor, then, leads her congregation through Sunday worship as Edward led the viewing party through Elizabeth's ceremony. Edward is acutely cross-pressured more than anyone else in the room. He seems to both most fiercely believe and yet also deny the potency of these practices. Edward defends them as powerful but can't quite articulate why. Edward tells the viewing room that they are entering an enchanted realm, and he seems to believe it, even to pine for it. Yet he gave it up to marry a divorced woman.

The pastor leads her people through the practices of faith. She bestows forgiveness on them in the power of the name of Jesus. She gives them over to their death and Christ's resurrection in the waters of baptism. She contends that these practices are powerful, imbued with a force; but she's not quite sure *how*. She is crossed up, maybe more than anyone else in the congregation. The American in Paris, watching the coronation with Edward, claimed the practice was crazy, but most people are happy to go through the motions, appreciating the pomp, safely buffered from any cosmic consequence. But the pastor, like Edward, feels the pressure of these colliding worlds, an internal tension she most often does a good job of keeping buried. The pastor is aware that in this Sunday morning hour she speaks of a kind of enchantment that she can easily walk away from, *never* tempted (not even once) to use the host to heal a sick dog or the baptismal water to fix a broken car. She'll leave all that for vets and mechanics.

### White and Black Magic

In Thomas Becket's time, if the medieval priests had a top-ten list of frustrations, "refusal to swallow the host" would be on it. People were sneaking the body of Christ out of the church to feed to their sick cows.[10] This is why it is now common for people to stick out their tongue to the priest, like a six-year-old with a sore throat, to confirm that the host has been swallowed. "The first Edwardian Prayer Book accordingly insisted that the bread should be placed by the officiating minister direct in the communicant's mouth, because in past

10. "In the eleventh century the consecrated host was often buried in fields to insure a good harvest." Paul Bernier, *Ministry in the Church: A Historical and Pastoral Approach* (Eugene, OR: Wipf & Stock, 1992), 119.

times people had often carried the sacrament away and 'kept it with them and diversely abused it, to superstition and wickedness.'"[11]

Failing fields and sick cows were enough for many people to seek this power, but the real fears in Becket's time were fire, famines, and plague.[12] For example, "as a protection against fire there were St. Agatha's letters, an inscription placed on tiles, bells or amulets. Fasting on St. Mark's day was another means of gaining protection; or one could appeal to St. Clement or to the Irish saint Columbkille. In 1180 the holy shrine of St. Werberga was carried round Chester and miraculously preserved the city from destruction by fire." In regard to famine, "there were exorcisms to make the fields fertile; holy candles to protect farm animals; and formal curses to drive away caterpillars and rats and to kill weeds."[13] The priest was happy to offer this kind of white magic, as long as people didn't wish condemnation on themselves by deceptively taking the most holy object—the host—to use for themselves, like a toddler playing with uranium.

Today we hear church bells and think their purpose is purely aesthetic, a kind of marketing, or even warning, reminding us that it's time for church. But for a peasant working a field near the Canterbury Cathedral, the dinging and donging would mean something very different. "The consecration of church bells made them efficacious against evil spirits and hence enabled them to dispel the thunder and lightning for which demons were believed to be responsible."[14]

Nearly everything the medieval priest did was to protect people from enchanted haunting. The priest always knew what he was doing, never struck with malaise of meaning. He had a deep sense of purpose because he had a clear vision of divine action, or he was himself a primary means of divine action. The priest was to constantly prepare people for entry into the sacred, to cross the line from the profane into the holy.[15] And this was heroic work, as Thomas Becket's veneration would witness, because the profane (or secular)

---

11. Thomas, *Religion and the Decline of Magic*, 39.

12. See Thomas, *Religion and the Decline of Magic*, 17–20, 38.

13. Thomas, *Religion and the Decline of Magic*, 35.

14. Thomas, *Religion and the Decline of Magic*, 34.

15. Peter Brown provides an example from Augustine's life in the fourth century: "Augustine grew up in an age where men thought that they shared the physical world with malevolent demons. They felt this quite as intensely as we feel the presence of myriads of dangerous bacteria. The 'name of Christ' was applied to the Christian like a vaccination. It was the only guarantee of safety. As a child, Augustine had been 'salted' to keep out the demons; when he had suddenly fallen ill, as a boy, he would plead to be baptized. These Christian rites, of course, might influence a grown-up man's conduct as little as the possession of a certificate of vaccination; but they expressed a mentality that had cut off, as positively 'unhygienic,' the pagan religion of the classical past." *Augustine of Hippo* (Berkeley: University of California Press, 2000), 30.

realm was filled to overflowing with forces of devils, demons, and all sorts of black magic. E. Brooks Holifield explains: "The clergy were specialists in the supernatural. They envisioned the cure of souls as a combat with Satan and his hosts; their pastoral methods were weapons in a warfare to force the enemy from his stronghold. They could assume command in that battle because they were stewards of mysteries that transcended the reach of most other people." The priest was a superhero in the medieval imagination, the first vampire hunter, the original Buffy.[16] He stood on the line between the profane and the sacred. And having been consecrated (having his essence bound to the sacred force), he had direct access to the warehouse of the supernatural, able to wield all its objects and substances, as Batman does with his utility belt. Keith Thomas explains that because the medieval church was a repository of supernatural power that could be dispensed to the faithful, "it was inevitable that the priest . . . derived an extra cachet from their position as mediators between man and God."[17]

This made the priest's prayers, words, and especially objects seem powerfully magical to ordinary people. It was imagined that a friar's coat, the church door keys, or even coins from the offertory had the power to chase away black magic, making them more valuable than Tom Brady's Super Bowl LI game jersey. Something wasn't holy because people simply consented to its importance; it was holy because it was infused with power itself. The medieval priest could never imagine a vocational identity crisis. He would find it unfathomable that pastors in our time are struck with a malaise of impotence or a sense that divine action is difficult to articulate and therefore unbelievable to most people. If the medieval priest had a crisis, it was the fear that the objects and rituals were *so* powerful that if he came into contact with his own darkness or disobedience, he'd be struck dead (this gives us a little insight into Luther's anxieties in the late medieval period). Becket's priests had magic. Every day they fought demons in fires, lightning, sickness, and the declarations of mad kings.

If the priest ever doubted this enchanted power, the significance of the Eucharist would bring him quickly back in line. As a matter of fact, in people's imagination it was the Holy Supper that was the very case in point that in-

16. Holifield continues, "Of course, they had to resolve a lot of mundane problems, as well. They instructed their people about oaths and vows, quarrels and vices, health and riches, clothing and recreation, alms and relief, and an array of other ethical and political questions. But the minister cared first for the conscience, a natural power with a unique capacity for giving 'supernatural' testimony. Such a faculty was especially susceptible to subversion by the forces of evil, but it was also the route of access to the sacred. For that reason, the cure of souls always impinged on the region of the supernatural." *A History of Pastoral Care in America: From Salvation to Self-Realization* (Nashville: Abingdon, 1983), 39.

17. Thomas, *Religion and the Decline of Magic*, 36.

deed the church possessed a warehouse of white magic. "In the . . . miracle of transubstantiation the 'instrumental cause' was the formula of consecration. Theologians refined this doctrine considerably, but their subtleties were too complicated to be understood by ordinary [people]. What stood out was the magical notion that the mere pronunciation of words in a ritual manner could effect a change in the character of material objects."[18]

A string of Latin words could turn one thing into another—presto, wine is blood, or an unimaginative girl is a goddess.[19] The Eucharist, particularly, was so powerful because what you received from the hand of the priest was a *host*. This grain and yeast carried a powerful guest, so much so that even though it *looked* like bread, it was now something completely other. It became the very flesh of Jesus himself, who turns water into wine and walks across liquid lakes. You take into your mouth part of a magical being who does magical things.

In this enchanted world the pastor knew exactly what he was doing by giving his people Jesus. He was taking them into the arcane mystery of deep enchantment. He was ushering them into the sacred place where they were protected from haunting evil spirits and where white magic cast out the dark.[20] Like the joke "When the boogie man is scared, he looks under his bed for Chuck Norris," so it was assumed that the demons of fire, famine, and sickness looked under their demon beds for Jesus lying in wait. What haunted the haunters was the Christ. And when you had the host, you had this Christ. The people honored and loved Thomas Becket because he protected the priests. And by protecting these priests, Becket gave the people the means of salvation by giving them the sources of protection from the devil. When the world is seen from this perspective, it is understandable how Becket's blood could be revered. It was a particularly potent white magic.

## When White Magic Is a Problem

This desire for white magic produced a vicious circle, though, that would eventually throw the whole system into question. People were frightened,

18. Thomas, *Religion and the Decline of Magic*, 37.

19. "Within Christianity, people have smuggled consecrated hosts to use against the evil eye and mumbled what they heard of the Latin consecration as an all-purpose charm (*hoc est corpus meum* is often thought to be the source of English 'hocus-pocus'), while at a yet more debased level of superstition whole churches now instruct sacramental rites according to the dictates of their own 'hearts,' deaf to the Lord's mandating word, 'Do this.'" Robert W. Jenson, *Ezekiel*, Brazos Theological Commentary on the Bible (Grand Rapids: Brazos, 2009), 114.

20. "The medieval Church thus appeared as a vast reservoir of magical power, capable of being deployed for a variety of secular purposes. Indeed it is difficult to think of any human aspiration for which it could not cater." Thomas, *Religion and the Decline of Magic*, 51.

so they raced to white magic and superstition. Thomas says, "It was also inevitable that around the Church, the clergy and their holy apparatus there clustered a horde of popular superstitions, which endowed religious objects with a magical power to which theologians themselves had never laid claim."[21] Holifield adds that "the clergy were not the only specialists in supernatural mysteries. They complained of competition from 'wizards and soothsayers' who used charms, love magic, fortunetelling, divination, and astrology to solve any problem. When pretenders claimed to have special access to supernatural beings, the clergy accused them of blasphemy and of implying that 'God hath provided a salve for every sore.'"[22] The propensity of people to reach for soothsayers made the church uncomfortable, so it doubled down, reminding the people of their sinfulness and the charged power of the church's holy things. This only made people seek more white magic to protect themselves and thus fall deeper into superstition, leading to more homilies of condemnation, corruption, and damnation. It was a cycle of anxiety. It was an age of great fears: "Fear of magic, of outsiders, of disorders, and of course of sin, death, and judgment."[23]

Inside this vicious circle, the contention that the church offered white magic never sat well with theologians (even in the Middle Ages). Nevertheless, the Eucharist was so powerful and the world so flooded with demons that to see it as other than magical was difficult. The church had to work hard to ensure that this perceived white magic wouldn't become diluted, sold as a cheap good. People were reminded that this holy meal was so powerful and so revered that to take it for anything other than its church-sanctioned purpose was to wish destruction and therefore eternal haunting onto your soul. People were reminded from the pulpit over and again that they were at great risk in eating such a powerful thing.

For most people in the middle ages, "celebrating" the Eucharist would be like us celebrating an appendectomy.[24] A little excited wiggle in your knees and a chipper happiness is not the appropriate reaction to an impending surgery in which a knife will slice open your belly. Rather, you enter surgery ready for

21. Thomas, *Religion and the Decline of Magic*, 36.

22. Holifield, *History of Pastoral Care*, 39.

23. Charles Taylor, *A Secular Age* (Cambridge, MA: Belknap Press, 2007), 88.

24. Roland Bainton shares what happened when the host was dropped. This gives us a sense of the power of the Eucharist: "One of the communicants so trembled that he dropped the bread. Carlstadt told him to pick it up; but he who had had the courage to come forward and take the sacred morsel into his own hand from the plate, when he saw it desecrated on the floor was so overcome by all the terror of the sacrilege to the body of God that he could not bring himself to touch it again." *Here I Stand: A Life of Martin Luther* (New York: Abingdon-Cokesbury, 1950), 206–7.

a frightening hell, knowing you'll be cut and probed. You allow the anesthesia into your body, knowing there is a small chance you'll never awaken. You'll choose it all only because the alternative is worse.

In the same way, the medieval peasant received the host with fear. Even if he snuck it out of the cathedral to feed to a sick cow, he'd only do so because he was desperate, risking condemnation, as a banker today might justify embezzlement to pay for his daughter's health care. The peasant paused before taking the host into his body, unsure if its holiness would strike him dead. But the risk of the sacred Eucharist meeting his sinfulness and striking him down was better than the alternative—demon possession and fires, whether of home and fields or eternal soul. In the centuries after Becket, the friction of the vicious circle became too intense to hold. The propensity to see the Eucharist as white magic led the church to show that it was *more than* magic, casting its sacredness against the profanity of the people. This only led people to fearfully avoid the Eucharist and run further into the superstition of other white magic. As Taylor says, "[People] were forced [to take communion] once a year, by the rules of the Church, but this minimum in fact remained a maximum for most people. . . . To take communion unworthily was seen as highly perilous, and the church's preaching reinforced this."[25]

The pressure on this vicious circle became too much, and reform followed. The only way to defuse the tension would be to directly oppose magic altogether. Demons and devils would need post-Galilean science, European Enlightenment, and Industrial Revolution to be exorcised from our imagination (allowed to pop back up only in movies and haunted houses).

Before science and philosophy could convince us that demons were only in our minds, magic itself needed to be devalued. Though theologians had been uneasy with magic for centuries, it wasn't until the Reformation took the bold step of blurring the line between the sacred and profane that magic and superstition would begin its slow fade.

It would begin with the bombastic courage to redefine the Eucharist. This was profound (and risky) because the Eucharist was proof that the church possessed a warehouse of powerful *things*. Yet in the Lutheran, Zwinglian, and Calvinist reconceptions of communion, the power of the meal was shifted from the transubstantiating *thing-ness* to its *representation* (so that God could be seen more clearly as a free actor).[26] For Luther the host was no longer magically

25. Taylor, *Secular Age*, 73.
26. Thomas explains the early Protestant opposition to the idea of a warehouse of powerful things: "Early Protestantism thus denied the magic of the opus operatum, the claim that the Church had instrumental power and had been endowed by Christ with an active share in his work and office." *Religion and the Decline of Magic*, 59.

Jesus: the real presence of Jesus was found in, through, and under it. It was just bread and would remain always so, even if Jesus meets us in eating it. For Zwingli the bread was only a representation, its power not in its *thing-ness* at all but in the minds and actions of those who ritualized it. Yet, regardless of how the different reforming traditions understood the Eucharist, they all agreed, and opposed Rome, that human beings had *no* control of divine power. God could not be captured in *things*, making *all* magic illegitimate.

The Reformation, though a distinctly theological movement, gained its deep and wide influence because it uniquely impacted people's day-to-day lives. With the Eucharist redefined and the line between sacred and secular blurring, more attention was given to the ordinary. Capital and material things of value were free to be reimagined as sacred.[27] Holiness not only was found in warehouses of the church but was worked out in our day-to-day lives. The heightened value of the ordinary allowed for the creation of institutions like the fire brigade and home insurance.[28] These new institutions were there to protect what was *now* holy—our ordinary farms and homes.

This new imagination of capital and social organization meant less of a need for fire and crop superstitions. Thanks to the Reformation, it became a true possibility, maybe for the first time, to live without the necessity of white magic. Calvinist societies didn't need bells to protect people from fire; they had systems for firefighting. They didn't need spells to turn vengeful neighbors passive; they had societal demands for decency and politeness. When these reforms took, *all* practices of magic were pushed to the margins, making superstitions in toto out of bounds.[29] Calvin had no tolerance for magic in

27. Here Thomas is affirming that these technological changes lead to a decline in magic. Similar to Taylor, he doesn't accept a simple subtraction story of social science rising and magic declining: "The decline of magic was thus accompanied by the growth of the natural and social sciences, which helped men to understand their environment, and of a variety of technical aids—from insurance to fire-fighting—by which they were able to increase their control of it. Yet the more closely Malinowski's picture of magic giving way before technology is examined, the less convincing does it appear. For the correspondence between magic and social needs had never been more than approximate." *Religion and the Decline of Magic*, 785.

28. "Despite initial hesitations, insurance established itself during the eighteenth century as one of the most basic sources of security for the English middle classes. . . . Nothing did more to reduce the sphere in which magical remedies were the only form of protection against misfortune. For, as Daniel Defoe remarked in 1697, the principle of mutual insurance made it possible for 'all the contingencies of life [to] be fenced against . . . as thieves, floods by land, storms by sea, losses of all sorts, and death itself.'" Thomas, *Religion and the Decline of Magic*, 782.

29. "The Reformation by contrast is justly commemorated for having robbed the priest of most of his magical functions. His powers of exorcism were taken away, and his formulae of benediction and consecration much reduced. The end of the belief in transubstantiation, the discarding of Catholic vestments, and the abolition of clerical celibacy, cumulatively diminished the mystique of the clergyman within his parish." Thomas, *Religion and the Decline of Magic*, 328.

Geneva. And while Lutherans and Puritans would concern themselves with protection from black magic for centuries, sure of witches and demons, this only made *all* magic problematic. For instance, Jonathan Edwards would continue to battle the devil in seventeenth-century America, not with *magic* but with self-control and order. The passion to move Christian faith into the whole of our lives and to lessen people's fear of the Eucharist led to a disenchanting that would eventually strike cross-pressured pastors in our time.[30] In a world of genomes, running water, penicillin, Geico, and sprinkler systems, where is the possibility of divine action?[31]

## Magic and Today

Though magic has been crowded out by the disenchantment that would bring our secular age, it still filters down to us like a recessive gene. When my wife, Kara, was growing up she wasn't allowed to watch *The Smurfs*. An early Protestant imagination, passed on through the centuries, convinced her parents that nearness to any magic, even on Saturday morning cartoons, was to dance with darkness. The poor Smurfs were just living in an enchanted time, not long from the days of Becket, where white and black magic always mixed. Today, some conservative Protestants oppose Harry Potter. They assume that its magic corrupts our ordinary sacred lives, infusing it with disobedient superstitions. My children are Harry Potter superfans, and I have no problem with it (likely because I unreflectively conceded to our secular age). I've allowed material scientism to convince me that there is no such thing as magic, leading my disenchanted mind to contend that demons can't get me, making Harry and Hermione only fun entertainment.

30. David Bentley Hart adds, "It is not the case that the Christianity of late antiquity or even of the early and high Middle Ages evacuated the world of supernatural or preternatural agency, or even that it regarded the gods of old merely as myths; it would be truer to say that the church subverted the ancient cosmology by subduing the ancient powers and demoting them to their proper place in the order of a redeemed creation. *Omnia corporalia regentur per Angelos*, wrote Thomas Aquinas . . . and he was doing no more than repeating the wisdom of centuries of Christian tradition, especially as enunciated by Dionysius the Areopagite." *The Doors of the Sea: Where Was God in the Tsunami?* (Grand Rapids: Eerdmans, 2005), 48.

31. Jane Bennett agrees with Taylor that it is more than science but also a kind of religious pietism that get us a secular age of disenchantment: "Modern science and 'ethically' oriented religions collaborated in disenchanting the world; they were sources of, even while they proffered solutions for, the problem of the meaninglessness that haunts us. Science progressively takes the spirit out of things and reduces them to uninspiring matter; otherworldly religions de-sanctify earthly life; and the vocationalism of the ascetic hard worker reinforces the sense that all worlds, in this life and in the hereafter, are rationally calculable." *The Enchantment of Modern Life: Attachments, Crossings, and Ethics* (Princeton, NJ: Princeton University Press, 2001), 62.

Yet as soon as I say this, I doubt it—so maybe while it is partially true, there is something more. Maybe my kids became superfans and I was allured because, having constructed a society to protect ourselves from demons and superstition, we've locked ourselves in a drab gray cell. While keeping us safe from the cosmic, the walls of thick materialism reduce our vision and flatten our experience. Harry and Hermione become a flash of a new enchanted color under the door of our disenchanted cell. Harry Potter, UFOs, eco-paganism, and quantum healing become distinct moves to *re*-enchant our world.[32] As we said in chapter 1, the age of authenticity is the search for spirituality inside this immanent frame. Locked inside this cell, we look within ourselves for something more, for a way to re-enchant.

In the age of authenticity, the "re" here can refer only to something like "reenact" rather than "return." There is no getting back to the world of Thomas Becket, and who would want that? The toothpaste cannot be put back in the tube; the line between the sacred and secular has faded. All-is-sacred has flipped to all-is-secular; there is no clear way to undo this. As James K. A. Smith says, "Even seeking enchantment will always and only be reenchantment after disenchantment."[33] We can seek for new enchantments, but those of the past are past.

It is no wonder the pastor feels caught in a malaise of meaning. The pastor is left to wonder what the liturgy and sacraments are good for. Can they possibly bear the weight of divine action in a disenchanted world? Squarely in the age of authenticity (when people can seek individualized re-enchantment at Comic-Con), the meaning system that can bear divine action feels to have imploded.[34] Rick Warren would build a twenty-thousand-member church

32. See Christopher Partridge, *The Re-Enchantment of the West*, vol. 2 (London: T&T Clark, 2005).

33. Smith, *How (Not) to Be Secular: Reading Charles Taylor* (Grand Rapids: Eerdmans, 2014), 61.

34. While agreeing with William Cavanaugh that there is indeed a sense of enchantment in our modern world, I think it is a re-enchantment. Cavanaugh says,

There is no question that things have changed in the last five hundred years. I am not sure, however, that describing the change is as simple as describing the way people experience the world. We need to take full account not only of the way people experience the world but of the categories that people use to describe the way they experience the world. It may be that we live in Descartes's world, not in the sense that the Cartesian mind-body dualism better describes our world, but in the sense that the way we describe our experience of the world has been shaped by Cartesian categories. We may have learned that the experience of shopping is a "secular" experience, one having nothing to do with demons or gods or supernatural powers. An empirical observation of the behavior of US shoppers on Black Friday, however, may indicate that the boundaries between the self and the world of material goods is not as buffered as Taylor describes it. There is a sense in which, as I have argued elsewhere, consumerism detaches the modern, affluent, Western

without a connection to historical liturgy or even the sacraments; why would we need them? The liturgy and sacraments *were* shelter amongst the downpour of demons. Like Edward at the viewing party, when the pastor gives the words of institution, she hears the response, "That's crazy!" But where this voice comes from she isn't sure; the pastor assumes her people think it—but does it disturbingly echo merely in her own head?

self from production of the goods we consume and the people who manufacture them; there is even a sense in which consumers are detached from the products they consume because their desires constantly move from one product to another. But to describe this process as "disenchantment" is to miss the "magic" that is associated with products in a world made of marketing, and to miss the fantasy construction of the self as one that transcends and consumes the material world. The very construction of the self as transcendent—and, in this sense, "buffered"—in other words, can be itself a kind of enchantment. ("The Invention of the Religious-Secular Distinction," in *At the Limits of the Secular: Reflections on Faith and Public Life*, ed. William A. Barbieri [Grand Rapids: Eerdmans, 2014], 123)

# 3

## keeping enchantment from flaring up

### *pastoring to private people*

It could have been the legacy of Martin Luther. He was always sure the devil was after him, even famously hurling an inkbottle at Satan as he approached his writing desk. This would lead to the tradition that followed him of never shying away from filling confessions and catechisms with devil talk. But still, though a lifelong Lutheran, my friend Jessicah never talked like this. She is one of the most rational people I know, even admitting that Luther's devil talk is the legacy of a medieval worldview. So I was shocked when at a dinner party she told one of the most frightening ghost stories I've ever heard. What made it so frightening was that it happened to her. She *experienced* this haunting; she wasn't retelling a story she'd heard from a friend who heard it from his cousin's neighbor. This was a first-person report.

When Jessicah was twelve years old her father joined the faculty of an old East Coast seminary (not far from the New Jersey city where Jonathan Edwards died). The seminary was built in the mid-1800s, its building surrounded by even older, colonial houses owned by the seminary. One of those old houses, right on campus, was her family's new home.

The day they moved in, the excitement of a new bedroom was too much, so Jessicah spent the day filling her walls with posters of puppies and boy bands while her parents unpacked the kitchen. After a long, exciting day, Jessicah crawled into her bed for the first night. As she settled herself, an uneasy feeling overtook her. Then, suddenly, the room turned ice cold and all at once, in complete unison, all the posters dropped forcibly from her walls. Jessicah shot out of bed and ran to her parents' room. As she explained the occurrence to her sleepy parents, a loud clanging and commotion started in the kitchen. They paused to listen, confused as to what it could be, and the blender started running. Jessicah's father ran downstairs to investigate and found every cupboard door wide open, and the blender was on . . . though not plugged in.

We sat open-mouthed, a chill racing up each of our spines at Jessicah's story. But her husband, Chris, the pastor of a local church, kept eating his ice cream and rolled his eyes.

"You don't believe it?" I asked.

"No. Come on," he responded with incredulity. "I've heard that story dozens of times. I don't believe it. I mean I'm sure something odd happened, but I think over the years and all the retellings the story has become more fiction than fact."

In the previous chapter we saw that divine action becomes obscured in a disenchanted world. This is the first blow to an overarching meaning system, a blow that starts moving the pastor toward malaise. Though it has its impetus in a deep devotion to upholding the sovereign freedom of God, the loss of magic makes it possible for us to create a world without superstition (or even the supernatural). Of course, individual people may still be prone to all sorts of superstitions: just watch professional athletes or old ladies at slot machines. But the larger institutions and the cultural imaginary we live within are constructed, mobilized, and validated beyond the enchantment of superstition. Few of us pray fervently for protection from the demons of fire or mark our doorways with symbols and sayings that repel evil spirits. Instead, we pay our taxes and are willing to give an extra fifty dollars when the volunteer fire department calls looking for donations.

Even Jessicah, who had this haunting experience, can happily live with a husband who doesn't believe it. This shows that the meaning system of enchantment is anything but overarching. But why isn't it? After all, those of us who heard Jessicah's story felt the chill race down our spines. Most of us even agreed that we were on Jessicah's side more than Chris's, that the paranormal is real—but obviously not real enough to hang chicken feet over the beds of our children. There must be more than just the loss of magic and demons that leads us into a secular age. This enchanted meaning system, like Windows 95, may still be able to run, but not at the pace of modern life. Jessicah lives a productive life, seemingly normal in every way. Yet she still believes in (though rarely thinks about) hauntings because she operates within a different meaning system. Chris also lives a productive life, faithfully pastoring his congregation, and yet doesn't feel any need to entertain or resist demons, ghosts, or magic. They can live happily together, both productive members of society, because there is more that produced our current secular age than just the loss of magic. Disenchantment met two other realities, further obscuring divine action and pushing the pastor into this malaise of meaning.

## The Two Added Realities

Breakthroughs in the cognitive sciences reveal that belief in God and a spiritual realm is natural. Justin Barrett, who works in the field of the cognitive science of religion, has shown that not only are we born to believe in god(s) but our brains are wired to assume the presence of agents.[1] Barrett calls this HAAD (hyperactive agency detection). His research shows that when we see something move out of the corner of our eye or something rustle the bushes, we naturally assume it is some kind of agent, some living being. (And when we look around that corner and see no agent, cognitive scientists of religion tell us that our minds have to do *more* work to explain it away as wind than they do to assume that the agent disappeared or was a ghost.) This natural tendency kept us alive in our long evolutionary voyage. Assuming that every shaking bush is a lion, even if we're wrong 99 percent of the time, keeps us from being an afternoon snack.

This natural disposition to see agents and gods makes it all the more necessary for us to look at the two other changes that allow enchantment to be pushed from the center to the very edges of our meaning system. Without these two other changes, enchantment would continue to be central to our imagination, rather than just popping up on the edges as it does today.

Cultural phenomena such as UFO hunting and séances are forms of "re-enacted" enchantment. For instance, something like cosplay allows people to "play" with enchantment, dressing like their favorite magical creature. But if a player is injured in their reenactment of "the battle of bastards" from *Game of Thrones*, getting a stray sword accidentally in the eye, the central meaning system beyond enchantment rushes quickly to the fore. The injured party is taken to an ophthalmologist, not to an old witch with a bag full of pulverized mushrooms, dog hair, and dew from a frog's back. Even re-enchantments like Wicca are powerful to individuals but small on a societal scale because these other two changes are the penicillin that keeps the flare-ups of enchantment from becoming a contagion.

1. See Justin Barrett, *Born Believers: The Science of Children's Religious Belief* (New York: Free Press, 2012); Barrett, *Cognitive Science, Religion and Theology: From Human Minds to Divine Mind* (West Conshohocken, PA: Templeton, 2011).

## Change One: The Dis-embedding of God from Public Life

The first change that keeps enchantment down, and in turn delivers a meaning system beyond divine action, is the dis-embedding of God from public life (even the conception that there is something called "public," in contrast to "private," is a constructed reality that helps cloud divine action). When magic was assumed, and the priest was a superhero, there was no real necessity for people to have a distinct private life cut off from others. Rather, everything you did, whether as a noble or peasant, priest or banker, played its part in, and even reflected, a higher or divine order.[2] Thomas Becket had to oppose King Henry, because the kingdom of England *must* be grounded in the higher kingdom of God. It was the king's duty, for the good of all, to rule his domain just as God ruled the heavens. The peasant too labored under the command of God, obedient to the lord of the field, in marriage, in trade, and in war, as a direct act of duty to the Lord in heaven.[3] There was no such thing as mere human action with no divine consequence. Everything you did had spiritual concern, because everything you did played its part in the earthly kingdom that was a direct reflection of the heavenly one.

Though preparing fields and milking cows was profane work, it was nevertheless a link in the chain of a strict hierarchical divine order. You would never conceive of yourself as having any part to play other than serving God and therefore your lord. (This is why Charles Taylor says there were no atheists in 1500; there was no way to conceive of your world without divine action, and enchantment, at its center.) Obviously, preparing fields and milking cows wasn't as important as the work of the priest (he had magic and knew the route into sacred time), but nevertheless it had its place, unimaginable outside the kingdom of God. The cathedral and the priest provided direct access to the sacred realm of the kingdom of God. The farm was profane compared to these sacred things, but nevertheless it had its place (and meaning) in the earthly realm that was to reflect the divine. This meant that everything you did—work, sex, childrearing—was done as a note in the symphony of the

2. Historians have a saying that connects to this point: "only the king was alone," meaning that one had to have significant power, even the perception of being a lord, to have a private life.

3. John Milbank says it like this: "Once, there was no 'secular.' And the secular was not latent, waiting to till more space with the steam of the 'purely human,' when the pressure of the sacred was relaxed. Instead there was the single community of Christendom, with its dual aspects of *sacerdotium* and *regnum*. The *saeculum*, in the medieval era, was not a space, a domain, but a time—the interval between fall and eschaton where coercive justice, private property and impaired natural reason must make shift to cope with the unredeemed effects of sinful humanity." *Theology and Social Theory: Beyond Secular Reason* (Malden, MA: Blackwell, 2006), 9.

kingdom of God. Therefore, "one could not but encounter God everywhere"; divine action was ever clear.[4]

How and why it was imagined like this will make more sense when we turn to the second change that keeps enchantment down. For now it is important to recognize that there was no place to go where people's attention and practices were not focused on God. There was no holiday from the grind of prayer, confession, and absolution (except a few church-sanctioned carnivals). And everything was everyone's business, because everyone was playing the same song. You had no right to privately play your own tune—not that you'd even consider it.

The meaning of magic could end and disenchantment could stick only because we were allowed to imagine something very different. Protestantism blurs the line between the sacred and profane, seeking to make everything equally sacred by turning us radically toward our inner lives, setting the conditions for us to imagine ourselves—in new, distinctly private ways—as having a private inner life that only God knows of. This radical turn inward, where what mattered was my heart (my private willful devotion), made the priest's prayers or the changing of a baby's diaper ultimately equal. But this equalizing was possible only if all magic was deemed disobedient, hypocritical, evil, and therefore only dark. Yet this in itself wasn't enough: the pull to magic was too strong, as we see in Salem.

Truly blurring the line between sacred and profane, and therefore keeping enchantment down, would necessitate a liberation of the people. They would need to be freed from seeing themselves as just links in a chain of being. They would need to see *themselves* as priests. With magic degraded and the Eucharist reimagined, the peasants were invited to think of their homes as mini-cathedrals and their families as small congregations. Responsibility for faithfulness switched from the powerful, who possessed the sacred things, to each of us. You were now lord of your own small domain (particularly in the New World), and even able to read your own Bible. You could give confession and receive absolution yourself; it was between you and God, privately interacted. (And remember, this was done not to lower the bar of commitment to God but to raise it.)

As the line between the sacred and the profane blurred, another line formed between the private and the public. It was never the intention for this line to be drawn; it was the result of turning the means of salvation over to the people. Making everything sacred by breaking the rigid chain of being eventually allowed us to imagine the public space free of any divine reflection or even

4. Charles Taylor, *A Secular Age* (Cambridge, MA: Belknap Press, 2007), 25.

responsibility. (And it now became possible, for the first time in the West, to be an atheist, to live in the world without the necessity of God, because the meaning system that was mobilizing society separated God into the private sphere.) The American and French Revolutions were both about much more than just producing societies without monarchs. Rather, inspired by God's law, these founders felt free to order a world by the will of the people. No longer did they need to order themselves as a direct reflection of God's own kingdom. Protestantism pushed its adherents to *will* to be near and faithful to God. In turn, we forged new societies from the will of the people and the action of strictly human agents. Jonathan Edwards would have supported this, though he never imagined from within his strict Puritanism how anyone could will to create anything but a new Israel. The Declaration of Independence and the US Constitution *may be* inspired by some vision for divine law (likely a deist one), but their power rested not in their direct reflection of the kingdom of God (in them being holy or sacred *things*) but in their encompassing of the will of the people.

Now that the order of society and the shape of our public lives were grounded in *only* human action (in our willingness, and not God's), divine action would become much harder for people to recognize. People now presumed that *they* constructed the world they inherited. With our society created solely by us, it was a short step to contend that any religious form was free to be practiced in the private sphere *but not* in the public. Too much public concern for the will of God could restrict the freedom of the will of the people. There needed to be a clear separation between a church created by the action of God and the state created solely by the action of the people. The public sphere would need to be free of God—something not imaginable to Edwards, let alone the medievals.

If this divide between the public and private had its origins in making all people priests and every home a cathedral, then the need for a pastor had to be redefined.[5] The pastor no longer had magical powers, but he could read;

5. "Luther stressed the task, or function, of ministry rather than its form. Roman medieval doctrine had established the view that the priest has an 'indelible character'—that is, that he is endowed with the never-failing power to mediate God's grace to a laity distinguished from the clergy by divine law. Luther destroyed this medieval Roman doctrine of priesthood in 1520, when he developed the concept of the priesthood of all believers by virtue of baptism. 'Whoever comes out of the water of baptism,' he declared in 'To the Christian Nobility' in 1520, 'can boast that he is already a consecrated priest, bishop and pope' (LW 44, 129). Luther no longer interpreted 'ministry' in terms of a 'holy order' metaphysically secured by an infallible sacrament. Rather, he considered it an essential *function* ordained by the sacrament of baptism and protected by a Christian community's proper call at a given time and place. Luther clearly distinguished between the 'spiritual estate' of baptism and the various holders of a special

he was no longer a superhero but now was just a learned man.[6] The pastor's authority shifted from a sacred consecration to an education, from being a divine thing to knowing important stuff. Harvard and Yale were founded to educate clergy; there was little sense that education was needed for much else.[7] One of Yale's most famous students was Jonathan Edwards.

Edwards still inherited an enchanted world, but unlike Thomas Becket, he fought the devil not with magic but with a degree from Yale.[8] Order, discipline, and study were what set the pastor apart. The discipline of being a learned man allowed for a kind of unity between private and public. Edwards was set apart, not by the power of oil and oath but by his education. And his education allowed him to do a very public act: to preach from the pulpit at the middle of the village. He was supposed to discern if people's individual and private experience of "awakening" qualified them to participate in the public life of the covenant. For Edwards, education wasn't about achievement of degrees; rather, long periods of reading and study (Edwards averaged thirteen hours per day) produced a disciplined will. And from this disciplined will he could call others through his preaching to search their hearts and discipline their own wills. The point of all this discipline was to keep the devil from finding a foothold in the private cathedral of the family, thereby corrupting our shared

---

'office.' Consequently, there are secular and spiritual offices, such as the secular function of princes and the spiritual function of priests; both princes and priests have their different duties." Eric Gritsch and Robert W. Jenson, *Lutheranism: The Theological Movement and Its Confessional Writing* (Philadelphia: Fortress, 1976), 110–11.

6. It is not that medieval priests couldn't read—of course they could—it is simply that their authority didn't rest in their learning. Many priests lacked education in Becket's time. E. Brooks Holifield adds, "Clerical education assumed paramount importance among Protestants because their emphasis on preaching required a clergy able to interpret biblical texts. Having rejected the older view of ordination, they turned to education as a means of giving clergy an authoritative status." *God's Ambassadors: A History of the Christian Clergy in America* (Grand Rapids: Eerdmans, 2007), 32.

7. "To a marked degree American colleges served as training schools for ministers. During the first fifty years of the [eighteenth] century, over half the graduates of Harvard and Yale went into the ministry. The proportion fell to roughly a third by mid-century, but even then more graduates entered ministry than law or medicine. In the first two decades of the century, 65 percent of the graduates of all the colonial colleges entered the ministry. The number fell to 40 percent between 1741 and 1760." Holifield, *God's Ambassadors*, 75.

8. "The forms of authority that defined the colonial pastor—official, personal, and rational— have continued to intersect with each other in varying ways throughout the later history. In the colonial churches, clergy bore authority by virtue of their office and education, though not without equal concern for the divine calling and the capacity to minister effectively. After the Revolution, the populist surge elevated personal charisma above authority of office and rational authority, while the spread of seminary education during the same period accorded more weight to competence and learning. Many twenty-first-century pastors believe, with good reason, that their authority has once again become more personal and less official: their authority depends more on who they are and what they do than on the office they occupy." Holifield, *God's Ambassadors*, 346.

public life. Education seemed to both distinguish between and perfectly link the public and the private. Up until the nineteenth century the clergy had a monopoly on education, giving the pastor importance and meaning.

Even today, we imagine that the pastor's distinction rests in her education, but this has been given over almost completely to the immanent frame. The meaning of her education has been pushed further to the edges. Today, the pastor's education is not to discipline the will but to qualify her for the profession. If people assume their pastor is special, it's because she's been to seminary and studied esoteric things that public education doesn't touch. In other words, she knows things about the Bible that they don't. Unlike Edwards's time, this education doesn't in itself embody the shape of a vocation (or provide authority). It doesn't give direct meaning to her actions (rather, the content of the seminary classroom and the practice of ministry have never been further apart). In Edwards's day, people expected, and even hoped for, long sermons with exhortations on all sorts of theological, scientific, and political perspectives. Edwards's education was on display weekly. E. Brooks Holifield says, "Preaching could make strenuous demands on congregations. The New England sermon was anywhere from forty-five minutes to two hours long."[9]

Today people will tolerate very little of this, refusing to sit through a long sermon. The pastor's education becomes a detriment, something that keeps her from being relevant. Education might lead people to respect the pastor, but its real objective is to provide the needed credentials that allow her to seek a profession. She's no different in that sense than a dental technician or mortgage broker. Most mainline churches still want this credentialing for their pastors (though this too is starting to fade). But the bulk of the pastor's education is often hidden, or even forgotten, in her day-to-day work.

When we scratch a little deeper, we quickly recognize that the power of the professional office of pastor rests not in a divine order or a disciplined will (bound to education) but solely in the strength of the institution. (And that strength is created by the will of certain individuals who support it with money and attendance.) Just as a CEO has the power of her office due to the societal or economic strength of the company, so too the pastor's power depends on the size and influence of the congregation. The CEO of Apple is more powerful than the owner of Ray's Waffles.

The perception of the pastor follows suit. For example, very rarely is the pastor of a small church assumed to be a star in her synod, presbytery, or network—no matter the depth of her spiritual life or theological imagination. The pastor's public importance rests not in the fact that she is a pastor and

9. Holifield, *God's Ambassadors*, 89.

plays a part in a divine order but rather in the fact that her church is big (in numbers, budget, or cultural relevance).[10] Rick Warren moderated the first 2008 presidential debate not because he is a pastor who can help the nation discern how the election of a president will reflect God's heavenly realm but because his church is huge (a voting bloc and collective of cultural will).[11] In our time, the credentialing of the degree gives the pastoral candidate the privilege of seeking such positions, licensed to build such a powerful institution, which in itself isn't bad and is in many ways necessary. There is no way for the church to be a cultural reality without being an institution. The pastor's job has always stewarded, and will continue to steward, the church's de facto institutional power—or lack thereof. This "lack thereof" opens the pastor to a malaise. When there is little direct connection to divine action, and no vision for something bigger, the pastor is left wondering why she didn't choose to run a different institution with more inherent power and possibility. That kind of thinking only makes it harder for her to connect to divine action outside of a private, personal call story. Spending time with seminarians will reveal that the call story is most often framed as justification for choosing a long and expensive educational-credentialing program over all sorts of other professional options.

This is perhaps saying it too strongly. Holifield reminds us that even in the late twentieth century, it was a vocation, not a profession, that energized pastors: "Uppermost in the motivation of most priests and ministers was the sense of divine calling. For some, this came as a gradual deepening of conviction, but for more than 70 percent of ministers it also included a particular experience of God's call."[12] The pastor today still feels a sense of God's

10. Holifield explains that this perspective started in the nineteenth century: "The tensions between populists and professionals occurred during a period when the ministry, in some parts of the country, was becoming a 'career' in which ministers expected to advance upward through several pastorates, moving toward larger urban congregations. [Enoch] Pond explained that ministers found their level—serving in 'higher or lower stations'—according to their merits. Others thought that ministers had become perpetual 'candidates' seeking higher salaries from wealthier congregations. They spoke of a clerical market in which the pulpit would, unfortunately, 'have its market-price, like that of stocks and manufactures.'" *God's Ambassadors*, 130, citing Pond, *The Young Pastor's Guide* (Bangor, ME: Duren, 1844), 343; Donald Scott, *Office of Profession* (Philadelphia: University of Pennsylvania Press, 1978), 72; and Phillips Brooks, *Statements of Facts* (Boston: Crocker & Brewster, 1854), 8, 13.

11. And the irony is that most pastors were serving small and even rural congregations, causing a further identity crisis because they couldn't build something big: "Most of the clergy served a smaller congregation—much smaller. The average American congregation in 1998 had 171 regular participants. Seventy-one percent of the local churches consisted of fewer than one hundred regularly participating adults, and the median congregation had only seventy-five." Holifield, *God's Ambassadors*, 342.

12. Holifield, *God's Ambassadors*, 331.

calling, but the blurring of divine action and the fragility of belief keep the call from being a deep well that pastors can draw from for vocational identity and direction in ministry. That's not to say that those in pastoral ministry no longer see themselves as called to a vocation, just that there are few external structures to help verify this calling other than immanent or cultural ones such as acquiring academic degrees, building a big congregation, writing a book, or maintaining an uberpopular podcast.

Enchantment is kept from reappearing because our day-to-day order is detached from the divine. The institutions and structures we live in, whether private or public, make no presumptions that they reflect God's act—the chain of being has been broken. Because this has occurred, the pastor has been left with *only* the hope of building a vital institution and therefore winning the right to speak into people's private lives (helping them live their best life now). It is no wonder that the entrepreneur becomes the core metaphor for the pastor. In our time, the pastor has to spend time and energy winning a cultural place for his congregation, not encountering (and inviting people into) divine action (he's unsure how to even do that). Divine action has become fuzzy, blurring the meaning of the pastoral and the purpose of the pastor.

## Change Two: The Division of the Natural World from Divine Purpose and Action

There are times when the pastor is nonetheless asked to represent, even call on, divine action. Few people may have a sense of the shape of divine action in their public or private lives. And yet a fifty-five-year-old mother asks her pastor if the cancer growing on her liver is a curse from God, a five-year-old requests prayer for her sick dog, and everyone wonders why a loving God would allow another earthquake to pound Central America and another drought to ravage Africa. What does the pastor say, other than that God causes none of this, which only makes it appear as if God does nothing at all? To assume that divine action is real and to lean into it opens the pastor to all sorts of other problems that she feels inadequate to address.

These problems appear because the second change arrives that keeps enchantment from flaring up. This change is to divide the natural world from "divine purpose and action."[13] People in Becket's time could assume that the kingdom of England was to reflect the kingdom of God because nature itself was embedded in a divine hierarchy (in a chain of being). Those people lived in a

13. Taylor, *Secular Age*, 25.

cosmos of linked orders that bore God's design.[14] The seasons were dependable not because of independent laws of nature but because nature was directed by the hand of God. The sun rose and snow melted because God oversaw God's creation, acting on it. To see the sun descend and rise again was all the proof needed for divine action. Magic worked, charging certain things with a force, because God was intricately engaged in the natural realm. God (or some other spiritual being) was responsible for the design and disruptions of nature, and never at a distance. "The great events in the natural order, storms, droughts, floods, plagues, as well as years of exceptional fertility and flourishing, were seen as acts of God."[15] Lightning wasn't just a random happening: when it struck near you it meant something. Because God directly acted in the natural world, meaning was everywhere. The nearby lightning strike wasn't just random—it was, for instance, a sign from God to leave the university and join the monastery. Happenings in the natural world could communicate God's desires or judgments. Everyone believed this, just as most everyone today believes in Newton's laws of gravity and Einstein's theory of relativity.[16]

The world was assumed to be part of an intricate cosmos, a system of natural and supernatural forces and beings that interacted and affected one

14. Charles Taylor provides further discussion on this point:
Embedding in society also brings with it an embedding in the cosmos. In early religion, the spirits and forces with whom we are dealing are in numerous ways intricated in the world. We can see examples of this aplenty if we refer back to the enchanted world of our medieval ancestors: although the God they worshipped transcended the world, they nevertheless also had to do with intracosmic spirits, and they dealt with causal powers that were embedded in things: relics, sacred places, and the like. In early religion, even the high gods are often identified with certain features of the world, and where the phenomenon that has come to be called "totemism" exists, we can even say that some feature of the world, an animal or plant species, for instance, is central to the identity of a group. It may even be that a particular geographical terrain is essential to our religious life. Certain places are sacred. Or the layout of the land speaks to us of the original disposition of things in sacred time. We relate to the ancestors and to this higher time through this landscape. (*Dilemmas and Connections: Selected Essays* [Cambridge, MA: Belknap Press, 2011], 218)

15. Taylor, *Secular Age*, 25.

16. Taylor adds to this: "Now, with advancing disenchantment (especially in Protestant societies), another model took shape, with relation to both the cosmos and the polity. In this, the notion of design was crucial. As this model manifested itself in regard to the cosmos, there was a shift from the enchanted world to a cosmos conceived in conformity with post-Newtonian science, in which there is absolutely no question of higher meanings being expressed in the universe around us. But there is still, with someone like Newton himself, for instance, a strong sense that the universe declares the glory of God. This is evident in its design, its beauty, its regularity, but also in its having evidently been shaped to conduce to the welfare of God's creatures, particularly ourselves, the superior creatures who cap it all off. Now the presence of God no longer lies in the sacred, because this category fades in a disenchanted world. But he can be thought to be no less powerfully present through his design." *Dilemmas and Connections*, 149.

another. Meaning was everywhere because the natural world was the staging area of cosmic action. Everything that happened was because some personal (spiritual or other) force caused it. When the fifty-five-year-old woman asks her pastor about her cancer, we're quick to claim that its cause is impersonal. It's just the odds, bad luck, the randomness of an impersonal order, or childhood exposure to some toxin or chemical.

Yet if this is so—and it might be—then it becomes much harder for her to trust that a personal God can act to heal her. It is less frightening to assume that it is just the odds or bad luck that makes her sick—it's nothing personal. She did nothing wrong, nor is some malevolent personal force after her. Yet, while this is less frightening, without a personal cause it is much harder to imagine (and explain) the intervention of a personal God in a presumed impersonal universe. And maybe more importantly, it becomes a challenge to provide meaning to her illness and death. She is stuck with a meaninglessness to her disease because, though deeply personal to her, her disease is only a fading echo in a dark, cold, impersonal universe where everything dies, swallowed in the tsunami of massive, impersonal time and space. If the cancer is caused by no personal force, how can a personal God affect her, other than by providing some banal comfort or cold indifference?

The pastor, then, must do something much more difficult than our ancestors had to: she must contend that a personal God can act in an impersonal universe and therefore challenge the theory that the universe is closed. The pastor will find it confusing or frustrating to point to divine action in a world that has no place for it. But this "no place" is not only societal (as we saw above) but stretches now to the natural realm. Unlike our ancestors, "we might say that [we've] moved from living in a cosmos to being included in a universe."[17] And a universe is much different from a cosmos. The universe is a closed system, where all causes are the result of impersonal forces (like laws of gravity, evolution, and particle collisions). "The shift from cosmos to universe—from 'creation' to 'nature'—makes it possible to now imagine meaning and significance as contained within the universe itself, an autonomous, independent 'meaning' that is unhooked from any sort of transcendent dependence."[18]

The enchantment of spirits and demons is upended and can never work itself to the center of our meaning system again, because now mystery is no longer that which escapes being but is just a riddle that has yet to be solved. It is mysterious that the universe is made up mostly of dark matter, particles

17. Taylor, Secular Age, 59.
18. James K. A. Smith, How (Not) to Be Secular: Reading Charles Taylor (Grand Rapids: Eerdmans, 2014), 35.

that we cannot identify. But this is no reason to return to an enchantment vision—dark matter is not on par with dark magic. For unlike our ancestors imagined with magic, we assume that one day this hidden mystery will be revealed and we'll know exactly what dark matter is. Mystery for those living in a universe is quite different than for those living in a cosmos. Mystery in the cosmos is haunted by transcendence and the powerful actions of the supernatural. But in the universe, mystery is just that which we haven't yet figured out (a riddle unsolved), making all the causes (of earthquakes, sick dogs, and ill mothers) impersonal.

Because the woman's illness is the result of impersonal forces, the pastor, somewhere deeper than she can admit, wonders whether to pray for a personal intervention. This tacit grappling can only leave the pastor with a sense of powerlessness experienced as a malaise—*What am I doing? What is the meaning of prayer? And how can a personal God act in an impersonal universe? Is it even right to pray for a sick dog? And why are the movements of tectonic plates beyond the wisdom and compassion of God?*

And though this all produces significant challenges, nevertheless some testify to some experience of divine action. Whether on a hill with pills in their hand or becoming a pastoral physician with a tumor in their brain, some claim the encounter with a personal force. What makes the pastoral (or better, the *ministerial*) remain significant, even up against these transitions, is its ability to host an encounter with personhood. It appears, both in lived experience and the tradition, that divine action comes in and through personhood. While divine action may be opaque, it nevertheless seems to come as an encounter of personhood that bears a death experience, which leads to transformation.[19] The questions we'll explore below are: How central is the pastoral to encounters of divine action? And how might we imagine divine action in an impersonal universe of disenchantment, a world very different from Becket's? But before we can get there, we must look more intently at the pastoral in relation to the self, and how deeply the image of pastor has changed.

19. In volume 1, I called this hypostasis, kenosis, and theosis.

# 4

## the force field of the buffer

### *Augustine and pastoring to selves*

I knew it—I swear I did—but it all disappeared when I stood in front of the whole class. I was in fifth grade, and we were in the middle of a poetry lesson. To my surprise, this was my day. In a short five minutes it would be my turn to stand in front of the class and read my favorite poem. I was unprepared, but I knew my piece. It was a Shel Silverstein poem that I'd read dozens of times to myself. Sitting silently in our book corner, I'd even let out a giggle or two as my eyes relayed it to my mind without as much as saying a word with my mouth. (This was, after all, a *silent reading* corner.) I wasn't a strong reader, not even close, but who would know? Reading words was something between my eyes and my mind; it was a private, inward act—yet in five minutes that would no longer be so. Soon it would be a public act, done as much by my mouth as my eyes, revealing the capacities of my mind.

I raced to our book corner, grabbed the Shel Silverstein book, and dashed through the pages until I found those funny verses. When my name was called, like a flipped switch I felt lit up by anxiety. Opening the book, I looked down at the words, and they blurred, appearing in Chinese or Akkadian or something; all I know is that *none* of those words made sense. The force of the confusion seemed to cut the wires between my mind and my mouth. I tried to vocalize the letters, but nothing connected; the sounds and the shapes were incoherent. I froze, unable to get even the first word out. I had the sense that if I could get just that first word, my mouth would know what to do with the rest. But that first word never came.

I stood there frozen, the anxiety in my body slipping into humiliation. I could hear the giggling. I had anticipated it, but the source was starkly different. I assumed they'd giggle at Silverstein's irreverent prose, not at *me*. Like a failed satellite TV signal, my mind wouldn't connect with my mouth, but my mind was wildly active. It raced into the other minds of my classmates. Though I couldn't read the words on the page, I was sure I could read their minds. They were thinking, *He's stupid*.

It was one of the most traumatic experiences of my childhood, good fodder for psychoanalysis or hypnotic therapy. It's possible that all my other personality shortcomings go back to that event, some deep form of compensation for my humiliation as an eleven-year-old. I doubt it, but it's possible. Regardless, it impacted my inner life, leaving a mark on my "self." To this day, whenever I'm surprised by being asked to read something out loud, I feel a stab of panic and anxiety that stings like it did in fifth grade.

As we mine the history of our secular age, exploring how it impacted and was impacted by pastors, few would guess that reading out loud plays a part in our story. But it does, going back to one of the most famous pastors and thinkers of Western civilization: Augustine, bishop of Hippo.

### Augustine and the Move Toward the Inner World

It's nearly impossible to tell the story of the Western world without putting Augustine at the center. When he was born, though, he was anywhere but central. Son of a pagan father and Christian mother in Thagaste of Africa, Augustine grew up on the fringes of the Roman Empire. It would be quite a story that would lead this boy not only into the pastorate but even more to the center of Western intellectual history.

The economic standing of Augustine's family is debatable. Most assume that his father, while a free man, was poor, though not too poor to scrape together enough money to get his eleven-year-old boy educated. At the same age as my fifth-grade self, Augustine was sent to a small school that was a long nineteen miles from home in Madaurus.

Maybe it was due to the pain of being sent away from home, but when referring back to these early student days Augustine would speak glowingly of his friends, but he spoke of his mother very little, and he said nothing of warmth about his father. Peter Brown explains: "Augustine, who will soon experience and express deep grief at the loss of a friend, will mention his father's death only in passing."[1] He continues, "Augustine . . . will hardly ever spend a moment of his life without some friend, even some blood-relative, close by him. No thinker in the Early Church was so preoccupied with the nature of human relationships; but then, few environments would have impressed their importance upon Augustine so vividly as the close-knit world in which he had grown up."[2]

This close-knit world of friends would give Augustine his first real sense of his inner world. My own inner world crashed on me with my failure to read a poem. For Augustine, it came at the same age, but instead of being delivered as humiliation, it came as guilt. Decades later in his *Confessions* (a book that is quite literally the confession of Augustine's inner world, which would over the centuries help turn the West toward a concern for inwardness), he reports that he snuck into a garden with a group of his friends and stole fruit that he didn't even want. It wasn't hunger or need that led to the deception but the desire, even delight, to do what wasn't permitted. This experience would lead Augustine to surmise years later that human nature itself is inclined to perversity, that indeed there is nothing in the nature of humanity itself that can save it.[3] Augustine's connection to his own inner world, starting when he was eleven, gave him no patience for Pelagius and his claims that sin is not intrinsic to the human will.

If Augustine was part of *The Little Rascals* while at the school in Madaurus, in Carthage he became a member of the Alpha Betas (yes, that's a *Revenge of the Nerds* reference). He'd arrived in the city a Christian, but really only because his beloved mother was devout. Augustine, like the most notorious frat boys, split his time between study and hookups. His days consisted of reading Cicero, racking up sexual exploits, and hanging out with his friends. Augustine takes us into his inner life in this period in the *Confessions*, giving us the most famous prayer of this classic work. He reveals again what he had experienced at eleven and concludes that the inner life is delighted by, indeed is inextricably caught in, sin. He prays, "Grant me chastity and continence, but not yet."[4]

These experiences in his youth would so mark Augustine because they stood in stark contrast to his deepest love, his mother Monica. As Brown explains,

1. Peter Brown, *Augustine of Hippo* (Berkeley: University of California Press, 2000), 19.
2. Brown, *Augustine of Hippo*, 20.
3. Brown gives us a sense of how the inner experience of childhood impacts the great thinker, leading him to see inwardness as central: "Augustine grew up a sensitive boy, acutely anxious to be accepted, to compete successfully, to avoid being shamed, terrified of the humiliation of being beaten at school." *Augustine of Hippo*, 23.
4. Augustine, *Confessions*, trans. Henry Chadwick (New York: Oxford University Press, 2008), 145.

"What Augustine remembered in the *Confessions* was his inner life; and this inner life is dominated by one figure—his mother, Monica." Augustine recognized that her strength came from her own inner life. When as a pastor Augustine looks back on his life in the *Confessions*, his mother, Monica, becomes the model of Christian life. Augustine will so lift up the inner life, even pastoring toward inwardness, because of Monica's faithfulness. Brown says it like this: "What Augustine says about Monica throws as much light on his own character as on that of his mother. . . . Occasionally, we glimpse a genuinely impressive woman—very much what her son would have liked himself to be, as a bishop: retrained, dignified, above gossip, a firm peacemaker among her acquaintances." These are virtues birthed from inwardness, traits that show that the inner self delights in God, who has overcome the self's desire for sin. Brown continues: "Above all, she was a woman of deep inner resources: her certainties were unnerving; the dreams by which she foresaw the course of her son's life were impressive, and she was confident that she could tell, instinctively, which of these dreams were authentic."[5]

Yet these dreams for Augustine must have seemed far from possible after he completed his education in Carthage. Toward the end of his student days he finally left his nominal Christian commitments and became a Manichaean (a gnostic religion that saw a cosmic battle between light and darkness, with disdain for the material). Of course, these commitments broke Monica's heart. But this only led her to be more committed to her beloved son.

Now a budding rhetoric teacher, Augustine knew that if he were to make a name for himself he'd have to get to Rome, leaving the African fringes of the empire for its heart. But he'd need to do so by himself, leaving his mother behind. So ditching her at the port, with a subterfuge of switcheroo, he sailed to Rome without her, free from her wishes and Christian piety, ready to take Rome like a bachelor arriving in Vegas.

In Rome, Augustine was showing his prowess as a rhetor, but everything else seemed to be failing, particularly his commitment to Manichaeism. After a turbulent year, Augustine received an opportunity that would change his life: an appointment as professor of rhetoric in Milan. If the Eternal City was a collision of multiple philosophies, spiritualities, and religions, Milan was under the sway of one man: the great Christian bishop Ambrose. Augustine entered Milan bearing the marks of Rome: unsettled on what he believed, leaving Manichaeism, dabbling in the skepticism of the New Academy; and of course he was the son of a Christian mother, whom he loved and missed. Yet what was settled was that he was a talented teacher of rhetoric. It was

5. Brown, *Augustine of Hippo*, 17.

argued that Ambrose was the greatest speaker in the entire world. As a professor of rhetoric, Augustine had to find this out for himself. Soon enough
Augustine discovered that not only was this true but even more profound than
the bishop's tongue was his compassion. Augustine says, "That man of God
received me like a father would and expressed pleasure at my coming with
kindness most fitting in a bishop."[6]

The sense of a fatherly embrace may have been reason enough for Augustine
to send for Monica. Within months she'd join her son in Milan, even more
taken by Ambrose than Augustine was. Yet truth be told, Monica assumed
Ambrose walked on water because of his impact on her son. "When Monica
arrived, Augustine's relations with . . . Ambrose became yet more complicated:
[Augustine says in his *Confessions* of his mother] 'she hastened to church
more zealously than ever and drank in the words of Ambrose as a fountain
of water. . . . She loved that man as an angel of God, because she had learnt
that it was by him that I had been brought so far as to that wavering state I
was now in.'"[7]

Augustine's wavering state would become sure with his conversion less
than two years after moving to Milan. Not surprisingly, it connected to inwardness, reading, and the voice of a child. Augustine reports that he heard
a childlike voice (maybe that of an eleven-year-old, the age he was when he
realized he delighted in sin) telling him "to take up and read." So picking up
Paul's Epistle to the Romans, he did. Reading Romans, Augustine recognized,
as Luther and Barth would after him, that God acts to transform the sinful
inner nature into Christ.

Ambrose baptized Augustine the next Easter. And this couldn't be more
fitting. Not only had Ambrose treated Augustine like the father he wished
he'd had, but it was Ambrose's reading that further solidified in Augustine
that the location of divine and human encounter was the inner life—the
"heart" of each person. After not being able to find the source of the voice
of the children, Augustine realized it was God speaking directly to his heart
to "take and read."

There is a certain pride in being the first to do something. And the more
ubiquitous the thing becomes, the more renown goes to the first. Little did I
know back in fifth grade that reading had always been assumed to be a rhetorical act; it was a spoken practice, done for an audience. I'd been taught that
reading was an inner, not a public, practice. It was something between my
mind and the page, not for others to hear. But when Augustine met Ambrose,

6. Augustine, *Confessions* (trans. Chadwick), 88.
7. Brown, *Augustine of Hippo*, 77.

no one would have imagined this. Words were for speaking, and speaking is done by a mouth to ears.

As Augustine got to know Ambrose, he became shocked that not only did the great bishop devour books, but he read them without so much as a noise. Augustine says in the *Confessions*, "When reading, his eyes ran over the page and his heart perceived the sense, but his voice and tongue were silent." He continues, "He did not restrict access to anyone coming in, nor was it customary even for a visitor to be announced. Very often when we were there, we saw him silently reading and never otherwise. After sitting for a while in silence (for who would dare to burden him in such intent concentration?) we used to go away."[8] Like watching someone put to use a common tool for some other unimagined but brilliant solution, the rhetoric professor was spellbound, recognizing that Ambrose used words not to win an argument but to feed and shape his inner life. Reading is to edify the heart, not to persuade an audience.

## The Self

Augustine now experienced a trifecta that would assure him that the inner world, the "heart," was the place where the divine encountered the human, and the Christian life was most directly expressed. His own inner delight in doing wrong, his mother's inner piety and resolve, and Ambrose's silent reading made it clear that the inner world was ground zero for our encounter with God.[9] As Charles Taylor adds, "Augustine makes the step to inwardness . . . because it is a step towards God."[10] He continues, "The idea that God is to be found within emerges with greater force out of Augustine's account of our search for self-knowledge."[11]

And this Augustinian breakthrough has never left us; pastoral ministry in the legacy of Augustine assumes that there is a self, an inner reality that must be addressed. Since Augustine, the pastor's job has been to impact, direct, and lead people's inner lives. It is not enough to sway people's action; the pastor is to do something more difficult. The pastor is to get deeper than behavior, treading inside the inner world of people's intentions.[12] The faithful Christian does Christian things—she prays and cares for the poor—but

8. Augustine, *Confessions* (trans. Chadwick), 92–93. See also Brown, *Augustine of Hippo*, 73.

9. Charles Taylor gives some background: "Augustine shifts the focus from the field of objects known to the activity itself of knowing; God is to be found here." *Sources of the Self: The Making of Modern Identity* (Cambridge, MA: Harvard University Press, 1989), 130.

10. Taylor, *Sources of the Self*, 132.

11. Taylor, *Sources of the Self*, 134.

12. To be fair, this turn toward the inner world that moves deeper than behavior is bound in Jesus's own words. For an example: "But I say to you that everyone who looks at a woman with lust has already committed adultery with her in his heart" (Matt. 5:28).

Augustine reminds us that this doing must come from a core inner desire for God. The Protestant pastor particularly is to help people's longing heart find rest in God. Whether with words or practices, the pastor's job is to shape people's inner life, sending them further inward to find the presence of God. Outward behavior is important, but it comes from the inner wellspring of the soul. The pastor could send them inward only if the pastor too could enter this inner world (again whether through Word or sacrament), directly addressing the inner self.

For the next fifteen hundred years, pastors sketched out for people the need to surrender this inner reality to God. Misuse of the sacrament can damn this inner self, and after the Reformation, the Word preached can save it. Just as silent reading could shape Ambrose's heart, so too can silently hearing the sermon shape the heart of each person. Not everyone in Jonathan Edwards's congregation could read, but they all could have their inner life encountered by the Word when preached. And they'd show that this inner life had encountered the divine by how they lived out their ordinary lives. Behavior was bound to the awakening of the inner life. So whether with fear or compassion, the pastor was able to enter people's open inner world.

But in our secular age this inwardness thrusts the pastor into a malaise. Pastors often have the uneasy sense that what was once open is now closed. The inner world, while more than ever an intricate edifice (thanks to modern psychology), nevertheless appears closed to the pastor. The modern self, able to be created in the first place thanks to the pastoral work of Augustine, has turned on the pastoral. The self is now buffered from both the pastor's holy things and her prodding. People seem fine negotiating their inner lives without the help of a pastor, not even recognizing the contribution that pastoral practice made to give us the inner life we now enjoy. People now have all sorts of other options to negotiate their inner selves, making the pastor feel obsolete. They have therapists, life coaches, Oprah, and sometimes even purpose-driven pastors who impact the inner life by staying out of it.

As we moved into modernity, it was as if the Augustinian Christianity that shaped the West gave us resources not only to build intricate inner worlds but to eventually build them with high walls and elaborate security systems that could keep out the transcendent.[13] Like a big house in an expensive neighborhood,

13. Charles Taylor believes that this Augustinian inwardness was carried to us in the West by many different forces, but that without Augustine there would be no Descartes, whose work is the next step to get to buffered self. Brad Gregory offers this on Descartes and inwardness: "Similarly, in 1641 Descartes related how he had sought in his own meditative solitude to sever the distracting influence of other people, whether past or present, in order to discover the foundations for truth. Having recognized how many false opinions he had regarded as true in

our inner lives are expansive but protected. They have curb appeal but are not open for visitors. And just like a big house in an expensive neighborhood, the walls and high hedges are there to keep intruders with evil intentions out. The self becomes closed and secured, not because people stopped believing in God, but because they so deeply sought God in their inner life that they feared demons would enter and turn an inner space made for God into hell. This move to create walls and hedges to keep things out came from a reverence for inner life. But we didn't see that eventually we would secure this inner world so extensively that we could keep even God out. Once this happened in modernity, there became a tangible sense, like in neighborhoods with expensive houses, that to achieve this safety you must lose the excitement of connection and engagement, making you safe but bored.[14]

In the same way, the modern self has been buffered from evil forces. To achieve this safety, it had to close down its porous openings. That has, thankfully, kept evil spirits from attacking the sacred inner world. But the collateral damage has been a buffering from the clear perception of divine action and transcendence. Personal encounter with divine action has been locked out of the compound of the self. We've entered a safe zone where we are so protected from demons that we can assume they never existed in the first place.[15] This assumption makes it easy for us to wonder whether divine action is just a leftover from a past time when the self lived in tents and tenements. Perhaps there was a time when the pastor was needed to help us embrace the inner life and protect it from the evil that haunted us. Some assume we've outgrown that now.

Back when Augustine was burying his beloved mother in Milan, before heading back to Africa and after he'd fast-tracked from convert to priest to bishop, these thoughts never would have crossed his mind. More than anyone else, Augustine developed this sense of inwardness, because he assumed

---

his youth, and so how dubious was everything he had inferred on their basis, he realized he had to start over: 'Everything had to be torn down to the ground and I had to begin anew from the first foundations, if I ever wanted to establish anything firm and enduring in the sciences.'" *The Unintended Reformation: How a Religious Revolution Secularized Society* (Cambridge, MA: Belknap Press, 2012), 115.

14. This is the malaise of modernity that Taylor references and develops.

15. Brown reminds us that Augustine held to an enchanted world, giving a central place for demons: "For Augustine believed in demons: a species of beings, superior to men, living forever, their bodies as active and as subtle as the air, endowed with supernatural powers of perception; and, as fallen angels, the sworn enemies of the true happiness of the human race. Their powers of influence were enormous: they could so interfere with the physical basis of the mind as to produce illusions. Into the turbulence of the lower air, below the moon, these condemned prisoners, awaiting sentence in the Last Judgment, were always ready to swoop, like birds, upon the broken fragments of a frail and dissident humanity." *Augustine of Hippo*, 310.

"a world cut off from perfection, and shared by human beings with hostile 'powers,' was part of the 'religious topography' of all Late Antique men."[16] Brown continues, showing us both Augustine's attention to the inner self and also how this inner world was open to forces from outside it:

> Augustine merely turned the Christian struggle inwards: its amphitheater was the "heart"; it was an inner struggle against forces in the soul; the "Lord of this world" becomes the "Lord of desires"—of the desires of those who love this world, and so come to resemble demons committed to the same emotions as themselves. "The Devil is not to be blamed for everything: there are times when a man is his own devil." In the same way, victory comes to depend on adherence to some inner source of strength: on "remaining in Christ," interpreted as an abiding principle within the self. For, when this "inner" Christ "sleeps," the boat of the soul is rocked by desires for the world; when this Christ "wakes in the soul," it becomes calm again.[17]

## The Challenges of the Buffered Self

Augustine's pastoral practice sent us inward, claiming that it is within us that we find divine action—God speaks to the heart. But as the above quote witnesses, this movement inward was not to enter a pressurized cabin, like on a Boeing 737, where all outside forces were locked out and we simply breathed over and again our own conditioned air.

Rather, for Augustine the journey inward was an *open* battle with devils and demons. Augustine's pastoral practice gave us an inner self, but this self, to use Taylor's language, was porous. It was open to encounter. God could get in; this is why the heart was the place to encounter God. But of course, because God could get in, so could all sorts of other evil forces. Once, when as a boy Augustine was sick, Monica had him salted from head to toe, like a pretzel, believing it would keep demons from entering him (I guess demons are more into sweet than savory).[18] So again, Augustine may have taken us inward, but this inwardness was open (even porously so) to divine action and transcendence more generally.

What Augustine couldn't have imagined is what we would inherit. The inward turn that was to open us to the act of God has been secularized—it is now possible for the inner self to be embraced and explored *without* God.

16. Brown, *Augustine of Hippo*, 240.
17. Brown, *Augustine of Hippo*, 240–41.
18. That I can even attempt a joke here shows how much I assume myself buffered from ontologically independent evil forces.

Augustine assumed (and this was shown to be true for nearly fifteen hundred years after him) that the more you attended to the inward, the more clear was God's presence.[19] This is not so for us; the more we turn inward, the more divine action becomes opaque and a personal God can be perceived to be merely a figment of our imagination (a cursory example: the academic field and profession with the most reported atheists is psychology; it has more than double that of physicists). In later modernity there seems to be a correlation between the intense focus on inwardness and disbelief.

We now pastor not to *porous* selves who are fundamentally open to spiritual forces, like Augustine, but to *buffered* selves. Metaphorically, the inner lives of people in our congregations are not located in tents or tenements, where the smells, noises, and motions of the spiritual are ambient, surrounding us whether we like it or not. Rather, people now live in big, quiet mansions, set back from the street, with security systems wired to trip if the self is invaded—particularly by any so-called spiritual force.

It isn't that we don't experience or even *want* the spiritual; it just now appears controllable. Because the self is buffered from encountering spiritual forces that it doesn't welcome, the spiritual is chosen as an accessory—and the spiritualities chosen are usually more fashionable than traditional religions. We may still—or especially—seek the spiritual because our buffered mansions are bland. But because we live in these mansions, we enter the spiritual only as an excursion, as a fashionable vacation that makes living in these buffered-mansion selves bearable.

Our selves are so buffered, then, that even (or especially) the act of God cannot coherently enter the high hedges of our intricate inner world without setting off some security system wired by the immanent frame.[20] T. M. Luhrmann, in her award-winning book *When God Talks Back*, shows just this. As an anthropologist, she has studied a small group of people (those in the charismatic Vineyard denomination) who speak often of God encountering their inner selves and to such an extent that they experience direct communication. They claim that God talks to them. She has written the book because for most Americans, even other Christians, this kind of talk is shocking. It sets off an alarm in our buffered selves that repeats over a siren: "They're crazy! They are out of their minds!" We modern people are buffered from such things. Today even if people encounter God in their inner world (which

19. Of course, this started to unravel with Descartes and then Kant. Taylor believes they are inheriting an Augustinian world. But it isn't until the late nineteenth century that we fully imagine this.

20. This way, most spiritual inclinations of people in our culture are away from a personal force called God to a feeling of inclusion or connection.

of course they do), they wonder if they really have. The alarm system of the buffered self flashes a signal of incredulity.

This is quite a pastoral challenge. Once, all it took to enter the inner self was the smells of the chapel, the words of institution, or the sermon preached. Your authority as pastor gave you a direct access card to people's inner lives, seen no more clearly than in confession. People expected (even yearned for) you to enter their inner self and set it right with the wisdom of the Word and the power of the sacrament.[21] The words of absolution set the inner life right; they were a blessed salve to the aching inner soul. Today, few people imagine that they need the stiff wind of the words of absolution to blow clean their inner life. On the contrary, they imagine that things cannot get inside of them. As buffered selves, we are free from anything or anyone encumbering the self—even the words of absolution. They are barely different from the announcement of free coffee that preceded them eight minutes earlier.

### Implications of Buffering for Pastors

Taylor tells us that this buffering of the self has two implications, which I contend more specifically name our pastoral challenge. The first implication when the self is buffered, Taylor explains, is that we perceive freedom differently. Following Augustine, Luther celebrated the freedom of the Christian. By taking up and reading Romans just as Augustine did, Luther recognized that the inner self was justified by the act of Jesus. This sets the sinner free from the possession of the evil one and the inner grind of self-justification. Freedom came to the porous self, freeing the inner life from the anxiety of works to be a slave to our neighbor. We are now to be possessed by a divine action that sends us into the world to proclaim the Word.

Yet when the self is buffered, Taylor explains, that freedom is reconceived. We are now free to disengage. Our buffer allows the ability to turn off and tune out. No one in Augustine's, Becket's, or Edwards's congregations would have ever assumed this. The pastor may have been a heretic or the devil in disguise, but apathy was not an option—demons and devils roamed too close to the self. Today most pastors feel the biggest issue they face is their people's

21. Keith Thomas gives us a little context on how this inwardness took shape. He discusses the spiritual practice of diaries and Catholic confession. We can see that this presumed a distinct self, but a porous one: "It was also possible for the godly layman to turn inwards, entrusting his doubts and uncertainties to a spiritual diary, and resolving his problems by recourse to prayer; the psychological function of the Puritan diary or autography was, as has often been pointed out, closely parallel to that of the Catholic confessional." *Religion and the Decline of Magic* (New York: Penguin, 1991), 188.

indifference. They seem disengaged—from attending, from listening, from serving, from caring at all. But this is only normal, Taylor would remind us. Once the self is buffered, living far from the curb in its own mansion, disengagement becomes the mark of the buffered self's freedom.

Taylor says it like this: "The buffered self is essentially the self which is aware of the possibility of disengagement. And disengagement is frequently carried out in relation to one's whole surroundings, natural and social."[22] American congregational life, particularly in the suburbs, feels like a constant ebb and flow of disengagement to reengagement and back to disengagement. Sometimes it's patterned—when I was growing up my dad would disengage every April through October to golf on Sunday mornings. And sometimes it is more sporadic, happening even within the service itself, as minds wander, feeling little impact on the self when the Word is being preached. Preaching has had to turn to self-help and humor (turns initiated by Henry Ward Beecher in the nineteenth century, as we'll see) because the self is buffered and disengaged. Humor, particularly, becomes a direct switch that can flip people from being disengaged to engaged—laughter is a sure sign that people are with you (the buffered self begins to coalesce in the nineteenth century, making it unsurprising that Edwards spent no time trying to be funny, while Beecher saw it as essential). For us, a lot of work needs to be done to engage otherwise disengaged selves.

But this goes deeper. Taylor's point is that the self is so buffered that it can disengage (for a time) not just from preaching but from all social connection or even from nature itself. Any environmental activist will tell you that one of the biggest issues is keeping people engaged. It's an odd challenge; after all, we can't live without a natural environment. But we are now *so* buffered that it becomes an actual option to care or not about clean air and water. Only a buffered self can assert, "It's my right to not give a crap." With the buffered self, freedom is freedom to disengage.

The second implication of the buffered self is interconnected with the first. Taylor explains that a buffered self that believes it is free (making it a right) "to not give a crap" assumes invulnerability. If you've read closely, you'll know that I've fallen into this trap myself. Just pages earlier, I made a joke about demons and their snack preference. I can make this joke, even publishing it in a book, because I assume that my inner life is invulnerable to the demons getting their revenge. I have to work really hard imaginatively to assume that dark forces will know I wrote it and place some bounty on my head. I just don't believe it, at least as an unthought presumption of the way the world

22. Taylor, *A Secular Age* (Cambridge, MA: Belknap Press, 2007), 42.

works. Of course, in the eyes of Becket's or Edwards's people, this makes me dangerously cocksure. But I assume, even as I write about its problems, that my self is buffered and cannot be encumbered by such forces. It isn't that I don't believe in demons and other ghouls. Instead, I just assume that I'm not "vulnerable to a world of spirits and forces which cross the boundary of [my] mind." Taylor continues, naming my own presumption of invulnerability: "The fears, anxieties, even terrors that belong to the porous self are behind it. This sense of self-possession, of a secure inner mental realm, is all the stronger, if in addition to disenchanting the world, we have also taken the anthropocentric turn, and no longer even draw on the power of God."[23]

It is easy for people to disengage because, in a sense, the buffered self is assumed to be stronger than God. The buffered self is so protected behind its hedges that the power of God, while maybe acknowledged at some level, is unneeded. In Becket's time people felt weak, fearing even communion, recognizing nevertheless that their vulnerable inner lives needed its power. Today it is often recovering addicts who can confess a vulnerability that leads to deep engagement, making them the ideal teachers in a secular age. Addicts have experienced a home invasion. The mansion of their buffered self has been overtaken by a force that took residence in it, throwing every room into chaos. Admitting their weakness, addicts engage prayer, confession, and communal life, for the very reason that they are vulnerable (to a relapse). Addiction can become a particular hell within a buffered self.[24] The haunting is born from within the free autonomy of the self, the chaos coming from deep within the inner self. But once out, it is caught, bouncing back and forth in the thickly buffered walls of the self. There are few porous windows to let the chaos out, and none until you confess that you're vulnerable and then start engaging in the program.

Yet most people in our congregations haven't hit rock bottom, ready to admit their vulnerability and the necessity of engagement. They assume, as do most pastors, invulnerability. It becomes very difficult, then, for the ancient and trusted practices of sacrament, preaching, and confession to enter the self. The pastor can sense that she is no longer really welcomed in the inner life of her people. People often assume that they don't need a pastor because they are unencumbered by any spiritual forces (they might need a therapist or financial advisor or social worker, but not a pastor). And when things do encumber us, they don't necessarily get to *us*, to our inner self (this is why we feel so invulnerable and the

23. Taylor, *Secular Age*, 301.

24. Actually, we can only have addiction when we have a buffered self. See Anthony Giddens, *Modernity and Self-Identity: Self and Society in the Late Modern Age* (Stanford, CA: Stanford University Press, 1991), for more discussion on this. Giddens is not using Taylor's language, but he does think that addiction is born from within modernity, which would connect their points.

pastor becomes less necessary than a good cardiologist or chiropractor). Things may get over the hedge, setting off the alarm, but they cannot get into the house of our self. Things may impact our physiological bodies, or the chemistry of our brains, and therefore affect our moods, but they never reach our *being*. We live with a strict buffer that makes the pastor seem tacitly unnecessary.

Taylor uses the example of melancholy. In the fourteenth century, to be overtaken by melancholy was to have the very *thing*—black bile. You felt sad, sullen, or gloomy because black bile had invaded you. And this black bile was an evil, put there by a demon, because it overtook your inner self with sadness. Feelings were not illusions of the mind but correlated to real things in the world. You felt melancholy because you (your inner self) were up against the thing.[25] Now, in a world of buffered selves, to have melancholy is to be depressed. And to be depressed is, of course, to feel despondent sadness, but it is not to *be* sadness (as in having sadness written into your essence). You're sad not because you have a thing, like black bile that has entered your non-material spiritual heart, but because your brain's chemistry is off. Your inner self is buffered; it is just your body (in this case, your brain) that is making you feel this way. It is not a spiritual state, like Augustine or Becket would imagine, but just a reduction in the amount of certain neurotransmitters (monoamines such as serotonin and norepinephrine).

As another example, when my son is in a terrible mood, every word from his mouth dripping with frustrated sarcasm and every word from mine returned with an aggressive eye roll, I think, "He's tired, he didn't get enough sleep. Or he's just hangry." These aren't signs that evil has overtaken his inner being. His self is buffered. This is just fatigue; a lack of sleep, food, or vitamin D; or the hormones of puberty.

## The Therapeutic and Divine Action, or When Sin Becomes Sickness

It is no wonder that in the early twentieth century, pastoral practice takes a distinct turn toward the therapeutic (we'll see this below in the story of Harry

25. Taylor explains: "Modern Westerners have a clear boundary between mind and world, even mind and body. Moral and other meanings are 'in the mind.' They cannot reside outside, and thus the boundary is firm. But formerly it was not so. Let us take a well-known example of influence inhering in an inanimate substance, as this was understood in earlier times. Consider melancholy: black bile was not the cause of melancholy; it embodied, it was, melancholy. The emotional life was porous here; it didn't simply exist in an inner mental space. Our vulnerability to the evil, the inwardly destructive, extended to more than just spirits that are malevolent. It went beyond them to things that have no wills but are nevertheless redolent with evil meanings." *Dilemmas and Connections: Selected Essays* (Cambridge, MA: Belknap Press, 2011), 220.

Emerson Fosdick).[26] It now seems that the most direct way into people's inner lives is through either proper science or pseudoscience.[27] Thanks to the legacy of Augustine, we still assume, no matter how enclosed in the immanent frame we are, that the pastor's vocation is to enter the inner world.[28] But the sacraments, absolution of sin, and Word preached seem no longer to penetrate the buffer. What does, however, is depth psychology and psychoanalysis (for mainline liberal pastors) or expressive self-help (for evangelical pastors). E. Brooks Holifield states, "By the end of the [nineteenth] century, the mainline liberals concluded that the key to unlocking the mysteries of religion and reality was 'in ourselves.'"[29]

Yet it's not quite right to say that they penetrate the buffer. Rather, what makes these therapies so powerful is that they don't penetrate the buffered self at all but instead reinforce its plausibility when its firm boundary starts to thin. Therapy is powerful in our secular age because it can go inward but without disturbing the buffer (mainly because it operates only at the level of epistemology and avoids ontology, essence, and, often, explicit moral categories).[30] And this can be good, as anyone helped by therapy will attest. I don't want to live in a world without psychology, therapy, and medication (if Owen's angst becomes too much, I'll take him to a child psychologist or family therapist, not a witch doctor or a church healing service).

Yet when these therapies are transferred to pastoral practice, we can see more clearly why although at one level they are deeply helpful, they can in turn add to the pastoral malaise in a secular age. These proper sciences or

26. For Fosdick's view of preaching as counseling, see E. Brooks Holifield, *A History of Pastoral Care in America: From Salvation to Self-Realization* (Nashville: Abingdon, 1983), 220.

27. Holifield provides some nice texture to this transition and its impact on Protestantism: "The introspective piety in the American Protestant heritage—the preoccupation with inwardness, rebirth, conversion, revival—was easily translated into a secular psychological piety. And the new vocabulary of the psychologists and psychotherapists then reshaped the older Protestant vision. The writings of pastoral theologians have reflected the transitions in the church and the culture. In their proposals concerning pastoral counsel and counseling, one can discern the broader Protestant journey 'from salvation to self-realization.'" *History of Pastoral Care*, 356.

28. James K. A. Smith says insightfully, "There is a certain irony, however: while the therapeutic was meant to throw off the guilt and burden of spiritual responsibility, and hence the scowl of the clergy and confessor, 'now we are forced to go to new experts, therapists, doctors, who exercise the kind of control that is appropriate over blind and compulsive mechanisms'" ([Taylor, *Secular Age*,] p. 620). In the name of securing our freedom, we swap submission to the priest for submission to the therapist." *How (Not) to Be Secular: Reading Charles Taylor* (Grand Rapids: Eerdmans, 2014), 107.

29. Holifield, *History of Pastoral Care*, 198.

30. Taylor's point is that sin as opposed to sickness provides goods and therefore moral formation. Sickness is just the absence of something, whereas sin is to be repossessed by something good, freed for something. "The difference is this: evil has the dignity of an option for an apparent good; sickness has not." *Secular Age*, 619.

pseudosciences presume a disenchantment that allows the true self to be independent of what it feels. Where confession demands that you admit an ontological state, that *you* (that your very being), in the essence of your nature (to echo Augustine), are sinful, the proper sciences or pseudosciences of therapy say something very different.[31] You might feel guilty, but what you feel comes from your brain chemistry or misinterpreted history. It isn't *you* that is sinful (if you *are* anything, you're sick). This makes your state just a feeling that you have, produced by your mind, not some outside objective reality that presses on you. It is just your brain that causes this because of its chemistry or your mind's interpretation of your past history. Your self does not need confession or an outside ontological force to bring healing and a new moral trajectory; you just need analysis or a pill.[32]

This is a huge change that undercuts the pastor. We as a culture follow Augustine into the inner world but then take a radical turn away from him, claiming that the self is (almost) always innocent—as opposed to Augustine's claim of its fundamental sinfulness and guilt. Taylor explains: "One of the most striking fruits of this sense of innate human innocence has been the transfer of so many issues which used to be considered moral into a therapeutic register. What was formerly sin is often now seen as sickness."[33] The pastor is unneeded, or needs to take on the practices of the proper sciences or pseudosciences, because no longer does healing "involve conversion, a growth in wisdom, a new, higher way of seeing the world."[34]

Or to say it another way, you no longer need the Word or host. They might offer some symbolic help to your enclosed, buffered self and therefore be worth partaking in, but they have no direct independent ontological force to transform your being. You are buffered from such things. You can now actually take a more radical step to assume, deep within the buffered self, that there is

31. While I believe it is right to say that these perspectives take little consideration of ontology, this is only directly. They do have implicit, often unaware, commitments to ultimacy that work from some sense of ontology. For more on this, see Don Browning, *Religious Thought and the Modern Psychologies: A Critical Conversation in the Theology of Culture* (Philadelphia: Fortress, 1987).

32. "Psychoanalysis may seem, and partly is, an intermediate phenomenon. Unlike behavioural therapies, or those relying mainly on drugs, it involves a hermeneutic, an attempt to understand the meaning of our unease. But its goal is the same; the hermeneutic delves into the unavoidable, deep psychic conflicts in our make-up. But these have no moral lesson for us; the guilt or remorse points to no real wrong. We strive to understand them in order to reduce their force, to become able to live with them. On the crucial issue, what we have morally or spiritually to learn from our suffering, it is firmly on the therapeutic side: the answer is 'nothing.'" Taylor, *Secular Age*, 621.

33. Taylor, *Secular Age*, 618.

34. Taylor, *Secular Age*, 619.

no such thing as an objective reality outside of your inner self.[35] Reality is just the buzzing of buffered minds in consent (welcome to *The Matrix*!). Although language and embodiment make it seem unlikely that we are just brains in vats, stuck in our Matrix pods, we now can imagine that this really could be.

Even if we don't go this far, the buffered self still seems to disbelieve the impact of any ontological other on our inner life. Particularly, we reject the idea of an ontological other that transcends the senses and comes with transforming grace through judgment. It now becomes a violation, or at least major buzzkill, to remind people that they are sinful. The modern moral order of the buffered self, cordoned off from ontological encounter, asserts that no one is allowed to judge anyone. People are not sinful, just sick, and it is rude to point out and judge sick people.

All of this means that the buffered inner life is no longer the amphitheater of divine and human encounter. In other words, the buffered self seems predisposed to lock divine action out of its inner world, radically reversing Augustine's vision and making things very difficult for the pastor. If God is to enter this space that Augustine helped make, then God must be stripped of otherness and made into a therapeutic crutch that the brave can outgrow. (This is why I said in volume 1 that Moralistic Therapeutic Deism isn't a misplaced understanding of faith but endemic to our time.) In the secular age of the buffered self, God may be a worthy symbol with therapeutic payoff, but if you don't need this God strategy, why use it—especially if it violates your disengaged freedom and makes you feel vulnerable. The pastor, then, walks a fine line. If at any time she uses anything stronger than a weak suggestion for people's deeper involvement (or even implies that people are vulnerable), naming at any point the ontological or moral necessity of community and its practice, she could be interpreted as being judgmental, having crossed the hedge and invaded the space of the buffered self. This could lead people to interpret the pastor and the entire church as abusive.[36] Telling people during Lent that they need to pray, instead of suggesting that it might be helpful to them, is invasive. During a stewardship campaign, suggesting that God cares and might not be happy with how you spend your money is a violation. Even

---

35. For an example of this in philosophy, see Richard Rorty.

36. And the fact that this is true shows that while we have moved behind the porous self, it remains in the genealogy of consciousness. People get so angry when these things are brought to the surface because at a deep level they still believe them. Taylor says it like this: "Think of the reaction of some people to the AIDS epidemic; or the way people with cancer are often told that they are stricken because of their bad life style (Susan Sontag protested against this). Some of the old attitudes are not beyond recovery, in a sense. It is just that in espousing them seriously one goes against the grain of the modern identity in a fundamental way. One adopts beliefs which most people will castigate as weird." *Secular Age*, 40.

asking people to get up and move seats so a closer sense of community can be experienced in a sparsely populated sanctuary may cause visitors not to return.

It is no wonder the pastor feels a malaise. But the malaise is complicated, because who can really live with no sense of an ontological other? As we said in chapter 3, in regard to cognitive science, it appears that the human spirit is wired to look for agents. When we're tired, grieving, overjoyed, or in a dark theater, we experience the world as porous; we are opened up by the experience. (The buffer is never as thick as we think.) Art and love also seem to invade the buffer. It's not a surprise, then, that we are a culture overwhelmed by entertainment and sex. These are two ecstatic ways to penetrate the buffer of the self with something that feels like transcendence but is too weak to demand transformation. It can make us feel, and even pull us temporarily out of ourselves, but won't actually upend the buffer. (Of course, when the yearning for entertainment is returned to a longing for worship, and sex to the expression of the deepest of unions, it moves quickly into the ontological—enabling true encounter.)

So the malaise of the pastor is compounded, because though divine action is pushed out of the buffered self and the core practices like confession, preaching, and communion are relativized, there remains a longing for something more—seen clearly in how alternative therapies have begun to attend to the spiritual in the last decade, with even the University of Minnesota, a bastion of immanent science, having a Center for Spirituality and Healing.

# 5

when ordinary life becomes so much
more than ordinary

*Jonathan Edwards and pastoring to those who don't care*

You'd be shocked too if your name appeared in the story of a famous American. I've never assumed that I came from a great line of people. Never once did I even dream that I was a Kennedy, or even a Kardashian (I mean, who would want the second one!). Because of this lack of imagination, I've never really had the sense that my name implicated me in either honor or derision. I've always assumed that I'm responsible for my own name (this in itself proves Charles Taylor's point about the rise of the self and its buffering).

But when I turned the page, it was there, staring back at me: "Root." Even now I have no clue if there is any relation, but it didn't matter. I felt implicated—and not in a good way. My name was attached to a villain.

It appears that no matter how talented a pastor you are in America, at some point some group in your congregation will turn on you, rallying an angry mob to oust you. Stay long enough and it happens to everyone, even Jonathan Edwards. And it was the guy bearing my name who led the revolt: Timothy Root.

The year was 1744, still a decade or two before revolutionary ambitions got white hot in the colonies. Edwards had just finished a successful decade and a half at his Northampton church. He arrived in Northampton in 1725,

after two stints at Yale (one as a student—starting at the age of thirteen!—
another as a tutor) and a meaningful but short pastorate at a Presbyterian
church in New York City. Jonathan came to Northampton as assistant pastor
to his famous and powerful grandfather, Solomon Stoddard. Stoddard was
a pillar of Puritanism, a major voice in New England church conflicts. But
four years after Jonathan arrived, Stoddard died, leaving the Northampton
church to Jonathan's solo charge.

Like Augustine with Monica, so the pastoral genius of Jonathan Edwards
can be traced back to his mother, Esther, Solomon's daughter. It's true that
Jonathan's father was a minister, but everyone agreed it was Esther who
possessed the deep intellectual capacities and piety. Like Monica before her,
she'd pour much into her son. But unlike Monica, she wasn't alone in the
task. Jonathan was the fifth of eleven children, but the only son. Esther and
Jonathan's sisters attended to his development in both intellect and piety. It
is hard to miss how mothers and sisters impacted these great pastors. Women
had been refused ordination since around the fourth century, but their impact
on the pastorate was immense. There simply is no Augustine, no Thomas
Becket, no Edwards, and (as we'll see) no Henry Ward Beecher without shaping and influence by women.

Jonathan, particularly, needed care from his mother and sisters because,
while he was gifted in mind, he was frail in body, suffering stomach pains and
ailments most of his life. So when he arrived in Northampton in 1725 to assist
his imposing grandfather, he was frail and thin; "sickly" was a fair description. He'd remain in this state the rest of his life. But this weakness was his
strength. It forced him into a strict discipline of thirteen hours of prayer and
study each day. A hoe and ax were never a temptation for Edwards; books
and a quill were all the heavy lifting he could muster.

In those thirteen hours each day, Jonathan began to pray for something
specific. Fearing that his grandfather had been too lenient, Jonathan believed
that a return to piety and a reform of the inner life was needed. Solomon was
one of the creators of the Half-Way Covenant, a way of allowing membership
without all the necessary piety. This allowed people to be part of the church
without being completely reformed in spirit and action.[1]

1. Mark Noll explains: "For his labors, Stoddard experienced five 'harvests' of souls in
Northampton. In general, however, those who followed his lead on church discipline showed
less interest in the unconverted. But Stoddard's concern for revival was shared by his grandson,
Jonathan Edwards, who became his colleague minister in 1724 and his successor when he died.
Edwards eventually repudiated his grandfather's ideas on the Lord's Supper, but his efforts in
the 1730s and 1740s to promote renewal marked him as his grandfather's heir in spirit as well
as in fact." A History of Christianity in the United States and Canada (Grand Rapids: Eerdmans, 1996), 87.

But with his grandfather lying in the Northampton graveyard, Jonathan began asking God to bring revival. In 1733 it came. In a period of six months, three hundred people were added to membership in the church.[2] To be a member in full covenant meant a complete commitment to bend *every part* of your life toward the holy. It was to live at the high bar of the pastor, even if you were a farmer or tradesman. Over the next decade, revival—the first of the great awakenings—spread throughout the colonies. Edwards played a central part; his sermons were preached and read across the Connecticut River Valley and beyond.

When Timothy Root came into Edwards's life in 1744, Edwards was considered by many to be one of the greatest theologians in the New World, and without a doubt a gifted pastor. Things were going swimmingly until he got word that some rambunctious young men, all between the ages of twenty-one and twenty-nine, were stirring up trouble.

This mischief was particularly disturbing to Edwards. Not only did it seem to be a stark example that some of the fervor of awakening was dissipating, but it also opposed Edwards's deepest pastoral conceptions. As a good (maybe the best) Puritan preacher, Edwards supported the ancient Augustinian turn inward, even doubling down on it. "Jonathan . . . insist[ed] that professions of faith must show evidence of being heartfelt. . . . True religion, he had long held, must involve the affections. The will must be radically transformed from its natural self-love to love for God."[3]

Augustine could have said this. But what Edwards assumed as evidence of true heartfelt-ness was distinct from Augustine, something imagined only after the Reformation (and intensified in the New World). According to Edwards, we show that indeed our affections are turned to God and not to ourselves by continually being reformed.[4] And we do this not by just going to church but by living out each minute of our ordinary lives in the village, fields, and home in direct obedience to God. We are to avoid in every way idleness, drink, and lewdness—all things that these young men were reported to be doing.

2. "During the 1730s various and scattered congregations had experienced spiritual revivals. But it was not until the English evangelist George Whitefield toured the colonies in 1739 that the Great Awakening really took on the dimensions of a mass social movement. Whitefield's powerful preaching ignited the spiritual sensibilities of thousands and his influence reached into virtually every congregation in the northern and middle colonies." David Harlan, *The Clergy and the Great Awakening in New England* (Ann Arbor, MI: UMI Research Press, 1980), 50.

3. George Marsden, *Jonathan Edwards: A Life* (New Haven: Yale University Press, 2003), 353.

4. For more on Edwards, see Nathan O. Hatch and Harry S. Stout, eds., *Jonathan Edwards and the American Experience* (New York: Oxford University Press, 1988); and Iain Murray, *Jonathan Edwards: A New Biography* (Edinburgh: Banner of Truth, 1987).

## When *What* Becomes *How*

The transitions between Becket in the twelfth century and Edwards in the eighteenth are immense, and they play a major part in getting us to a secular age, where divine action becomes opaque.[5] From the twelfth to eighteenth century we not only go through a Reformation, reinforcing Augustine's inward turn, but a whole New World was founded (at least from the European perspective). The New World was "discovered" by mainly Catholic Italians, Spaniards, and Portuguese, but it was Protestants who settled its northern coasts. Edwards's ancestors imagined it as a New Israel in a New England.

There are at least two radical transitions to highlight here that move like undercurrents in Edwards's story, eventually floating us into a secular age and a malaise in our own pastoral identity.

### The Affirmation of Ordinary Life

First, after the Reformation we see a new affirmation of ordinary life. I've mentioned this many times throughout, but this was ultimately as much a *rejection* as an affirmation. Both Lutheran and Calvinist Protestants "rejected the belief that some sorts of activities were qualitatively superior than others."[6] For instance, by affirming Augustine's inwardness and the ability of each individual to read the Bible and stand before God's justifying action themselves, Luther rejects that some people are spiritually dependent on what *other* people do. What the priest and pope do is *not* superior in kind to what farmers and housemaids do. All are the same in God's eyes, for God meets us not just in sacred enclaves but in our ordinary lives. The Reformation asserts that what matters is not *what* you do but *how* you do it.[7] This was earthshaking!

---

5. I've been trying throughout this project to show these pastors as transitional figures moving us to a secular age. Marsden give us some sense of how Edwards fits into that category: "Edwards, for all his openness to the new age and his ardent support for Whitefield's work, was in some respects a person of another era. Much ink has been spilled on whether Edwards was essentially a medieval or a modern. The answer is that he was both. Like Whitefield and Franklin he was looking for a revolution, but he was thoroughly committed to the age of Constantine in a way that they were not. Caught between two eras and determinedly and sometimes brilliantly trying to reconcile the two, he spent the rest of his life in an agonizing struggle to fully affirm the new without giving up anything of the old. He would be trying to pour new wine into old wine skins." *Jonathan Edwards*, 213.

6. Ruth Abbey, *Charles Taylor* (Princeton, NJ: Princeton University Press, 2000), 89.

7. Charles Taylor says it like this: "Thus ordinary life is to be hallowed. But this doesn't come about in the manner of the Catholic tradition, by connecting it to the sacramental life of the church; rather it comes about within this life itself, which has to be lived in a way which is both earnest and detached." *Sources of the Self: The Making of Modern Identity* (Cambridge, MA: Harvard University Press, 1989), 223.

Becket was murdered, and in a very gruesome way—pieces of his brain bobbing in his blood on the cathedral floor—because he defended the importance of *what* priests do. He kept corrupt King Henry from controlling the distinct, enchanted deeds priests singularly offered the people. The Reformation blurred these lines by pulling down the hierarchy of deeds. The Reformation claims that no one deed is necessarily greater than another. What counts is not the essence or even function of the deed itself but *how* the person does it. A farmer who prayerfully harvests his field, or even, Luther would add, a hangman who responsibly executes, is faithful.[8] Ruth Abbey, commenting on Taylor, says, "What mattered was that one carry out one's deeds worshipfully, to the glory of God. From this perspective, even the most menial activity could become sanctified, if practiced with the appropriate attitude."[9] Edwards is disturbed by the deeds of these rambunctious young men because, as their pastor, he must be concerned about their attitude. If they are spending their time doing lewd acts or even wasting time, then it reveals that the affections of their hearts are turned toward sin.

I vividly remember one sermon from my childhood (and maybe just one!). I was somewhere around the age of eleven or twelve, probably within six months of my reading failure. The pastor in my conservative Lutheran church told us it was disobedient, even an offense to God, to waste time. All time, he explained, was God's because God had entered into time and made every part of it God's domain. He explained that if our hearts were turned toward God, then we'd be responsible to use every minute in obedience to God.

This blew my eleven-year-old mind. I felt convicted and stuck. I had become a time-wasting savant, honing my skills to perfection with the practice of nearly six hours per day in (boring) school. Time wasting was my art form! I was terrible at reading and math, but I excelled at daydreaming and other distractions. My pastor was echoing a deep Protestant commitment: time was equalized, and there were no profane and sacred times. All time was equivalent—it was all God's now, meaning how I spent each minute revealed the state of my heart. I was in big trouble! Lucky for me, this was just a one-off, a kind of throwback Sunday sermon, a little echoing of Edwards that wouldn't return. Thankfully, the pull of the secular age on our religious life was too strong.

---

8. This isn't to insinuate there was no ethic, though ethics in Lutheranism has had an interesting history. The idea is that if your heart was really turned toward God, then deeds that were disobedient to the Ten Commandments could not be done. For instance, you couldn't faithfully lie and steal. However, in a Nazi prison cell, Dietrich Bonhoeffer would discover that there was a faithful way to lie.

9. Abbey, *Charles Taylor*, 89.

Taylor explains that this commitment to the *how* over the *what* is essential to laying the seeds of a secular age. In our time, these seeds have sprouted. For instance, people can assert that they are spiritual but not religious only because the *what* has been replaced completely by the *how*, to a level that would make even Calvin or Luther blush.[10] People all over our culture say, "I don't need to go to church, take communion, or care about baptism; that's not *what* I do. I think what matters is *how* you live your life, and I live mine spiritually." They can even go further, explaining that all the "*what you dos*" of religion get in the way of an inner life that cares for others or for the environment. Religion can keep you from living *how* you should, they assert, by oppressing you with *what* you should do.

In the shadow of the radicalizing of *how* over the *what*, it becomes nearly impossible even for a Protestant pastor to disconnect herself completely from the *what*, unless she takes an extreme step and furiously deconstructs confession, Bible reading, prayer, and more. (Some pastors have tried this; it was big in the early 2000s when the emerging church movement moved in this direction.) Yet what most pastors discovered is that no matter how hard they tried to deconstruct the *what*, it is inextricably laced within their vocation. To completely evacuate the specificity of the *what* in order to respond to the demands of the secular age necessitates leaving the church. And if the pastor can't do this, completely shaking off the *what* in favor of the *how*, then she is always under the threat of being perceived, ironically, as a blockage to people's genuine (authentic) spiritual journey (more on this below).

The way to compensate for this unease and remain in the church is to become obsessed with the *how*, but in a very different way from Jonathan Edwards. Edwards was concerned with *how* you did your deeds because they revealed if your affections were holy. If your inner life was encountering the divine presence, then it would be clear in *how* you lived your ordinary life. But for most pastors today, the obsession with *how* revolves around *how* successful others—those with big churches and platforms—are doing things: *How* can we (I) be relevant? *How* can we get people to come?

We inherit a world of disenchanted *whats*. Unlike a medieval priest, the pastor can't assume that her job is to enact the Mass, recognizing its divine power whether or not human minds are present to give it significance. The

10. "Mistrust of institutions leads to such well-known expressions as 'I am spiritual, but not religious'—which often means I have spiritual yearnings but I do not want to submit them to institutionalized patterns." Bert J. Schreiter, "Spirituality as Platform and Forum for Encounter," in *Renewing the Church in a Secular Age: Holistic Dialogue and Kenotic Vision*, ed. Charles Taylor, José Casanova, George McLean, and João Vila-Chã (Washington, DC: Council for Research in Values and Philosophy, 2016), 192.

practices in themselves have been emptied of their transcendence. But so too has the *how* of people's deeds. Few pastors feel it is right to be checking in on people's inner affections by pointing out their deeds at work and home. Most often *how* people live in the boardroom and bedroom are off limits. Instead, the pastor turns her focus to the *how* of building the church, even able to copy all sorts of other "successful" pastors' *how* with little concern for their theological commitment.[11] In the end, oddly, these *hows* are bound in an immanent frame that has blocked out divine action. The pastor today doesn't need theology (attentive reflection on divine action), because she has silently succumbed to the immanent frame, disconnecting the *how* from divine action itself. The pastor today is in a difficult place where the practices of the *what* have been disenchanted and the *how* of our deeds has been made private. They are personal in the sense that they are our own business and no one else's, to such an extent that we agree across the culture that it is wrong to judge *how* anyone lives their life. But judging for the sake of connecting people to divine action was one of the core pastoral tasks for Edwards.

Yet in this radicalizing of *how*, we shouldn't miss that this move to the *how* was once imagined as a gift from an acting, present God who justifies sinners, bringing forgiveness and love. It was an experience of divine action that allowed a shift from the *what* you do to the *how* you do it. Yet now the *how* of your own deeds means you're free from needing God at all, as long as *how* you live your life makes you happy and not a jerk (to echo Moralistic Therapeutic Deism). The radicalized *how* makes it possible to live *how* you want to such an extent that you don't need God. This is a major current that gets us to our secular age. The freedom of the Reformation's affirmation of the *how* makes it possible, with some twists and turns, to void divine action in toto. The kind of atheism represented by most people in our culture can grow in the soil tilled by a Protestantism that separates the *what* from the *how*.[12]

11. There is another side to this *how*. Many pastors feel the tension of the desperate and many pulls on them by the *hows* of the congregation. E. Brooks Holifield explains these tensions: "What the May-Brown study revealed was that the ministers in this fragmented profession faced heavy and conflicting demands. Congregations wanted clergy who could meet an 'endless variety' of expectations. Some wanted good pastors, others good preachers, and still others money raisers, builders, or promoters. Laypeople wanted ministers with 'personality,' clerics who were poised, tactful, and socially at ease, filled with self-assurance and enthusiasm, and able to get along with people. They sought 'spirituality' in their pastors, devotion to the Christian 'way of life' and 'evangelistic zeal'—but they also favored 'executive ability.' A recurring assumption was that they could find such qualities especially in young male pastors. May was struck by 'the young-man obsession.'" *God's Ambassadors: A History of the Christian Clergy in America* (Grand Rapids: Eerdmans, 2007), 222.

12. This is one reason that atheism doesn't become a real option until the nineteenth century. It finds its foothold in Paris—a Catholic locale—but only after the Reformation, the

## Being Polite

This leads us directly into the second transition. The sermon on time wasting that I heard when I was eleven was a one-off because the *how* linked with the immanent frame had lowered the bar of time. My pastor could play the part of Edwards for twenty minutes, telling us that every minute was God's, but most people, other than my eleven-year-old self, just didn't believe it. But this wasn't the case in the decades after the Reformation.

When time was equalized and the *what* was replaced by the *how*, the bar on time was raised. For Calvinists particularly, every minute mattered. "The consequence of this . . . was that the worlds of production and reproduction acquired a new significance. Working with dedication and diligence became more important than the sort of work one did."[13] Again, we can understand why Edwards was disturbed by Timothy Root and his buddies loitering; it revealed that not only their own souls but also society were under threat.

Max Weber, from whom Taylor adopts the concept of disenchantment, believed that this mentality was the origin of capitalism.[14] It was not the desire to make money that moved Calvinists to work hard every minute, producing and reproducing capital, but the desire to obey God. What mattered was the heart's dedication and diligence; it didn't matter if the hands were busy trading silks or selling buttons. If the *how* was really to replace the *what*, and the heart was truly dedicated to God, then reforms would need to stretch into the whole of society.[15] A new society would need to replace the old one. Where the medieval world was ordered by an art of violence, this new society would need to be "polite."[16]

---

Counter-Reformation, and the disenchanting of the world. For more on this, see Michael Buckley, *At the Origins of Modern Atheism* (New Haven: Yale University Press, 1987).

13. Abbey, *Charles Taylor*, 90.

14. See Max Weber, *The Sociology of Religion* (Boston: Beacon, 1963).

15. "Calvinism drained 'the calling' and everyday life of any sacramental significance, while rendering it a kind of testing ground for the reality of election. Meanwhile the Counter-Reformation tended to clamp down on or try to control lay spontaneity and therefore negatively encouraged the rise of a more secular lay sphere." John Milbank, "A Closer Walk on the Wild Side," in *Varieties of Secularism in a Secular Age*, ed. Michael Warner, Jonathan VanAntwerpen, and Craig Calhoun (Cambridge, MA: Harvard University Press, 2010), 62.

16. The move into a polite society for the sake of commerce further made faith a private endeavor. Early New York City is an example. From its beginning it was a hub of commerce (making money). This clear focus allowed it from its start to be pluralistic and diverse, because religion, for instance, was a private affair. Taylor explains the larger point: "So within the framework of polite society, there come to be a set of normative limits on the action and intervention of churches, and the playing out of religious differences: largely overlapping with those with which we have become familiar in contemporary society. State power should operate independent of ecclesiastical control, and public order should be maintained without disturbance by ecclesiastical doctrinal strife, whether this originates from below, among sects,

The elites of the old world saw themselves as warriors (remember the knights who opened Becket's skull?). They were often eager for war and valued its honor codes as the framework for *what* they did in the world. Yet Taylor explains that the elite "members of a 'polite' society were dedicated primarily to the arts of peace."[17] Politeness as modeled by the elites would be the expectation because it produced a dependable and stable environment in which commerce could thrive. This was not done in order to make money but rather was the environment to work out your salvation, diligently giving every minute to God. Taylor explains further how politeness and commerce go together: "The more a society turns to commerce, the more 'polished' and civilized it becomes, the more it excels in the arts of peace. The impetus to moneymaking is seen as a 'calm passion.' When it takes hold in a society, it can help to control and inhibit the violent passions. Or put in other language, moneymaking serves our 'interest,' and interest can check and control passion."[18]

Trade is easier when there is peace. Commerce in the market is more efficient with established rules of properness and cordiality. Ways of speaking, eating, and defecating that are done politely are good for society. They are good for business, we would say today, because *how* you do something is now more important than *what* you do. This is why, Taylor shows, etiquette books for the commoner didn't arrive until between the seventeenth and nineteenth centuries, which seems late. And their advice is shocking, reminding people to never blow their nose in a tablecloth or to always avoid defecating on the steps. This starkly shows how little manners were considered before this time.[19] But now, into the seventeenth century, doing something undignified revealed a life that was undisciplined, which in turn revealed a heart not eagerly seeking God. It is from this time that we hear that "cleanliness is next to godliness," because in a real way the discipline of cleanliness shows that our heart is dedicated to God, for it seeks discipline and order.

Because of this releasing of the *how* into the whole of society, the Protestant pastor is reimagined as a man of manners.[20] For example, "In 1827, Samuel

---

or from above by gratuitous state coercion or persecution." *A Secular Age* (Cambridge, MA: Belknap Press, 2007), 238.

17. Taylor, *Secular Age*, 235.

18. Taylor, *Secular Age*, 180.

19. See also Norbert Elias, *The History of Manners* (New York: Pantheon, 1978).

20. Conrad Cherry gives us some examples of this focus on manners and politeness for the pastor: "After the Civil War, pastoral theologians began to emphasize virility, toughness, and physical stamina rather than etiquette as the virtues appropriate to the grimy new world of city and industry. But the seminaries did not completely give up the aim of smoothing the ragged social edges off of ministerial candidates. In the early 1930s, the average seminary student still had been reared by parents with two years of high school and by fathers who were either farmers or manual laborers. This typical family background led Union Seminary professor William

Filler, a teacher at Princeton who had previously been the pastor of the Wall Street Presbyterian Church in New York City, where he was admired for his 'cultivated and graceful' bearing, published *Letters on Clerical Manners and Habits*, with instructions on proper decorum in pastoral conversation."[21] In the mid-nineteenth century the pastor was a man of manners and the church a place of politeness and order; just decades after the appearance of Filler's book, Mark Twain's *Adventures of Huckleberry Finn* would despise the church as a society of manners.

Today most pastors feel embarrassed by this legacy of the church as polite and the pastor as a bastion of manners. Young pastors, particularly, hate when people assume that they don't drink, swear, or watch HBO (one of the reasons hotel restaurants are filled with cigar smoking and Scotch drinking at pastors' conferences). Now in a secular age, with its attention to authenticity, this leftover conception of politeness and manners seems restricting at best and at worst reveals the pastor as inauthentically dull.

It is no wonder that, around the year 2010, Nadia Bolz-Weber and Mark Driscoll were pitted against each other as *the* model of the pastor in the twenty-first century. Theologically and politically they couldn't have been more different, but where they were similar (and therefore worth pitting against each other) was in their equal rejection of the pastor as polite. Both refused it as part of their pastoral identity. Manners would be far from the center of the churches they led.

Bolz-Weber used crass language and tattoos to upend the image of the mainline pastor as a polite gentleman in loafers. Driscoll embodied the bravado of a WWE wrestler to upend the image of a mannered, hair-parted-perfectly evangelical pastor in khakis. Driscoll even went so far as to outright reject not only the Calvinist call for manners but even the art of peace, asserting that this focus only turned Jesus into a "Richard Simmons, hippie, . . . a neutered and limp-wristed popular Sky Fairy" (Driscoll has never feared being offensive).[22] This placed Driscoll more in the vein of the knights who went

---

Adams Brown to encourage seminary faculty in 1934 to counsel students 'on those matters of personal decorum in which men with faulty social background are deficient.'" *Hurrying toward Zion* (Bloomington: Indiana University Press, 1995), 187.

21. E. Brooks Holifield, *A History of Pastoral Care in America: From Salvation to Self-Realization* (Nashville: Abingdon, 1983), 119.

22. "Mark Driscoll Says Just Grow Up," Relevant, September 9, 2010, https://relevantmagazine .com/god/church/features/22807-mark-driscoll-wants-you-to-grow-up. Driscoll isn't all wrong. Charles Taylor explains: "Along with drink (also aiding and abetting it) were other favored activities: cruel sports, gambling, sexual promiscuity . . . long-standing male forms of conviviality outside the family. The new understanding of order was family-centered, and it often involved identifying the male as the source of potential disruption and the female . . . guardian

swinging for Becket's head than of Jonathan Edwards. Driscoll aggressively sought to recover the warrior image, making the pastor appealing to all those video gamers raised on *Call of Duty* and *Grand Theft Auto*, who were bored and agitated by politeness and peace.

With sarcastic, edgy humor, deep witness, and colorful tattoos, Bolz-Weber too made it possible to be a pastor beyond politeness and therefore more relevant in a secular age. The tattoo has now become a ubiquitous staple for any pastor under forty. Of course, this is in part because of its fashion in the culture. But even more so for young pastors, I believe, the tattoo is a signal that she rejects the image of the pastor as polite and mannered. In its own way, this reveals (quite tacitly and quietly) that the link between the politeness and properness of *how* you live and divine action has been cut, and perhaps for good reason. Its connection led to a lot of pharisaical pastoral misbehavior. But with this gain comes a loss, making the connection between pastoral practice and divine action much harder to name. Behavior and obedience to God, if anyone even feels comfortable still talking like that, are much harder to describe.

We have a name we use, most often disparagingly, for this kind of focus that drives hard for a polite and disciplined society. We call it "puritanical," after Edwards and his forefathers and foremothers. No one would ever be tempted to describe Bolz-Weber or the church she founded with that word. "Puritanical" is seen as morally strict, and Edwards's Northampton church was this—all needed to rise to the bar of holiness. Edwards was such a respected pastor because he lived this out, even going "beyond typical Puritan rigor. He resolved 'to maintain the strictest temperance in eating and drinking.' On this he was constantly experimenting with himself, seeing how much he needed to eat out of necessity and avoiding all excesses that would dull his mind or rouse his passions. Throughout his life observers commented on his strict eating habits and often emaciated appearance." George Marsden continues, "Though he lived in the midst of the world, he did so as an ascetic. Few better illustrated the Protestant ideal of what Max Weber called 'worldly asceticism.'"[23]

So for Edwards, both personally and pastorally, divine action was bound in *how* you do things. When everyone is concerned with *how* they do things, flourishing (of capital or in family life) witnesses to our nearness to God. We are still light years away from a prosperity gospel—we'll need a heightened expressive individualism mixed with a hyper-consumerism to get to that—but

---

of this ordered domestic space." *Dilemmas and Connections: Selected Essays* (Cambridge, MA: Belknap Press, 2011), 53.

23. Marsden, *Jonathan Edwards*, 51.

the base cells for all these realities are possible (*not* inevitable) because of this turn toward flourishing through peace and politeness.

Augustine and the turn inward may have made the self important, but this self was never cut off from others. And for Puritans, other people, like these young men who did not participate in flourishing through politeness, could put us all at risk. Because of this Calvinism, Edwards's pastoral responsibilities stretched deep. Not only did he need to preach sermons that touched the heart; he also needed to do this so that production and reproduction could flourish through the dedication and decency of the people. The puritanical was good for business and brought us near to God.

For the next two hundred years, the pastor is assumed to be essential. Without the pastor prodding others to be decent, society as a whole could not flourish (particularly economically). This assumption will come to its climax with Harry Emerson Fosdick in the early twentieth century. Fosdick's period was the last in which it was assumed that society needed pastoral chaplains to keep us flourishing. After this, most people could imagine flourishing not only without God but also without any pastors reminding us to be diligent, dedicated, and decent. The drive for fame and riches in a full-blown consumer society was fuel enough to keep us engaged and motivated (though newly haunted by a lack of meaning).

### A New Morality

This focus on puritanical politeness creates the possibility of a whole new kind of morality. Before the Reformation, what was right, proper, or good was bound in the higher order. The good was intricately connected to "design." King Henry II argued that because it was designed, the lord should rule his domain as God rules the heaven, and because all God does is good, so too are all the king's deeds good.[24]

The *what* was higher than the *how* because the moral was based in the hierarchy of design. But as we said, the Reformation toppled this hierarchy, replacing the *what* with the *how*, forging a modern moral order. Now what is right, proper, and good is based not on the design of heaven (and the ways its order falls to earth) but on how we organize society for individual mutual benefit. If your salvation is dependent on (or at least reflected in) *how* you work, then any actions by an individual or laws by a government that would keep you from this are *wrong*. Taylor says it like this: "The idea of moral

---

24. The divine right of kings is more complicated than this, but it is enough to make my point about design.

order which is expressed in [the] Declaration [of Independence], and which has since become dominant in our world, is what I have been calling the Modern Moral Order. It is quite different from the orders which preceded it, because it starts from individuals, and doesn't see these as set a priori within a hier-archical order. . . . Its members are not agents who are essentially embedded in a society which in turn reflects and connects with the cosmos, but rather disembedded individuals who come to associate together."[25]

Young men loitering or the king of England's taxation without repre-sentation are immoral because they threaten the fruits of my dedication. "Thus the 'moral' is bound up with (and [eventually] perhaps reduced to) the 'economic.'"[26]

This modern moral order lives on with us today, and is even heightened, adding to a further division between people's imagination and divine action. Most people assume that anything is permitted as long it doesn't violate two things.

One, it doesn't hurt anyone. And by this we mean that it doesn't oppose mutual benefit. "Mutual benefit" means that instead of being led by a set of higher norms, we are guided by the ethic that it is wrong for us to do anything that keeps people from pursuing their own happiness and advancement. Most people, even in our churches, assume that there is no real transcendent or timeless law to which they must correlate their lives. Rather, they are free to do whatever they want as long as it doesn't hurt anyone or deny others the mutual benefit of doing whatever *they* wish.

Of course, this ethic becomes tricky when we enter an age of authentic-ity. In this age, my own definition of what it means for me to be human is the highest pursuit.[27] In the age of authenticity, something is *wrong* when it opposes or restricts someone else's freedom to define his or her own identity. For instance, on episode 7 of season 34 of *Survivor*—yes, I've watched them all—the whole tribe turned on Jeff Varner because he outed Zeke, revealing to the group (and the national audience!) that Zeke was transgender. The indignation of the other contestants was high, revealing that something im-moral had just happened; an ethical line had been crossed. And perhaps it had, because Varner violated a moral code that claims that no one can infringe on or oppose another person's chosen identity.

The way that this modern moral order takes shape around chosen identity makes it complicated for pastors. If the church or the pastor tries too hard

25. Taylor, *Secular Age*, 447.
26. James K. A. Smith, *How (Not) to Be Secular: Reading Charles Taylor* (Grand Rapids: Eerdmans, 2014), 142. See also Taylor, *Secular Age*, 221.
27. See volume 1 for more on this.

to shape a person's life, it will be a violation of the modern moral order. It will likely be seen as a power move to restrict another's mutual benefit (or as we colloquially refer to it, someone's "freedom"—though this is not the true theological definition of freedom[28]). Just listen to the testimonies of ex-Christians. The common thread that led them to leave the faith usually does *not* surround theism, Christology, or even a practice like communion. Rather, it is the perception (or experience) that the church put an imposition on their identity. This is seen as *wrong* (and outrageous) because it violates the mutual benefit of the modern moral order, which, ironically, was created in major part by Edwards's puritanical forefathers.

Sensing this tension in our modern moral order, most pastors avoid saying anything about ethics, goods, or morality—unless it can be supported squarely by some political or ideological group that will provide cover. This allows a closed spin on the immanent frame to reign, and thins out divine action. (A "closed spin" is a construal of life bound in an immanent frame that blinds us to divine action. In other words, it is the presumption that there is no divine action in the world.) What is good has no correlation to the transcendent. Faith, particularly in the mainline, has no real connection to daily life (which is shocking, because we can only get to this point at all because the *how* of daily life was tied together with divine action). Taylor says, "In short, the buffered identity, capable of disciplined control and benevolence, generated its own sense of dignity and power, its own inner satisfactions, and these . . . tilt in favour of exclusive humanism."[29] In other words, it created an ethic without the need for divine action.

But there is also a second violation that comes from this Protestant legacy. Just watch *The Bachelor* (I promise I've missed most of those episodes) and you'll see it. People are justified in losing control, calling out one another, even with a finger in their face, if this other has been "rude." Today, to be rude means that you callously (often laced within the interpretation of violence and victimization) oppose my own identity, threatening my unique expression of who I am.

It's "rude" to tell someone they're wrong, because that's *their* position; it is bound in their experience. It is rude to cut someone off when they're talking, because they're not necessarily trying to communicate their ideas or feelings, but they're expressing—broadcasting—their identity, and you've stopped them from this recognition. That's r-u-d-e! When this perceived rudeness is

---

28. Bonhoeffer's sense of freedom is to always be bound to others—we are free *for*, not free *from*, others. Here he is drawing from Luther. This allows him to be able to talk about obedience as the shape of discipleship.

29. Taylor, *Secular Age*, 262.

experienced, you are justified in defending yourself—if you're punched, it's right to punch back. To add to the point above, it is hard for the pastor to say anything to the congregation about morality without walking very gently on broken glass, fearing that too much exhortation will be labeled as rude victimizing.

Rudeness meant something very different in Edwards's Northampton. To be rude was a revelation that the affections of your heart were far from God. Timothy Root's rudeness was a tumor that Edwards feared meant cancer, not only for Root's soul but for the whole village, if it was not cut out. Rudeness was so threatening because it showed that your dedication was not to God, and therefore you were far from divine action. For Edwards, then, there was a significant moral structure for rudeness that was bound to divine action. Rudeness was not being a blockage to someone's expressive identity but instead a sign that rot had entered the soul (to change the metaphor). Each heart needed to surrender inwardly to God's Word, but this would have the result of reordering people's ordinary lives, leading them to discipline themselves and their children so that their inner lives would submit to the will of God.

A rude child revealed undevout parents—the rot was the child's rudeness, but the moisture that made it possible was undedicated, distracted parents. Your duty, and therefore the first place you lived out the *how* of your deeds, was in marriage and family.[30] This all seems harsh, even punitive, but we should remember, first, that in many ways we still believe this—of course, without the direct connection to divine action. When a teenager shoots up a school or commits a crime, or a child falls into a gorilla cage at the zoo, we publicly blame, even shame, the parents. We echo the legacy of our Protestantism, but without any of the practices of reconciliation, forgiveness, restoration, and mercy that were bound up in the experience of divine action. In its place you receive derision on CNN or Fox News. Second, while most definitely harsh, without this focus it would be unlikely that both marriage and parenting would have ever become compassionate. Rudeness revealed spiritually inept parents, but the coating that prevented this rot of rudeness was to double down not on punishment but on love. Love and support of children was the route to a

---

30. Taylor both nuances and develops this thought: "The nature of this change has often been misunderstood. Some critics have taken the historians of family life to have been making the preposterous claim that before modern times, people didn't really love their children and never married for love. . . . It is not the actual place of affection but the sense of its importance. What changes is not that people begin loving their children or feeling affection for their spouses, but that these dispositions come to be seen as a crucial part of what makes life worthy and significant, whereas previously these dispositions were taken as banal, except perhaps that their absence in a marked degree might cause concern or condemnation." *Sources of the Self*, 292.

flourishing society—as social theorists today still believe.[31] The coddling of our children today is another legacy of our Protestantism.

This focus on marriage and family delivers to us the more prominent conception of puritanical. Today, when we use the word "puritanical," most often we are referring to sexuality. A puritanical person would never watch *Game of Thrones*, wear a string bikini, or be caught paging through *Maxim*. A disciplined and polite society, where the *how* is bound to the dedication to family, would, of course, uphold sexual purity.

Augustine was never concerned with this. Once he even said that the only trouble a man could get into when young was with his penis—meaning that this kind of trouble wasn't really trouble at all.[32] But not so for those pastors after the Reformation. Now the inner passions and desires were linked to decency, discipline, order, and politeness. "Viewing the human condition as a warfare between flesh and spirit, [Edwards] had a firm conviction that sexual impurity was incompatible with the spiritual sensibilities he sought. Indeed, he often preached that to be driven by short-term pleasures of physical lust was the epitome of self-love."[33] The inward attention, added to by decency and politeness located in marriage and family, made open sexual behavior at best crass and at worst depraved. Regardless, it was out of bounds in Edwards's Northampton.

## Back to Timothy Root and the Young Folks' Bible

So you can imagine the shock when Pastor Edwards is told that this group of a dozen or so young men, all of whom but three are members of his church,

31. For the clearest example of this, see Don Browning, *From Culture Wars to Common Ground: Religion and the American Family Debate* (Louisville: Westminster John Knox, 1997). More recently, see Brad Wilcox, *Why Marriage Matters*, 3rd ed. (West Chester, PA: Broadway, 2011).

32. Peter Brown explains how Augustine sees vandalism as a deeper issue than sexual activity. This presumption has changed a great deal as we've passed through Protestantism. "Nothing shows Augustine's preoccupation with the will more clearly than the way in which he recounts his adolescence. His African readers tended to think that a boy was innocent until he reached puberty: 'as if,' Augustine once said, 'the only sins you could commit were those in which you use your genitals.' These, indeed, are the sins that seem to have interested the average reader of the *Confessions* ever since. Augustine, however, treats them as not very important: in his eyes they paled into insignificance before a single act of vandalism. The pointless robbing of a pear-tree is what really interests this great connoisseur of the human will: he will analyse this one incident with fascinated repulsion; 'For what could I not have done, seeing that I could enjoy even a gratuitous act of crime?'" *Augustine of Hippo* (Berkeley: University of California Press, 2000), 166.

33. Marsden, *Jonathan Edwards*, 106–7.

and led by Timothy Root, are "passing around books on popular medicine and midwifery, quoting from them to each other in a lewd joking manner and using the information in them to taunt young women about their menstruation."[34]

Marsden takes us further into Edwards's thinking, helping us see why this was such a problem: "The case was not simply one of an overzealous pastor trying to stamp out minor expressions of illicit sexuality when he learned that a few young men were making erotic use of books on sex and midwifery. Edwards abhorred sexual indulgence as especially distracting from the vastly higher beauty of spiritual things."[35] So Jonathan couldn't let this stand; he needed to bring it to the church for discipline.

After preaching a sermon on Hebrews 12:15–16 ("See to it that no one fails to obtain the grace of God; that no root of bitterness springs up and causes trouble, and through it many become defiled. See to it that no one becomes like Esau, an immoral and godless person, who sold his birthright for a single meal"), he called a church meeting, setting forth the parameters for a disciplinary hearing. All of this was pretty standard. These colonial Puritan villages were known for church discipline trials; how else could you get to a decent, polite society where all could flourish in the name of Jesus?

But Edwards made a big mistake. Telling the community that the hearing would happen at his house, he announced a list of names, not discriminating which men would be witnesses and which were the accused. To be wrongly marked with this kind of lewd behavior would disturb anyone, but it was especially disturbing for Puritan Calvinists, whose decency and politeness were marks of their election. This led some of the leading families to wonder who Edwards thought he was. He had just recently requested a raise, and now he was indiscriminately painting everyone with the same messy brush!

The blowback was intense. But Jonathan couldn't relent. As Marsden writes, Edwards reminded his people that it was "not . . . a gender issue, but . . . contagious public speech that threatened souls. Young men had created a lascivious underground and were corrupting other young people. Most of those involved were church members who had been taking communion. Those who were promoting a profane culture among the young had created stumbling blocks that endangered the eternal destinies of their neighbors."[36]

At the trial, the testimony given by Mary Downing and Bathsheba, a slave of Major Seth Pomeroy, confirmed that this lewdness led to an undisciplined and indecent society. One of them stated that those who were laughing at the book saw girls pass and were "ready to kiss them, and catch hold of the girls

34. Marsden, *Jonathan Edwards*, 293.
35. Marsden, *Jonathan Edwards*, 293.
36. Marsden, *Jonathan Edwards*, 296.

and shook 'em. Timothy Root in particular," they testified. But Root went further. He not only tried to kiss the girls; he also called these books "the young folks' Bible." Marsden remind us, "In a Calvinist community where there were few sacred objects [because all of ordinary life was made holy] and where the Bible was the highest authority, this was serious sacrilege."[37]

Root's actions and attitude convinced Edwards something had to be done. After all, he was acutely aware that it was these exact young men who just years earlier, in their teens, were awakened to the Lord. Edwards himself had led them to the inner light in the first Great Awakening. Jonathan worried that his answer to the prayer for revival was unraveling before his eyes, thanks to the bombastic Timothy Root.[38]

But even more was unraveling than Jonathan could see at the time. Smoldering under this controversy over the "young folks' Bible" and Edwards's mishandling of the situation was resentment over his request for a raise. The pastor's salary was connected to town taxes in those days, and people are always annoyed by requests for a tax hike. Surprisingly, the buffoonish Timothy Root played a part in fanning those coals hot enough to burn. Across New England people were becoming more and more weary of taxation, especially if it came with an air of detached elitism. This allowed even a mook like Root to seem relatively sensible.

During the initial church meeting, Timothy and his brother were asked to wait as the elders, led by Edwards, discussed the matter. This didn't sit well with the impatient Root, so the comments started to spew. He said loudly, "What do we do here? We won't stay here all day long." When rebuked and told to show respect, Root responded, "I won't worship a wig." When challenged further, Root stated that these elders "are nothing but men molded up of a little dirt." Marsden adds that such a comment shows "how a Calvinist low view of human nature might make one a revolutionary."[39] The very sinfulness that Edwards highlighted led Root, and then other, more respected townsmen, to wonder if Jonathan's own heavy hand of discipline and longing for a raise were not corrupt.

A new spirit from a new generation was budding. They'd use this very drive for a decent and polite society to mobilize against crown and wig for

37. Marsden, *Jonathan Edwards*, 298.
38. Harlan explains why Edwards would hold so tightly to the Great Awakening: "Edwards' millennialism was inspired by the revivals of the Great Awakening. The millennium would, he believed, be inaugurated by an outpouring of God's spirit and it would consist of a renewal of 'the hearts and minds of mankind.' It would come 'neither by a reconstruction of the temple nor through its destruction, but as a renewal of the nature of those who dwelt within.'" *Clergy and the Great Awakening*, 120.
39. Marsden, *Jonathan Edwards*, 299.

the sake of liberty. Timothy Root demanded his own, departing the meeting for the pub, shouting as he left, "If they have any business with me . . . they may come to me; I ben't obliged to wait any longer on their arses, as I have done." He added, "I don't give a turd, I don't care a fart!"[40] (yep, that's surely my relative!).

## The End for Edwards

From this incident, Edwards lost his grip on the congregation. For the next four years, no new members joined the church. Eventually, a 200–23 vote sent one of America's greatest preachers and thinkers packing. Any pastor who has been painfully ousted should take some comfort that you join the likes of Jonathan Edwards, who also felt the stab of congregational revolt. Whether in the fourth, twelfth, eighteenth, twentieth, or twenty-first century, churches are never utopias, and to echo Bonhoeffer, anyone who wants them to be seeks not the real church but its idea.[41]

Edwards's Calvinism kept him from idealistic dreaming. After all, he had to push so hard for a disciplined and polite society because of his very realistic anthropology. He knew that while the inner heart could will for God, it was, as Augustine taught, caught in sin. But as Edwards contemplated what was next in his life, idealism and even fantasy may have gotten the best of him. Passing on pastorates from New England to Scotland, he chose the West. He set out for the rugged forests of Indian Territory, a missionary to the Housatonic—not a great choice for a sickly bookworm. Yet by God's grace and human determination (the great trait of the Calvinists), Edwards did significant ministry there. But the wear and tear of these years was intense. So when the College of New Jersey in Princeton (later renamed Princeton University) came looking for a new president, Edwards was ready to return to the comforts of the colonies and a life with his nose back in books.

In 1758, Edwards would be installed as president, making the new Nassau Hall (built in 1756 and still standing today) his stomping grounds. But this settled life as an academic was, alas, not meant to be. In March, the same year as his installation, Edwards would be dead at fifty-four. A big supporter of science, particularly seeing great advantage in inoculations, Edwards inoculated himself against smallpox to encourage others to do the same.[42] But

40. Marsden, *Jonathan Edwards*, 299.
41. See Dietrich Bonhoeffer, *Life Together* (Minneapolis: Fortress, 1996), 35–37.
42. We lack the space to discuss Edwards's fascinating connection to science. He is such a transitional figure because, though he inherits and affirms an enchanted world, he's also

when this small dose made its way through his sickly body, it won. The great American pastor was gone. To this day, you can find his body at rest in the Princeton cemetery. Next time I'm there, I'll visit, though Edwards might roll over when another Root stops by with a "hello."

---

drawn to Newton and new science. This draw makes sense and fits his Puritanism. Taylor again shows that the flat narrative of atheism is wrong. "The Puritan theology of work and ordinary life provided a hospitable environment for the scientific revolution. Indeed, much of Bacon's outlook stems from a Puritan background. The support given to the Baconian vision by Puritans has often been commented upon." *Sources of the Self*, 230. For more on this, see Robert W. Jenson, *America's Theologian: A Recommendation of Jonathan Edwards* (Oxford: Oxford University Press, 1988), chap. 3.

# 6

## when a pastor was America's greatest celebrity

*Henry Ward Beecher and pastoring by personality*

I know this sounds weird, and there is no way any scientific instrument would verify it, but I've always thought that time was different in LA—yeah, like on the island in *Lost*. I lived in Los Angeles for almost four years, and yet I'm not sure I ever experienced a weekday. Of course I did, more than a thousand of them. But it never felt like it. Even when I was busy with work, grinding out a nine-to-five, the city had a tangible buzz, a saturated feeling of excitement and possibility pulsating from its core. I think it was partly the sun. Seventy-five degrees and sunny every day of the year has a way of tricking your brain into thinking it's Saturday. But it was more; the pulsating possibility seemed to come directly from the entertainment industry. Even living across town in Pasadena, I could feel the ambiance from Hollywood blanketing everyone from the valleys to the beaches. The intoxicating vibe of the entertainment industry and all the celebrity allure seemed to bring the whole city to the speed of the weekend.

Yet Los Angeles is not the birthplace of American celebrity, nor is radio, film, pop music, or television its first medium. Not surprising to most, New York City is the place of celebrity's origin. But perhaps most astounding, celebrity's first medium was the sermon.

America has always been a land of famous men; no country can throw off the ancient regime of the monarch and choose to create a society solely from

97

the will of the people without leveraging tales, legends, and fables of ordinary citizens doing extraordinary feats. The Pilgrims, Washington, Adams,
Jefferson, and even Paul Revere would be on the lips of all Americans after the
revolution. But none of these legendary figures ever drew screaming crowds,
large paychecks, constant front-page news, or the gossip of scandal. (No one
would ever mistake the reception of John Adams for that of Justin Bieber.)

One of the first persons in the New World to receive something like Beatle-
mania was pastor Henry Ward Beecher. He was so famous that Walt Whitman
and Mark Twain wanted nothing more than to be in his presence, overwhelmed
by his personality.[1] They saw themselves as just small men hoping to live in
the shadow of the great preacher's celebrity light.

### Profile of a Pastor

When Henry was a boy, no one would have assumed that either fame or legend
awaited him. (Though if you had to pick, you'd go with legend.) Henry was
the son of esteemed pastor Lyman Beecher. Lyman was a pastor cut from the
cloth of Jonathan Edwards. Though born a decade after the great American
preacher's death, Lyman saw the world through the same Calvinist lens, even
receiving a Yale education, just as his hero had.

Lyman embodied what French diplomat and scholar Alexis de Tocqueville
would call "the political priest" when he visited the country in the 1830s.
Lyman not only assumed an enchanted world and great concern for damnation but also saw it as his primary calling to prod people to uphold holiness
in their ordinary lives. He drove them to raise their children in the piety of
the Calvinist reforms and work for a flourishing society—all to the glory of
God. This passion won Lyman the title "the moral leader of the nation."
But it was much more than just talk. Lyman would not only father thirteen
children, but more than half of them would be important pastors, authors,
or fighters for abolition. The best example of this is Lyman's daughter Harriet Beecher Stowe, who penned the American classic *Uncle Tom's Cabin*.
This book would intimately take white Northerners into the evils of slavery.

Harriet's closest sibling, both in age and affection, was Henry.[2] While it
was clear from early childhood that Harriet was destined for greatness (if her
gender wasn't a barrier), the same could not be said of Henry. He wasn't dim

---

1. See Debby Applegate, *The Most Famous Person in America: The Biography of Henry
Ward Beecher* (New York: Doubleday, 2006), esp. 370–72.

2. "The two were so close they seemed almost like twins—'always hand-in-hand. They
are as lovely children as I ever saw, amiable, affectionate, and very bright.'" Applegate, *Most
Famous Person in America*, 33.

but was not even close to the sharpest knife in his family drawer. This gave Henry the space to flex a personality much different from the rigid Calvinism that his father expected. As a matter of fact, you could see the imagination and ministry of Henry Ward Beecher switching the American pastoral identity, shifting the pastoral imagination onto new tracks. Henry would be the first (at least with any significance) to discard the parts of the Calvinist tradition that grated against a message of acceptance and love. Henry ministered in a time very different from his father's. If Lyman was continuing the legacy of Edwards, asserting that all ordinary life demanded the rigor of seeing everything (all the time) as sacred—needing the constant attention of willed commitment, or hell would dawn amongst us—Henry would be one of the first to upend, and therefore relativize, this perspective. Henry decided hell, fear, damnation, and rigid asceticism need not be preached.

## A Loss That Directed

As we saw above, a key plotline in the early life of Thomas Becket was the death of his mother, ending his education and sending him back to London from Paris. Henry's childhood, too, would be marred with the loss of his mother, though Henry was much younger. "One cool July night, just as Henry turned three, his mother disappeared into her bedroom and did not come out. Suddenly the house that had been brimming with high spirits was now hushed with fear."[3] The fever that had taken Roxana's life would also burn out the warmth that had filled the Beecher home. Roxana played a key role for the family that stretched far beyond her duties as a mother and wife. Roxana balanced Lyman's rigid reforming Calvinism with affection, compassion, and kindness.[4]

With Roxana gone, Lyman was lost in more ways than one. With children ranging from the teen years to nine months old, he was out of his depth. So almost exactly a year after Roxana's death, Lyman returned from a trip to Boston with a new wife. Like Henry's beloved sister, this new mother bore the name Harriet. But while his sister reflected, almost in every way, Roxana's

3. Applegate, *Most Famous Person in America*, 29.
4. "In an age when few women possessed formal education, Roxana was a skilled artist and a genuine intellectual, fluent in French, with a passion for history, math, and science, and whose most treasured possession was an imported English encyclopedia. Roxana's piety equaled Lyman's, but in contrast to her high-strung husband, she was by nature 'calm and self-possessed,' with an 'easy and gentle temperament that could never very strictly enforce any rules,' as her eldest daughter recalled; 'at the same time, in sudden emergencies she had more strength and self-possession than my father.'" Applegate, *Most Famous Person in America*, 26.

personality, the same could not be said about Harriet Porter Beecher, their new mother.

Things started well. The younger children, thirsty for the affection of a mother, particularly welcomed her, soaking up her presence. But soon enough it became clear that she was the stark opposite of Roxana. Harriet Porter Beecher was overtaken by the darker elements of Calvinism. She felt a two-ton weight of divine consequence on the back of her ordinary life, threatening to break her. This heaviness moved her in and out of severe depression. Fearing damnation, contemplating suicide, fearing more damnation, and frantically disciplining the children to save their mortal souls was her pattern. It was experiences like these that gave momentum to the flipping of the social imaginary, in which the "all is sacred" was flipped to the "all is secular." Experiencing such fanatic spiritual pressure, people in the nineteenth century sought ways of living without divine consequence in their ordinary lives and beyond the constant prodding of a pastor (and/or his wife).[5]

Henry and his preaching would be core to this transition, stemming in major part from his childhood. Henry reports, "I don't remember a year of my life, after I was seven or eight years old, . . . that I did not go about with a feeling of sadness; a feeling that I was in danger of exile from heaven—all because I was a sinner, and I didn't want to be."[6] Henry watched the divine consequence of our ordinary lives break his stepmother. "Soon [she] was spending more time cloistered in her room, praying intently and suffering from vague maladies. All the children found their new stepmother forbidding and gloomy, but little Henry was particularly intimidated by her."[7] He said years later in reflection, "I was afraid of her. . . . It would have been easier for me to lay my hand on a block and have it struck off than to open my thoughts to her."[8]

The loss of Roxana's affection, mixed with the rigidity of Harriet's cold discipline, led the growing Henry into conflict with Lyman and eventually

5. "New England, it has been said, is the child of a superstitious mother and a philosopher father. This fusion of the supernatural and the hyper-logical is at the heart of Lyman Beecher's theology. In seeking to impose the rule of divine law on an unruly universe, Calvinism takes the great unanswerable questions of life—Why is there so much pain in the world? Is there a higher power in the world? What happens when we die?—and poses them, as Harriet later observed, 'with the severest and most appalling distinctness.' Lyman and his fellow divines mercilessly drilled their parishioners in these impenetrable questions, casting a morbid pall over the culture in general and over the Beecher house in particular." Applegate, *Most Famous Person in America*, 36.

6. Henry Ward Beecher, "Bringing Men to Christ," *Christian Union*, vol. 7, no. 25 (June 18, 1873), 482, quoted in Applegate, *Most Famous Person in America*, 40.

7. Applegate, *Most Famous Person in America*, 33.

8. Quoted in Applegate, *Most Famous Person in America*, 33. See also William Beecher and Samuel Scoville, *A Biography of Rev. Henry Ward Beecher* (New York: Charles Webster, 1888), 77.

into a departure from the reforming drives of Calvinism. Biographer Debby Applegate says, "The greatest barrier between Henry and his father was religion. Before her death Roxana's cheerful piety had calmed her husband's deep-seated anxiety and lightened his morbid theology, but under Harriet Porter's chilly influence, the dark, authoritarian aspects of Calvinism permeated the parsonage. The endless round of religious rituals that had once seemed merely gloomy now became utterly bleak."[9]

The only way Henry knew to fight this gloom was with humor and personality. He was the life of the party in a New England without parties. From the age of seven or eight, when he was overwhelmed by the thoughts of damnation and experiencing hell at home, he found solace in being liked. Beginning in childhood, Henry had an insatiable drive to connect to people, giving and receiving affection. This was most acute when it came to women. "This . . . triangle of influences—an idealized absent mother; a distant, critical stepmother; and a bevy of smart, strong-willed sisters and aunts who doted on the boy but had little time to spoil him—bred in him a lifelong craving for the affection of attractive, intelligent women."[10] This was a trap that Henry would fall into, making his coming popularity as infamous as famous. But before that could happen, the world would need to change, and Henry would play his part by shifting the image of the pastor.

## The Changing World

In the 1830s the air was infused with newness. If the late 1960s had a foreshadowing cousin, it was the 1830s. Like the late 1960s, it was a time of exponential growth in college attendance, coming on the crest of a baby boom. Much like after World War II, after the War of 1812 a large generation was produced and came of age just as "the old generation of founding fathers was dying, symbolically passing the revolutionary mantle to this rising generation. . . . 'There was a breath of new air, much vague expectation, a consciousness of power not yet finding its determinate aim,' Ralph Waldo Emerson recalled forty years later."[11]

It was in this environment, so colorfully described by Emerson, that Henry came of age, making his way through Amherst College and Lane Seminary. Our secular age was just coming into vision, and divine action was becoming

9. Applegate, *Most Famous Person in America*, 35.

10. Applegate, *Most Famous Person in America*, 34.

11. Emerson, "Historical Notes on Life and Letter in New England," in *American Transcendentalists, Their Prose and Poetry*, edited by Perry Miller (Garden City, NY: Doubleday, 1957), 5, quoted in Applegate, *Most Famous Person in America*, 77.

much fuzzier. Just as in the late 1960s, it was a time where the Romantic thought of European poets and philosophers hit the dry, hard land of American puritanism. Henry's childhood made him open to Romanticism's drive to feel exuberance and acceptance by moving beyond the authority of tradition—which Henry had felt was too harsh since he was seven years old.

The year Henry graduated from seminary, Emerson offered a prediction that would find its clearest fulfillment in the arc of Henry's coming ministry. To an audience at Harvard College, Emerson "called for a new sort of minister . . . one who rejects the 'timid, imitative, tame,' and instead cultivates originality, courage, and, above all, 'self-trust.' The orator who offers his own 'frank confessions,' predicted Emerson, will find that audiences 'drink his words.'"[12] By the 1850s, drink Henry's words they would.

Yet two things would need to converge in this post-1830s environment to bring Emerson's prediction to fruition in Henry. First, Henry would need to see a "new path to salvation based on acceptance rather than judgment." Thanks to a thirty-year-old senior at Amherst named Moody Harrington, Henry began to see Christ as a *personal* friend and mentor. This Christ came not with judgment but with acceptance. Moody showed the younger Henry exactly this kind of relationship, helping the freshman see that Jesus too offers this kind of companionship. Henry wanted nothing more than to believe this. It was in "stark contrast to the legalistic theology he'd grown up with, in which God was a stern judge and Christ the sacrificial scapegoat."[13] Yet it would take another mentor, just a few years older than Henry, to convince him that there were ways other than Lyman's of reading the Bible.

At Lane Seminary, Henry met a talented biblical scholar named Calvin Stowe. Stowe would eventually marry Henry's beloved sister Harriet. But first he'd leave his impression on Henry. Drawing from the new German text criticism that gave attention to original language and culture, Calvin Stowe helped free Henry from seeing ordinary life as a constant battle to keep each of its molecules sacred. Rather, Henry began to see that it was possible, even obedient and faithful, to seek happiness, for Jesus was a friend who accepts us. Indeed, ordinary life was important—central, as Henry's Puritan ancestors had taught across New England. But now Henry was convinced that ordinary life was indeed *so* central that it needed to be enjoyed.[14] This was a big move that would eventually allow for *all* sacred sense of ordinary life to

12. Applegate, *Most Famous Person in America*, 135, quoting from Emerson's "American Scholar" address, which was given to Harvard students in the summer of 1837.

13. Applegate, *Most Famous Person in America*, 81.

14. "Immersed in the New Testament, he focused less on the Lord as lawgiver and more on Jesus Christ as soul mate—'a Christ that never was far from me, but was always near me,

be perceived as secular. Henry's preaching would do its part in freeing us from divine consequence, encouraging us to enjoy life by finding a friendly Jesus.

Henry's life exemplifies Charles Taylor's take that the cold but firm grip of divine consequence and constant pastoral prodding would give way to something very different. In the nineteenth century, we more fully entered a world we could not return from, where divine action was no longer bound in things (like the Eucharist, relics, coins, and church keys) but was bound completely in minds. The Reformation started us down this road, and Lyman's hero, Jonathan Edwards, took us further, asserting that it was our urgent duty to *willfully* obey God. Edwards told us that we were but sinners in the hands of an angry God. If this was true, being a pastor was serious business; constant study and prayer were needed to battle the devil, who sought to corrupt our ordinary lives. But Lyman's son would discard these unhappy thoughts, creating a completely new mold for being pastor.

Yet it is important to see that Henry's new mold was not to water down or abandon God but to more directly encounter God. As Applegate says, "After a lifetime of believing that being good and being happy were incompatible, it was intoxicating [for Henry] to think that happiness might lead to goodness and that Christ was sent to make mankind happy rather than vice versa."[15]

Henry's new mold was cast from a belief that divine action came not through duty to doctrines and traditions but through positive feelings—Henry was the first to so successfully mix Calvinism with Romanticism. "Beecher's transcendent experience of the divine was not like love, it was the actual feeling of love that he and Jesus Christ shared. You cannot know Jesus, he maintained, 'until you have been intimate with him.' And like Christ, a 'preacher is in some degree a reproduction of the truth in personal form,' as Henry put it."[16] This is a major statement that we shouldn't miss: Henry asserts that Jesus comes to us as an experience of love and acceptance, as a friend. Standing in our time, few of us would doubt this; we can even trace similar elements back to the desert fathers and mothers or saints like Julian of Norwich in the fourteenth century. Yet what's fascinating is that Henry upped the ante. He called for a change in the conception of the pastor. Henry claimed that the pastor is to witness to this divine action by personifying acceptance and friendship. It is the pastor's task, Henry believed, to run at the speed of intimacy—and this was very different from pastors before him.

---

as a companion and friend, to uphold and sustain me.'" Applegate, *Most Famous Person in America*, 171.

15. Applegate, *Most Famous Person in America*, 134.

16. Applegate, *Most Famous Person in America*, 274, quoting Beecher, *Yale Lectures on Preaching* (New York: J. B. Ford, 1872–73), 1:113, 3.

## A New Speed

Henry worked out the new pastoral mold in Indianapolis. It took two distinct shapes. First, after months of preaching, "Henry the talented orator" came to the surface. His impact was as great as Edwards's; people hung on every word. But the ethos couldn't be starker. Edwards's meetinghouses were filled with awe. People were overtaken by the preacher's learning that blanketed the congregation with the importance of their obedience. They were solemn and serious. Edwards pastored by pressing learning and discipline.

Beecher's church was far from that. People hung on every word, just as they did with Edwards, stomachs hurting and tears flowing, but for Henry's listeners the stomach pain and tears came not from the fear of hell and the pressure of pastoral prodding but from exuberant laughter. Henry was extraordinarily funny. It could be argued that Pastor Henry Ward Beecher was the first stand-up comic; he was a Jerry Seinfeld or Sarah Silverman almost two hundred years before them. He's even responsible for creating the style that these two great comics of the future would come to master. Henry didn't so much tell jokes as "put human foibles in such an ironic light that people couldn't help giggling. The effect was often so subtle, so dependent on a knowing tone of voice, a roll of the eyes, or a slight shrug of the shoulders, that it is hard to find the humor when reading the sermons on paper."[17]

But read them on paper—in newspapers—people did, which convinced thousands that Henry was something you *had to see*. When he moved to New York to become the first pastor of Plymouth Congregational Church in Brooklyn (built by railroad and other industrial tycoons), Henry was launched into stardom. But the point was never to be funny—though it might have been to be loved; Henry had an insatiable desire to be loved. Rather, in the early days in Indianapolis, Henry had stumbled onto a whole new conception of preaching. He retired the belief that it was the pastor's duty, particularly in the sermon, to prod the people into obedience. "Henry realized [that] the point was not to outline 'correct' doctrine but to motivate the audience psychologically."[18]

We had now entered into a new stage. Divine action was no longer bound in any *thing*, not even doctrine or the sermon, maybe not even in the obedient behavior of the listener. For Edwards, doctrine and exegesis were powerful; only a learned man, covering his feeble soul with the Kevlar vest of understanding and prayer, could preach. The point was to release the powerful Word among weak people. The preacher needed to be a serious man able

17. Applegate, *Most Famous Person in America*, 213.
18. Applegate, *Most Famous Person in America*, 171.

to control this force. But Henry realized those days were over.[19] The sermon now needed to enter the personality of the listener. And Henry realized that the only key that fit the lock of individual personality was personality itself. Luckily for Henry, he had personality in boatloads.

In New York, Henry soon became the most famous man in America. A nation wrestling with the evils of slavery coupled with a burgeoning newspaper business saw Henry as the conscience of the country. He was the single most in-demand speaker in the nation; the first time Abraham Lincoln made it to New York, his first stop was to hear Beecher preach. Later Lincoln tapped him to use his oration skills to sway support for the Civil War. Henry was as committed as his sister was to fighting slavery, but he did so as a celebrity. He was a personality that used personality to persuade. This would win Henry high speaking fees, a hefty salary, and columns and stories all over the nation's newspapers.

This all leads us back to Indianapolis and the second distinct shape of Henry's new mold of being pastor. If Edwards operated at the speed of learning and discipline, Henry downshifted completely, casting the pastor as no different—living at no different speed—from any other man or woman. Edwards spent thirteen hours each day alone in study and prayer, preparing himself to be a vessel of the Word, readying himself to deliver a message of divine consequence through direct pastoral prodding. Henry, on the other hand, spent all of his time at the general store, floating on the river, or joining a group of men hunting and fishing. "Before long the young Reverend Beecher seemed to know everyone, high and low. 'He was universally popular,' testified the pastor who succeeded him."[20]

The days of direct, heavy pastoral prodding were ending, at least when it came to divine consequence. Entering a nascent secular age through the Romantic spirit of acceptance, Henry would still use his pulpit to speak of flourishing, echoing his Puritan legacy, and prodding the nation to end slavery. But this prodding would no longer come from a set-apart holy man, consecrated by enchanted oil or a Yale degree. Rather, Henry's prodding was done as "one of us." Henry threw off any sense that he was a class above or beyond, as so many clergy embodied. "Nothing about him seemed ministerial. Instead of the white cravat that marked a Presbyterian minister as surely as a white

19. Applegate says of Henry: "He insisted that he still believed in theology, as one friend noted, but it was 'as he believed in the human skeleton; it was useful and necessary in its place, but should be kept out of sight.' He retained the mantle of Congregational orthodoxy, but he insisted on redefining its terms to suit himself. He cloaked challenging new ideas in familiar language, to make them easier to swallow, and gave old ideas new resonance with his vivid illustrations and unexpected connections." *Most Famous Person in America*, 214.

20. Applegate, *Most Famous Person in America*, 151.

collar signified a Catholic priest, he wore open-throated shirts, tied loosely with a black stock or tie. He was the first minister in those parts to sport a workingman's soft, wide-brimmed felt hat (and in summer a jaunty straw hat) instead of the stiff top hats of professional men."[21] Henry also introduced new practices, like the church social, that we still live with today. The church social allowed Henry to both stage and distribute his down-to-earth, folksy personality. "At these [socials] he was at his best—joking, singing, teasing, and leading old-fashioned games imported from New England."[22]

## A New Wardrobe for a Profession

Henry broke the mold of the pastor, forging a new one in its place. Now the pastor wasn't so much a professional as a personality. He wasn't supposed to reveal his difference from ordinary folk in dress or manner, for he no longer possessed magic or even was exclusively educated. Henry shifted the pastoral identity from learned, serious professional to your beloved uncle. The point was no longer to show your difference but to show your sameness—living at the very same speed.

Whether he knows it or not, Rick Warren's Hawaiian shirt is an homage to Henry Ward Beecher. Warren's Hawaiian shirt serves the same purpose as Beecher's hat, broadcasting that *this* pastor is down to earth, one of us, a personality we should allow to impact our own personality. This pastor's prodding (if you can even call it that) will be done as a friend, helping you find purpose. Henry Ward Beecher locks away the stick, shifting pastoral nudging to the carrot.[23]

For Edwards, the stick was there not because he was a masochist but because our ordinary lives bore divine consequence—making divine action at times frightening but always present. Thankfully, with this shift to personality, the stick is retired (until it returns in fundamentalist enclaves). But once pastoral prodding is directed toward personality by personality, divine action in our ordinary lives becomes much harder to name.

21. Applegate, *Most Famous Person in America*, 172.
22. Applegate, *Most Famous Person in America*, 173.
23. E. Brooks Holifield discusses Washington Gladden's 1898 book, *The Christian Pastor and the Working Church*: "Gladden captured the new style of ministry when he called for pastors with a 'genius for friendship.' The route to success was not preaching, wrote one minister, but rather 'the attraction of the man as a whole.' His 'enthusiasm' would 'charm' the youth, and his 'popularity' would draw new members. Gladden intended his ideal of 'the pastor as Friend' to suggest the qualities that could inspire 'confidence and affection' in the urban parish. In place of the 'reserve' of the antebellum cleric, the 'social gifts' of the modern pastor would ensure influence." *God's Ambassadors: A History of the Christian Clergy in America* (Grand Rapids: Eerdmans, 2007), 163.

Edwards saw himself as the first, or lead, priest amongst a priesthood of all believers. The stick was there to raise *all* up to the speed of priesthood, giving them direct access (an awakening) to the sacred. Edwards could boldly herald divine action because he lived with holiness and called all others to do the same. Edwards was the Sherpa, conditioned by his thirteen hours of study and prayer every day to walk the congregation up the steep hill of holiness, clearly pointing out divine action along the trail of their ordinary lives.

Beecher flips the script, and most Protestant pastors have been reading off his ever since. If Edwards was pushing his people up the hill of holiness, making priests of them all, Beecher layman-ized the priesthood, making the pastor just like one of the people.

This legacy lived on past his own life. Like many pastors who would follow in the mold that he created—the mold of being loved, of being a personality able to persuade personalities—Henry experienced fame and excess turning on him. In the same newspapers that made Henry a star, it was huge news to reveal his love affairs with women in his congregation. These affairs eventually got him ousted from his church. Beecher was the first celebrity—his star would shine bright and fizzle through phases of scandal and cultural ridicule, but he died, in 1887, still a wildly famous orator and cultural influencer.

It is not an overstatement to credit Beecher, together with the nineteenth century itself, with finally accomplishing what the Western spirit of reform had sought for hundreds of years: to eliminate ecclesial hierarchy. But, unfortunately or not, to do so it had to end the dream that the whole of society could be pious priests. It relinquished the belief that everything could be sacred, and it lowered the bar for all. The pastor now ran at the speed of the shopkeeper and eventually, one hundred years after Henry, the entrepreneurial business leader.

But this was (and continues to be) for good reason. As one of the people, Beecher could more clearly claim God's love. God, Beecher could say as a regular bloke, wants us to feel loved, to be happy and not miserable. Instead of having us cough up blood as we climb the hill of holiness, this God wants to be our friend—just as your pastor does. A down-to-earth, friendly pastor could more clearly communicate that message. But this wasn't devoid of the prophetic. Preaching with flare and humor, Henry could claim that God wants us to end slavery, forging a world where all can flourish, where all ordinary people are loved and able to seek happiness.[24]

24. "Growing numbers of clergy no longer felt bound to 'speak from a text of Scripture.' They sought 'the truth of God' in 'the circumstances of daily life.' Some of the most eminent preachers, from Henry Ward Beecher to Phillips Brooks, practiced a style of pulpit oratory that conveyed, in Brooks's phrase, 'truth through personality.' The preacher was to 'be natural' and

This has great merit, and I mean not to belittle it, but it also opens up a problem that we feel more acutely in our time. When the pastor is laymanized and one of us, it becomes much harder for her to call attention to divine action. It is not impossible, as we'll see in part 2. Pastors as divergent in time and background as Martin Luther King Jr. and Nadia Bolz-Weber have found important ways to witness to divine action, even in a pastoral age of personality. But as we'll see, both needed to take on particular visions of divine action next to their pastoral practice, embedding their own personhood in these visions to clearly lead their people into divine action.

Beecher played an important part in the dawn of our secular age, for now people were more free to wonder what happens when love and flourishing can be produced from our own personality, solely by our own will. How do we conceive of, or even spot, divine action, when personalities can make us happy and political movements make people free? It's a short step to conclude that the personality of a therapist or the work of a community organizer is much more effective than that of a pastor. Once this drive into pastoral personality is connected with the conception that nature is impersonal, as we saw above, divine action becomes much fuzzier and faith more fragile for the pastor and her people alike.

After Beecher, these changes to the pastorate have given us problems that we didn't anticipate—and big ones at that. We can all get to the same speed thanks to the impersonal, the disenchanted, and the private—by all living in a solely material world. But these equalizing forces make it *much* harder for people to perceive divine action in both their lives and the world, framing our shared downshifted lives in immanence.

This downshifting of the pastor has led us all into the speed of the immanent frame, making it much harder for the pastor as well as her people to perceive, practice, and proclaim divine action. The immanent frame pulls us all toward what Taylor calls "a closed spin." This makes the pastoral task of witnessing to the concreteness of divine action in the world a challenge.

But even so, who would want to return to the past and a world organized around multiple speeds or harsh punitive pastoral prodding? Not Taylor, nor myself. Maybe this isn't necessary. But to see if this is the case will be the task of part 2. For now we need to continue with our story.

---

even 'buoyant,' to avoid the rigid forms of earlier doctrinal sermons, and to engage the audience through stories and illustrations." Holifield, *God's Ambassadors*, 161.

# 7

## the pastor as chaplain of a secular age

*Harry Emerson Fosdick and pastoring
at the end of the denomination*

For the TV fans out there, the period from *Boardwalk Empire* to *Mad Men* is the very time frame in which *the* most important pastor of the first half of the twentieth century did his work: from the early 1920s to the 1960s. And, like those shows, it all unfolded in New York and New Jersey. For Harry Emerson Fosdick, people utterly loved him or feared him. To some, he was a saint, but to others he was Satan in a nice suit.

In his memoir *The Pastor*, Eugene Peterson tells about meeting Fosdick. Growing up in a conservative Pentecostal environment in Montana, where traveling preachers came in and out of the community, making impassioned calls to return to old-time religion, Peterson was taught that Harry Emerson Fosdick was (we might say today) Voldemort. Fosdick's name so represented evil that it should not be named. But later on, at New York Biblical Seminary in the 1950s, the young Peterson was asked to write a profile of a contemporary American religious leader. Peterson says, "I chose Harry Emerson Fosdick. In the world in which I grew up, Fosdick was the enemy—the incarnation of unbelieving liberalism that was eroding the foundations of the Christian faith in Christian America. . . . Fosdick was . . . the Antichrist [according to] many of the evangelists who came through our town in my youth."[1]

Peterson found something very different from the devil when he met Fosdick. Arriving at Riverside Church, the retired "elderly man with rosy cheeks

1. Eugene Peterson, *The Pastor: A Memoir* (San Francisco: HarperOne, 2011), 87.

approached . . . with . . . a welcoming smile, extended his hand, and said, 'Hello, Mr. Peterson, I'm Harry.'"[2] Peterson explains that he "had just read a book by Fosdick, *The Meaning of Prayer*. It was the best book on prayer I had ever read. Could the Antichrist have written this? That was hard to believe. I was curious . . . to find out what was behind, or not behind, all the vicious invective that surrounded the name Fosdick in my memory."[3]

What was behind this vicious invective was that Harry Emerson Fosdick ministered on a significant fault line of our secular age. His ministry would represent a transition that would finally and completely say goodbye to one world and hello to another, seen clearly in people's divergent views of him. Not only did some call Fosdick an antichrist, but others, like Martin Luther King Jr., called him the greatest preacher in America and an inspiration to King's own rhetorical development.

### Fosdick: The Early Years

In terms of family background, Fosdick was more like Augustine than Jonathan Edwards or Henry Ward Beecher. And maybe that's fitting, for Fosdick's ministry was responding to a world much more like Augustine's. Christianity was unhooking and dis-embedding from a strict political or national identity. Both Edwards and Beecher (as well as Rick Warren, as we'll see below) were the sons of pastors. As with Augustine and Becket, Fosdick's father wasn't a pastor, bishop, or theologian. Frank Fosdick was a teacher and principal in western New York.

Like all the pastors we've explored, Harry was influenced by the important role that his mother, Amy, played in his life. He felt such affection for her that he quoted often a line from the Talmud: "Since God could not be everywhere, he made mothers."[4] If Augustine had known of this line, he would have either written a theological treatise against its metaphysic or gotten it tattooed on his back, probably arched around a giant picture of Monica.

It was in this family environment that Harry would learn to wrestle with the faith. Harry was born in 1878; the Protestantism of his youth was building toward an explosion. Back in the last decades of the nineteenth century, the young Harry could never have guessed that he'd be the spark that, in the first decades of the twentieth century, would send it into pieces.

2. Peterson, *The Pastor*, 88.
3. Peterson, *The Pastor*, 87.
4. See Robert Moats Miller, *Harry Emerson Fosdick: Preacher, Pastor, Prophet* (New York: Oxford University Press, 1985), 21.

But while the tension was building between liberal and conservative Christians (some of its earliest antecedents going back to the days of Beecher), a focus on the global missionary movement seemed to allow at least some loose ligaments of union. Henry's own conversion experience came through the missionary movement. As a fuzzy-headed seven-year-old, Harry sat in church listening to Albert Tennent preach, "Go ye therefore and teach all nations." In that moment, Harry felt the Spirit come upon him, and he was sure that he would be a missionary in a foreign land, preaching the Word and harvesting souls as well as adventures.

Soon after Harry's conversion and calling, his family moved to Lancaster, New York. There were no Baptist churches in Lancaster, so at about the age of eleven (the same age I was for my reading failure and for my pastor's sermon on time wasting), Harry moved equally between the Presbyterian and Methodist churches. The first seeds of a kind of denominational transience were beginning in America, and the Fosdicks were on the cutting edge. His whole life, Harry would embrace this fluidity, somehow opposing Calvinism (like Beecher before him) while pastoring a large Presbyterian church, before starting a distinctly nondenominational church with, Harry demanding, no creedal commitments.

By the time Harry was in high school and the family settled in Buffalo, Protestant churches were split between conservatives and liberals. But this split was not like it is today, where one Methodist church in town is liberal and another conservative, or where whole denominations come down on one ideological side or another. Rather, in the last decades of the nineteenth century, that split took place within individual churches. Harry's own Buffalo church was a case in point. One pastor was a liberal and the other was a conservative, and they alternated their weeks of preaching.

Sunday meals at the Fosdicks' revolved around debating their differences. Harry and his father went back and forth in an intense but collegial debate, mother and siblings thoroughly entertained. Harry's parents leaned conservative, as did Harry. But as an educator, Frank Fosdick demanded that all his children reason about and reflect on what they believed. Harry became particularly good at this and was a top student throughout high school and college, winning a sterling reputation as a student, leader, and rhetor at Colgate University.

### Declarations of Unbelief

Fellow students, professors, and administrators saw Harry as a star. But Harry felt an internal battle. The late nineteenth century was one of the first times in the West when someone could assert, as a statement of faith, that they didn't believe. This simply wasn't possible in Edwards's or Becket's day. This is the major plotline of Charles Taylor's description of a secular age (this is what he means by secular 3, and here in the late nineteenth century we see its earliest arrival). Taylor wants us to understand how we got to an age where unbelief becomes a legitimate option. It takes disenchantment, inwardness, a buffered self, an affirmation of ordinary life, and a modern moral order to produce the possibility that some could herald unbelief and not be ostracized or burned at the stake. Here in the late nineteenth century, even in a place like Colgate or Buffalo (not just in Oxford or Paris), a person could claim unbelief.

Harry had one of these very people in his life. Uncle Charles was Frank's half brother. He was a mysterious man of adventure to whom any boy would be drawn. Dark piercing eyes; long, shoulder-length hair; and all the marks of battle—a Civil War vet, Uncle Charles had a saber scar across his crooked nose, and a Confederate bullet was still lodged in his leg. He not only oozed mysterious escapades but also wrote about them in boys' adventure novels. Along with all this, Uncle Charles was known for his impious proclivities and bold assertions of unbelief.[5]

Now at Colgate, Harry started to have his own doubts. As many college students even today experience, these accepted statements of unbelief actually become plausible when injected with the study of the natural sciences. You can understand the pattern; you have an Uncle Charles in your life who boldly states that there is no personal God who cares about what you do. You're not sure you buy it, the mysteries of childhood and its attachment too strong to go with the reduction, the haunting of transcendence too vivid. But Charles reminds you, either directly or indirectly, of the bravery of his unbelief and the bold freedom it earns him. That has appeal; there is a little sizzle to the reduction, not unlike the excitement of vandalizing a park bench. Someone like Uncle Charles makes unbelief plausible but far from inevitable. You now know someone who doesn't believe in God or transcendence, contending that all is material, but that's all it is until freshman biology or physics 101. Now, in the lecture hall, unbelief seems to grow teeth and seems logical, noble, and grown-up.[6] It takes the first, an Uncle Charles and all those cultural transitions named above, to get to the second, seeing the natural sciences as support for a godless, solely material, and closed universe.

5. In part 2 of *A Secular Age* (Cambridge, MA: Belknap Press, 2007), esp. chap. 7 ("The Impersonal Order"), Taylor discusses how Brits who suffered in World War I trenches never returned to church and wrapped themselves in unbelief. He shows how this was not the case in America, although I think it is plausible that the Civil War did that for some, including Uncle Charles.

6. Taylor discusses this in chapter 10 ("The Expanding Universe of Unbelief") of *Secular Age*.

Edwards spent big chunks of his thirteen daily hours of study reading and reflecting on Newton and his laws. Edwards was a big proponent of the Enlightenment and the arrival of the natural sciences. But never did science lead him (or Roger Bacon, Galileo, Kepler, or Copernicus) to unbelief. The natural sciences only seem inevitably bent toward unbelief when they are coupled with the culture that arrives in the late nineteenth century, right around the days that Harry was matriculating at Colgate.[7]

In these choppy waters, Harry swam into his sophomore and junior years, determined to discover if it was "possible to remain a Christian without reject-ing all that nineteenth-century science and scholarship were disclosing about the universe and man, pre-Christian religions, and Christianity itself, especially the authority of scripture as interpreted by the new higher criticism." Robert Miller continues: "Because the old orthodoxy was not now for Harry a live option . . . the real decision for him was between the New Theology and no formal, institutional religion at all."[8]

By his senior year he had made his decision. The conversion experience as a seven-year-old and call to ministry couldn't be shaken; ministry was Harry's destiny. But following this path meant a decision for the New Theology. One place was the bastion of this new liberal theology, a place where religious experience was put directly in conversation with the new scientific disciplines: Union Seminary in New York City.

### The Slums

In the summer of 1901 the most significant pastor of the twentieth century and Gotham's greatest preacher would arrive in New York City as a student. It didn't take long for both the city and the seminary to enter Fosdick's DNA, though neither easily. For the rest of his life, both would be as core to him as his left arm.

New York City, since its days as New Amsterdam, has been a place where the ultrarich blended with the devastatingly poor; since its beginning it has been held together by the pursuit of money. But the disparity between the rich

7. James K. A. Smith says something similar: "If someone tells you that he or she has converted to unbelief because of science, don't believe them. Because what's usually captured the person is not scientific evidence per se, but theorem of science. . . . Indeed, 'the appeal of scientific material-ism is not so much the cogency of its detailed findings as that of the underlying epistemological stance, and that for ethical reasons. It is seen as the stance of maturity, of courage, of manliness, over against childish fears and sentimentality' [Taylor, *Secular Age*, 365]. But you can also under-stand how, on the retelling, the convert to unbelief will want to give . . . the impression that it was the scientific evidence that was doing the work. Converts to unbelief always tell subtraction stories." *How (Not) to Be Secular: Reading Charles Taylor* (Grand Rapids: Eerdmans, 2014), 77.
8. Miller, *Harry Emerson Fosdick*, 37.

and poor was never greater than after the Civil War. In a new industrial New York City, the rich became opulent, moving into enclaves like the Upper East Side. And the poor immigrants that came to feed the monstrous machines were stacked in slums. This became a huge offense to the kind of Protestantism birthed from Puritanism. The issue wasn't that some were extraordinarily wealthy. The modern moral order of mutual benefit never looked down on those who profited from *how* well they ran their business. The issue was the "mutual" piece of the puzzle. An urban, industrial America, seen most vividly in New York City, didn't seem to allow *all* to benefit mutually. Machines were crushing some while exalting others.

Part of the new liberal theology that drew Fosdick to Union was speaking out boldly against this, asserting that theology and ministry must attend to these practical societal issues.[9] The modern moral order had made human flourishing, particularly economically, central. A flourishing society was a polite one of manners, cleanliness, and piety. Poverty was an attack on a flourishing society because it was assumed to allow impoliteness and indecency to fester. People in poverty seemed to use crass language, with rampant chaos in their streets and homes. Some strongly held that a Protestant theology that attended to the *how* needed to concern itself with a social gospel.

At Union, Fosdick would be taught that a big piece of the pastor's job (especially for liberals) was to remind barons of industry that it was their job to participate in and support flourishing. In the 1920s Harry did just this, becoming close with John Rockefeller Jr., the richest man in America. Harry's brother, Raymond, on Harry's recommendation, came to work for the Rockefellers as John Jr.'s right-hand man.

John Rockefeller Jr. was all about making money. But making money was for the purpose of mobilization. It was not necessarily a task of authenticity, where you used your money to express yourself, turning heads as you lived the lifestyle of the rich and famous (some, of course, did this, including Cornelius "The Commodore" Vanderbilt, who refused any charitable giving and despised the poor, but this was perceived by most as unbecoming and brutish). Rather, money was for the mobilization of institution building. Philanthropy justified your wealth. Whereas in Becket's day heavy was the head that wore the crown, in Fosdick's time, after the Industrial Revolution, the elite rich bore

---

9. That is, the social gospel, which Mark Noll explains: "Better known, however, was the informal, loosely organized Social Gospel movement, which was a force from roughly 1880 to the start of the Great Depression in 1929. Its leaders also attempted a Christian response to the rapid social changes of the period, but one in which an analysis of corporate entities supplemented the appeal to individuals." *A History of Christianity in the United States and Canada* (Grand Rapids: Eerdmans, 1996), 304.

the duty of providing libraries, museums, and parks—which, of course, you put your name on.[10] But the point was to provide for the public good. That was your responsibility.

It was the pastor's job to remind people of this responsibility, participating in practical actions that would bring flourishing to all—though this flourishing was now being pushed further into exclusively immanent realms. Nevertheless, the pastor was the consciousness of the industrial age. And religion was still valued—even with the arrival of some people's expressed unbelief—because of its ability to check human excess and remind us of our better angels.

Harry learned the need for this responsibility firsthand, spending his first summer in New York City serving the poor at the Mariners' Temple mission. Miller adds, "[Fosdick's] eyes were open to the truth of Walter Rauschenbusch's dictum: 'We rarely sin against God alone.' This awareness had come to Rauschenbusch while ministering near New York's 'Hell's Kitchen' where, he reported, 'One could hear human virtue cracking and crumbling all around.' Fosdick's concern for . . . New York's poor and disinherited [awoke that summer]."[11]

The pull of the new liberal theology that inspired pastors like Fosdick was a strong push away from metaphysical conceptions and transcendent musing and toward concern for immanent conditions. For instance, where Edwards reminded us that we were sinners in the hands of an angry God, Walter Rauschenbusch, the founder of the social gospel movement, told us that our sin was social and material.[12] Now the link between flourishing and divine action was becoming faint within theology and ministry itself, fading under the friction of the machine's ability to mold our imaginaries toward immanence. Let me explain this further by returning directly to Taylor.

## Taylor's Triads and What This Has to Do with Us

Taylor provides us with two different triads that he uses, in broad strokes, to tease out our transitions—I'll call one the "ages" and the other the "Durkheims."

10. David Brooks discusses this in *Bobos in Paradise: The New Upper Class and How They Got There* (New York: Simon & Schuster, 2000).

11. Miller, *Harry Emerson Fosdick*, 44.

12. "The most important exponent of the Social Gospel was Walter Rauschenbusch (1861–1918). . . . Rauschenbusch's main concern was to search the Scriptures for a message to the troubled circumstances of industrial society. The results were published in 1907 as *Christianity and the Social Crisis*, a work that recalled the prophetic denunciations of Old Testament prophets as well as New Testament injunctions about the dangers of Mammon. Rauschenbusch followed this work with other influential volumes. . . . In these works Rauschenbusch combined a prophetic ideal of justice with a commitment to building the kingdom of God through the power of Christ." Noll, *History of Christianity*, 306.

The "ages" triad is the movement from what Taylor calls the ancien régime to the age of mobilization to the age of authenticity. This has connections to, though doesn't map directly onto, his second triad, which is the movement from a paleo-Durkheimian to a neo-Durkheimian to a post-Durkheimian understanding of the function of religion and faith. We'll have to leave all these Durkheims for our discussion of Rick Warren in the next chapter. By spending some space with the "ages," we can get a better handle on how this period impacts pastoral practice and obscures divine action, seeing its strong currents within the story of Fosdick.

We've already discussed the concept of the ancien régime without using that label. This is the period of medieval Christianity where the questions of religious necessity or purpose couldn't even be formulated, because there was no divide between the organization of our lives and God.[13] As a matter of fact, historical philosopher Peter Harrison has shown that the label *religion* wasn't something even used before the Enlightenment.[14] The thought that it had a separate or distinct function was not even imagined. So whether common, royal, or political, our so-called ways of life and ways of faith were one whole cloth.[15]

This starts to divide most dramatically with the Declaration of Independence. The American Revolution was not only an overthrowing of King George and his taxes but, even more so, an overcoming of a whole ancient age of organized life. It makes sense that deists were central in this revolt. For what was needed, as much as Washington's military tactics, was the audacity to believe that it was possible to create a new order without direct reflection of divine design (this is why it was an open debate whether, after George was ousted, America would need its own king). Taylor reminds us that now in the age of mobilization, "Sovereignty comes from the people, not from the king; but the king's sovereignty comes from above, from God; so democracy is already an implicit rejection of God."[16]

It's not that God was unnamed. Taylor explains that the kind of deism that Jefferson, for instance, represented (and seemed to mix well enough with a New England Puritanism) was providential.[17] This meant that we could mobilize any way of life that we the people thought best—as long as it conformed to

13. For more, see Taylor, *Secular Age*, 438.
14. See Peter Harrison, *The Territories of Science and Religion* (Chicago: University of Chicago Press, 2015).
15. For more on these "collective rituals," see Taylor, *Secular Age*, 438.
16. Taylor, *Dilemmas and Connection: Selected Essays* (Cambridge, MA: Belknap Press, 2011), 228.
17. Taylor, *Secular Age*, has a whole chapter on this (chap. 6, "Turning Points").

God's broad laws or design.[18] But when these deists said "laws," they were thinking not of Luther or Moses (i.e., a law/gospel hermeneutic or the Ten Commandments) but of Newton and his static laws of the natural universe, like gravity. God was no longer an actor, confronting people with calls for transformation, changing water into wine, picking one ruler over another, and bringing direct protection or judgment. It was up to the people to act. God gave us, in a sense, a list of ideals. It was up to us to mobilize a world that honored them.

The American Constitution could even (shockingly, when looked at from the ancien régime) separate the church and state because we'd entered a new age of mobilization.[19] Our political and social orders were no longer tied directly to divine action. A ruler no longer received authority by divine right of blood. Rather, it was we the people who mobilized, with our vote, who represented us. It was we the people who created our own system and the institutions that support it. Life, liberty, and the pursuit of happiness are divine ideals, but they have no form. It is up to us, not God, to mobilize the kind of world that we should live in. Responsibility for the shape of social lives shifted to us—God was happy to sit it out (and to eventually become impersonal altogether).

This sense of mobilization was embedded in the new liberal theology that drew Fosdick to Union. We know God's law or design, but it is solely our responsibility to enact it. Our action and God's could be equated (hence Karl Barth's point that liberal theology is just speaking of ourselves in a loud voice), leading one of Fosdick's teachers at Union, George Albert Coe, to assert that democracy and the kingdom of God were the same.[20] Our mobilized forms of life were one and the same as God's action, because although God was not active, God set up ideals for us to mobilize.

18. "In the United States, for example, Jefferson indeed traced the sovereignty of the people to an endowment by the 'Creator,' but the Creator he had in mind was religiously quiescent, a deity whose presence or absence would make no difference to the practical conduct of affairs. Insofar as modern states appeal to deity, they appeal to a deity invented especially for the purpose of not interfering. The God who would make a difference to public affairs is explicitly banished from them by the founding ideologies of all modern states. Thus James Madison insisted on religious freedom in order to 'multiply sects,' the purpose of the multiplication being so to balance them against each other that none could achieve public influence." Eric Gritsch and Robert W. Jenson, *Lutheranism: The Theological Movement and Its Confessional Writing* (Philadelphia: Fortress, 1976), 188.

19. Robert W. Jenson adds, "America has no foundation but the Enlightenment and the Puritanism of which Enlightenment was the secularization." *America's Theologian: A Recommendation of Jonathan Edwards* (Oxford: Oxford University Press, 1988), 195.

20. See George Albert Coe, *A Social Theory of Religious Education* (New York: Charles Scribner's Sons, 1927).

The job, then, of a Fosdick-like pastor was to remind his people of God's ideals, helping them take responsibility to mobilize these ideals so that society could flourish (mobilization shifts the eschatological horizon from eternity to time; the liberal pastor no longer tries to get people to heaven but instead plays his part in society flourishing). The pastor was the conscience of the Industrial Revolution. Industrialization had no correlation to the divine being; it was solely and completely the making of people—secular through and through. The pastor's job was not to fight this form[21] but to remind people of their responsibility within it. The pastor's job in dress, manner, and preaching of the Word was to help support the best liberal democracy by reminding the people of their responsibility to mobilize their private and public lives for flourishing. The pastor was to tell them to remember God's ideals. (You can already sense why some will find this new theology deeply problematic and yearn for a return to the "fundamentals" of faith.)

The ancien régime was *not* devoid of corruption, yet its whole form was to echo the bold nearness of divine action. In the age of mobilization, the direct link between God and the forms of political and societal life are severed, most particularly after the Industrial Revolution. There is nothing inherent in the forms of society itself that mediates the divine. People's social imaginary is no longer shaped by the nearness of God's action, allowing some people, like Uncle Charles, to doubt it completely. The American liberal theology that would be the mother's milk of the early twentieth-century pastor responded in turn, providing a theology that sought more the mobilization of religious institution building than the encounter with the divine being. As a whole society, we were now walking an exciting tightrope without a divine net. Yet the pastor was to play the part of a safeguard, keeping the modern moral order from snapping by creating socially engaged institutions (like Mariners' Temple mission) and sermons that reminded people of responsibility.

The pastor was an important person, given esteem because civic religion played an important part in the age of mobilization.[22] We feared that without continued reminders of God's ideals our flourishing could be upended and our form of life could be lost. And why wouldn't it? It was forged not from the mold of heaven but solely from the will of the people (it's little wonder that we've had to almost divinize the founders).

---

21. Stanley Hauerwas critiques liberal Christianity for succumbing to liberal democracy, assuming that our job is to concede to this form of life as inevitable or God's desire. This is a consistent motif in much of Hauerwas's work, having it clearest origin in his famous *Resident Aliens* (cowritten with William Willimon) (Nashville: Abingdon, 1989).

22. See Robert Bellah et al., *Habits of the Heart: Individualism and Commitment in American Life* (New York: Harper & Row, 1985).

Mobilization necessitates responsibility; it demands that people engage and participate. Democracy is a participatory sport.[23] Even if this responsibility is tied solely to the immanent frame, we need to feel some obligation to continue to renew and reenact it. Its existence is bound only in our collective will (in our day, the campaign to get out the vote uses stickers and celebrities to remind people that we have a responsibility). Religion played an important part in the early twentieth century. Taking this role risked chaining it to the immanent frame. The pastor and religion kept people invested and engaged in the social forms of flourishing we'd created (warning them against the threats of drinking, gambling, and greed).

The American way of life and Protestant Christianity became connected, with some, like the fundamentalists, linking them more and more as the age of mobilization reached its conclusion. Even today it is not surprising to see rhetoric that fuses Protestant Christianity with America when our way of life is threatened, like when airplanes are flown into buildings, the country goes to war, or a travel ban is debated. Pastors today often feel either a sense of tension themselves or disgust with their colleagues when a national crisis or patriotic moment leads to a fleeting return of the pastor's civic importance.

In the age of mobilization the pastor, then, was placed on a pedestal. But it was a wobbly one, teetering on civic religion without clear attention to divine action. The fall would be hard and fast when the age of authenticity arrived the year of Fosdick's death. The age of authenticity asserted (as we discussed at length in volume 1) that everyone is free to define for themselves what it means to be human, and any religious or spiritual way of life with meaning needs to "speak to me." In other words, all established forms of authority that the age of mobilization used to keep people renewing and reenacting our way of life began to be doubted. We started to recognize that indeed these mobilized ways of life are more corrupt than we'd assumed, never delivering the life, liberty, and happiness they promised. No institution or authority, not even playing by the rules and obeying your pastor, would get you to fulfillment. It was only *you* and your authentic pursuits that mattered now. Any outside force that tried to determine how you lived were "fascist pigs" (as asserted by hippies in the late 1960s). And almost no one was more impacted than the mainline pastor and his civic religion. All those Uncle Charleses who didn't believe, though avant-garde and few in number in the late nineteenth century, became sages and prophets in late 1960s.

23. This is why Robert Putnam's book *Bowling Alone: The Collapse and Revival of American Community* (New York: Simon & Schuster, 2000) drew such wide acclaim. If people are not "joining" the form of life we've mobilized from, our own collective willing is at risk.

## The Breakdown

With the experience at Mariners' Temple mission under his belt, Fosdick dove into his first semester at Union. Since Harry had walked onto the Colgate campus, he'd been a star. Everyone predicted the highest success and prominence for Fosdick. Harry bathed in these prophecies, assuming nothing less himself. But Union was no joke. Not only was its faculty world-class and demanding, but its student body was packed with shining lights just as bright as Harry.

By November 1901, it was clear that something wasn't right. Blurred vision, stomachaches, insomnia, crushing fatigue, and suicidal thoughts struck Harry one after the other. The pressure of Union coupled with the relentless pulse of the city was threatening to crack this young stalwart. So he left the city for home. But the crippling anxiety wouldn't pass. Early in 1902, locked in his parents' Buffalo home, he placed a razor to his throat and pressed. One quick jerk down and it'd be over. Luckily, his father, Frank, walked in at that moment and intervened.

Harry spent most of the first half of 1902 at the Gleason Sanitarium. There he regained his footing. Three major consequences of the ordeal would direct his future. First, in the sanitarium he learned to pray. The God that came to him as a seven-year-old returned. He explained years later that without this experience he would have never written *The Meaning of Prayer*, the devotional book that launched him into national recognition and sent a young Eugene Peterson to meet him in the 1950s. This devotional emphasis seemed to make Fosdick particularly dangerous to his fundamentalist enemies. His genuine yearning for God's healing was cognitive dissonance, particularly next to the other two consequences of his time in the sanitarium.

Second, Harry discovered without a doubt that the new psychological sciences saved his life. Harry now had a new sense of what it meant to be a pastor in the age of mobilization. The pressures that led one to drink, divorce, gamble, and more were often there in the first place because of psychological distress. If people were to flourish, attending to their psychological issues would be key.

This realization led to the third consequence: the time in the sanitarium made Harry a preacher. He said, "Until then I had intended to teach about religion rather than to preach the Gospel, but henceforth I wanted to get to people, real people, with their distracting, anxious, devastating problems."[24] Harry came to see preaching as the vehicle for pastoral care. He once told

24. Quoted in Miller, *Harry Emerson Fosdick*, 49.

an associate that he determined whether a sermon was good by how many people requested a one-on-one counseling meeting with the pastor after hearing it. To his critics, the new sciences seemed more normative than the Bible, and sin was minimized to just sickness (which we've already discussed in chapter 4).

Harry never imagined himself or his ministry as being about authenticity— we'd need to wait for Warren for that. But Harry was indirectly helping to set the conditions for the dawning of the age of authenticity by interlacing the psychological with the religious and by seeing divine action and ministry itself as working toward freedom from such distress. As a good liberal, Harry saw experience as more essential than tradition. He didn't preach just to deliver the Word, contending it was alive to do its own work, as Edwards may have assumed. Rather, Harry saw preaching as a direct way to help people experience relief, freedom, and an overall feeling of acceptance. Preaching, Harry believed, was not the pastor standing in as the medium of God's words. Rather, for Fosdick the preacher molded his sermon to talk to each individual, providing a psychological balm.[25]

## The Hell of the Suburbs

Harry was assured that this was a necessary direction because after graduation in 1904, he was called as pastor to a church in Montclair, New Jersey. If there was a ground zero for the cultural discontent of the early twentieth century, it was this perfectly groomed, wealthy bedroom suburb of New York City. If there was any place Fosdick would be assured that preaching needed to go therapeutic so our societal flourishing could continue, it was here. Novelist Walker Percy, decades after Fosdick was in Montclair, writes words Don Draper could have said: "What, after all, is the use of not having cancer, cirrhosis, and such, if a man comes home from work every day at five-thirty to the exurb of Montclair and there is the grass growing and the little family looking not quite at him but just past the side of his head, and there's Cronkite on the tube and the smell of pot roast in the living room, and inside the house and outside in the pretty exurb has settled the noxious

25. "'I am commonly thought of as a preacher, but I should not put preaching central in my ministry. Personal counseling has been central.' Fosdick gave this surprising assessment in his autobiography and also on many other occasions. A pastoral letter informed his congregation that in times of special need his study door was open to them for personal consultation. 'I would rather help individuals than preach sermons,' he assured the flock. 'Were I not a minister,' he once reported, 'I should probably be a psychiatrist.'" Miller, *Harry Emerson Fosdick*, 251.

particles and the sadness of the old dying Western World, and him thinking: Jesus, is this it?"[26]

"Is this it?" This question would haunt the twentieth century and eventually overthrow the age of mobilization. The age of authenticity that would replace it demanded the question never be hidden as it had in the age of mobilization, buried under duty, responsibility, and civic religion. Rather, the centrality of all these commitments would be thrown off, using the practices of bohemianism, to find something more.[27] Is this it? Is there not more? What is my purpose? These questions, which had their hidden origin in the time of Fosdick, would be made explicit in the age of authenticity and in the ear of Warren.

By the 1980s almost all suburbanites would admit that they were looking for something more, seeking purpose. And Warren, to return to Percy's quote ("Jesus, is this it?"), believed Jesus was indeed it, but a Jesus that spoke to those in the age of authenticity. Warren would sense this shift better than anyone, deciding to build his church not in Los Angeles, New York, or Chicago but in the Montclair of Southern California: Orange County. The point of the church's founding was not to play its part in producing a flourishing polite society, calling people to their institutional responsibilities—this was dead, now meaningless! (If that were its goal, then a location in the heart of a city would be best). Instead, the aim was to be a resource to help people authentically find the purpose they were seeking.[28] While the city had a deficit in mental health and economic equality, the suburbs faced a scarcity of meaning. Warren, then, would deliberately strip his church of any signs of civic religion and the age of mobilization, refusing, for instance, to put Southern Baptist in its name (and therefore moving beyond the fundamentalist-modernist conflicts that had become so central to Harry's story). Warren's church would move beyond the mobilizing institutional structures of the past age; calling it Saddleback Community Church would be enough to communicate that it was different, a hub to find the purpose *you* were seeking. Pastors who directly or indirectly follow Warren's lead have even gone so far as to refuse to call their churches "church," instead using names like Tapestry, Mosaic, Wit's End, The Font, Jacob's Well, Spirit Garage, The Hub, and so on. The word "church" signals a past age, and therefore, they imagine, it is irrelevant to those seeking meaning and purpose in the age of authenticity.

26. Miller, *Harry Emerson Fosdick*, 55. This quote is a good example of what Taylor means by the malaise of modernity.

27. See volume 1 for more on this.

28. Of course, as time goes on, Warren and most famous megachurch pastors will do much to help flourishing. Warren even uses his fortune to fight AIDS in Africa. But these churches have their origins not in a pursuit of a social gospel, or even in institution building, but in helping expressive individuals who are seeking authenticity to find it in Jesus.

## Back to the City, and into a War

For Fosdick, living squarely in the age of mobilization, the appeal to return to the city was too great to resist. By 1915, with exceedingly popular devotional books giving him a national reputation, Harry headed back to Union, this time as a professor. In 1918 three Presbyterian churches consolidated, calling themselves First Presbyterian. When we hear "consolidation" today, particularly within the mainline, we imagine dying institutions combining resources to stay afloat. But this was not the case in 1918. As with corporate mergers today, the consolidation made First Presbyterian big and powerful.

Harry, along with another professor from Union, was invited to fill the pulpit. Soon enough, Harry was called as pastor and crowned the greatest preacher in New York City since Henry Ward Beecher. Like Beecher, Harry became famous. His sermons were printed in the paper and broadcast to the country over the radio. Miller explains how deep the fame ran: "Some who flocked to hear Fosdick preach did so only because it was modish, much like going to Carnegie Hall or the Belasco Theatre or Yankee Stadium."[29] Miller goes on to explain that Fosdick's fame was on par with Babe Ruth, the Sultan of Swat, who was belting home runs in the Bronx at this very time and was soon to be an American legend. As a matter of fact, here in the early 1920s, it would be better to say that Ruth's fame was on par with Fosdick's. The preacher still held more esteem than the star athlete in the American consciousness—a thought that barely makes sense to us today.

But this popularity made Fosdick a target. The tension between liberals and conservatives was now branded as a fight between modernists—those like Harry who turned to the sciences in ministry and read their Bible through a historical-critical method—and fundamentalists—those who sought a return to a commonsense reading of the Bible and a Puritan-like commitment to a Christian America.

The tensions came to a head in 1922 when Harry preached a sermon called "Shall the Fundamentalists Win?," which was reprinted and distributed across the country. In the sermon, Harry doubled down on the age of mobilization and the place of Christianity within it. He claimed that the Bible was not the literal Word of God but the historical record of God's unfolding *will*. In the logic of mobilization, the Bible wasn't step-by-step directions but instead revealed the *will* of God that we as human beings could *willfully* mobilize. Following suit, Harry asserted that Christianity was a religion of progress, development, and improvement—in other words, the constant movement into

29. Miller, *Harry Emerson Fosdick*, 97.

flourishing. Sin, redemption, and the need for transformation were minimized. In this kind of mobilized age, it is a short step between flourishing and an *exclusively* human flourishing that sees no need for the otherness of God's action. As a matter of fact, most liberals found too much talk of God's action unintellectual, a primitive belief, and embarrassing to state in public. Harry was not without piety and wouldn't go that far, but his modernist commitments led him to nevertheless minimize divine action, allowing flourishing to be co-opted by the immanent frame. Fundamentalists and modernists were both fighting a war in the age of mobilization, both making distinct cases for how religion should function in America. Neither realized that by mid-century the age of mobilization would be over and, for most of the American public, their fight irrelevant.

Yet in the 1920s Harry's sermon was a significant victory, a sign that the modernists would win the war. It would help to more firmly impose the immanent frame and take us further down the road of a secular age in which divine action is opaque. Yet while the modernists won, Harry lost. The general assembly of the Presbyterian Church gave the local presbytery permission to investigate Fosdick, including a hearing. Showing Harry's cultural importance, and the significance of the pastor at this time, John Foster Dulles, who was part of the counsel for the US at the Versailles Peace Conference, represented him.

Dulles's beloved father was a liberal Presbyterian pastor, so John was happy to successfully defend Harry. But the tension was too much, and Harry resigned from First Presbyterian, even after Dulles's victory. Watching the conflict from a distance, John Rockefeller Jr. became adamant that the fundamentalists not take the country and the faith backward. Therefore, he supported the modernists. Now, with the greatest preacher in America without a pulpit, Rockefeller opened his wallet, funded a new church in the Morningside Heights neighborhood of the city, and called it Riverside Church. Rockefeller intended the church to be the bright star of liberal Christianity. It was there that Harry would spend the rest of his career and where he would come to be known as the greatest preacher of the first half of the twentieth century.

As Harry's career came to an end in 1946, no one could imagine that the fundamentalists, who had departed losers in the religious culture wars of the 1920s, would see new opportunities to come back onto the public stage in the 1950s. And no one would have guessed that because of their losses in the 1920s they would be more able than the mainline liberals to respond to a new age of authenticity that would end the mainline liberal hegemony and radically change the image of the pastor.

# 8

## when purpose becomes mine and authenticity becomes king

*Rick Warren and pastoring in a post-Durkheimian age*

In the spring of 2005, a few weeks before Easter, gunshots rang out and bodies fell as Brian Nichols escaped from a courthouse. A fugitive on the run, he came across Ashley Smith. Nichols jumped from the shadows, put to Smith's head the weapon that had just killed four, and demanded that she hide him in her apartment. For the next seven hours she was a hostage, her life hanging by a precarious thread as a desperate man with nothing to lose threatened her. Yet, to everyone's shock, Nichols surrendered, leaving Smith's apartment after a friendly breakfast of pancakes and eggs.

When the authorities asked Smith what happened, amazed that a sure incident of inevitable violence had led to a peaceful ending, she told them, "I asked him if I could read." The police returned, "And what did he say?"

She reported that Nichols answered, "What do you want to read?"

Smith retrieved her Bible and a book called *The Purpose Driven Life*. She read out loud the chapter for the day, called "Using What God Gave You." After starting with a Bible verse and a Danish proverb, Rick Warren says in the chapter, "God deserves your best. He shaped you for a purpose, and he expects you to make the most of what you have been given. He doesn't want you to worry about or covet abilities you don't have."

For some reason, Nichols was infatuated, asking Smith to read it over and over again. Soon the dynamic of hostage and captor was broken, and they started to talk as friends. They shared stories of their families and questions they had about God. But what really energized their conversation was purpose. Nichols even asked Smith, "What do you think mine is?" Smith boldly returned, "Maybe it's to minister to people in prison, maybe that's what God wants you to do, and he brought you here to my apartment so that you could know that."[1] The thought of purpose was so powerful that with the last pancake gone, Nichols surrendered not only to the police but even more so to his purpose.

Smith was soon being interviewed by every three-letter network in the country, making stops on CNN's *Larry King Live*, NBC's *Today Show*, ABC's *Good Morning America*, CBS's *The Early Show*, and Fox's *Hannity and Colmes*. And on every one she mentioned pastor Rick Warren and his book. It was the perfect pre-Easter story. The publicity made the already well-selling book a juggernaut (it's sold more than thirty million copies to date) and launched the already well-known pastor into celebrity.


### Warren's Background

There are interesting threads that connect Harry Emerson Fosdick and Rick Warren. Both are Baptists who see their vocation solely as pastors, especially, in a significant way, a pastor to pastors. Fosdick lived this out not only by continuing to teach at Union but also by giving large amounts of time to one-on-one meetings with pastors and by speaking at conferences. Warren started a whole organization to support and train pastors. His book *The Purpose Driven Church* laid the groundwork for *The Purpose Driven Life*. And as pastors in the twentieth century, Fosdick and Warren both sensed a huge need to impact the spiritual lives of the laity in a more practical way than someone like Jonathan Edwards would have assumed that he should. Both Fosdick's and Warren's national prominence were achieved by writing chart-topping devotional books (Fosdick's *The Meaning of Prayer* and *The Meaning of Faith* were nearly as popular in their time as Warren's *Purpose Driven Life* is today). But it is there that their similarities end. The deep changes that arrived in the second half of the twentieth and the early twenty-first centuries shifted the conception of the pastor, the church, and the function of religion and faith.

1. See Jeffery Sheler, *Prophet of Purpose: The Life of Rick Warren* (New York: Doubleday, 2009), 184–85.

Rick Warren was a product of the fundamentalism that saw Fosdick as a Nucky Thompson with a Don Draper smile—a devil in a nice New York tailored suit. After the modernist victory in the 1920s, few would have guessed that the 1950s would bring the beaten fundamentalists back onto the national scene. After World War II and its new conservative ethos, some fundamentalists reinvented themselves as neo-evangelicals, holding to the core of biblical faith, while engaging, even embracing, culture. Rick Warren would bear this desire in his being, holding a conservative evangelical theology while making his main mission to engage the culture on its own terms. When Warren moderated a 2008 presidential debate between his friends John McCain and Barack Obama, the transition of the American pastor was complete. Eighty years earlier, this would've been unimaginable. It was no longer a big-steeple mainline city preacher who was the image of the American pastor but the son of a Southwestern fundamentalist.

Warren, like Edwards and Henry Ward Beecher, is the son of a pastor. Jimmy Warren was the youngest child of a moderately religious farmer in Depression-era Texas. With a failing economy and elderly father, Jimmy was sent to a Baptist high school in Shreveport, Louisiana. By the time he was a senior, he had heard the call and was preaching weekly. But self-doubt, bad advice, and World War II sent the young Jimmy out of the ministry and to Southern California. There, Jimmy met Dot, the woman who would become Rick Warren's beloved mother.

If Jimmy came from a moderately religious background, Dot's pedigree was true fundamentalist stock. Baptist preachers ran throughout her linage, and they were the kind, one would assume, who weren't fans of Harry Emerson Fosdick. Rick Warren's heritage is securely planted in the Southwest and California. The last great American pastor of the twentieth century (and first of the new century) would, for the first time, come from somewhere other than the Northeast. This signals the change sweeping across society, moving us into a secular age. The age of mobilization had its hubs in urban and industrial centers of the East; the new age of authenticity would have its "capitals" in the sunny new track suburbs of the Southwest, most particularly California. The sprawling valleys of Los Angeles and San Francisco are ground zero of the age of authenticity. Rick Warren was born and raised here.

After marrying Dot, Jimmy volunteered in her parents' congregation. Just as back in high school, Jimmy again heard the call, and this time he had the appropriate support to follow it into the pastorate, starting with a small church in San Jose. Rick's childhood was equal measure strong family and church life, both feeding his confidence. The family moved often. Jimmy was called from one ministry to another up and down the West Coast. Finally, in 1965

Jimmy accepted the position as director of mission for the Yokayo Baptist Association, which was part of the mission board of the Southern Baptist Convention. Moving the family to California's Redwood Valley, Jimmy and Dot gave Rick an idyllic environment in which to grow up. Rick watched his father care for pastors, with many spending respites at their home.

The family was filled with laughter and piety—a stark difference from the family that Henry Ward Beecher grew up in. Henry became a cutup to survive his austere and stern father. Rick became a jokester because Jimmy was always running some practical joke or another. But like Beecher, Warren was also close with his sister, Chaundel. She and her husband partnered with Rick in the founding and forming of Saddleback Church.

## The Dawning Age of Authenticity

Rick was fifteen years old when Harry Emerson Fosdick died in 1969, and the counterculture was in full force in San Francisco, just up the road from the Warrens. Rick was never tempted to participate, but his life wasn't absent of the impact of the counterculture. As I mentioned in detail in volume 1, there is clear resonance between the counterculture's pursuits of authenticity and conservative evangelicalism. Rick became deeply aware of the ways that the age of authenticity placed each individual on their *own* journey, a voyage to finding meaning and purpose, one that emphasizes individualism and the affirmation of ordinary life. Some of the counterculture's outward marks directly impacted Rick as well, particularly music and hair length.

The year following the summer of love, Rick, like most good evangelical teenagers, spent his summer working at camp. He was mostly doing grunt work but also playing his guitar and sharing his testimony around the campfire. This won Rick a reputation with the Northern California Southern Baptists. Soon he was playing music and giving messages at youth rallies and evangelistic events. Christian rock—an evangelical creation that blended biblical commitment with new cultural forms—became an infatuation. Jeffery Sheler, Warren's biographer, says, "The music was a catchy blend of Gospel lyrics set to a rock 'n' roll sound, and Rick embraced it enthusiastically. Being a worship leader would allow him to harness his previous passion for rock music and put it to sacred use. It seemed to him the best of both worlds."[2]

Combining the best of both worlds became a new strategy for evangelicals in the age of authenticity. And music had long been a way of connecting with

2. Sheler, *Prophet of Purpose*, 57.

the authentic movements of the Spirit. Warren had experienced how even (or maybe *particularly*) in secular music there was a deep drive toward the pursuit of spirituality. The rock and folk music scenes manifested the clearest outward sign of the arrival of the nova effect (more on this below). Warren now saw that as a worship leader he could connect with this inner emotive drive for an authentic spirituality, bringing the old-time biblical religion in the new casing of rock riffs.

This was the start of a new phenomenon in which the worship leader at times outstrips even the pastor. For Edwards, Beecher, and Fosdick, music was essential. For Edwards particularly, singing together was a communal act of worship done to a holy God; the hymns taught the content of the faith. But now music became a directly individual emotive experience. Its objective became feeling something spiritual in your *own* heart. In the age of authenticity, with its heightened expressive individualism, more often you feel something spiritual in the worship leader's riffs and strums than when the preacher reads the sacred text. It would take a few more decades for a phenomenon like Hillsong to have its enormous impact. But Warren was riding on the shifting currents as they began in the 1970s.

In high school, Rick and some friends started a Christian club at school, calling it Fishers of Men. Its aims were equal measure support for living a Christian life in a now non-Christian environment (this opposition or alien sense was sharpened to a point by the legend of the modernist-fundamentalist wars in which Harry Emerson Fosdick was central) and to reach the unsaved.

That such a group met on the public school campus reveals further shifts into our secular age. It has been a common thread of evangelical youth ministry since after World War II to make a push into public school campuses. Since the late 1940s, Young Life and its much smaller predecessors like Miracle Bible Club saw the public high school as a mission ground. But here in the 1970s, even evangelical denominational groups (not just parachurch movements) saw it as necessary to plant a Christian flag in the public schools.

## Back to the Durkheims

This takes us back to Charles Taylor's triads, picking up on his second set. In the previous chapter we called these the Durkheims and explained that they map closely onto the first triad, which we called the ages (the age of the ancien régime, the age of mobilization, and the age of authenticity). The Durkheims get their name from the French thinker Émile Durkheim, who is one of the founding fathers of sociology.

In 1912, Durkheim published his classic *The Elementary Forms of Religious Life*. In it he asserts that religion plays an important part in society; it functions to bring forth solidarity in practice and camaraderie in belief. Religion is a kind of glue that holds the functions of a society and the actions of individuals together. Durkheim wasn't concerned with whether religions actually attended to a real God, encountering divine action. Rather, he focused only on religion's social function.[3] Taylor, who affirms the genius of Durkheim but turns him against himself, shows with this triad how the social function of religion adds to the opaqueness of divine action.

Taylor adds three prefixes in front of Durkheim to further draw out our transitions—"paleo," "neo," and "post." Most of us think of the diet when we hear "paleo." But Taylor uses "paleo" to refer to ancient, hence the ancien régime. In a paleo-Durkheimian time, there is no divide between the functions of the social, political, and religious life. They are all the same, so embedded that they're basically one. You can't be French and not be Catholic; your participation in the Mass is inseparable from your loyalty to the king. There are simply no seams between your public life, private life, and religious commitments. The pastor or priest has a central place in the functioning of the whole society.

But this changed with the age of mobilization. When we hear "neo" we might think of *The Matrix*. "Neo" simply means "new" or "revived." When Keanu Reeves's character awakes from his pod, he is new—Neo. The decision that "we the people" can mobilize our own way of life—matching in intention, but not in form, God's own design—signals entry into a whole new function of religion matching the conception of the age of mobilization. We enter into a neo-Durkheimian dispensation. Yet this is where the ages and the Durkheims don't completely overlay. The age of mobilization creates the conditions for an eventual neo-Durkheimian age. But it would take years to get to its essential outgrowth in religion: the rise of the denomination.

The denomination, as the religious form of the age of mobilization, reenacts, now in a religious form, the functions of the age of mobilization.[4] People

---

3. William T. Cavanaugh elaborates on Durkheim's position: "Functionalism is indebted to the work of Emile Durkheim, who thought that religion is a matter of social function, not mere belief. Religion is the way that a social group represents itself to itself. . . . For Durkheim it does not matter, for example, if no one consciously believes that the national flag is a god. What matters is whether or not the flag serves to organize people in such a way that ritual boundaries between the sacred and the profane are reinforced. The empirical fact that people will, in certain times and places, kill and die for the flag is what makes nationalism a religion; it does not matter at all that the same people believe that the flag is an inanimate piece of cloth without 'supernatural' powers." "The Invention of the Religious-Secular Distinction," in *At the Limits of the Secular: Reflections on Faith and Public Life*, ed. William A. Barbieri (Grand Rapids: Eerdmans, 2014), 109.
4. Charles Taylor gives us more background: "So in one way, a denominational identity tends to separate religion from the state. A denomination cannot be a national church, and its members

are free to decide for themselves how they'll organize their religious lives. There is no reason for conformity across the society, because God has been lifted and separated from our public life. In the age of mobilization, identity becomes central. But identity is conceived of differently from how we think of it today.[5] When we hear "identity" we think of an individual person's chosen self-definition. Against the backdrop of the age of mobilization, "identity" means something constituted through a collective group whom you or your parents *will* to be part of.

From the mid-nineteenth to the late twentieth century, the denomination was the hub of religious power. This is why it was a big move to have Harry Emerson Fosdick cast from his Presbyterian pulpit in 1922 (those who did so assumed that to kick him out of the denomination was to flatten to nothing his religious power). People's affiliation with their denomination had every sense of being free, but nevertheless it was often stable because it was a central piece of your collective historical identity.

If you grew up Lutheran, it was a good bet that you'd marry a Lutheran and confirm your kids as Lutherans even if you didn't totally believe everything the Lutheran church said. It didn't matter; being Lutheran was part of your historical identity. (Similarly, you didn't believe everything those politicians did in Washington, but you were still a devoted American.) You could think this way because more than likely your mother and her mother were Lutheran; it was part of a collective historical identity. The ancien régime

can't accept and join whatever claims to be the national church. Denominationalism implies that churches are all equally options, and thrives best in a regime of separation of church and state, de facto if not de jure. But on another level, the political entity can be identified with the broader, overarching 'church,' and this can be a crucial element in its patriotism." *Varieties of Religion Today: William James Revisited* (Cambridge, MA: Harvard University Press, 2002), 75.

5. Robert Joustra and Alissa Wilkinson explain our transition to a different form of identity: one of recognition.

This mythology, Taylor argues, has ushered in a politics of equal recognition—that is, the push for every person's identity to be seen and explicitly acknowledged by the social structure as equal to and as worthy as everyone else's. "The underlying premise here is that everyone shares in this," Taylor says. "The forms of equal recognition have been essential to democratic culture." Because we say that everyone is equal, we then must continuously recognize and affirm every distinct way of being human. . . . Of course, we've always been socially dependent on one another for recognition. But in the past, that often took quite a different form. I knew I was recognized and my existence was validated when I filled my role properly. And that role conformed to a set of socially derived identities on which most people agreed, if only implicitly. So I knew I was "doing" life right if I filled the role that I was born into—woman, or farmer, or royalty, or whatever—based on how it had always been done. Our recognition was social because we agreed on roles. (*How to Survive the Apocalypse: Zombies, Cylons, Faith, and Politics at the End of the World* [Grand Rapids: Eerdmans, 2016], 105, 108, citing Taylor, *The Malaise of Modernity* [Toronto: Anansi, 1991], 46–47)

assumed that religious life was history in whole. The age of mobilization shifts this to assume that religion is (just) *part* of your history. And as we'll see, in a post-Durkheimian age religion would be completely severed from people's conceived history, fading into one's individualized and completely buffered sense of the self as a completely self-chosen identity.

Yet here in the age of mobilization, religion had a place in your history, and therefore the pastor was an important person, guiding a major part of your history and therefore your functions in the world. The pastor was there at the most solemn or significant moments of your life—like birth, baptism, wedding, and death. While this seemed secure, the denomination was a product of mobilization, meaning all it took was conflict and initiative for a group to decide that they couldn't be *that kind* of Methodist, or *that kind* of Presbyterian. Therefore, they were free to mobilize themselves in a new way, creating a new denomination. This was no longer a threat to society as it was in the ancien régime, which had led the Pilgrims, because of persecution, to flee to the New World. Yet what was often not an option—except for the very few like Fosdick's Uncle Charles—was to decide to have no denominational identity and therefore no connection to any religious group (even tangentially), believing religion had no function in your life. A neo-Durkheimian dispensation shifted the function of religion to a collective historical identity. It would take the post-Durkheimian period, and its redefinition of identity away from a collective history, for the Uncle Charleses to become the norm.

When our lives are no longer completely embedded in the religious social practice and political organization of the ancien régime, what it means to be American or British is to identify with the nation. It is to have part of your identity squarely rest on a collective historical national identity (U-S-A! U-S-A! U-S-A!). We don't need direct religious functions to hold us together (as they did in the ancien régime); we simply need people to take on responsibility and the duty to uphold our way of life—whatever that means. The modern Olympics and the World Cup can work only in an age of mobilization—they can be created only during this period (the first modern Olympics was in 1896 and the first World Cup in 1930) because you need a sense of chosen—yet taken for granted—national identity for it to work.[6] In other words, you need a sense that people in other nations are, for the most part, *like you*—mobilizing their own societies through their own willing. The only difference is that you

6. Charles Taylor explains why religion in America has seemed to hold on longer than in other Euro-Atlantic countries. He holds that America was the only country that was forged without the ancien régime, having a distinct break with it that, say, Canada (which is still in a commonwealth) didn't. In this environment religion took a new function, one that was more open to the age of authenticity. *A Secular Age* (Cambridge, MA: Belknap Press, 2007), 525.

identify with different nations. Because religious function has shifted to the neo from the paleo, we can make friends and compete with people from other nations (enjoying games together). What makes us different is not our gods or fundamental religious practices but our national historical identities.[7] Divine action has nothing to do with it.

The denomination, as an invention of the age of mobilization, assumes the same.[8] I'm Presbyterian because my parents or I have chosen it. We have identified with the collective and its concrete institutions. Which denomination I pick is a mobilized choice, initiated from someone else's decision. In a paleo-Durkheimian age you had little to no choice in your religious life— you actually had no religious life at all, because all of life was bound in the functions and visions of faith. But in a neo-Durkheimian time, religious affiliation is connected to consenting choice, to your willingness to identify. The national identity of the age of mobilization allows for the Ryder Cup and those star-spangled golf pants, just as the denominational identity of the neo-Durkheimian dispensation allows for youth gatherings and trienniums in filled stadiums. This turn to denominational identity may create rivalries, producing a level of competition between Methodists and Presbyterians, say, but in the end we assume we're the same. We've just chosen to identify with a different denomination (and its institutions) because of choice or heritage (no wonder theology is perceived as meaningless to most people, even pastors). This "being the same," thankfully, moves us into peace—the threat level for another Thirty Years' War is nil[9]—but in turn this "being the same" makes it much harder for people to sense, or even validate, experiences of divine action. It becomes easier (and more peaceful), we're told, to just move beyond or ignore divine action and find meaning somewhere else.

Of course, sometimes the rivalries do become hot, but most often over social issues and not conceptions or experiences of divine action. I oppose a certain social issue because it threatens my chosen identification with the denomination. I can't, in good conscience (even in my understanding of the authority of Scripture), identify with this group if its position on sexuality,

---

7. These national historical identities have their concrete manifestation in the different ways society *chooses* to mobilize its way of life.

8. "The denomination clearly belongs to the Age of Mobilization. It is not a divinely established body . . . (though in another sense, the broader 'church' may be seen as such), but something that we have to create—not just at our whim, but to fulfill the plan of God. In this, it resembles the new Republic as Providentially conceived in its civil religion. There is an affinity between the two, and each strengthened the other." Taylor, *Secular Age*, 450.

9. At least within Christianity, maybe not with other religions, this "not same" dynamic becomes a strategy for some who wish for conflict. If our Muslim neighbor is not like us, it is easier to ostracize them.

poverty, or gender differs from mine. This is why the most heated fighting happens inside the denomination, threatening to tear it apart. I have identified with the denomination, willing to be part of it, but if it no longer connects with my own identity or, worse, feels like a violation of it, then I'll need to leave for a denomination that more clearly connects with my identity (including my understanding of my practices like reading Scripture). Or I could mobilize a group within the existing denomination to take it over, shifting it to more readily fit something people like me can identify with.

The neo-Durkheimian dispensation gives us the phenomenon of First, Second, Third, and so on, Presbyterian Church. In a neo-Durkheimian age it is hard to have a true *status confessionis*. (A *status confessionis* claims that the very heart of the gospel is at risk, that part of the church has accepted and followed a false gospel.) Conflicts now are most often propelled by a group's social sensibility and not by the revelations of divine action. This is why a pastor is much more at risk for talking about politics than theology in the pulpit. My point here is that the organization of religion into denominations has direct parallel with a national identity in the burgeoning nation-state.

### Back to Warren

It is this linking of national identity with denominational commitment in a neo-Durkheimian dispensation that unconsciously prompted Rick Warren and his friends to start the Fishers of Men on their high school campus. In a real sense it was a simple, faithful, and naive initiative, something only possible, of course, in the remnants of the age of mobilization. Rick and his friends were simply mobilizing from their own will a religious gathering, a kind of denomination if you will.[10] But why did Rick and his friends feel the need to do this on the public school campus?

The principal of Ukiah High School couldn't figure that out, so he refused the Fishers of Men official club standing. What the principal didn't realize was how some evangelicals were taking steps to link the national identity of the age of mobilization with the Christian religion. Sensing Christianity's loss as the age of authenticity and a post-Durkheimian period began to dawn, the on-campus club became a direct strategy to continue the neo-Durkheimian

10. By denomination here I mean a "kind among others," the way a one-dollar bill is a unique denomination among other bills. And this is the moral code of the denominational movement of the neo-Durkheimian age; any religious group is only one kind among many others. Yet what evangelicals sensed in the 1970s was that religion, particularly their kind, was becoming a two-dollar bill.

dispensation by infiltrating the supposed secular institutions with religious collectives, mobilizing religious practice within their secular walls.

From thousands of similar clubs to See You at the Pole, evangelicals in the 1970s, 1980s, and 1990s saw this as a core strategy. Many didn't recognize, and wouldn't have cared, that this strategy was embedded deeply in the age of mobilization and a neo-Durkheimian sense of national identity and a denominational sense of religion. Merged with the aim to witness to Jesus was the goal to fortify a strong Christian element in the DNA of the national identity, keeping a denominational space from shrinking in a post-Durkheimian age.

In the 1980s the Moral Majority and the Righteous Right would come to epitomize this strategy, making all political issues into religious ones and fighting for a Christian national identity. They would seek to uphold neo-Durkheimianism, seeking institutional and denominational power more than the act and being of the living Christ. This had the impact of turning off many (both Christians and non-Christians). This move to uphold a neo-Durkheimianism seemed to be antithetical to the new spiritualities being fashioned from the age of authenticity. This gave some anecdotal evidence that organized (mobilized) forms of religion were indeed no place to find authenticity, meaning, or purpose.

After gathering signatures of petition for the club, Warren got the district attorney involved, finally taking his case to the school board and winning. "A few months after the club's launch, Rick wrote an article for *Hollywood Free Paper*, an underground newspaper published by the Jesus Movement in Southern California, describing the drawn-out battle . . . and the considerable influence he believed the club was having at school."[11] Rick now had his first taste of notoriety. Within weeks he received mail from all over California, asking his advice on how others too could start a Christian club, securely placing a Christian group (or denomination) inside the walls of the secular public realm. These evangelicals were not making a case to return to the ancien régime, in which faith and social life were one unit and divine action was everywhere; rather, in a neo-Durkheimian way they were fighting for a denominational space and overall respect for their own desire to mobilize their religion.[12]

Even as a high school student, Rick Warren became a trainer and resource provider, helping all those who wrote to him by creating a document titled "How to Start a Christian Club." Attaching a practical help sheet to the district attorney's letter, he gave high school students what would come to

11. Sheler, *Prophet of Purpose*, 59.
12. This mentality has even affected the way we define faith. This is the central argument of volume 1.

be his forte: direct practical help (resources) in building an initiative. The worship leader now found another dimension to his calling. If music made people feel something, directly impacting them, then so too did direct practical resources. Rick was becoming a master at connecting the practical entrepreneurial spirit with the emotive pulls of the worship leader. Yet while the fusion of entrepreneur and worship leader would never leave him, he would let go of an overcommitment to the denominational focus of neo-Durkheimianism.

### But . . . the Long Hair

High schooler Rick Warren was now a minor celebrity in his small California Southern Baptist world. By the winter of 1971, at the age seventeen, he was traveling the coast preaching to hundreds of young people. Yet getting his preaching license wasn't absent drama. The conflict pushed him down a new road that would lead him to eventually embrace a post-Durkheimian world.

After reviewing his application, a committee of pastors and deacons interviewed Rick. Overall, the committee was enthusiastic and positive, happy with Rick's answers. But toward the end of the meeting his own pastor stood and proclaimed that he couldn't support Rick, explaining that his hair was too long and his overall appearance looked more counterculture than faithful Christian. At the end of a neo-Durkheimian time (and as a sign that a post-Durkheimian age was pressuring and replacing the neo) Christianity was becoming more and more defined as a subculture, making dress and hairstyle, for instance, important as a way to mark in-group commitment.[13]

Rick met the pastor's challenge, explaining that his appearance gave his preaching *authenticity*, asserting that his mission was to convert young people and that his long hair and wire-rimmed John Lennon glasses were a key tool. Angering his pastor, the committee sided with Rick, approving his license. He had now taken a small but significant step outside the neo-Durkheimian conventions, but it would take a few other experiences to turn this small step into a big leap.

In the summer before Rick's senior year of high school, when he now had his license in hand, "the California Southern Baptist Convention launched an ambitious and, for its time, innovative campaign to reach unsaved young people with the Gospel and to train and motivate young Southern Baptists to do street evangelism."[14] The streets their feet walked would become the

---

13. See Christian Smith, *American Evangelicalism: Embattled and Thriving* (Chicago: University of Chicago Press, 1998).
14. Sheler, *Prophet of Purpose*, 65.

center of the counterculture movement in Southern California, the soil of the new age of authenticity. Spreading out on Hollywood and Sunset Boulevards, they invited strung-out hippies to tent revivals. Their primary goal was to save these lost youth. But their secondary aim was to make the surrounding neo-Durkheimian Southern Baptist congregations and their pastors, like Rick's own, more open and welcoming to the authenticity-seeking young people.

That summer three things entered Rick's bloodstream and would never leave. First, he learned how to preach to authenticity seekers who were done with a neo-Durkheimian denominationalism. Second, he saw just how stuck most churches were in this denominational commitment and recognized that they needed help and vision to escape it. And finally, Southern California became intoxicating to him. So after finishing his senior year, he moved south, matriculating at Cal Baptist in Riverside. But Rick's education came less in the classroom and more in hands-on youth ministry.

Taking a job at a Baptist church, Rick was transformed from traveling youth evangelist to youth pastor. It was his job to move the young people into discipleship. In the name of Jesus (he'd rejected neo-Durkheimianism) he claimed that his job was to make not good Southern Baptists but disciples. "After a few months on the job he saw the youth group more than triple in size."[15] With a mind bent toward the entrepreneurial, Rick was beginning to do the same with discipleship as he had with his Fishers of Men high school group; he was starting to forge a discipleship resource that would eventually become "purpose driven." By the time his work at the church was done he'd have more than ten thousand young people on his mailing list.

As the 1980s approached, mailing lists were no joke. The Religious Right would achieve political power, and the California governor, Ronald Reagan, would even win the presidency, thanks to direct mail.[16] Rick's ability to garner ten thousand addresses showed that he had all the makings of an entrepreneur and that a big church was in his future. Yet when Rick headed to seminary in Texas, few saw this future clearly. Rather, people's eyes were clouded by

15. Sheler, *Prophet of Purpose*, 81.
16. "Each week Warren and his team would analyze the responses and add addresses to a growing database of potential invitees. From the survey responses they identified four common complaints that people had against churches: the sermons were boring and irrelevant; church members weren't friendly to visitors, they were more like a clique; churches were more interested in people's money than in people; and parents worried about the quality of the church's child care. 'What we discovered was that what most churches offered was not what most people wanted,' Warren explained. 'People's hang-ups about church were not theological; they were sociological. They said, I don't have anything against God. I just don't see it relating to my life.' Warren was determined to use those findings to design a church that would meet the 'felt needs' of the community and would overcome the barriers that prevented people from attending church." Sheler, *Prophet of Purpose*, 106.

denominational politics. When Rick Warren sat in classes at a Southwestern Baptist Theological Seminary, a coup was commencing. Just four hours south of Fort Worth, in Waco, the historic 1979 Southern Baptist Convention was taking place. Systematically, the conservatives were taking over the denomination, voting out any moderate from office. Basically, anyone who would have had a soft spot for Harry Emerson Fosdick was ousted. It was a war for denominational control, a battle for power in a neo-Durkheimian world.

But Rick Warren knew something in his bones that these leaders didn't: the neo-Durkheimian world was ending, and a new dispensation was here. Rick knew it because of his time on Sunset Boulevard, rubbing shoulders with the authenticity seekers. He was sure of it because of his work in youth ministry, building programs and talking about discipleship.

Just four hours away, Rick had no desire to participate in the convention. Reflecting on that time years later, Rick said, "I just wasn't interested in denominational politics, then or now. . . . I was more interested in the work I was doing, preparing for the ministry and, later, building a church. All of that denominational stuff, it meant nothing to me."[17]

As we read these words now, in the second decade of the twenty-first century, they don't sound as profound as they are. For historical comparison, Fosdick wondered if denominationalism was a problem in the 1920s and started Riverside as a non-creedal church that was not denominationally specific. But even so, Fosdick had no sense that he could be indifferent to denominationalism and its functional structures; he never imagined that he could simply assert, like Warren, that it meant nothing to him.[18]

So Warren is doing something unimaginable before the 1980s: he's rejecting that the church, the pastor, and therefore the function of religion in our lives has anything to do with the denomination. And he is doing this, not to return to a theocracy or an old vision of the ancien régime, but to fully embrace the authenticity revolution. It no longer matters that people identify with a denomination, finding footing for their life history within it. Rather, what matters is that people feel engaged and supported as they search for their purpose. The church is no longer a collective community that holds a broad identity but is instead a *resource* to help *you* (*individually*) finally find the

17. Sheler, *Prophet of Purpose*, 91.

18. *The State of Pastors* reports that most pastors are not opposed to their denomination but find much less direct connection. "Denominations are important, but not typically influential. Half of church leaders say their affiliation is very strong, but just one-quarter says their denomination has a lot of influence on their ministry activities." Barna Report, *The State of Pastors: How Today's Faith Leaders Are Navigating Life and Leadership in an Age of Complexity* (Ventura, CA: Barna Group, 2017), 61.

authentic purpose you've been seeking. And if there was anything that Rick was good at, it was creating resources. He now began to imagine a church that was, from top to bottom, a resource. Church should help people live the purpose God had for them by serving at every level as a resource to that goal.

Warren and the megachurch movement he'd help to create were not directly opposing enchantment or the mystery of the church—even as they chose to design their buildings more like malls and office complexes than cathedrals.[19] It's wrong to assume that they were resisting an ancient Christianity (though they maybe were ignorant of it). What they opposed was the denomination-alism of the age of mobilization. They were agreeing with the culture that it was an inauthentic form and devoid of true spirituality. This is why Rick would refuse to have "Southern Baptist" anywhere in the name of Saddle-back Community Church—you'll have to look hard to find any mention of Saddleback's denomination.

But in opposing the neo-Durkheimian, whether aware of it or not, Rick embraced a transition into the post-Durkheimian, which conceded much to our secular age, as Taylor has described it. No longer seen as part of a de-nomination, the church could freely be seen as a resource. But what legitimates a resource, particularly in the age of authenticity and its post-Durkheimian dispensation, is *growth* or the number of people using it (for us this has evolved, with online tools, to likes, views, and retweets). There are no other mechanisms to judge its veracity. No longer is there a hierarchy—whether consecrated or mobilized. What validates it is numbers—or better, growth. This is why the legend of Saddleback always begins with forty people in a school gym and ends with twenty thousand on 120 acres.[20]

The more Rick thought about the church as a resource, the more he became enamored with growth—or maybe it was the more he thought about growth, the more he saw the church as a resource. Whether it was the chicken or the egg, by his last year in seminary the budding movement of church growth (a truly post-Durkheimian, post-denominational discipline) was Warren's passion.

One of the earliest fathers of the church growth movement was Robert Schuller. Those raised in the 1980s or 1990s might have memories of Schul-ler in a light blue robe, beamed into your living room on a Sunday morn-ing. Schuller's Crystal Cathedral was the TV church of the nation. He had

19. Though it is hard to assume that sacramental tradition could take some of the initial bold steps that Warren and others did. Sacramental traditions, like Lutheranism, can follow in their footsteps, but it would be harder to assume they could initiate this church revolution. It was Baptist and other less sacramental traditions that created these unique pastors.

20. This is true of any big church. See Rob Bell, *Velvet Elvis: Repainting the Christian Faith* (Grand Rapids: Zondervan, 2005), for the Mars Hill version.

built an opulent building by growing his small Reformed Church in America congregation to ten thousand members. He did this by stripping it of any outward denominational ties and thinking of it like a retail business.[21] In *Your Church Has Real Possibilities*, Schuller gave pastors a how-to guide "in which he compared the process of growing a large and vibrant congregation to that of building a successful retail business. Just as in retailing, . . . factors such as good location, high visibility, adequate inventory, convenient parking, strong consumer service and sound cash flow were important ingredients for a church's success."[22]

Warren read the book, and in the summer of 1978 he went to Schuller's conference, eager to get inside Schuller's methods. The entrepreneur sensibility that had been alive within him since high school now found direction. He was convinced by the church growth methods, feeling no apprehension in throwing off denominational ties in order to grow. But it was more than just ambition that motivated Warren; he also saw in these strategies a way to gain new converts "rather than [just] attracting people from other congregations or by birth rate." As Warren's friend Steve Williams says about Rick's participating in the church growth conference, "It was there for the first time that [Rick] caught the vision of doing church for the unchurched"[23]—in other words, in a fully post-Durkheimian time.

## Post-Durkheimianism

If we most often think of cavemen and Keanu Reeves when we hear "paleo" and "neo," we tend to link "post" with something like *post*modern. "Post" might be the most straightforward of the Durkheimian triad. We have a good sense of what it means, as compared to "paleo" and "neo." "Post" means "after."

Postmodernity was all the buzz in the early 2000s. Pastors were asked how they'd do ministry now that all metanarratives and truth itself were liquidated

---

21. Robert Jones adds about Schuller: "In 1957, when Schuller invited Dr. Norman Vincent Peale, a popular proponent of Christian 'positive thinking,' to speak at Garden Grove, the masses of people who flocked to the service caused a traffic jam on Interstate 5. Schuller's devotion to Peale's style of ministry—which emphasized making people feel good about themselves rather than 'teaching' or 'converting' them—proved to be a wild success. 'I decided to adopt the spirit, style, strategy and substance of a "therapist" in the pulpit,' he remembered later. It was the foundation for the 'theology of self-esteem' that transformed Schuller into one of the most influential Christian pastors of the late twentieth century. Schuller was one of the pioneers of a new conservative Christian trend that explicitly tied Christian worship to consumer culture." *The End of White Christian America* (New York: Simon & Schuster, 2016), 23.

22. Sheler, *Prophet of Purpose*, 94–95.

23. Sheler, *Prophet of Purpose*, 95.

by the heavy weight of "post." Pastors were told that all they'd assumed about epistemology had changed. If modernity was a kind of knowing built on rationality and empirical truth, we were now *post* all of that. We were now living *after* truth and a single consented-to story. Epistemology, pastors were told, was all the rage. But all this postmodern stuff may have been more sizzle than substance. Pastors were taken into the philosophical debates about truth, perception, hermeneutics, and texts. But the *post* they may have been feeling was bound not in epistemology but in the Durkheims.

Pastors stayed ostensibly connected to the esoteric conversation because they sensed that underneath the epistemological hubbub was a dynamic change in the function of religion. We had entered not so much into a postapocalyptic time without truth or narrative as into a post-Durkheimian age where faith, spirituality, and religion were being renegotiated, taking us further yet into our secular age.

Like the paleo- and neo-Durkheimian, the post-Durkheimian dispensation comes onto ground cleared by the ages. If the neo-Durkheimian dispensation and its denominational focus were made possible by the age of mobilization, then a post-Durkheimian time feeds off the new age of authenticity.

As we've said, both in this volume and the last, the age of authenticity, which arrived en masse during Rick Warren's high school days, asserts that everyone has the right to define for themselves what it means to be human.[24] No religious institution, denomination, or even national identity can impose on you what it means for you to live a life of meaning and purpose. If you don't want to fight in Vietnam, run your family business, or be a Presbyterian, then you shouldn't.[25] There is only one duty you have: to follow "what speaks to you."

Identity now shifts from being planted in a collective history to individual expression. My identity is no longer necessarily tied to a history but is that which I decide to express to the world. I'm called first and foremost to express (loud and proud) how I live out my own individual way of being me (and the new morality is that no one should oppose my right to express my identity—this is the ethics of authenticity that Taylor develops in the Massey Lectures and beyond).[26]

24. Taylor explains that this has been a growing cultural reality since the late 1960s, but it had its antecedents in the thought of eighteenth-century philosopher Johann Herder. See *The Ethics of Authenticity* (Cambridge, MA: Harvard University Press, 1991).

25. Taylor explains that the age of authenticity and post-Durkheimianism required "the triple attack that the family-religion-patriotism complex of the 1950s suffered in the era of civil rights, Vietnam, and the expressive revolution." *Dilemmas and Connections: Selected Essays* (Cambridge, MA: Belknap Press, 2011), 160.

26. Taylor explains how the modern moral order evolves as we transition into an age of authenticity: "One shouldn't criticize the others' values, because they have a right to live their

I'm now free from any and all conforming molds. Taylor calls this transition the move into an expressive individualism, and in volume 1 I showed how the consumer society that was created after World War II shifted hard and fast toward *expressiveness* (over duty) in the late 1960s and beyond. It is now only by being me (my individual expressive identity) that I'll discover meaning and purpose. There is no longer any transcendent referent to meaning and purpose that does not begin and end with me. I may be able to find spirituality, but its epicenter will be not outside me but within me. "Thus the injunction would seem to be: let everyone follow his/her own path of spiritual inspiration. Don't be led off yours by the allegation that it doesn't fit with some orthodoxy."[27] There is no longer even a weak connection to design, as in the age of mobilization and a Fosdick-like liberalism. It is only within myself and next to my own chosen identity that I can find significance.

And this is no more important than when it comes to religion and spirituality. What moves you individually is what has veracity. There can be no legitimate spirituality or even religious function without having expressive meaning, giving you, individually, a purpose. Taylor says, "For many people today, to set aside their own path in order to conform to some external authority just doesn't seem comprehensible as a form of spiritual life. The injunction is, in the words of a speaker at a New Age festival: 'Only accept what rings true to your own inner Self.'"[28]

It is on this ground cleared by the age of authenticity that we move from a neo- to a post-Durkheimian time. In a post-Durkheimian world, we are unhooked—this is its key component. There is no external institution or societal form that shapes and controls our religious commitments.[29] Our religious functions and committed spiritualities are bound to nothing other than ourselves. This is why being a pastor in the post-Durkheimian age is so hard; to use a bad analogy, you can eat only what you kill. Neither the denomination nor the larger society delivers people, or more significance, to your door. This leads to great insecurity and competition between pastors; it assumes

own life as you do. The sin which is not tolerated is intolerance. This injunction emerges clearly from the ethic of freedom and mutual benefit, although one might easily cavil at this application to it." *Secular Age*, 484.

27. Taylor, *Secular Age*, 489.

28. Taylor, *Secular Age*, 489.

29. "The expressivist outlook . . . [says] the religious life or practice that I become part of must not only be my choice, but it must speak to me, it must make sense in terms of my spiritual development as I understand this. . . . Within this framework of belief, I choose the church in which I feel most comfortable. But if the focus is going now to be on my spiritual path, thus on what insights come to me in the subtler languages that I find meaningful, then maintaining this or any other framework becomes increasingly difficult." Taylor, *Secular Age*, 486.

that those with the bigger church are more talented, because people follow only what speaks to them. Heritage, history, or a sacralized society are long gone. As Taylor says, "A thoroughly post-Durkheimian society will be one in which our religious belonging would be unconnected from our national identity. It will almost certainly be one in which the gamut of such religious allegiances will be wide and varied."[30]

Yet a post-Durkheimian period should not be confused with the end of religion and spirituality; it rather is the exponential surplus of spiritual options. The tightly organized forms of paleo- and neo-Durkheimian religion have exploded like a massive star. In the post-Durkheimian dispensation, we live inside a supernova effect, where a massive buffet of frenetic spiritual options is set before us, none formally ruled better than any other, yoga as significant as communion, Martian chat rooms as important as the preached Word. Whatever speaks to you is worthy of exploration and commitment until it no longer does. Divine action is opaque, not because religion and spirituality have been darkened, but because the light of the nova explosion is so intense and inner-directed that a vision for divine action becomes washed out. When Rick Warren claims to be uninterested in denominations because his concern is for searchers and seekers, he intuitively and coherently is stating that he will create a church for those unhooked from organized religion. Warren denies the neo-Durkheimian to free himself to create a true resource for the post-Durkheimian searcher.

Robert Schuller was right. Sensing this nova explosion in the late 1970s, he knew that a church that desires to draw seekers needed to take the form of retail because not only were all religious forms assumed to be equal in value but, even more so, the market was flush with options. The key was to make the church a legitimate choice in the marketplace by upping its visibility.

The pastor needed to now become an entrepreneur because the religious market was far too crowded (due to the nova) to assume people had any loyalty to any religious function or form that didn't help them in their own seeking. The new pastor being forged from Warren's genius would no longer bemoan the nova effect and the crowded market but would engage it, providing the church as a key resource in helping all searchers find the purpose they individually were seeking.[31] The age of mobilization and the denominationalism

---

30. Taylor, *Dilemmas and Connections*, 256. Taylor contrasts the post-Durkheimian and neo-Durkheimian periods: "In the post-Durkheimian age many people are uncomprehending in face of the demand to conform. Just as in the neo-Durkheimian world, joining a church you don't believe in seems not just wrong, but absurd, contradictory, so in the post-Durkheimian age seems the idea of adhering to a spirituality which doesn't present itself as your path, the one which moves and inspires you." *Secular Age*, 489.

31. "Virtually all [megachurches] offered a conservative biblical theology, an informal 'seeker sensitive' style of worship with lots of up-tempo music, a variety of social and outreach ministries,

of the neo-Durkheimian dispensation tended to mold the pastor, in dress and form, into a politician (even today, this still holds on in places), organizing initiatives and institutions. Fosdick carried himself, in dress and manner, like a politician, building institutions as he went. Yet in the age of authenticity and its unhooked post-Durkheimianism, the mold of the pastor shifts to the visionary CEO, now in a polo or Hawaiian shirt, finding ways to make the church a resource for those unhooked religious consumers looking for what speaks to them.

Being a visionary CEO was essential because, counterintuitively, Schuller and even more so Warren knew that the more everything was about seeking individual expression, the more size mattered. The arrival of the nova effect and its surplus of individual options didn't mean that there is no sense of collective gathering in a post-Durkheimian period. Rather, there is a desire to find associations, thus making all sorts of new, large gathered groups seeking spirituality important. People rush to all sorts of things, like U2 concerts, Taizé, or Saddleback. Yet the drive to participate is unhooked from any obligation other than my own search for significance, meaning, and ultimate purpose.[32]

The pastor needed to be a great entrepreneur because inside the nova effect growth mattered more than ever. For the church to be a resource for your own individual pursuits of meaning and purpose, you needed to feel like you belonged—not to something historic, ancient, or even institutional but rather to something emotively vibrant, even exciting—something authentic. Rick Warren, the worship leader and Christian rock connoisseur, understood how

---

and a comfortable modern facility that more resembled a concert arena or a shopping mall—complete with food courts and information kiosks—than a traditional church. More than just places of worship, they often functioned as community centers, providing a wide range of opportunities for social networking, recreation, community service, counseling and support groups, and other programs." Sheler, *Prophet of Purpose*, 27.

32. "Of course, they won't necessarily sit easily in these communities as their forebears did. And in particular, a post-Durkheimian age may mean a much lower rate of inter-generational continuity of religious allegiance. But the strongly collective options will not lose adherents. Perhaps even the contrary trend might declare itself." Taylor, *Secular Age*, 516. There seems to be a lack of intergenerational connection in churches that most deeply embrace post-Durkheimianism. One thinks particularly of the resources coming out of Fuller Seminary's Fuller Youth Institute, which has most directly worked with these kinds of churches. E. Brooks Holifield shows that pastors were overall spending less time with children, exacerbating the intergenerational divide. This was likely the impact of reimagining the pastor as CEO. "Clergy spent less time with children than they once had. Catechizing no longer occupied much of the Protestant minister's time. . . . Catholic priests gave more time to children than Protestant ministers, mainly because many of them remained responsible for parochial schools. Catholics and Protestants alike spent most of their working time with middle-aged or older adults." *God's Ambassadors: A History of the Christian Clergy in America* (Grand Rapids: Eerdmans, 2007), 340.

you could feel a deep sense of belonging while nevertheless being unhooked from obligatory denominational or religious functions.[33]

So the pastor as entrepreneurial CEO has become key in this post-Durkheimian age, because the entrepreneur can convince people that his product has just the thing you (individually) need. And while it is just for you, there are *many, many* others who use or participate in it. This connects us with a growing gathering of others who, just like us, are individually finding meaning and purpose. The bigness becomes the new authority in the post-Durkheimian dispensation. I'm sure that I'm not being duped or, worse, wasting my time, because this feels good. But how can I trust my feelings? Not because generations of my people have worshiped like this, or because it is part of my national identity, but because ten thousand or, better, twenty thousand other people feel what I do. And we're all here by our own individual free choice, unhooked to find meaning and purpose anywhere we please.

### The Beginnings, Balloonings, and Ballyhoo of Saddleback

Jonathan Edwards prepared for his ministry with thirteen hours per day in his study, Henry Ward Beecher found his pastoral stride by spending hours talking with ordinary people at the general store, and Harry Emerson Fosdick came to grips with the dark night of his soul in a sanitarium. It wasn't the study, general store, or sanitarium that would be the birthplace of Warren's church. Rather, it was a university library full of US Census data and demographic research. Each day in the summer of 1979, Rick poured over the material, seeking the perfect place to plant his flag and start his church.

In a post-Durkheimian fashion, Rick didn't wait for denominational approval or submit himself to a bureaucratic process. As the exceptional entrepreneur he was becoming, he took his destiny into his own hands, choosing for himself the perfect locale for the post-Durkheimian church he envisioned as a resource for unhooked purpose seekers.

But to say it this way isn't to insinuate that there was no sense of God's movement. Sheler explains, quoting Warren, how the demographical study of the entrepreneur met the leading of God: "One afternoon [Rick] came across a

33. Eugene Peterson, who in many ways was the yin to Rick Warren's yang in the 1980s and 1990s, says prophetically about this type of pastor: "Pastors are subjected to two recurrent phrases from the people to whom they give spiritual leadership. Both are reminiscent of Baalism, enough so as to earn the label 'neo-Baalism.' The phrases are: 'Let's have a worship experience' and 'I don't get anything out of it.'" *Five Smooth Stones for Pastoral Work* (Grand Rapids: Eerdmans, 1992), 183.

report identifying Orange County as the fastest-growing county in the United States, and the fastest-growing part of the county was called Saddleback Valley." Describing the moment years later, Warren said the discovery "grabbed me by the throat and made my heart start racing. I knew that whatever new communities were being started at such a fast pace there would also be a need for new churches. As I sat in the dusty, dimly lit basement of that university library, I heard God speak clearly to me: 'That's where I want you to plant a church!' My whole body began to tingle with excitement, and tears welled up in my eyes. I had heard from God."[34]

By 1980, Saddleback Community Church was founded, having its first official service in the Laguna Hills High School theater. Only forty people showed up, but this was a start. Using direct mail and advertising, Warren began to quickly grow the church. By the very next week, the numbers jumped from 40 to 240. A perfect storm was brewing, a demographic avalanche in a sunny hub of post-Durkheimianism meeting a high-energy pastor with his finger on the pulse of people's unhooked spiritual searching.

By 1982 Saddleback was becoming the resource people wanted. Rick's sermons were shifting more in the direction of spiritual searching, becoming in themselves resources people could use. He was no longer preaching traditional sermons; gone was the form of the Reformers or Edwards. Now in its place were messages like "How to Handle Discouragement," "How to Survive under Stress," "How to Feel Good about Yourself," "How to Stay Calm in a Crisis," and "How to Keep On Keeping On." The "How to" of each message showed the post-Durkheimian attention to individual seeking, offering people resources for their own individual journeys. Never were these presented without Jesus and the Bible. But Jesus became the answer to the *how*, making Jesus one with the rest of the constellation of spiritual options in the nova effect. Warren just wagered that Jesus was the best in the buffet of spiritualities. And it's hard to argue with his results.

In 1992 the church surpassed the five thousand mark. "The secret to Saddleback's growth, Warren would one day write, was in fact no secret at all. From the beginning he had made effective use of direct mail and local-media advertising to promote . . . the church's seeker-sensitive ministries." But more important, Warren insisted, "was the word-of-mouth testimonials of people whose lives had been changed by accepting Christ and through the help they received from the church's various support groups and other Saddleback ministries that attracted newcomers."[35]

34. Sheler, *Prophet of Purpose*, 97.
35. Sheler, *Prophet of Purpose*, 156.

Saddleback had now proven to be the perfect resource for searchers in the age of authenticity. The church you'd now pick, if you picked a church at all, was the church that worked. But unfortunately for the many pastors not as talented as Warren, the only church that would work—that is, giving you help in your individual spiritual pursuits—was the one big enough to possess the resources you needed to feel connected and supported in each and every phase of your life. This made exercise classes as important as Sunday school. By the early 1990s, the creation of massive churches from nothing, by Warren and others, changed the image of the successful pastor from a denominational leader (often people had no sense of what denomination someone like Bill Hybels or Leith Anderson belonged to because it was usually none, as in the case of Hybels) to an entrepreneurial CEO, delivering the resources people could use. The pastor now needed to be able to run a Walmart-style congregation in which each individual could find all the resources necessary in those individual pursuits of meaning and purpose.[36]

By the mid-1990s, "how to find purpose" became a central focus, playing a major part in ballooning the average attendance of Saddleback to over ten thousand. Rick had come up with a practical discipleship strategy back in his youth ministry days. He now fleshed it out further by using the analogy of a baseball diamond, moving from membership (first base) to maturity (second base) to ministry (third base) to mission (home plate). Using this strategy, the church could be purpose driven, not settling for denominational lethargy and the assumptions of neo-Durkheimian significance.

Soon Warren was sharing these strategies at the Saddleback pastors' conference, teaching others who were feeling the impact of post-Durkheimianism how to reinvent their churches beyond denominationalism. Twenty years after its start, more than four hundred thousand pastors from 162 countries were in Warren's Purpose Driven Network. Warren's impact on the image of the pastor and the direction of ministry is unquestionable.

When Rick drove into the Saddleback Valley back in 1980, he repeated a mantra, first to himself and then to anyone who would listen, stating that his goal—his purpose—was to build a church of twenty thousand on

36. Kevin Vanhoozer has some direct words to say about this transition: "Too many pastors have exchanged their vocational birthright for a bowl of lentil stew (Gen. 25:29–34; Heb. 12:16): management skills, strategic plans, 'leadership' courses, therapeutic techniques, and so forth. Congregations expect their pastors to have these qualifications. . . . In these circumstances, it is hardly surprising that newly installed pastors so often complain that their seminaries failed to prepare them for the 'real work' of ministry. Meanwhile, seminaries race to catch up to new expectations, reforming their curricula in ways that result in an even greater loss of theology in the church." Vanhoozer and Owen Strachan, The Pastor as Public Theologian: Reclaiming a Lost Vision (Grand Rapids: Baker Academic, 2015), 1.

fifty acres. This goal directed every step through the 1980s and 1990s. In 2005, the same year that *The Purpose Driven Life* saved Ashley Smith's life, Saddleback celebrated its twenty-fifth year. Angel Stadium in Anaheim was rented out to celebrate. Rick not only met his goal but surpassed it. On just its twenty-fifth anniversary, the post-denominational church started for seekers had reached twenty-two thousand members on a 120-acre campus—which was too small to house everyone for this twenty-fifth anniversary celebration.

It is hard to know what is more impressive, the number of people and acres or the short amount of time. Only in a post-Durkheimian age of authenticity, when disenchantment, inwardness, a buffered self, an affirmation of ordinary life, and a modern moral order has set in, could something so new have such spiritual and religious significance. Only in a secular age that does away with both paleo- and neo-Durkheimianism, making all belief contestable, could a church like Saddleback exist (its size, its non-denominationalism, its seeker emphasis).

## Conclusion to Part 1

This brings our story to completion, and now our work has just begun. Throughout these eight chapters we've told the tale of how divine action has become opaque, adding to Taylor's argument by showing how the pastor was impacting and impacted by these transitions. We've sketched how Augustine, Thomas Becket, Jonathan Edwards, Henry Ward Beecher, Harry Emerson Fosdick, and Rick Warren all played their parts in recasting the pastor in response to the currents of our coming secular age.

We've told this long story to elicit, in the necessary detail, why some pastors, like the one who approached me at the conference, feel loss or have lost their practice. Other than becoming the next Rick Warren or settling for dying denominational forms, they find it difficult to imagine their vocation. Divine action has been pushed to the far edges of our lives and has become unbelievable to most people—maybe even most pastors.

Having now lived in the problem, then, our next step is to cast a new vision for how we can imagine divine action in our secular age. Rick Warren's story may help us move forward. In 1979, Warren said that God spoke to him, telling him that the Saddleback Valley in Orange County was the place to start his church. In the early 1990s, the attention on moving all people into ministry seemed to serve as a catalyst, propelling the congregation to the next level. While almost none of us possess the same skill as or serendipity of Rick Warren, attending to a speaking God who calls us into ministry may be a way to reimagine divine action in our secular age.

In part 2, we'll turn from biography, history, and philosophical genealogy to theology. But as a bridge into this constructive theological work, we'll first turn to Michel Foucault's discussion of pastoral power. Exploring Foucault's famous lectures will help us close out our discussion of the pastoral challenges by placing us on new theological ground. This bridge will shift the primary subject of our discussion, from the pastorate and its challenges in our cultural realm, to God and God's nature as minister. If my contribution above was to place these six pastors in Taylor's story, revealing what our secular age is doing to pastoral practice, then my contribution below, through a dialogue with Foucault, Robert W. Jenson, and Old Testament texts, is to show that God is a minister, and therefore ministry is the form of divine action. Pastoral identity can be regained, then, through hearing, speaking, inviting, and participating in encounters like Paul Kalanithi's.

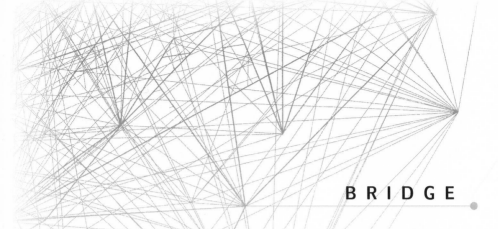

BRIDGE

# winter
# lectures
# in paris

# 9

## Foucault and the rise of pastoral power

On January 11, 1978, a group of students awaited the arrival of one of the world's greatest philosophers, Michel Foucault. This would be the first of thirteen lectures, given every Wednesday, called "Security, Territory, Population." (From their title, these lectures couldn't seem less relevant to our discussion and concerns.) As Foucault walked toward the lecture hall, he carried a reputation matched by almost no one. He was renowned by intellectuals worldwide for his philosophical work on sexuality and punishment. Foucault had become a master of following in the footsteps of his hero, Friedrich Nietzsche. Like Nietzsche, Foucault would mine history for the DNA of our cultural ideas. Not dissimilar to how Charles Taylor uses history to explore how we should understand secularity, so Foucault uses history to examine our conceptions of sex, power, and punishment.

But as Foucault organized his lecture notes and the room fell quiet, preparing for his first words, all that work was behind him. On these Wednesdays he'd explore government, teasing out how we got to the governmental practices to which we concede our lives. And here is the connection to our topic: for Foucault, the shape of governmental power is embedded in the pastoral. He cleared his throat and began the lecture, proceeding to unpack the essential place of pastoral practice in the Western imagination. Stretching back thousands of years, he mined what the pastoral is and where it came from. The esteemed Foucault revealed to his rapt audience over these thirteen weeks of lectures that Western governments were birthed from the pastoral practice. We have the world we do—concerned about law and truth—because of the

153

way pastoral power has shaped our imaginations. Though Western civilization has moved toward a closed spin, blind to divine action—and this was
represented no more clearly than in Paris itself—nevertheless, it was all built
on the foundations of the pastoral.

If we join Foucault's journey to sketch the DNA of Western governmental
power, sitting in class with him for a session or two, we'll get a better sense of
the pastoral, readying us for the theological work necessary in part 2.


## The DNA of the Pastoral

Foucault is no apologist for Christianity. Like Charles Taylor, he's a Franco-
phone living in a post-Catholic milieu (Foucault in Paris, Taylor in Montreal).
But where Taylor is not shy to claim his Catholic commitments, Foucault once
said, "If I were not a total atheist, I would be a monk."[1] Maybe it was this
call of the desert that led him to see things that others missed.

Most often we assume the Greco-Roman world as the birthplace of our
societal and political lives. Athens and Rome gave us democracy, senates, and
public debates, after all. But Foucault thinks this view is a mistake. Rather, the
fundamental DNA of the power of the modern state is in the deserts of the
Mediterranean East. It is not the robed philosopher with his skilled rhetoric
who is central, but the dusty shepherd attentively tending a flock. Deep in the
DNA of our social imaginaries is, not the shadowy figure of a philosopher,
but a shepherd. The kind of power that we are wired to follow, Foucault wants
to show, is not purely rational or logical but pastoral.

I'm tempted to give you paragraphs of examples from the weird phenomenon of American politics. But without space, another TV example will have
to suffice. On the hit HBO show *Veep*, the brilliant Julia Louis-Dreyfus plays
ambitious Selina Meyer. We watch with hilarity as she tries to climb the slip-
pery pole of politics, thinking of only herself and the intoxicating beacon
of the Oval Office. The most humorous scenes are when Selina is forced to
interact with the populace, shaking hands with or hearing stories from normal
people. We know that she cares little for people, but to gain power she must
(clumsily) wield the pastoral, faking concern for every boring Ohio factory
worker she meets. The whole comic engine of the show is built on the juxtaposition of the politician's self-centeredness and the need to be perceived as
pastoral. The humor is in the hypocrisy.

To show why we find this hypocritical, Foucault returns to the desert to find
our cultural origins. Foucault shows that the role of the shepherd was central

---

1. David Macey, *Michel Foucault* (Islington, UK: Reaktion, 2004), 130.

to the people of the desert in the Mediterranean East. These were pastoral societies built on keeping and overseeing sheep and cattle.

Foucault explains that, embedded in this pastoral ethos, the people of the Eastern Mediterranean took a more radical step. For example, Israel uniquely, in contrast to the Greco-Roman world, experienced God as *shepherd*, asserting that divine action itself is ministry. God came to the world not as raiding king or ruler but as a shepherd who acted pastorally, keeping and overseeing his people. It is little wonder that when Israel wanted a king like the other nations, God refused (1 Samuel 8). God reminded them that kings "lord over," and they are but people of a shepherd. A king would corrupt the pastoral and ministerial at the heart of God's own being, which they were to reflect. It is little surprise that when God relented and allowed them a king, the king after God's own heart was a shepherd boy. He was so schooled in the pastoral that he was not even available when, like an ancient-day *America's Got Talent*, the prophet Samuel comes to town. This sense that there is but one God, and that this God is a pastor who ministers, is shockingly unique to the Greco-Roman mind.

On February 8, 1978, a pasty, turtlenecked Foucault walked into the classroom lacking his usual energy and charming demeanor.[2] Nevertheless, with precision he drew out the three elements of pastoral power, connecting them to this shepherd God.

### The Pastor in Motion

Looking vaguely ill, Foucault read from his notes:

> What is it, then, that characterizes this power of the shepherd? . . . What are its specific features? I think we can summarize them in the following way. The shepherd's power is not exercised over a territory but, by definition, over a flock, and more exactly, over the flock in its movement from one place to another. The shepherd's power is essentially exercised over a multiplicity in movement. The Greek god is a territorial god . . . with his privileged place, his town or temple. The Hebrew God, on the other hand, is the God moving from place to place, the God who wanders. The presence of the Hebrew God is never more intense and visible than when his people are on the move, and when, in his people's wanderings, in the movement that takes them from the town, the prairies, and pastures, he goes ahead and shows his people the direction they must follow.[3]

2. I've added a number of dramatic details about Foucault being sick and students' experience of it. This is all speculative and done for the sake of contextualization. However, we do know that Foucault was ill during this lecture. After giving the three points listed here, he says, "Good, listen, I feel lousy. I cannot go into all this, and ask you if we can stop now." Foucault, *Security, Territory, Population: Lectures at the Collège de France* (New York: Picador, 2007), 129.

3. Foucault, *Security, Territory, Population*, 126.

This shepherd God is in motion. When the people are on the move, the shepherd God beckons them to follow. The shepherd God is a leader, directing the people down a new path. It is no wonder, then, that Paul Kalanithi, the neurosurgeon struck with cancer, would be transformed into a pastor. He sees his calling no longer as staying in the territory of disease and cure but as traveling with his patients as they journey for meaning in sickness and hope in the shadow of death.

Foucault wanted his students to see that our view of political power (both ancient and modern) is more pastoral than territorial. Today the politician must speak of a journey, of where she will lead the people. It is out of a desert, or into a new morning, that the politician will take us. Political power, born from the pastoral, is bound not in the space of now but in the vision of what's next, in the idea of who we can be and where we can go.

### The Pastor as Beneficent

Foucault, now flushed and sweating, went on to the second element of pastoral power, explaining to his class that it is a beneficent power. It is charitable and good from top to bottom. Cutting off at the pass his class's criticism, he clarified, "You will say that this is part of all religious, moral, and political descriptions of power. What kind of power would be fundamentally wicked? What kind of power would not have the function, purpose, and justification of doing good?"[4]

Foucault contrasts pastoral power with the Greco-Roman polis, which was only *in part* beneficent. For the Greco-Roman mind, "power is characterized as much by its omnipotence, and by the wealth and splendor of the symbols with which it clothes itself, as by its beneficence. Power is defined by its ability to triumph over enemies, defeat them, and reduce them to slavery. Power is also defined by the possibility of conquest and by the territories, wealth, and so on it has accumulated. Beneficence is only one of a whole bundle of features by which power is defined."[5]

But not so with the shepherd God of Israel. This God, in both act and being, is a pastoring shepherd. Beneficence—generosity and goodness—makes up every molecule of Yahweh's being. This God is mighty because this God is good. And this God is good because this God is inextricably a pastor, coming to the world as minister. Care for the poor and weak is the continued refrain of the prophets, because the prophet is to point out where the political power of Israel has departed from the pastoral by seeking its own strength over the

4. Foucault, *Security, Territory, Population*, 126.
5. Foucault, *Security, Territory, Population*, 126.

benefit of the weak (making them like all other nations). When the weak are cared for, the society is most fully living out of the pastoral—most directly obeying the shepherd God. Prophets call the king to be obedient to Yahweh and his law. The king is to exercise his own power only and finally as a pastor, charitably leading his people to still waters.

The class (now sure Foucault is running a fever) listens as he explains how state power, because of its pastoral DNA, gets caught in many conundrums. Applying Foucault's point to American history reveals the difficulty of this—the United States must defend itself and its interests, but only by being beneficent. This becomes very tricky and demands loads of spin. To give an unambiguous example, the war against Hitler was right from beginning to end because Hitler threw off all duty of beneficence and, with little guise, modeled his power completely on the Greco-Roman conception.[6] It was German atrocities in both World War I and World War II that led a reluctant America to enter the European theaters of both wars. Watching a nation wield its power for a reason *other than* beneficence was enough to sacrifice soldiers to the fight.[7] Americans wanted no booty or land, just to make the world safe for the pastoral power of democracy. The European theater of World War II can be seen as a fight between pastoral and Greco-Roman political power.

To give Foucault's ideas a contemporary example, think of the phrase "drain the swamp," which suggests that some people think the powerful of Washington have been more loyal to victory, wealth, and territory than to the beneficence of the people.[8] Pastoral power is the power of care; the shepherd is responsible to feed the flock. If we're going to spend trillions on defense, it must be justified as being used not for the sake of wealth and territory but for safety. We feel the clash of a culture war because the colliding sides both operate from hidden pastoral power. Both sides hold that the politician's responsibility is to care for the people. The clash comes in whether that means

6. This is a sometimes overstated but nevertheless present connection between Friedrich Nietzsche and the Nazis. It is assumed that Nietzsche's return to Greco-Roman power inspired the Nazis. While often overstated—some claiming that Nietzsche is responsible from his grave for National Socialism—it is true that the Nazis admired Nietzsche and through him sought to mobilize a world without pastoral power, solely in the foundation of Greco-Roman force.

7. The greater motivation for entering WWII was the bombing of Pearl Harbor. This secret attack on American soil was a violation of our own territory (remembering that Foucault is discussing territory), but its real ethical atrocity was that it was a sneak attack with no concern for people, even the Japanese soldiers who killed themselves as kamikazes. This all seemed outside pastoral power.

8. Foucault says it this way: "This is precisely the difference between the good and the bad shepherd. The bad shepherd only thinks of good pastures for his own profit, for fattening the flock that he will be able to sell and scatter, whereas the good shepherd thinks only of his flock and nothing else." *Security, Territory, Population*, 128.

protecting them from hardcore terrorists or from hunger. For some, caring for the people means slaying the lion that would bloody the sheep, and for others, it means being led to green pastures to receive full stomachs.

Beneficence reveals that the "essential objective of pastoral power is salvation of the flock."[9] This shepherd God calls to the people to come (to move) to him, to leave all else behind and find their rest in him. He invites them to be his flock so that they might share in his goodness and receive his gifts. This God who is a shepherd has his being in becoming (as Eberhard Jüngel has said and we'll develop below) because his desire is to be a pastor to a flock. God longs to give them salvation, which is the goodness of his own being, by keeping watch over them and directing them further and further into the goodness of his love.

Foucault concludes this second point by mentioning a rabbinic commentary that claims that Moses was called to lead the Hebrews out of Egypt because he was a shepherd (and I would add, a lowly, powerless one at that). Not coincidentally, it was when seeking for a lost sheep, for the beneficence of the lost little one, that Moses stumbled into a bush that burned but was not consumed. Here God told Moses his name: I am who I'm becoming, I'm the one who moves (acts as minister). I will come to my people as their shepherd. You will know me as a ministering pastor who leads you from the toil of Egypt to a new land of milk and honey.

The rabbinic commentary put these words in the mouth of the God who is a pastor: "Since you [Moses] know how to pity the sheep, you will have pity for my people, and I will entrust them to you."[10] Moses was called because, as a broken man in a far country, he had learned to be a shepherd—and thus to do ministry. He received God's name because he had learned to minister to the sheep.

### The Pastor Cares for the One as Well as the Many

Every sentence now seems strained. As Foucault pauses before his third point, some students wonder if he'll be able to continue—only the most daft among them are unaware that the flu has struck their professor. But his third point needs to be made. So, gathering his strength, he continues, explaining that "pastoral power is an individualizing power."[11] This is not to say that it is not collective, even communal. The shepherd oversees the whole flock. It

9. Foucault, *Security, Territory, Population*, 126.
10. J. Engemann, "Hirt," in *Reallexikon für Antike und Christentum* (Stuttgart, Germany: Hiersemann, 1935), quoted in Foucault, *Security, Territory, Population*, 127.
11. Foucault, *Security, Territory, Population*, 128.

is Israel that is precious to God's heart. It is only the flock that the shepherd is leading; only through community can you be led by the shepherd God. There is no singularly individual path, no sense that every sheep is loose to find its own way to water. The voice of the shepherd comes to the whole, for the whole's benefit.

But with that said, what drives the shepherd God is not the economics of possession. The shepherd does not do a cost-benefit analysis and decide that it is not worth losing the entire flock for one lost sheep. That "pastoral power is individualizing power" means, rather, that the shepherd understands that each sheep is under his care, and therefore when it needs finding, he must be willing to risk all in search for the lost one. Lost ones matter to this pastoral God. To steal a line from John Caputo's *The Weakness of God*, this shepherd God's math goes like this: $1 > 99$. As we said above, Moses is looking for a lost sheep when he encounters the bush that burns but is not consumed. The shepherd God, who is a minister, reveals his act and being most directly in the Old Testament not as a king or ruler but as a shepherd looking to pastor lonely sheep.[12]

Foucault's point, as he suffers under his fever, is that only from the desert, from the logic of the shepherd, would we assume that it is the politician's responsibility to care for all people, seeing each one as worth attention and not just as a cog in the machine of territorial possession and expansion. If you need an illustration of a society devoid of pastoral power, in which people are but parts in a machine, watch the beginning of *Mad Max: Fury Road*. Or think of Negan's Saviors on *The Walking Dead*. These stories of post-apocalyptic societies imagine what would be if the institutions that Foucault believes carry the DNA of the pastoral were lost. Season 7 of *The Walking Dead* can be interpreted as a fight between pastoral and Greco-Roman power. It contrasts Rick's crew, building a society and sacrificing for the care of others, with Negan's will to power that smashes distinct personhood and demands total allegiance. Negan's people even lose their names for the sake of security, territory, and advance (everyone is Negan, saying when asked, "I'm Negan").

In Greco-Roman power, the people owed everything to the ruler. Caesar was owed complete and unquestioned devotion. Not so for the shepherd. From

12. Owen Strachan adds, "The kings of ancient Israel were to rule not with an iron fist, or by way of overbearing authority, or by consulting only the oracles of their own mind. They were to be kings of a different kind. They would become great by embracing humility, discernment, and wisdom. The Israelite king was in reality an 'under-king,' one who ruled only by the gracious calling and provision of Yahweh. The monarchical leader of God's people was not high and mighty, but lowly and meek, charged with modeling these attributes to the people." Kevin Vanhoozer and Owen Strachan, *The Pastor as Public Theologian: Reclaiming a Lost Vision* (Grand Rapids: Baker Academic, 2015), 52.

the desert, this was reversed: instead of the people owing the ruler everything, "the shepherd owes everything to his flock."[13] The modern politician shouts, "I work for you. I'm up at 5 o'clock in the morning fighting for the people of my district!" Our suspicion is that he fights for reelection, not for our needs. But if he wants reelection, he must wrap himself in the cloak of pastoral power and proclaim that he owes us his time and energy. The pastor is accountable to care for his people. Period.

With his last bit of strength, Foucault reminds his class that pastoral power is always risky, even precarious. And this is so because it has a vision of salvation. Salvation is to be reunited with the care of the shepherd—the sheep has been saved, for the shepherd who loves it has found it. And it is only the shepherd, never the sheep, who goes looking. The shepherd searches, sacrificing safety and power, navigating the trails and passes that could bring the perils of beast or bandit.[14]

### Cultic versus Service and Pastoral Power

After a short summary, Foucault is cooked, saying to the class, "Good, listen, I feel really lousy. I cannot go into all this, and ask you if we can stop now. I really am too tired."[15] Foucault may be exhausted and feeling not at his best, but this lecture has done us a great service. It has given us a sense of the theological lifting we'll have to do in part 2. Most specifically, it has articulated how ministry must again become a central category for us to think about divine action—but now in our secular age. We'll explore how our secular age itself opens up new skylights to divine action through the pastoral or ministerial—but of course this must be deeply reimagined. This will help us recognize, again returning to the introduction, why Kalanithi became a pastoral surgeon and the abandoned-young-man-turned-minister experienced the ministry of a pastoral song caring for him when he was lost in self-hatred and anger.

Yet before we can move on, we need to deal with the rest of Foucault's story. When the flu is gone, Foucault will return to show how Christianity

13. Foucault, *Security, Territory, Population*, 128.

14. Kenneth Bailey draws us a picture of sheep and need for a shepherd: "Sheep have a special problem. They have no defenses. Cats have teeth, claws and speed. Dogs have their teeth and their speed. Horses can kick, bite and run. Bears can claw, bite and crush. Deer can run. But the sheep have no bite or claws and cannot outrun any serious predator. They can butt other sheep, but that ability will not protect them from a wolf or a bear. The sheep's only security is the shepherd. Indeed, 'you are with me.'" *The Good Shepherd: A Thousand-Year Journey from Psalm 23 to the New Testament* (Downers Grove, IL: InterVarsity, 2014), 49.

15. Foucault, *Security, Territory, Population*, 129.

does something very unique with the pastoral commitments of the Hebrews. Foucault's last words before succumbing to chicken soup and a nap reveal where he'll be going when he returns: "The sacrifice of one for all, and the sacrifice of all for one . . . will be at the absolute heart of Christian[ity]."[16] This sense of pastoral sacrifice, Foucault shows, became a distinct obsession of Western Christianity.

Western Christianity intensifies the importance of pastoral power by seeing Jesus through the sacrifice of the cross (Eastern Christianity does something different, focusing on resurrection, bending it more toward the mystical and therefore connecting the church less with political power and reform).[17] Both the East and the West saw Jesus as the fulfillment of the pastoral, revealing that he is the fullness of the shepherd God—the true good shepherd. Jesus is on the move, bound by no territory (not even death); he claims that he can tear down the stones of the temple and build it again in his body (John 2:19), and he gives his Spirit to his followers so their bodies too might be a temple of the Holy Spirit (1 Cor. 6:19). Jesus is beneficent, no longer calling us servants (John 15), but instead calling us friends whom he will serve, dying so that we all (both collectively and individually) might live (2 Cor. 5:15).

Foucault points out that the Hebrews have a pastoring God but no pastors. They have priests who manage divine things (offering sacrifices in the stone temple) and rabbis who teach the law. But only Christianity, Foucault claims, has human agents who pastor, embodying the shepherd God by reenacting the drama of sacrifice in their bodies (by breaking the bread, ministering to the sick, etc.).

Western Christianity vibrantly affirms that from the sacrifice of one comes salvation for all. This led to a heightened view of the pastor, leading to abuse of the role. Attention to sacrifice moved medieval Christianity to lock the pastoral into the cultic, seeing *things* as the location of divine action. Priests dispensed the pastoral where it was needed through cultic activities like the Mass, which sought to elevate all to the holy.

The Mass was the reenactment (the actual reexperiencing) of Jesus's cosmic sacrifice. The rites and ceremonies themselves possessed the power of the pastoral—making people think that they were magical, for these pastoral acts directly delivered the divine being. The host, Thomas Becket's blood,

16. Foucault, *Security, Territory, Population*, 129.

17. Not surprisingly, Western Christianity has a long legacy of connection with the political (both in opposition and support), while the East does not. The sacrificial has also given the West a reforming spirit that has been missing in the East, allowing, for example, the metropolitan of Moscow to be good friends with Vladimir Putin—without any sense that the church must reform corrupt political systems.

or church keys mediated by the pastor brought encounter with the being of God. It was the priest's job to distribute these holy things, giving the priest the power to give or take away the pastoral.

Before the Reformation, the pastoral was linked—some might even say fused—with cultic *things*. The pastoral was found solely locked within the holy words of the priest and the things he controlled. The weight of responsibility that pressed on the pastor was on the *things*. The cultic things possessed the ontological weight of divine being, and therefore the priest needed to be protected and honored. When the priest gave the host, he gave the warrior or peasant *God himself*, the *real* sacrificed body of Jesus.

The Reformation radically separated the pastoral from the cultic, freeing God from *things*.[18] But it did not minimize sacrifice. Rather, in a new way, the Reformation loaded sacrifice onto service. After the Reformation, the pastor was to serve the people by prodding them to see how their ordinary lives bore divine consequence. Through pastoral leadership, he was to encourage each sheep to reach the devotion of the priest. This kind of service would call for a whole different sense of pastoral responsibility.[19] The burden for the pastor

18. This is a helpful historical overview of the use of terms. It doesn't change Foucault's larger point about the pastoral, but it is helpful to understand the use of descriptors. Wilhelm Pauck says,

> In this connection, we must mention that the Reformers customarily spoke of the minister as pastor (shepherd, in relation to certain New Testament passages, e.g., John 10:2 and 10:16; Heb. 13:20; 1 Peter 2:25), but they called him most frequently "preacher" (*Prediger* or *Praedikant*). The term "pastor" came into general use only during the eighteenth century under the influence of Pietism, especially in Lutheranism. The German Reformers also adhered to the medieval usage and called the preacher *Pfarrer*, i.e., parson (derived from *parochia*—parish, and *parochus*—parson). The common people most generally called the ministers "preachers," but they also continued to use the terms to which they had been accustomed under Roman Catholicism, i.e., "priests," et cetera. This was natural in view of the gradual transition from the old order to the new. In certain regions, basic structures relating to the organization of the parishes and to the polity of the church developed by Roman Catholicism were preserved in the changeover to the Reformation, not only in certain parts of Germany, but chiefly in the Scandinavian countries, especially Sweden, not to speak of England. Here, the old names and tides of the ministerial office were naturally retained. The term "minister" was gradually introduced into English-speaking countries by the Nonconformists and Dissenters. Dependent upon Calvinism, they distinguished the Protestant "ministry" from the Anglican "clergy." ("The Ministry in the Time of Continental Reformation," in H. Richard Niebuhr and Daniel Williams, eds., *The Ministry in Historical Perspective* [New York: Harper & Brothers, 1956], 116)

19. "The Reformation as well as the Counter Reformation gave the religious pastorate much greater control. . . . The pastorate had never before intervened so much, had never had such a hold on the material, temporal, everyday life of individuals; it takes charge of a whole series of questions and problems concerning material life, property, and the education of children. So, there is an intensification of the religious pastorate in its spiritual dimensions and in its temporal extensions." Foucault, *Security, Territory, Population*, 230.

was no longer on handling divinely charged things but in prodding minds, through serving them, to seek God.

The burden (or joy) of the pastor's responsibility then shifted from things (and their ontological impact) to consent.[20] Now the pastor's job was to serve each person so that they might consent to an epistemological shift, raising their commitment to the level of God's plan. At its worst, the care of the pastor could be used as a device to win consent, the pastoral care given to win commitment.

This dark side was possible because the pastor's job from the Calvinist Reformation forward was to help people *will* to be saved, moral, and pious. Pastoral power was bound in epistemological consent rather than ontological encounter. Foucault states, "The pastor must not simply teach the truth. He must direct the conscience."[21] When the pastor prods people for commitment instead of handling holy things—seeing his core practice as preaching to minds as opposed to giving the actual sacrificed body of Jesus in bread—it is only logical that concern would shift from encounters with being to what people know. The move of the pastoral from the cultic to service had the effect of elevating epistemology over ontology.[22]

As the secular age dawns and the world is disenchanted and depersonalized, we begin to doubt the possibility of encountering divine being. Or at the very least, when epistemology becomes overly inflated, divine action becomes very difficult to imagine as something more than what our minds consent to. When service is chained to an overcommitment to epistemology, the temptation is for the pastor to focus on either foundationalism (biblical inerrancy, doctrinal purity, moralism) or politics (a *kind* of social justice without an eschatological horizon).

Both options are based in service. The pastor serves her people by helping them *know how* to read the Bible correctly, or the pastor serves his people by raising their consciousness so that they might *know how* the system oppresses. Both strategies, while at one level helpful, often concede to an overinflation of epistemology and the loss of ontology. Often neither can speak directly about

20. It is not that consent is foreign to Christianity. Rather, Larry Siedentop shows that Paul is doing something very different by focusing on will. In the modern era, consent is distinguished from collective or communal will. "Paul creates a new basis for human association, a voluntary basis—joining humans through loving wills guided by an equal belief. . . . Love creates what Paul calls a mystical union in the 'body of Christ.' The metaphor conveys what, in his eyes, is distinctive about Christian association. An unseen bond of wills joined by conscience identifies this mystical body, distinguishing it from associations founded on birth, gender or social status. Human agency acquires a new independence and dignity." *Inventing the Individual: The Origins of Western Liberalism* (Cambridge, MA: Belknap Press, 2014), 62–63.

21. Foucault, *Security, Territory, Population*, 181.

22. This shift would allow for the obsession of Western philosophy to concern itself with epistemology. Descartes moved the West in this direction.

how *human* beings encounter the *real* being of the shepherd God. In other words, both have a hard time with divine action; this is part of the legacy of shifting pastoral power from the cultic (and its heavy ontology) to service. In part 1, I told the story of how things like cultic sacrifice and magic became downgraded. This was never to disparage these realities, but only to describe the world we now live in.

In part 2, we'll do the important work of exploring whether it is possible in this world that we inherit to keep the pastoral on the footing of service and yet connect it to the ontological. It appears that in our secular age there is no way back to the cultic imaginations of Becket's time—there is no way for us to live again with belief that things are haunted or holy or that the natural world is just a direct reflection of God's design. But without some way of imagining ontological encounter with the being of the shepherd God, belief, transformation, and even grace itself are washed away.[23] We are left with a shell of the pastoral. Working from within the shell, the pastor feels all the expectations of pastoral power (thanks to the history that Foucault has traced) but with no direct connection to the pastoral being of God. The pastor is easily frustrated in our secular age, because while pastoral expectations remain, the connection to divine action is severed, making it hard for her to know how pastoral service is any different from any other helping profession (which, Foucault argues, also inherited the pastoral).[24] The truth is that without attention to divine action, it isn't different.

23. Paul Bernier give some more context to the place of the cultic, giving us hope that in part 2 we can reimagine service outside the cultic and yet hold to the ontological: "Challenging our tendency to associate Christ's ministry with only 'the sacrifice of the cross,' and to see it mainly in cultic terms, is the fact that one of the most striking features of the early Christian decades is their strongly a-cultic character. We begin to see an active and reflexive cult only in the middle of the second century; the earliest decades of the church are not characterized by an institutionalized ritual of worship. This has unavoidable implications for our study of ministry in these decades. It makes it difficult to maintain that cultic functions were central to Christian ministry in the primitive church." *Ministry in the Church: A Historical and Pastoral Approach* (Eugene, OR: Wipf & Stock, 1992), 13.

24. Here Charles Taylor points to two things central to our discussion: (1) how the early church too was centered on service, making it impossible for us to get back to service without flattening ontology, and (2) how the pastoral (as Foucault discusses it) has been distributed beyond the church, leaving the pastor with confusion on what kind of service to provide. "Scholars agree that the Christian church which arose in the ancient world was a new kind of religious association, that it created around itself new 'service' institutions, like hospitals and hospices for the needy. It was heavily engaged in the practical works of charity. This kind of activity remained important throughout the long centuries of Christendom, until in the modern era, these institutions have been taken over by secular bodies, often by governments. Seen within the history of Western civilization, the present-day welfare state can be understood as the long-term heir to the early Christian church." *A Secular Age* (Cambridge, MA: Belknap Press, 2007), 737.

## The Rub of Expectations

On February 22, just two weeks after the chills got the most of Foucault, he explained to his class how Christianity, right after the Reformation in Western Europe, added four elements to pastoral power.[25] These four elements became central to the Protestant pastoral imaginary, and without attention to divine action, can breed only frustration or embarrassment in the pastor.

### Analytic Responsibility

Foucault jumps into this lecture by tackling responsibility. "First there is the principle of what I will call *analytical responsibility. That is to say, at* the end of the day, at the end of life in the world . . . the Christian pastor, will . . . have to account for every sheep. A numerical and individual distribution will make it possible to know if he really has concerned himself with every one of his sheep."[26] Foucault's point is that each sheep needs to be counted; it is the pastor's job to know where every sheep is, aware of those who are saved and those who are lost. It is the pastor's responsibility to locate each sheep, the pastor's job to be in your business, deciding if you are saved or lost. The pastor does this not to torture the sheep but because it is his responsibility: "any missing sheep will be counted *against him.*"[27]

If the Protestant pastor is to serve and sacrifice for the sheep, he must know where they are and what they are up to. Today, pastors can still feel this pull of responsibility but are aware that in most middle-class settings it isn't welcome. Our modern moral order asserts that it is wrong to judge anyone. Living in the age of authenticity, where each of us gets to name for ourselves what it means to be human, judgment becomes anathema. The pastor somehow is to bear analytical responsibility, but without ever laying judgment. This is a tension that seems unresolvable.

### Exhaustive and Instantaneous Transfer

Continuing, Foucault adds, "The second principle, which is also completely specific to Christianity, I will call the principle of *exhaustive and instantaneous transfer.*"[28] Building on the first principle, Foucault explains that pastors need

25. Throughout this lecture Foucault explains that he's leaning on post-Reformation thought, but he makes no real distinction between Protestant and Catholic pastors, using more analogies from pre-Reformation periods. I believe these principles are heightened by Protestantism and make more sense inside its arrival and changes.

26. Foucault, *Security, Territory, Population*, 169 (emphasis added).

27. Foucault, *Security, Territory, Population*, 169 (emphasis added).

28. Foucault, *Security, Territory, Population*, 170 (emphasis added).

to locate each sheep, getting in your business to see whether you are lost or loyal (becoming familiar with your actions, attitudes, and behaviors) because the pastor must see "every merit or fault, as his own act. . . . This is the principle of the exhaustive and instantaneous transfer to the pastor of the merits and faults of the sheep."[29] This is intense! The pastor is not only concerned that you use your ordinary life to glorify God for *your* own good; if you refuse, choosing drink or money over God, it is also a mark against the *pastor*. The pastor has failed to shepherd the sheep, because they are scattered. The Protestant pastor is to serve the sheep, and if he fails, it is as much on the pastor as the sheep. It is not enough for the sheep to simply partake in the cultic, ingesting the host and being blanketed by divine action. Rather, every part of the sheep's ordinary life must bear the marks of heaven. And it is the pastor's job to serve the sheep so that this might be.

It is little wonder that pastors can feel a dark powerlessness that chases them into depression. They somehow have to be aware of the inner life of each person, but without making judgments. But powerless to say much, the pastor has the people's commitment (or lack thereof) transferred to him. It can feel like a powerless sandwich to be stuck between analytic responsibility and exhaustive and instantaneous transfer.

### Alternate Correspondence

The third principle builds on this transfer of merit. Foucault calls it *alternate correspondence*. "If in fact it is true that the sheep's merit constitutes the shepherd's merit, then can we not also say that the shepherd's merit would not amount to much if all the sheep were always perfectly worthy of merit? Is not the shepherd's merit due, at least in part, to the sheep being recalcitrant, exposed to danger, and always about to fall?"[30] Jonathan Edwards reminded his people that they were but sinners in the hands of an angry God, that their souls were indeed in danger. It is the pastor's job to remind her people again and again that there are wolves in the woods. It becomes a classic mark of the Protestant pastor, and one that Henry Ward Beecher rejects, to serve the people by reminding them of the spiritual danger they face. But if God is only a benign pal (who doesn't act), a logo or idea, and each of us is OK to do with our lives what we want, then what dangers do we face? And why would a pastor's service matter? The dangers we face are no longer spiritual; demons and divine consequence have been extracted from our lives. The only perils we face that need the pastoral (and of course this is an illusion) are

29. Foucault, *Security, Territory, Population*, 170.
30. Foucault, *Security, Territory, Population*, 171.

economic or self-help—finding our best self or the right parenting practice. Rick Warren has built a huge church making purpose (and lack of it) the alternate correspondence. He tells his people not that there are demons and judgment nipping at their heels but, more ominous for the modern person, of the threat of a purposeless life.

### Sacrificial Reversal

The fourth and final principle of responsibility, Foucault says, "is that of *sacrificial reversal*, which is once again completely specific to the Christian pastorate."[31] If the three other principles seem to set the pastor apart, this one does the opposite. The pastor locates and evaluates the sheep because he is ready to die for them. Or to say it less dramatically, it is not to lord over them that moves the pastor to locate and evaluate, but to minister to and care for them. The pastor seeks to give them protection from the wolves that circle. And this care comes not from a pedestal but from being one of the sheep, from being lost just like the rest of the flock. The pastor is no better than her people; she is one of them, once lost but now found. The pastor stands in a difficult place, only because she needs to be both one of her people and yet also different from them. This difference is not in consecrated being but in hearing a call to serve and sacrifice for the sheep. The pastor is to remind the sheep through testimony that she too was lost, was scarred by wolves, but is now found by the same shepherd God that calls to them.[32]

### Summarizing These Four Principles

It is no wonder that to most pastors, pastoral power feels like wearing clothes from college; they are so familiar and yet don't quite fit. Whether coming from her people or herself, the currents of pastoral power still are present (its location in our political imaginary is a stark witness). Somehow, the pastor is still supposed to care for each person in his congregation, counting, warning, and sacrificing for them, and yet never without simultaneously being one of them. Most contemporary pastors are stuck between Edwards and Beecher, not sure how to negotiate pastoral power. Edwards was a master of counting, warning, and sacrificing for his people. Beecher was epic at being

---

31. Foucault, *Security, Territory, Population*, 170 (emphasis added).

32. "It is good, then, for the pastor to have imperfections, to know them, and not to hide them hypocritically from his faithful. . . . Consequently, just as on one side the pastor's merit and salvation are due to the weaknesses of his sheep, so too the pastor's faults and weaknesses contribute to the edification of his sheep and are part of the movement, the process, of guiding them towards salvation." Foucault, *Security, Territory, Population*, 172.

one of them. Beecher realized that as divine action became more opaque in the nineteenth century, the only way for pastoral power to have coherence was to focus solely on being one of them.

In our day all pastors have to negotiate pastoral power without a shared sense of divine action. It is no longer clear why you'd exercise pastoral power. Yet, strangely, people seem to still welcome it—maybe because it echoes back to them from the political. But for whatever reason, it isn't rare for pastors and their pastoral power to be called on after tragedy or before remembrance (just think of 9/11 and 9/11 memorials). But the role's connection to divine action is much harder to name and claim.

Other than these times of civic religion, why would a pastor count, warn, sacrifice, and be one of the people? The direct connection to the divine action of a ministering God seems severed. Instead, if we're going to exercise such power, it is for something very different from encounter with divine action. We exercise pastoral power to build a twenty-thousand-person church on 120 acres, like Warren, or to lead a march of thousands for justice in Washington.

In great irony, our secular age has made it so that pastoral power has coherence only within the immanent frame itself. Pastors feel embarrassed, or like raging fundamentalists, to exercise the pastoral for the sake of encountering the shepherd God, claiming that pastors count, warn, and sacrifice for the sake of divine action. Instead, pastoral power is only laudable when it is used to build movements through huge churches or popular blogs and books. When the immanent frame makes divine action opaque, the pastor is always tempted to press the clay of her identity around the mold of business leader or political activist. But this only leaves most pastors—those who can't build large churches or organize significant movements—frustrated, not sure what they are doing. Our secular age has kept pastoral power intact but cut it off from divine action, giving the pastor tacit, and for some a tangible taste of, confusion.

## Moving Forward

So how then does the pastor serve in this secular age? How can we find divine action—encountering its ontological impact—in and through service? At this point, the longing may be for a new profile. Who is the ideal pastor for the secular age? The temptation in moving into part 2 is to provide a profile of the pastor that follows the Warren type, continuing our progression of archetypes. The temptation might be now, as in a Madden football video game, to "make" a pastor, scaling the attributes and skills necessitated by the secular age and building the ideal. But this would avoid the source of the malaise, which is the opaqueness of divine action. We must speak of God's being in and through God's action in order to have something to talk about in a pastor's identity and function in this age. People find it impractical to talk about God, but the only way to get to something practical is to talk about God.

This doesn't mean that I won't have direct things to say about what a pastor can do in our secular age. Through theological discussion on God's action I'll make important points on what pastors do and why they are still needed. Yet my overall hope is to show that this need is based not in culture or nostalgia but on divine action itself. And this is because the shape of divine action reveals that God *is* a minister. Therefore pastoral service, framed biblically, can return the pastor to divine action, because to be in ministry is less about certain skills or personality characteristics and more about joining the action of God, which brings us into encounter with the being of God.

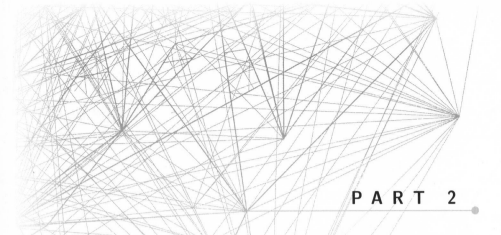

PART 2

# the God who is a ministering pastor

# 10

## the weird God of Israel who arrives

We started this book with two people. Even before introducing the first of our many pastors and the ideas of Charles Taylor, I introduced a talented young man dying of cancer and an old man bearing the marks of exclusion. The young man was a pastoral physician; the old man was a retired pastor. These are two people living in a secular age, in a time when divine action is opaque, who nevertheless confess a real encounter with the presence of God.

Paul Kalanithi, the talented neurosurgeon, in a crude irony is dying of a brain tumor, and yet he finds something profound. In embracing his own experience of dying, he discovers something that he was not taught at Yale Medical School: how near God is when we minister to another out of weakness, how the closed spin of the immanent is made wide when we become a minister.

The old man also encounters the concrete presence of the living God. Years before age sets in, like Israel in the desert he blames God for his exclusion, readying himself to end his life. In the heavy quiet, as the dark abyss of his suicide approaches, a song breaks the silence. This is not simply an inner religious experience—it's too real, happening directly on the plane of his own history. Someone, *some person*, is behind him, he assumes. Yet he can see no one. But again the song comes, a personal force meeting him with words. This is enough to send him from death into new life.

Now an old man, having lived his life out of the event of this personal force coming to him, he discovers that these words spoken to him by God were the very chorus of his beloved nanny. When he was but an infant so long ago, she became his minister, embracing his broken person. The song was the timeless sound of her love mediating the presence of God. On that hill, when he cried out like an Old Testament prophet, accusing God of abandoning him, it is in this song of ministry that God spoke to him. *It was I who led you out of Egypt. It was I that sent to you a scared girl to minister to you. It was I who sang you a song of love from her lips.* Somehow, ministry seems to move fluidly across time and space, while remaining always personal (always mediating an encounter with personhood). The old man is shocked when he discovers that it was his nanny's song that he heard God speak. The ministry to an infant reached forward to a suicidal young man and then formed the life of a pastor.

In both these people's lives, not only is divine action present as they live in a secular age, but God's action comes to them as ministry (as a sharing in the personhood of another, like Ananias and Paul, as we discussed in volume 1). Ministry seems to have a mystical power (in cruciform shape) that is nevertheless historical; it seems to move fluidly across time and space. Because it does, it turns death into life. But how can this be?

It's possible that the act of ministry can do this because it correlates with God's own being. It can give a dying person mercy, a calling. For another, a song of ministry can be the known and unknown tissue of life. This kind of action constitutes the fullness of God. In other words, what makes God God is the action of ministry. These actions reveal the very being of God. Even over and against the closed spin of the secular, the pastor is never far from divine action if the focus is on ministry, as we'll explore below.

Michel Foucault has argued from the level of political theory that Israel, and then Christianity, experiences God uniquely as a shepherd. Other Eastern Mediterranean people imagined their rulers as shepherds (as compared to the Greco-Roman world), but only Israel saw their God as a shepherd in act and being, as the God who acts in history with the Word that gives God's own being to God's people. This shepherd is a minister, traveling with his sheep, caring for every need of his sheep. To call God shepherd is to presume that God is a minister, and to say God is a minister is to say that ministry is the constituting reality of God's being, given to the world through God's action. *Then we know God through actions of ministry.* It is in this kind of action that both of these men experienced the living God.

Therefore, we'll have to explore whether it is possible to imagine God's being through the act of ministry. If it is, then we'll have a helpful way of imagining divine action in our secular age of disenchantment, buffered selves, new moral orders, and post-Durkheimianism. We will see divine action as the event of ministry. If we can broaden or, better, deepen our conception of ministry,[1] shaking it loose from a clerical operation to constituting it as the state of God's own being that we are invited to share in, we may find new ways of helping our people recognize, claim, and participate in God's being, even, or most particularly, in a secular age.[2]

## Story of Your Life

*Time Flies When You're Alive* is a little-known one-man play by Paul Linke that explores his wife's battle with breast cancer. Most of the play revolves around Linke's homily at his now-dead wife's funeral, this experience of loss somehow bending time. The play had moderate success but mostly ran to small rooms. Yet one night, in one of those small rooms, sat the science fiction writer Ted Chiang. This little-known play inspired Chiang to write a novella called *Story of Your Life* that would win him awards. In 2016 it was made into an Oscar-nominated movie starring Amy Adams and Jeremy Renner called *Arrival*. Linke's play was about time, regret, and the shape of our lives. Chiang wondered how this all worked, and particularly how language and words shape our experience of reality.

Charles Taylor has reminded us that we once lived in a world where apocalyptic *events* were anticipated and assumed. Happenings that would shake all we knew were ever present; strange raiders with new gods, prophets with new omens, and voyagers meeting new worlds were familiar and expected. The puncturing of history with a new event was laced within our ancient ancestors' plausibility structure. Not so much for us. Our loss of historical

1. This quote by Eric Gritsch and Robert W. Jenson shows how complicated "ministry" is to comprehend. I use "ministry" to refer to the "common ministry," though I'll continue to address the impact of this common (theologically infused) ministry on "special" ministry. Gritsch and Jenson say, "There is, then, a 'common' ministry, exercised by all who are baptized, and a 'special' ministry, carried out by those who are called to the public office of the word. In his theological battle with Rome, Luther stressed the common ministry; in his controversy with the 'leftwingers' of the Reformation, he emphasized the special ministry." *Lutheranism: The Theological Movement and Its Confessional Writing* (Philadelphia: Fortress, 1976), 111.

2. There is significant debate about whether ministry is an office or a function. Many trace this slippage back to the Reformation. John N. Collins says, "In particular, within the Lutheran tradition, the question of ministry was never satisfactorily resolved. A tension has remained from the beginning, and has expressed itself within different churches at different periods, as to whether ministry is an office as such or whether it is a function confided to some in the church for the purposes of good order." *Diakonia Studies: Critical Issues in Ministry* (London: Oxford University Press, 2014), 121. I suppose I'm susceptible to this slippage, particularly with regard to forms of ministry based in human action. Yet I'm also trying something different, seeking to first locate ministry in the act and being of God, therefore placing it more in the function category of human action—not for ecclesial or political purpose but because it is the shape of divine action.

perspective, coupled with the relative strength of our institutions and tech-nological abilities, leads our maybe-growing apocalyptic itch to be scratched and distanced by all those dystopian TV shows.

Yet if there is an event that could shake us to our core, a single arrival that could melt our institutions, stripping us naked to face an unimagined and unprepared future, it is the arrival of aliens. It is the perfect immanent frame–bound nightmare, which is why a high percentage of our alien-arrival stories play out with a battle for earth and ensuing warfare. These stories reveal that something in us is still open to the event-full (the events that are so full of meaning that they change our sense of the world and our very existence). Locked in the immanent frame and stuck in a flat but massive universe, we have a hard time imagining the arrival of angels or demons, but highly technologically advanced space travelers in shiny ships is plausible.

So it's on this canvas that Chiang paints his sci-fi masterpiece, avoiding all of the common tropes of explosions, gunfire, and Will Smith. Instead of a military hotshot, the protagonist of Chiang's story is a linguistics professor named Louise Banks. Banks narrates Chiang's story. In the movie, the receiver of this narration is not primarily the audience but Banks's daughter, who, like Linke's wife, is dying. But the time jumps are confused, and this narrated story somehow begins before it starts.

Banks is narrating a story to a daughter before the arrival of aliens, though the daughter appears to be born after it. And it has to be that way; the girl's father is Renner's character, Ian Donnelly (Gary Donnelly in Chiang's story), a fellow scientist Banks meets and falls in love with at the scene of one of the arriving pods.

But the incoherence of this sequence is Chiang's whole point: this event has shaken time, recasting destinies and remaking a future. And it all happens through *word*. Banks and Donnelly's job is to figure out why these heptapods, as they're soon called, are here. What is the meaning of this event? There seems to be no way to crack the code until, like the author of the Gospel of John or Albert Einstein, they start thinking about *light*.

While Banks is a linguist, Donnelly is a physicist and explains Fermat's principle of least time. It's the idea that light, when refracted between two points, will always take the fastest route. *But how does it know this fast route?* Banks wonders. Then she realizes that a "ray of light has to know where it will ultimately end up before it can choose the direction to begin moving in."[3] It must somehow know point B, its goal and end, even before it begins.

3. Ted Chiang, *Stories of Your Life and Others* (New York: Tor, 2002), 101.

This breaks the code. Banks has figured it out: the heptapods' *word* is an event—it comes fully realized. Their word doesn't need a verb, a tense, and an object, all coming one after another to move the hearer or reader from past to present to future. Rather, the heptapod word encompasses all this as a single event. The heptapods experience not past, present, and future but the fullness of the event in the word.

Their word is not bound in causality, where one word or sentence is like a billiard ball that hits the next, causing it, sometime after the first was hit, to hit the second and then later hit the third. Rather, the heptapods experience all events at once, not necessarily free from time (not timeless or beyond history), but rather all time becomes full, becomes *now*.

So time becomes free from the scrim of causality. (*Causality* is the sense that *this* leads to *that* and *that* leads to *this* and that's all an event is. An event is just a link in a causative chain that gets us from then to now. But now here, we are *just* at a point that will be another link in our causative chain to nowhere particular.) But this causative cage, which is not too different from Taylor's immanent frame, is not how the heptapods experience events. Because their word leads them to experience all events at once, they're free from flat, cold causality, which leads to the view that events are not value neutral. All events (especially big ones like alien arrivals and the birth of a child) possess an intrinsic teleology. These events have an aim; time and history are going toward a goal. The heptapods' word allows them to experience the encounter, aim, and end of an event all at once.

Recognizing this, Banks is able to learn their language, and as she uses it, the most salient events of her life become compressed. At the same time that she is experiencing the heptapods, she is *not* remembering or foreseeing the birth of her daughter but is experiencing it. All events now weave together through word, delivering the end even in their beginning. The event is teleological or, better, eschatological; it is radically transforming history and therefore encompasses Banks's beginnings and ends at once. She experiences her daughter's birth and tragic death simultaneously. Chiang leaves us to wonder: If we were able to really perceive the ends of events when they begin, would we choose them? Would Banks choose to have a child, and to experience the overwhelming joy of the events of love, if she knew the event of losing her? Or does she realize it even before it happens?

Like Linke, Banks will experience at her own daughter's funeral all events compressed, somehow knowing, even experiencing, that she would lose her before it happened, because the event was written into her being before it occurred. And somehow this isn't just complete sci-fi; many of us, like Linke, have felt as Banks. Some of us, like the old man, have, for instance, realized it was her song all along, the event of her ministry experienced somehow all at once. He always knew this song, even before he knew it. Even in the immanent frame, where time is frozen in causality and the wormholes that pastors like Thomas Becket once led people into on Good Friday are paved over, we still experience the compression and twists of time. It is more mysterious than we culturally admit.

Yet today it seems to hinge more on teleological events than on religious practice. Or, we could say, today we have a hard time recognizing that the practices of faith open us to eschatological events, yet we remain aware of the possibility of time twisting. Rolex has a commercial they show often during the British Open golf tournament that recaps the greatest shots of the past. The commercial ends with the tagline "It isn't just time, it's history." The commercial testifies that we experience something more than just basic flat time, even in a secular age. Rather, there are moments, events, happenings that we experience as so full—as having a fullness, as Taylor would describe—that they do something to time. These points in time might be a collective ecstatic event like a sporting event or concert, or a deep personal experience like the birth of a child or the loss of a loved one. These moments are written into us so deeply that they become history, core events, shaped as the narratives of our identity (of who we are). To echo the Rolex commercial, these moments aren't just causative points in time but are events that deliver a transformation, becoming a history.

To give an example of such a moment of fullness, during the first few years after getting married, I had the weirdest experience when I'd be prompted to retell parts of my personal history before knowing Kara. I had this odd feeling that in times when she couldn't have been present, she was. My life was so redefined by our union that somehow she bled back into my history, writing herself into past moments. I somehow thought that, though she wasn't there, she was. Like Banks experiencing her daughter's death at her birth, Kara now infiltrated my history so fully that she somehow became present in the past. The event of encountering her personhood was heavy enough to bend time. This shows that even in the secular age, time is more malleable than we often assume. It is nowhere near as flimsy as it once was before the Reformation, but neither is it as rigid as the immanent frame often states.

## To Israel

Before you write this all off as a long excursion from a fan of *Arrival*, here's the link: this compression of events is how Israel experiences God, revealing

God's being as the act of ministry.[4] To understand Israel's conception of God is to understand God as the one who arrives. God is *the* event with an aim (telos), delivering a history.[5]

As Robert W. Jenson has said, whoever God is, God is the one who arrives in the event of freeing Israel from Egypt and raising Jesus Christ from the dead.[6] These are not only ways or times God acts; these are also so central, reframing history, that they become essential revelation of who God is. The

4. James Thompson shows how central Moses and the story of the exodus was to early Christians, particularly Paul: "Paul continues to contrast his ministry with that of Moses in 3:7–18, a midrash on the story of Moses' glorious face (Exod. 34:29–35). In 2 Corinthians 3:7–11 Paul does not deny that the ministry of Moses was glorious, but he insists that his ministry of the new covenant is more glorious than that of Moses. In 3:12–18 he contrasts his own boldness with that of Moses, insisting that Moses placed a veil over his face so that the Israelites would not see the end of that which was losing its glory. The contrast is not only between Paul and Moses but between the Israelites, who were unable to see the glory, and the community of faith, made up of those who have turned to the Lord (3:16)." *Pastoral Ministry according to Paul: A Biblical Vision* (Grand Rapids: Baker Academic, 2006), 140.

5. "Unlike the Hindus, Greeks, Confucians and Taoists, the Jews thought of time as the dimension in which their lives would find meaning. The Jews insisted that God had made a covenant with them and that by this covenant he had assured them of the advent of a better world. Their faith in the coming of a Messianic Kingdom made them an expectant people—a people who looked to the future rather than the past. For them the present and the past received their meaning from the future—from the end time which was slowly and in enigmatic fashion being realized. Their eschatological view of history gave particular events a universal meaning—a moral and spiritual significance." Eileen Cantin, *Mounier: A Personalist View of History* (New York: Paulist Press, 1973), 41.

6. Robert W. Jenson, *Systematic Theology: The Works of God* (Oxford: Oxford University Press, 1999), 2:97n7, referencing Taylor. Here Jenson is wrestling with material from Taylor's *Source of the Self*. I'm not aware of any place in which Jenson deals with Taylor's secularity thesis, as I'm doing here. But this shows a little crack to begin relating them. Jenson says, "God is whoever raised Jesus from the dead, having before raised Israel from Egypt. Since these statements identify God, they have a specific status among true statements about him. The way or ways in which they fit him display how he is a this one who is not that one, how he has identifiable particularity; they display what we may call his hypostatic being." *Systematic Theology*, 2:63. Carl Braaten explains this core point of Jenson's that will be central to my work below:

It is important to add that for Jenson the Christian understanding of the identity of God as the agent who raised Jesus beyond death into lasting life presupposes Israel's answer to the same question, "Who is God?" For Israel God is "whoever rescued us from Egypt." In Christian faith they are the same God: the One who rescued Israel from Egypt is none other than the One who raised Jesus the Israelite from the dead. Jenson puts the matter as succinctly as language will allow: God is what happens with Jesus. We cannot speak of the God of the gospel without speaking of Jesus. Is Jesus God? To say "yes" could be misleading. It might suggest that we already know who God is apart from Jesus, and then in recognizing something divine in him, we feel justified in calling him God. Jenson prefers to say that God "is" Jesus, so that in identifying the latter we simultaneously identify the former. ("Eschatology and Mission in the Theology of Robert Jenson," in *Trinity, Time, and Church: A Response to the Theology of Robert W. Jenson*, ed. Colin Gunton [Grand Rapids: Eerdmans, 2000], 304)

faiths that come from Jerusalem do not simply reason about God, seeking
logical ways to explain how a metaphysical reality is understood in a physical world. This kind of thinking has its place (particularly in Athens), but
this is not the legacy of the people of the desert. Those who experience God
as shepherd claim that to know God is to know God's acts. To say who God
is, is to say what this God has done. To claim what this God has done is to
point to the happening of an event.[7] That's what the Old Testament means
when it says, "the God of Abraham, Isaac, and Jacob." This is the God who
arrives in time. "According to Jenson, the distinctive feature of the biblical
God is that he transcends time not by being immune to it but by being personally faithful to his promises in and through it."[8] To say it again, for the
faiths coming from Jerusalem, God is whoever freed the people from Egypt
and raised Jesus from the dead, revealing God's being through the acts that
minister freedom and new life.

From these two events of exodus and resurrection, time seems compressed
all over the place (see Deut. 5; Pss. 78; 106). In anticipation of his resurrection,
Jesus is on a hill with Moses and Elijah (Mark 9). In Matthew 22:44 Jesus
points out that David (in Ps. 110:1) says, "The Lord said to my Lord, 'Sit at
my right hand, until I put your enemies under your feet,'" acknowledging the
event of Jesus's own messianic lordship long before it happened, like Banks
with her daughter's birth. Throughout Genesis, the name Yahweh is in the
mouth of people who could not know it until, in the book of Exodus, God
arrives in the event of the bush that burned but is not consumed. But the
writers of Scripture have little concern for the use that violates their time-
line, for the events of God's arrival to Abraham or Moses are but different
sections of an accordion's bellows, all held together by the revealed telos of
the event to make them a nation of ministers. When the event occurs, the

7. Old Testament scholar Walther Zimmerli affirms these points: "Not one of the 78 (or
80) passages under question in the book of Ezekiel offers us a description of Yahweh's essence
or being. It is always a matter of Yahweh's intervention, either in the history of the hostile
nations or of the people of God themselves. . . . In this sense to know Yahweh does not mean
to encounter some part of Yahweh's transcendent being, but rather to recognize his beneficial
deed on Israel's behalf. Yahweh's fundamental beneficial deed on Israel's behalf, however, is the
leading out of Egypt. It is no accident that his act already completely dominates the statements
in Exodus 6:7 and 7:5." *I Am Yahweh* (Atlanta: John Knox, 1982), 44.

8. Scott Swain, *The God of the Gospel: Robert Jenson's Trinitarian Theology* (Downers
Grove, IL: InterVarsity, 2013), 129. Gerhard Forde critiques Jenson's position: "In spite of the
excellence of Jenson's work, I find myself saying on the whole, 'almost.' Or perhaps I should
say 'too far.' When one builds heavily on the attempt to erase the timelessness of God, one all
too easily slips into the tendency to attempt explaining the timelessness away. One goes too far.
The systematic threatens to 'flatten out' once again into its own variation of a timeless scheme.
One reiterates the rejection of timelessness, but nothing 'timely' ever happens." "Robert Jenson's
Soteriology," in Gunton, *Trinity, Time, and Church*, 136.

bellows is pushed together, giving a sense of time's compression, making what is to come known.

Israel is not that different from Banks; her story is the overlapping of events, the fusing of arrivals. For Banks this is the arrival of her daughter and heptapods; for Israel it is the arrival of the promise given by Yahweh to Abraham and to Moses. Which comes first? For both Banks and Israel, it's hard to say. They are events that, while having their own distinct points in the causality of time, are interlaced in the eschatological aims of God's action.

## Arrival of God to Abraham

If forced to answer, Israel would likely say that the exodus came first, and Banks the birth of her daughter.[9] Even though they happen second in the causality of time (after Abraham and the heptapods), it's these second-but-first events that make the first-but-second ones meaningful. Israel is made into a people, and Banks into a mother, by these so-called second events. While second, they are first, because the teleological impact makes them primary. Yet as soon as they'd say this, they'd both admit that without the initial arrival of God to Abraham and heptapods to earth, the origin-forming event could not be.[10]

Israel has a story very different from all its contemporaries. What makes Israel so odd is not its creation story (though we've used it as a religious ideological football).[11] All Eastern Mediterranean people have creation stories, some of them shockingly similar to Israel's.[12] Yet for most of these people there is a kind of fused causal continuity (a lack of arrival if you will) between the myth of their creation story and the life of their civilization. For example, Marduk created, and bam, there are the Babylonians. Just as there never was a time with no Marduk, so there was never a time with no great civilization of Babylon—until of course there isn't any longer and Marduk disappears with the civilization he forged. These gods never arrive; they just are, as are the people who managed their story. And because they never arrive, there is no radical arriving event. With no event, there is no sense that these gods are moving in history. Their job is to protect the continuation of a civilization—for instance, to make casual time serve the Babylonians.

9. That's why the movie starts with this event.

10. Banks meets her daughter's father only because of the arrival of the heptapods.

11. David Congdon highlights this and also supports where I'm headed below: "What interests the Hebrew scriptures is not the world as nature but the world as history. History is the space in which God acts." *The God Who Saves: A Dogmatic Sketch* (Eugene, OR: Cascade, 2016), 233."

12. See Peter Enns, *The Evolution of Adam: What the Bible Does and Doesn't Say about Human Origins* (Grand Rapids: Brazos, 2012).

But this is not how it works with Israel. Their story is built around a time when there was no Israel—this is radically and profoundly different. The world was going on, the sun rising and setting, tides coming and going, and yet Israel was not. The Babylonians couldn't conceive of this; the history of Marduk and the history of the Babylonians were essentially one and the same, both somewhat timeless and ahistorical.

Yet Abram is secure and safe in the house of his father, living happily in the causative continuity of his father's gods, just as Banks is happily living alone, moving back and forth from lecture hall to study. Then, as disruptive as a space pod on the horizon, a God whom Abram does not know *arrives*. Abram experiences a radically different kind of God, the only true living God, because this God comes as an arrival, and like in Chiang's story, speaks. The Old Testament says "living God" to communicate that this God is altogether different, because unlike all other gods, this God is an actor in history. We know this because this God speaks.[13] Jenson says it well: "The God of Israel is a talkative one. There is a terrible hymn that talks about the silence of eternity. It cannot be right, for the Jewish God cannot keep his mouth shut! He is talkative! And he moreover expects to be answered!"[14]

This God comes arriving as an event that happens—this is unique.[15] For the rest of Abraham's life this God will be coming and going, arriving with a word, seemingly gone, arriving again with a word. Abraham experiences this living God as the event of arrival, as the one who comes with a word, changing Abram to Abraham.

13. Jenson, drawing from Einstein's theory of general relativity, explains how God doesn't just create stuff but *makes* histories, because (as I'll argue) God is a ministry, interacting with that which God speaks into being: "The removal of certain distinctions between time and space by relativity theory—and indeed already by the first beginnings of modern science—pre-reflects the theological fact: God does not create spatial objects that thereupon move through time; he creates temporal-spatial objects, that is, in a more precise language, he creates histories. We must only avoid the suggestion of popular appropriations, which in calling time a fourth 'dimension' tend to use 'dimension' in a pictorial sense, thus obliterating time's distinction from space." *Systematic Theology*, 2:46.

14. Jenson, *A Theology in Outline: Can These Bones Live?* (Oxford: Oxford University Press, 2016), 15.

15. Cantin gives us a nice discussion of the importance of monotheism for this historical understanding of arrival and its telos: "As long as men believed in a plurality of gods, they would believe also in a plurality of histories. Whether conflict or cooperation was the rule among the gods, historical events would result from a plurality of divine wills. However, in a world dominated by a single deity, all events would be unified and would somehow fall under a single dominion. The working out of history would no longer be a matter of chance; it would no longer be a manifestation of the interaction of the gods, but it would manifest the will of the one God, or result from the interaction of men and God." *Mounier*, 41.

And this word, like the words of the heptapods, is the interlacing of events, is what we call promise.[16] God's arrival calls Abraham to leave his father's house and to see through the window of God's word, or, better, experience even before it has happened, that he *is* the father of a nation. "How, then, can God be known to Israel . . . before the story ends? We have already indicated the answer: God's being-in-anticipation can be known to Israel before the end of Israel's history under the mode of promise."[17]

Just as Banks sees that she is a mother when she takes up the words of the heptapods, so Abraham sees that he is a father when God speaks. Though Abraham *is* childless and remains so for a long time, he nevertheless knows, because he has experienced it through the event of God's arrival, that he *is* the father of a great nation. This is only true inside the event of God's own being, where time is compressed and events interlaced. But to Abraham this makes it truer than a baby bump and an ultrasound. Though it has not happened, it has, for though it seems impossible, the event of God's arrival delivers God's telos. The promise has unveiled the future; it has brought what *will be* to be experienced *now*. The event comes with the power to compress the bellows of history.

Abraham believes. He has faith that is reckoned unto him as righteousness (Gen. 15:6) because even after the bellows has decompressed, he believes what he has heard. Even when God has departed, Abraham knows it not as a fever dream or apparition but as a historical happening in a time that for now has arrived only in God's own being.[18] Abraham is righteous because he seeks to live from within the history of God's coming, never forgetting the compression of time and the aims to which this event points.

## God's Being in Becoming

To say that God is uniquely the arriving God—a living God who makes himself known as an event in history[19]—is to claim that *God's being is in God's*

---

16. This is why the teleological dimension is eschatological.

17. Swain, *God of the Gospel*, 90, commenting on Barth's and Jenson's theology.

18. I'm seeing Abraham's faith through a lens similar to Gritsch and Jenson when they say, "In Reformation language, 'faith' is *not* the label of an ideological or attitudinal state. Like 'justification,' the word evokes a *communication-situation*; the situation of finding oneself addressed with an unconditional affirmation, and having now to deal with life in these new terms. Faith is a mode of life. Where the radical question is alive, all life becomes a *hearing*, a listening for permission to go on; faith is this listening—to the gospel." *Lutheranism*, 41.

19. By claiming that the winners of history write history, postmodernism critiques the idea that God's acts are historical. Identity, it would say, is bound in events that we story, and so deconstruction is always necessary. Yet Walter Brueggemann claims that the story of Israel and

*becoming*. I know to say it like that is to rival the most complicated of sci-fi movies, seemingly as mind-bending as space-time in *Interstellar* or genetics in *Gattaca*. To say it like this is simply to claim that the only way for us to know God (and therefore experience God's being) is to encounter God's historical arrival. Abraham has no preconceived ideas of God. How could he? He can't know this God until the event of God's arrival. It isn't until God arrives with calls and promises of action that Abraham has any sense of God's being.

If it isn't the esoteric phrase "God's being is in becoming" causing discomfort, but instead the word "historical," fearing a Hegelian error,[20] then we can follow Walter Brueggemann, who says, "The God revealed is an actor in historical experience, and if 'historical' is a stumbling block, it is enough to say that God participates in a 'narrative drama.'"[21] By arriving and speaking, God becomes a (*the*) player in the narrative, an actor in the drama. It is only by giving attention to what this player *does* that we can discern who this player *is*. It is only in the event of God's coming that we can know this God at all.[22]

That's what's so unique about Israel's story. Abraham is the righteous man of faith because, though he has no preconceived ideas about God, no innate data to draw on, he follows a God whom he knows only through God's actions of arriving and speaking. As we'll see, this is also true for Moses. The event of God's arrival is the revealing of God's being, even the giving of God's name, though Moses is much more reluctant than Abraham to follow. God's arrival is becoming, not because God is incomplete and becoming a better and better God, but rather because God is an event toward a telos. God is

Jesus is different: "Karl Popper has said a remarkable thing about history-making—namely, that all history is written by the winners, the people on top, with one exception. That exception, says Popper, is the history of Jesus and his community. I would extend Popper's observation to say it is the history of Yahweh and the community of Yahweh that writes history from underneath (cf. Ps. 82)." *Hope within History* (Atlanta: John Knox, 1973), 58.

20. This Hegelian stump over history has much to do with the conception that Hegel locks God's free act in historical processes, making God essentially the *Geist* of history; but it also has something to do with our unease with Marxism. It is obvious that Marxism needs the Christianity it denies to forge its perspective. Cantin explains Mounier's contrasting of Christianity and Marxism, helping us anticipate what we'll explore below, an "immanence of transcendence" in the acts of ministry: "The most radical difference between Christianity and Marxism, and Mounier insists that this difference is crucial, is that for Marx, history is purely immanent, while for the Christian it is the 'immanence of a transcendence.'" *Mounier*, 45.

21. Brueggemann, preface to *I Am Yahweh* by Walther Zimmerli (Atlanta: John Knox, 1982), xv.

22. T. F. Torrance supports this historical perspective: "The unity of eternity and time in the incarnation means that true time in all its finite reality is not swallowed up by eternity but eternally affirmed as reality even for God. . . . The Word of God has taken historical form and is now never without that historical form." *Incarnation: The Person and Life of Christ* (Downers Grove, IL: InterVarsity, 2008), 9, 13.

moving. "God is moved being," as Eberhard Jüngel says, because God is acting in history for a particular future—a future in which humanity participates in the very being of God by receiving God's acts of ministry.[23] To return to Jenson, God's primary *doing* is to free Israel from Egypt and resurrect Jesus from the dead. These acts are the revealing of God's being.

A pastor reminds her people to await the *coming* of God, to prepare them in the waiting for the possibility of God's arriving. In the impatience of our secular age, where any waiting quickly turns into disbelief, the pastor in a secular age holds a space to wait for God's becoming. The pastor's primary focus, then, isn't to build a church of size and reputation but to attend to revelation. The pastor focuses on how, even in this secular age, God arrives to reveal himself in the lives and stories of the community that the pastor leads. One of the pastor's primary dispositions, then, is to lead in a stance of discernment.

Brueggemann moves us in this direction when he says, "The revelation is never in a vacuum, but always in a context of decisive impingement."[24] As we said above, time gets compressed, but never obliterated, in the events of God's arriving. God's arriving happens in time, producing a history. "There is no spaceless and timeless knowledge of God. We cannot therefore think of a static eternal God apart from the living God who actively makes himself known to us in time and space in the history of Israel and above all in Christ."[25] God makes himself known not in a psychic state but in an encounter with historical bodies where God fulfills God's promises. For revelation to be the revealing of God's being, it must happen in the context of a time and place.

## What Context?

But existence is nothing if not the incredible surplus of times and spaces, meaning there are too many contexts to calculate. Recognition of these *many* contexts has played its own part in spinning the immanent frame closed in our secular age; the plurality of contexts makes divine action highly questionable. For instance, our secular age asks, "Isn't your belief in God just based on the family and community you grew up in?" It's *just* the socialization of your context.

23. See Jüngel, *God's Being Is in Becoming: The Trinitarian Being of God in the Theology of Karl Barth* (Grand Rapids: Eerdmans, 2001), 14–15.

24. Brueggemann, preface to *I Am Yahweh* by Zimmerli, xv.

25. Robert Walker, introduction to *Incarnation: The Person and Life of Christ* by T. F. Torrance (Downers Grove, IL: InterVarsity, 2008), xli.

So then what makes one context the location of God's arrival and not another? And doesn't this particularity violate the modern moral order, which
says everyone should equally benefit? If God shows up in one context and
not another, doesn't that make God an arbitrary and unfair jerk, just further
supporting the 1 percent? Those who ask these questions and make such
statements aren't wrong; to answer the question of particular context reveals
something of God's being. And Brueggemann has already told us what to look
for when he said that it is "in a context of decisive impingement."

This is why we can say that God's being is constituted as the event of ministry: because God arrives not only in a historical context but in particularly
conditioned historical contexts. The heptapods arrive on earth and not some
other planet seemingly because earth possesses just the conditions they need
to bring forth their arrival. The earth possesses a group of creatures that the
heptapods are able to teach their language to. Because their language is a
teleological event, they know that in three thousand earth years they'll need
saving. So they elect, with their arrival, earth, humanity, and Louise Banks to
receive their word. The conditions are right for their arrival. But though right,
these conditions *can't be* made or manipulated. How could they be? Earth,
humanity, and Banks, like Abraham, have no sense that there are such beings
until they arrive. To claim God as event who arrives in a context is to always
uphold God's freedom.[26] Abram is secure in his father's house and Banks is
secure teaching her classes when the event elects them.

Brueggemann's point about God's arriving is similar. The conditions are
right for God to arrive; Israel is crushed, and Jesus is dead. The decisive impingement is the condition that sends God arriving, revealing that this God
is an acting minister. God is the one who ministers freedom to Israel, the one
who ministers life back to the dead Jesus. It is in these impossible impingements that *this* God arrives, *this* God who has a personal name, though not
yet revealed when he calls out, like a pod on the horizon, for Abram to come
and learn the word of this living God.

In a sense Abraham is just like Banks, though, as we'll see, with an important
twist. Abraham is elected to receive a word from the God who is the event of
arrival. Yet this word is not for him, just as it's not for Banks. Participating in
the event of the arrival and learning this word reveals promise—both Abraham
and Banks will be parents. But this is not the whole point; rather, they have

26. John Zizioulas explains how God's revealing of himself in history constitutes God's
freedom: "We can recognize a person as a person only in freedom, so all the knowledge we have
of persons depends on whether and how they reveal themselves. We cannot know anyone as a
person by force, so if someone does not wish to divulge their identity, we cannot know them as
persons." *Lectures in Christian Dogmatics* (Edinburgh: T&T Clark, 2008), 28.

been elected to receive the arrival for the sake of learning the word that will save—not them, but those long yet to come. The event of God's arriving is ministry because it always acts to save. (This keeps ministry—even the practice of ministry—ever close to soteriology. But what conditions this soteriology, as we'll see more below, is the shape of the arrival; it comes to those in need, providing the love and mercy of a God who is a minister. It is salvation that makes us right or holy, but only because God lovingly invites us to find our being in God's being by experiencing God's loving *acts* of ministry.)

Just as Banks is elected to learn the heptapod language so that humanity might save the alien creatures in the future, so Abraham is given the word of God for the sake of saving. Not only will Abraham, through his own seed, participate in forging God's nation of ministers, but he will also teach them the word of this God's arrival through his own history so that they might receive saving from Egypt through the very ministry of God's being through act.

Just as the heptapods' arrival is for saving in a future that can't be conceived, so too is the arrival of God to Abraham. Yet here is the twist: Abraham is to learn the language of the event of God's coming so that God might save Israel from Egypt. The heptapods arrive seeking saving; the God who comes to Abraham is the savior. This God is the minister, revealed not in *God's* conditions of impingent (as it is with heptapods) but in Israel's. God comes arriving not for God's sake but for ours. We discover that it is in these very contexts of our decisive impingement that God most fully reveals himself by most fully acting. It is in these events that we learn God's personal names (Yahweh; Jesus Christ) because God acts to save by revealing God's being of love.

A lover who acts for another in conditions of impingement is a minister, giving the presence of his or her being as an act of salvation. God's arrival to Abraham is the act of a lover because, as we'll see, the God of Abraham, Isaac, and Jacob reveals God's personal name to Moses. The revealing of the personal name keeps us from imagining the saving action as anything other than the invitation of persons to share in the personal being of God. Because God is the loving minister who arrives with and for persons, personal names become essential—there is no way to minister without personal names; the pastor names things rightly, as Eugene Peterson says.[27] The pastor awaits God's arriving by creating a space where people address each other with personal names. The pastor of the small church may feel insecure in our secular age,

27. Eugene Peterson, *Five Smooth Stones for Pastoral Work* (Grand Rapids: Eerdmans, 1992), 48. See chapter 13 below for a further discussion of Peterson's position and why properly naming things is central to pastoral practices.

where the entrepreneur is the model. But she need not, for the pastor who begins to discern God's arriving, most particularly in a secular age, does so by creating a space of personal names, a space where people know each other enough to narrate their stories, sharing their experience of decisive impingement and their yearning for something more.

This kind of arriving for the sake of personal names is an additional twist from the heptapods. Their arrival moves from general to specific. They come to multiple locales, arriving at twelve different cities, because their aim is general (earth) to general (humanity) to finally, as a last resort, particular (Louise Banks). But the act of God reveals God's being as minister because the arrival moves in the opposite direction. God comes to the particular, to the person with a name, speaking to Abraham. Through this personal speaking and hearing, God's saving ministry moves out into the general—from Abraham to his family to a nation, and from a nation to all humanity and all creatures everywhere. There is no such thing as ministry in general (there is really no such thing as generic love). Ministry is always done as an event in particular places to particular persons with particular names. It is the pastor's job, especially in a secular age, to steward these particularities.

So to echo Brueggemann again, the context where God arrives is conditioned by "decisive impingement." God acts in the contexts where people need the ministry of God's action, for God's being is that of a minister. It is in time—it is in times of needing ministry—that the event of God's arriving is near. This is why, as we'll see in the final chapter, prayer is so important. To assert that God is an arriving God whose being is in actions of becoming is to see that God moves for the sake of ministry to a people decisively impinged by slavery and to a unique person decisively dead.

For a few weeks last school year, Maisy, my nine-year-old, fretted about how hard school was, the reading and math challenging her abilities and the social pressure intensifying. I told her that, when things are at their hardest, we must together open our eyes and ready ourselves for God's arrival. It is when we need ministry, impinged by impossibility, that the God who comes in the act of ministry arrives, calling to a dying surgeon to share in God's being by being a minister, giving a song to a broken man. The life of faith is not to assume that every impinging circumstance will bring God's arrival, but it is to open your eyes and anticipate that our God, who is a minister, may just move over these waters of impossibility. And so we must call out to this God, listening for his word. And when God comes, we must tell others of the arrival, for right in our places of death God has ministered life.

The context of God's arrival is where and when people are crushed and bondage and death are heaviest. Brueggemann agrees, saying, "Not incidentally then, the key formulae are found especially in the Exodus narrative."[28] The pastor is *not* the one who saves people from any or all of the impingements. Rather, the pastor is the one who reminds the community that though God seems absent, nevertheless the God who is a minister arrives right here in the middle of such events of impingement, when things seem so hard.

The secular age tempts us to give in to a closed spin in the immanent frame that we inherited and therefore to see divine action as implausible (we sketched this history through the six pastors of part 1). Now in a secular age, the pastor can never free people from the immanent frame. But the pastor can, as a primary element of his vocation, help his people be open to God arriving, even in his immanent frame. The pastor does this by inviting people with personal names to share their stories of impingement as a way to infuse the community with the spirit of ministry. It is when hearing the stories of decisive impingement (lost jobs, cancer diagnosis, addicted children) of those we know by name that the community is prepared for the God who arrives as minister.

We can find this God in our own experiences of bondage and death because God's being is in the arriving to Israel in Egypt and through Jesus in the tomb. We begin to talk about divine action in a secular age by attending to these contexts of our lives that seek and experience ministry. We can trust that God will come to Maisy, because God is the one who liberates Israel from Egypt and raises Jesus from the dead. It is the historical acts of ministry in time that give me the words to tell her at bedtime that God is an acting minister, present when things are hard, fulfilling God's promises revealed to Abraham and the prophets.

---

28. Brueggemann, preface to *I Am Yahweh* by Zimmerli, xv.

# 11

## encountering a speaking God
## who identifies with events

It was in his blood but not something he'd call his own. It would have been hard for him *not* to imagine himself as a Christian. His father was a pastor, and the Bible an essential part of his people's story. For generations his people had read this book and served in pastoral leadership. All people in his community talked of a personal God who spoke to them in prayer and got them through the day. It was real; he saw its impact, but he had never experienced it himself.

Growing up in segregated Georgia, he felt more called by the cries of humanity than the Word of God. Yet it was the 1940s, and the pastor, particularly in the black community, still held major esteem. The secular age was shifting people's perception of the pastor but had not yet ruled the pastor culturally insignificant. So the young Martin Luther King Jr. decided he'd study for the ministry. He would make this personal God who moves throughout history, speaking to people in prayer, his academic focus. But that was about it—it was all academic—until 1954, when Martin took his first pastoral position at Dexter Avenue Baptist Church in Montgomery, Alabama.

In December 1955 Rosa Parks refused to give up her seat on the bus. Her resistance and arrest kicked off the Montgomery bus boycott and the civil rights movement. The bus boycott's core strategist would be E. D. Nixon, and its vocal leader Pastor Martin Luther King Jr.

As the boycott launched and King became central to it, tension mounted. The pressure to do right by the African Americans of Montgomery was enough to bend his back. But when the threats came on his and his family's lives, he wasn't sure he could go forward. One night the phone rang, startling Martin from sleep. On the other end of the line was a man threatening to kill him and blow up his house. Hanging up, he knew sleep was no longer an option. The boycott wasn't going as planned, and now the threats were becoming more and more ominous. The pressure was more than bending his back; it was readying to break him in two. Sleep was no salve, so coffee would have to do.

Sitting at his kitchen table with the coffee cup before him and the incredibly difficult task ahead of him, he felt like Moses, inadequate to accomplish it. Throughout his seminary education and PhD work at Boston University, King had studied personalism, exploring God's personal nature and what this means for how we conceive of human beings.[1] But these were only intellectual ideas. They seemed important to the old black men and women of his youth; their conception of God's personal name somehow gave them the strength to stand under the torch of incredible oppression. But now that this torch was bearing down on *him*, he could only reluctantly follow their lead, turning to pray.[2] "At his kitchen table he bowed down before the God of his parents and ancestors and sought divine guidance, comfort, and assurance."[3] It was his last resort, a cry of desperation.

Divisive impingement arrived in double dose. The people of Montgomery, like those in Egypt, cried out for freedom. Not only that, but God's overly intellectualized servant, who doubted more than believed, succumbing to the cross-pressure more often than not—as a boy even denying the bodily resurrection—was feeling powerless, ready to give up. But it is in powerlessness (in the cross) that the ministering God of the exodus and resurrection moves, bringing the event of God's speaking.

1. Rufus Burrow explains, "By the time King attended college, seminary, and graduate school some of his most important religious and ethical convictions—e.g., that God is personal and persons are sacred—had already been shaped through the influence of his family and black church upbringing." *God and Human Dignity: The Personalism, Theology, and Ethics of Martin Luther King, Jr.* (Notre Dame, IN: University of Notre Dame, 2006), 1.

2. "From the time he was a boy, King believed God to be personal, although as an adult, especially during the Montgomery struggle, he did not know from a personal, existential standpoint what this really meant. He knew as well as anybody what it meant intellectually or academically. But he recalled a time when he had not been as conscious of the personal character of the God of his faith and of his ancestors. At times, he thought of God in a more abstract and academic sense. But his struggle alongside his people for freedom and dignity helped to reestablish and anchor his belief and trust in a personal God who hears, is affected by, and responds to prayer and other human endeavor. Reflecting on his own personal sufferings and persecutions reminded King of his earlier dependence on the personal and loving God of Jesus Christ, the God of his parents and grandparents." Burrow, *God and Human Dignity*, 104.

3. Burrow, *God and Human Dignity*, 105.

At that kitchen table, with midnight coffee cooling, God spoke. King testifies in his book *Stride toward Freedom*:

> I was ready to give up. With my cup of coffee sitting untouched before me I tried to think of a way to move out of the picture without appearing a coward. In this state of exhaustion, when my courage had all but gone, I decided to take my problem to God. With my head in my hands, I bowed over the kitchen table and prayed aloud. The words I spoke to God that midnight are still vivid in my memory. "I am here taking a stand for what I believe is right. But now I am afraid. The people are looking to me for leadership, and if I stand before them without strength and courage, they too will falter. I am at the end of my powers. I have nothing left. I've come to the point where I can't face it alone." At that moment I experienced the presence of the Divine as I had never experienced Him before. It seemed as though I could hear the quiet assurance of an inner voice saying: "Stand up for righteousness, stand up for truth; and God will be at your side forever." Almost at once my fears began to go. My uncertainty disappeared. I was ready to face anything.[4]

God had arrived! The event of God's coming had spilled into the dimly lit kitchen, with a word that called King into ministry, revealing God's personal being as the one who ministers the promises of freedom in and through God's own presence. God *said* to Martin, "I'll be at your side, ministering to you as you minister to my people." "The kitchen experience," as King would call it, would be "the most important night of his life, the one he always would think back to in future years when the pressure again seemed to be too great."[5] It was the *most* important night of his life because it was the event of God's arriving and speaking.

King would think back to that night because it revealed something essential about the act and being of God that, even up against the pressures of a secular age, he could hold onto. "After the kitchen experience it was clear that God was '*that power that can make a way out of no way*.'"[6] This would be the very refrain that King would use in a sermon, "Thou Fool," preached in Chicago in 1967, right in the hottest heat of the civil rights movement. This power to bring a way out of no way, to free Israel from Egypt and Jesus from the tomb, is the event of ministry. King now knew that this God made

4. Burrow, *God and Human Dignity*, 105–6.
5. David J. Garrow, *Bearing the Cross: Martin Luther King, Jr., and the Southern Christian Leadership Conference* (New York: William Morrow, 1986), 57, quoted in Burrow, *God and Human Dignity*, 106.
6. Burrow, *God and Human Dignity*, 106 (emphasis added), quoting King, "Thou Fool," sermon, Mount Pisgah Missionary Baptist Church (Chicago, Illinois), August 22, 1967, King Library and Archives, 3.

a way by entering impossibility, bearing the "no way" so that "a new way" (an advent of a new future), where God ministers eternally to God's people, might dawn. Because this God arrives in death, "in the no way," to bringing life, "a new way," this God is the event of ministry.

## But in a Secular Age?

What King discovered at the kitchen table was that it is in the confession of a death experience (as we explored in volume 1) that God often arrives. In part 1 of this volume, we went to great length to show how divine action becomes opaque in a secular age, leaving the pastor in a malaise. Yet what King discovered, and preached about so beautifully in "Thou Fool," was that the lens to see divine action is through death and impossibility. God arrived in that kitchen when it was darkest, and in Egypt when the decisive impingement too much.

Acknowledging this context of decisive impingement is a necessity if the pastor is to have a way of talking about divine action in a secular age. I've said it as directly as possible in the previous chapter: God arrives and acts not in some metaphysical transcendental state but in history. This is not to oppose transcendence (and therefore violate the heart of Charles Taylor's project) but to see transcendence in a deeply incarnational sense, as Taylor affirms.[7] It is to imagine the transcendent in time, as a historical transcendence, as Ray Anderson[8] and Emmanuel Mounier argue. "We usually think of that which is transcendent as something beyond us, as something which is at a distance. But transcendence does not necessarily involve a spatial distance. . . . The true distance is spiritual and creative of presence."[9]

God moves in time. God's acts may do odd things to time, compressing it as it births a history through promise, but this only testifies that it happens in time. The Christian faith (particularly in the West) has never added psychedelics to its practices, using natural herbs or other chemicals to expand the mind and see visions—a little peyote trip before the prayers of the people. It's not that trippy dream states are evil or unusable for the God of Israel. *Breaking Bad*'s fly episode was not that different from Daniel's dreams or John's vision on Patmos. But these dream states are never ends in themselves. They

7. See Taylor's conversation on excarnation in *A Secular Age* (Cambridge, MA: Belknap Press, 2007), chap. 20.

8. See Ray S. Anderson, *Historical Transcendence and the Reality of God* (Grand Rapids: Eerdmans, 1975), a dissertation written under T. F. Torrance.

9. Eileen Cantin, *Mounier: A Personalist View of History* (New York: Paulist Press, 1973), 73.

reveal God's coming act in time, unveiling how God is moving history toward the eschatological telos of God's promise. So it's in neither individual consciousness nor experience but in reality itself that God moves, unveiling that God is a personal reality who speaks. And God speaks not only to Abraham and Moses—premodern, ancient people, living long before the immanent frame—but to our contemporaries, like Martin Luther King Jr., whose feet rest squarely in a secular age.

But how can this be? The secular age, as we've described it through Taylor, has framed reality in immanence, freeing us from a speaking God as a consequence of making us immune to demons and devils. As nicely stated as Robert Jenson's or Eberhard Jüngel's theology might be, and as powerful as King's sermons, how can we say that God is an actor in history, coming to speak to midnight coffee drinkers? This seems unbelievable in the shadows of a secular age, something to reduce to psychological transference.

## Between Religious Experience and Ideology

There nevertheless seem to be two sanctioned ways within our secular age to tend to the spiritual or religious. But both options seem to intentionally or tacitly deny the eventfulness of God's arriving with a speaking word in history. Starting in the nineteenth century, forms of liberalism focused on religious experience. There was no need for an arriving God. Such thoughts were ruled antiquated by the immanent frame. But we could still experience God, or have some experience we called God, just not in time, not as a personal reality in (and with) a history. It was just a subjective feeling. This subjective feeling could be shared, and had been for centuries, producing a history of religious experience (think here of Adolf van Harnack), but it was no longer a history of God's otherness that arrives and acts.[10]

As the nineteenth century gave way to the twentieth, this focus on religious experience met expressive individualism and, as we said in part 1, exploded like a star, creating a nova of all sorts of *spiritual* experiences that now didn't even need to tip their hat to centuries-old religious forms, giving no concern even

---

10. Karl Barth's whole project is to oppose this. For Barth divine action isn't an experience or an ideology but an event. Colin Gunton explains: "Barth is referring to revelation as something that happens; not to subjective experiences but to events that are God, and specifically the events that come to expression in the story of the life, death and resurrection of Jesus Christ. Because this revelation is where God happens among men, it is impossible to distinguish between God's word and himself, between what God does and what he is. There is no other reality lying behind it: it is God himself." *Becoming and Being* (Eugene, OR: Wipf & Stock, 2011), 129.

to subjective experiences within a collective experience.[11] Now whatever spoke to you—whatever floated your boat—was a legitimate spiritual experience.

Before we brush this off too quickly, there is something to it; experience does matter.[12] Abraham and King had experiences. There is no way to encounter the arriving God outside of experience. The train image at the back of the *Four Spiritual Laws* booklet—where the engine is fact, the coal car faith, and the caboose feelings—makes the point that feelings are auxiliary. This doesn't work. There are no facts that aren't interpreted through our own or our community's feelings, and no faith is disconnected from feeling our way into our experiences.

But that little diagram is just a setup for the second option. Rightly recognizing that biblical faith cannot succumb to an ahistorical conception and be bound in solely religious experience, a conservative perspective arises. It seeks to protect God from liberals and their religious experience by turning God into an idea and Christian faith into an ideology. The Bible is no longer the interpretive history of God's arriving but a litmus test of who holds to the idea and supports the ideology[13]—no wonder enemies are imagined everywhere. A once-loyal friend can be made an evil betrayer with one word to a journalist, which *may* reveal that he no longer is completely committed to the ideology.[14]

---

11. Charles Taylor explains that this turn to individual spiritual experience was birthed, at least intellectually, by William James: "James's stress on personal religion, even his insistence that this is what religion really is, as against collective practice, can seem entirely understandable, even axiomatic, to lots of people." *Varieties of Religion Today: William James Revisited* (Cambridge, MA: Harvard University Press, 2002), 13.

12. Here I'm following Luther. Mark Mattes explains the place of experience in Luther: "Unlike his contemporaries and forebears, Luther has no confidence in either metaphysics or mysticism to establish God's goodness, in spite of the fact that both approaches influenced his theological development. Luther's is a highly experiential theology—not that experience is a criterion for truth but that sinners can never detach emotionally when doing theology, and at some point in their lives all sinners will do theology." *Martin Luther's Theology of Beauty* (Grand Rapids: Baker Academic, 2017), 54.

13. John Zizioulas gives us a sense of different ways that Scripture and doctrine have been perceived in the East and West. Some branches within the West have even more radicalized this view and turned the Bible into an ideology. I personally am following more the Eastern perspective here, connecting Scripture to a person's eventful experience of the living God. Zizioulas states, "The West tended to regard revelation as primarily rational or intellectual, and the Scriptures and the Church simply as a repository of truths, available as individual units of inert information. In the Orthodox tradition, however, Scripture and the Church are regarded as the testimonies of those prophets and apostles who have experienced the truth of Christ. But truth is not a matter of objective, logical proposals, but of personal relationships between God, man and the world." *Lectures in Christian Dogmatics* (Edinburgh: T&T Clark, 2008), 7.

14. I'm thinking here of Jonathan Merritt's interview of Eugene Peterson: Merritt, "Eugene Peterson on Changing His Mind about Same-Sex Issues and Marriage," Religion News Service, July 12, 2017, http://religionnews.com/2017/07/12/eugene-peterson-on-changing-his-mind-about-same-sex-issues-and-marriage.

This reduction of God to an idea and faith into an ideology, whether it is done knowingly or not, becomes a legitimate, forfeiting response to the secular age. Once God is turned into an idea, God no longer arrives and personally speaks as God did to Martin at his kitchen table. We can forget about divine action and just fight for an ideology. Like a butterfly in a book, divine action is flattened for the sake of control. We claim that this God once moved, but now all we have is God as a specimen, traits and attributes logged in a book.[15]

Italian physicist Carlo Rovelli makes a similar point, claiming that the universe itself is constituted in events. To make this point, he contrasts the difference between a kiss and a stone.[16] A stone is an object; it is statically located and lodged in time and space. Therefore any description of it must become impersonal; objects are frozen into ideas. But a kiss is much different. A kiss is an encounter that can't be captured, because it's a happening, an event that impacts your being. You can't find a kiss outside the event of its arrival. To say that God is event is to say that God is more like a kiss—an arriving, personal happening—than a stone. God always breaks free of our ideas, can never be caged in an ideology. God is an event of arriving.

## The Event Horizon

But in the shadow of a secular age, where divine action is opaque, how can we speak of a God who arrives in time? How could a pastor point to divine action? Not by attending solely to religious or spiritual experience, or to the Bible as ideology, but by focusing on event. But to speak of the event of God's arriving is to start by speaking of the personal events of God's seeming absence.[17] This, like a jujitsu move, is to use the weight of the secular age against itself. It seems nearly impossible in a secular age to speak of the presence of God without being pushed into one ditch or another. We're tempted either to hollow out God's personal nature like a pumpkin, leaving only a religious

15. This is simplistic, but is partly the reason you don't find a list of God's attributes in Barth's dogmatics—as you do in conservative evangelical projects. Barth is seeking to speak only of a God that is moving and living; the turn to attributes too often pins God to a page.

16. He discusses this on Krista Tippet's radio show *On Being* (March 16, 2017). See also his book *Seven Brief Lessons on Physics* (New York: Riverhead, 2016).

17. David Congdon discusses this, and he names some theologians who are also impacting my thinking: "With Luther and Bonhoeffer, Jüngel rethinks God beyond the polarity between absence and presence. If God is to be understood in the crucified one, then God's being 'can no longer be sought in the alternative of *present* or *absent*.' The place where God is most radically absent—namely, the cross—is paradoxically the place where God is most radically present. God is present to Jesus precisely in the moment he experiences the depths of divine abandonment." *The God Who Saves: A Dogmatic Sketch* (Eugene, OR: Cascade, 2016), 126.

or spiritual experience as a shell to then fight for some identity politics, or to ossify God into an idea, making God a hard ideological object with which to beat people who again don't share some identity politics. The opaqueness of divine action in our secular age makes falling into either of these ditches always a risk for the pastor, sometimes even over and against your best efforts.

The only way, in my mind, to walk the precarious trail between these ragged ditches and not hide in the fetal position from the impact of our secular age is to focus on event. We claim divine action not as religious experience or as ideology but as the encounter with a personal event. The pastor in a secular age becomes always interested in event-full-ness (I'll show what this looks like soon).

But to simply state that divine action is event and leave it at that won't solve our problem; it will leave people just as confused, drawing the pastor, even over and against her desire, to fall back into one of the ragged ditches. Divine action is too opaque, and therefore our pastoral work a walk too precarious, to hope this attention to God as event will keep us from falling into either of these ditches. So to truly respond to our secular age and attend to God as event begins, ironically, by attending to the events of God's seeming absence—theses events of midnight coffee where hope and strength are failing. It is attending to events of nothingness and death (of decisive impingement, as Walter Brueggemann says, or the *theologia crucis*, as Luther asserts) that gives us pastoral direction, making it possible, counterintuitively, to witness to the event of divine action.[18]

An event is, by definition, an occurrence in time and space—a kiss must happen somewhere at some time. To say that God is event is to claim that God arrives, that God is a living happening. To say that King experiences the event of God's absence is to claim that in a particular place and time—at midnight in his kitchen—he's overcome, not just with feelings or generic experience, but with a historical reality, that the bus boycott is failing and that real, historical threats of murder have been proclaimed. "I am at the end of my powers. I have nothing left," King confesses at the table at midnight. This is an event that changes the flow of his history, adding a new line to his story. Sure in his own power, he has expected that he can lead the bus boycott. But at midnight in the dark, a new event arrives, relaying that this is impossible; it is as sure

18. Eberhard Jüngel says, "God's being is a being in the act of suffering. But even in suffering God's being remains a being in act, a being in becoming. God persists in the historicality of his being. And this persistence of God in the historicality of his being allows this being to remain even in death a being in becoming. In giving himself away God does not give himself up. But he gives himself away because he will not give up humanity." *God's Being Is in Becoming: The Trinitarian Being of God in the Theology of Karl Barth* (Grand Rapids: Eerdmans, 2001), 102.

as dead. The event communicates that King has no strength to produce the future he hopes for, and he must confess it. But this becomes just the condition, to echo his sermon, for "that power that can make a way out of no way."[19]

This is an event because no matter what happens next, it will be a major part of his story. This occurrence sets the terms for his future and therefore forges a part of his identity. His identity is *not* the ideologies he's chosen to associate himself with—this is the error of identity politics—but the events that he experiences. Too often today we imagine "identity" as the composite of someone's *own* chosen self-definition. You define who you are through the expression of your desires and "likes," through ideas you associate with. This gives us a kind of ahistorical sense of identity, binding identity in something like consumer choice, a volition built on pure want and the choices you make to get these wants. Yet this is an illusion; identity isn't really forged through your choices but is forged through the events you live through. You don't really get to choose the identity you want. Rather, to have an identity is to have particular events you identify with produce a narrative you can speak,[20] telling the story of your life.[21] Your identity gives you a speakable history.[22]

My own identity is the story of events I identify my being with—the events of falling in love with Kara, of Owen's and Maisy's births, of the day my acceptance letter from Princeton came. These are events that are placed into a story that gives me my identity.[23] And I tell them, expressing my identity by speaking of these events' concrete location in a time and space, as well as

19. King, "Thou Fool," sermon, Mount Pisgah Missionary Baptist Church (Chicago, Illinois), August 22, 1967, King Library and Archives, 3.

20. Alistair McFadyen says something similar: "A person is sedimented from past relations as a unique organizational source of communication with a unique identity which guides future communication and relation." *The Call to Personhood: A Christian Theory of the Individual in Social Relationship* (New York: Cambridge University Press, 1990), 115.

21. To think of identity as simply the choice I make to express who I am through my desires is to lose something significant about the moral character of our lives. Yet to think of our identity as an event that we identify with causes us to be pushed into moral evaluation of these events, wondering if there are goods or evils that form through these events, wondering if we must let go of identifying with an event because it simply is not *good* for us.

22. It is not that individuals have to speak this history to have an identity, a presumption that would exclude those with cognitive disabilities or forms of dementia from having any identity. This would be short-sighted. Yet even people with cognitive disability and dementia have others who speak their history or remember on their behalf. Their identification might not be driven by cognition, but their very presence and inclusion in a community becomes their identity. For more, see John Swinton, *Becoming Friends of Time: Disability, Timefullness, and Gentle Discipleship* (Waco: Baylor University Press, 2017).

23. Scientist Jonathan Haidt explains the centrality of story for the mind: "The human mind is a story processor, not a logic processor. Everyone loves a good story; every culture bathes its children in stories." *The Righteous Mind: Why Good People Are Divided by Politics and Religion* (New York: Vintage, 2012), 328.

how these events arrived to direct my future. These events are a gift, and if I were living in another time than this secular age, I may be conditioned (and maybe should still be even today) to see these events as coming solely from the hand of God. But I know where babies come from. My disenchantment doesn't undercut the importance of these events, but it leads me to assume (even me, the seminary professor) that they were my doing, not really God's. This is why in a secular age, particularly, we must follow the paradigm of the exodus and begin with events of decisive impingement.

And these kinds of events are as clear in my life as those listed above. I have other events that are also part of my story, events that are hard for me to speak of but that I nevertheless identify with, even if I wish I didn't have to. These events too are part of me, because I'm more than just the story I tell myself; I'm the composite of events that encounter me, even some behind my back.[24] These are events like when I failed to read the poem and knew I was stupid in fifth grade, or when my dad called on Memorial Day 1999 to tell me my parents were divorcing. These events are also part of my history. When they arrived they gave me, for better or worse, a new future. So while I wouldn't choose them, and some of them I even try hard to forget, they are painted on my being. They are events that make me, because they direct my history, steering the rudder moving me through time and space.[25] I identify with them even if I wish I didn't (this in itself shows that identity is something much different than consumer choice or association with ideologies).

There is a narrative necessity to my existence. I live out of the story I tell myself about myself. But these negative events reveal that my being is more than simply a story (never just a collage of likes, ideologies, and interests). I

24. This is why it is always wrong for a white person in America to say, "Racism and slavery has nothing to do with me. It happened way before I was born." That's always wrong because even events that we don't give room to in our individual or even communal stories impact us. Just because I refuse to tell my own story within the history of a racist nation doesn't mean it isn't an event that affects my future. They have to matter to me because they happened; their historical reality makes them have something to do with me. It is a particular form of oppression to say to people that they need to get over a historical happening. Jeffrey McSwain discusses the need for people of privilege to confess their racism, saying that from the logic of the *simul* it is much better to confess the possibility of this sin than to assume innocence. McSwain, "*Simul* Sanctification: Karl Barth's Appropriation of Luther's Dictum *Simul Iustus et Peccator*" (PhD diss., University of St. Andrews, 2015).

25. Douglas Knight adds, "So far I have suggested that being is constituted by the whole economy of action in which we give and receive our identities. Now we must say that appearances add up to create beings. What we come to be is really a matter of the accounts that other people render of us. We demand that others speak and tell us who they are. We want them to spell out for us the relationship they have with us, and that they want with us, and what we have to gain from them. Their accounts either give or withhold our being from us." *The Eschatological Economy: Time and Hospitality of God* (Grand Rapids: Eerdmans, 2006), 23.

can't be reduced to some story another tells, or even I tell, about me. I'm even more than I can tell about myself. I can self-edit my fifth grade failure from my story, but still somehow, like soft clay, the weight of that event presses its mark on my being (for all its weirdness, and in many ways perpetuation of distorted views of identity—this is what psychoanalysis taught us in the early twentieth century).

And yet while I'm more than a story, in one way or another I'm always in pursuit of a story about existence that is true, that correlates with the event-full-ness of reality itself. I'm bound in a reality of events that happen, arriving to encounter my being. It's not story that constitutes my ontology (my being) but the fact that I am, that I exist in the time and space—in particular times and particular spaces, like Memorial Day 1999 and Mrs. Gentar's classroom in 1985.[26] I have being because of events in time and space. I no doubt make sense of these events through a story; I have storied the events of my history, not because I am a story but because I am—in time and space.[27] I'm a person with a history.[28] In fact the only way to make sense of the events of my reality is to narrate them, but even so, the narrative doesn't replace reality; the story is never more than my being.

Despite what some narrative and post-liberal theologians have argued, God is not ontologically a story.[29] God is an event of arriving, a personal being that shows up. To Israel, God is the God of Abraham, Isaac, and Jacob, a living, personal God who moves in history, making God's identity (who God is) bound to acts in time and space.[30] This God is a living God because this God

26. This echoes Martin Heidegger in *Sein und Zeit* (San Francisco: HarperSanFrancisco, 1962).

27. Robert W. Jenson shows how this is connected to God's own being: "The life of any person is both one event and many events. Therefore, to grasp myself whole, I must grasp the mutual dramatic coherence of the events of my life. At this point we may make the demand more specific: I must grasp the faithfulness of each of my acts and sufferings to all the rest. But as a creature, I do not have this faithfulness in myself; I have it in the coherence of God's intention for me. Moreover, as a fallen creature I actively fight against dependence on God and so against my own coherence with myself. Thus in daily experience I am threatened by absurdity, by disintegration of my life into a mere pointless sequence of happenings." *Systematic Theology: The Works of God* (Oxford: Oxford University Press, 1999), 1:222.

28. Congdon echoes my point here about identity: "True humanity is historical. There is nothing behind or above one's history. . . . Each person is a historical being whose being is thus only ever in becoming. People are inseparable from the historical moments in which they exist in relation to God, the world, and themselves." *The God Who Saves*, 18.

29. For a discussion of this, see Terrence Tilley, *Story Theology* (Wilmington, DE: Michael Glazier, 1985).

30. "Israel's and the church's God is thus identified by specific temporal actions and is known within certain temporal communities by personal names and identifying descriptions thereby provided. . . . It is the metaphysically fundamental fact of Israel's and the church's faith that its God is freely but, just so, truly self-identified by, and so with, contingent created temporal events." Jenson, *Systematic Theology*, 1:46, 48.

identifies with events, making the happenings of these events God's identity. We can know who God is by spotting the events that God identifies with. Because God is an event of specific happening in time, story or narrative becomes central. To know anything about this God is to rehearse these events in the only form we have[31]—story.[32] That's why Brueggemann says that the pattern of the exodus becomes paradigmatic, revealing God's being in God's action.

God is the one who identifies his own unique being with the particular events of exodus and resurrection. Because God arrives as an event in history, God identifies with events, and these particular events of exodus and resurrection reveal God's being through God's action. Because God identifies with these events, they reveal God's identity. God is who frees Israel from Egypt and raises Jesus from the dead. God's own being can no longer be extracted from these particular events; they are part of God's story that reveals God's being. We cannot talk about God's being without talking about the historical events that God identified with through God's action, just as I cannot talk about myself without telling stories of Maisy, Owen, and my parents' divorce. There is no way of talking about God disconnected, and cordoned off, from God's action. We can only know God as God has chosen to reveal himself, and this is always within a history of encounter.

Because God identifies with events, there is good news of healing, transformation, and salvation for me. The God who is an event is able—willing—to identify with those painful events in time and space that I wish were not part of me, that scar my being, and that shift my future somewhere dark. God gives his very presence to these events. God makes my painful events part of his own history because God encounters me in time and space with a word. And if these events are part of God's own history, then they are determined by God's own destiny, bound in God's own life and inner history—which, as we'll see, is the loving communion of God's ministering to Godself as Father, Son, and Holy Spirit. For Paul to say that "it is no longer I who live, but it is Christ

31. Jenson argues that God's own identity is based on dramatic coherence, in stories of action. He explains the ramifications of this: "The proposition that God's self-identity lies in dramatic coherence is in any case mandatory for those who wish to worship the biblical God. For if we cannot construe the biblical God's self-identity in this way, then we cannot construe it at all; then we do not know any one such reality as the biblical God. Otherwise than dramatically, the Bible's theological descriptions, accounts of divine action, and worshipful invocations are too mutually conflicted to suggest referral to a same someone." *Systematic Theology*, 1:64.

32. Scott Swain states Jenson's perspective, which I'm seeking to follow: "Narrative represents God as the sort of God whose being takes its concrete form in a temporally ordered dramatic plot." *The God of the Gospel: Robert Jenson's Trinitarian Theology* (Downers Grove, IL: InterVarsity, 2013), 69.

who lives in me" (Gal. 2:20) is to say that the event that I identify with—that makes my identity—is Christ himself. My own painful events are now Christ's.

The exodus and resurrection reveal that God particularly chooses to identify with those caught in impossibility, weighed by a heavy death experience, like Martin Luther King Jr. Because God identifies so fully with the event of the crucified Jesus, all historical events of death become concrete places with which God identifies.[33] So now any death experience, as Paul saw,[34] becomes the place where God is present, ministering a new future called *resurrection* and a new identity called *being in Christ* (Gal. 2:20). But this has only given us the proper stance for our jujitsu move, readying us to use the weight of the secular age against itself to direct our pastoral practice.

### The Black Hole of Event

The ramification of these thoughts takes us back to address our secular age through the event of God's seeming absence, readying us now to put our jujitsu stance into action. God chooses to identify with (to locate himself in) events of God's absence (that'll make your mind spin as much as that God's being is in becoming!). Think of it like this: exodus and resurrection reveal God's direct presence; God comes speaking and moving, fully identifying with these events. These events are the happenings that reveal God's presence and future. But these events that reveal God's presence come only after the event of God's seeming absence, just as God is seemingly absent to Abram and the earth spins with no Israel until God arrives. To say that God arrives is to say that there are events in which God seems absent—like when the diagnosis of cancer comes to Paul Kalanithi, or when the events of rejection become so identified with the being of a man that pills and death feel like his only option.[35]

In Egypt, Israel is in the heaviest and longest of oppressions. Within the event of their slavery, Israel *cannot* be perceived as God's people, for they are godforsaken in Egypt. And Jesus, from the event of his crucifixion, cannot be God's Son, for he is dying mercilessly on a tree. It appears, for this living

33. Jüngel has made a very similar point in claiming that God identifies with perishing in the perishing Jesus. See his *Death: The Riddle and the Mystery* (Philadelphia: Westminster, 1974). All perishing, as his colleague Jürgen Moltmann argues, is the location of God's identification. Moltmann makes this point more with regard to the historical (even Hegelian) vein, than does Jüngel. See Moltmann, *The Crucified God* (Minneapolis: Fortress, 1974).

34. See part 2 in volume 1 for more on this.

35. McFadyen says something similar: "Entering into the death-orientation of another, being open to a closed person, means following the path of death oneself for the sake of life. Paradigmatically, it means following God in Christ, restoring and maintaining communication, celebrating and proclaiming the power of life in its apparent contradiction." *Call to Personhood*, 171.

God, *the events that bring his presence arrive on the horizon of his absence.* It is the event of God's perceived absence that sets the stage for God's coming presence.[36] If identity is bound in the events with which one identifies, then the God of exodus and resurrection is the one who arrives when nothingness and death are insurmountable. When you are locked in the horizon of a death event, certain God is absent—it is then that God arrives!

If you want to watch a bad movie from the late 1990s, check out *Event Horizon*. It's too bad to even recap its plot, but its name comes from a term coined in physics that was made popular by Stephen Hawking. Building off Albert Einstein's theory of general relativity and the observation of black holes, Hawking surmised that there would be a point in space where the massive gravitational pull of a black hole would be so intense that nothing could escape it, not even light. A spaceship traveling toward a black hole, like in *Interstellar*, would have all sorts of options—its history in its own control because the ship could determine its own next event, determining its own future. The ship could turn right or left, head for this galaxy, that planet, or another star. But Hawking theorized that if this ship got too close to a black hole—particularly these massive black holes that appear to be at the center of each galaxy—entering its gravitational horizon, the pull would be too strong and the ship would be sucked into the nothingness. When the ship hits the point of no return, its history would be tied to the pull of the black hole, and it would have entered the event horizon.

The God who identifies with exodus and resurrection arrives when human action is rendered impossible, when the gravitational pull into nothingness is so strong that there is no possible identity outside the event of the black hole of death (Eph. 2:5: "even when we were dead through our trespasses, [God] made us alive together with Christ"). This is what Martin Luther King Jr. encounters at his kitchen table. God arrives when human act and being are caught in the event horizon of nothingness—as in Egypt and the crucifixion.

For example, this God comes speaking after Sarah's womb is dead and her identity locked in the event horizon of nothingness, when she is assumed to

36. When I say that God is seemingly absent, I mean to highlight the "seemingly." I mean something like Jüngel does when he imagines the *deus absconditus* within a sacramental reality. The seeming absence brings the presence. Jüngel says, "In so far as God reiterates his own objectivity in the creaturely objectivity which is foreign to him, God's being-as-object is sacramental reality. God's being-as-object as sacramental reality signifies an honour for the creature which 'in its objectivity becomes the representative of the objectivity of God Himself.' . . . Because God is the *deus revelatus* [revealed God] who graciously honours his creature, in his sacramental being-as-object he is the *deus absconditus* [hidden God]." *God's Being Is in Becoming*, 65.

be nothing but a god-cursed woman with no future.[37] In the same way, God comes speaking only when the events of Israel's past have long been forgotten and pharaohs who do not know Joseph have imposed an identity of subhuman slaves. And God comes acting when Jesus is three days dead, the event of his violent demise proof that his identity is as just another pretender. God arrives not in psychic states or ideas but in events in time and space. But these events are, first, experiences of nothingness (not religious experiences), of God's absence. This is the jujitsu move that uses the opaqueness of divine action in our secular age against itself, claiming, like I told Maisy, that when things get impossible and God seems absent, ready yourself to receive the event of God's arriving.

This new event (of God's action) inside the event horizon of nothingness provides a profound new identity. Sarah remains a barren woman, but because her barrenness is now the location of God's arrival, she is blessed (graced); out of nothingness comes new life. Isaac is the (personal) event of promise. Because God has heard the cries of Israel, rescuing Israel from the nothingness of death, Israel is more than ever God's people. They are given a new identity that transforms Israel from a nation of slaves to a nation of ministers. The event of nothingness is the stage on which God arrives, and therefore is not to be obliterated or erased from identity when God comes. Even though she is pregnant, Sarah remains barren; this is central to her identity. It is God who gives her an impossible child right in her barrenness. She is now forever known as a barren mother as witness to God's arriving in nothingness.

What led Martin Luther King Jr. into the event horizon of God's arrival was not his own spiritual vitality or even his goodness but his death experience. In that kitchen God showed up speaking, but only because King was pulled into the event horizon of nothingness. The concrete, lived experience of impingement was what led to the eventful encounter with the living God, because this God acts as minister. It is the confession of impossibility that opens our eyes, even in a secular age, to see the possibility of the arriving God. God comes to us with spoken word and is found near, identifying most particularly with the events we wish had not happened. God gives us a new story, a new history written on top and through these negative events. God turns our mourning into joy (Ps. 30) and our death into life, and transforms us into Christ (theosis), not because we are made gods, but because while we are yet creatures, our history is Christ's, our story God's own. God bears our events (in the cross) while God's event (of trinitarian love) is given to us.

37. T. F. Torrance highlights this: "In other words, Jesus seeks to be yoked together with people in their awful burdens of sin and guilt that he may bear them." *Incarnation: The Person and Life of Christ* (Downers Grove, IL: IVP Academic, 2008), 135.

At the kitchen table, King laments: "I am at the end of my power. I have *nothing* left." From this confession of nothingness King continues: "I could hear . . . [a] voice saying . . ." When Martin confesses that *he* can't do this—that there is no way that he can lead, bringing a new history to the people of the South—is when God arrives, speaking a ministering word of new possibility. Martin has tried to move himself away from the pull of the black hole. With the power of his courage he's tried to avoid the event horizon of nothingness. But at the kitchen table he lets go. Pulled into the nothingness, he finds something incredible. To enter the event horizon of God's own being is to confess your death experience. It is like Hawking's theory, to admit that you're being pulled toward the nothingness of a black hole. But just as physicists today believe that the monster black holes at the center of each galaxy, frighteningly able to eat whole solar systems, are actually there to create something new, a kind of hidden engine of new creation, so too are our own events of nothingness. They are monstrous, but in God's sovereignty they are forced to serve God by becoming the stage on which God plays out the revealing of God's being through God's acts. Out of the event horizon of nothingness comes the arriving of God, who speaks words of new possibility, giving himself to us as minister. This is what King means when he speaks of "that power that can make a way out of no way." And the "no ways" of our secular age are the very place where we begin to await divine action.

### Into Pastoral Ministry

It will be very difficult in our secular age for the pastor to witness to divine action if he succumbs to religious experience or turns God into an idea. The immanent frame will impose such cross-pressure on these accommodating stances that they simply will not be able to stand without either a disengaged ambivalence (whatever works for you!) or a church like Saddleback that can meet almost all your needs and wants.

The way to perceive divine action in a secular age is to give your attention to events, willing to be present in them. This makes the pastoral task quite different from that of a therapist. The pastor, for centuries, has been the one invited to both share in and help discern the meaning of life's events; in the pull of the privatization of religion we've lost this. But now that many of the cultural structures of the past are absent, sharing in people's events as a way to discern meaning may be as important as ever. For instance, the pastor needs to stand with people when the event horizon of nothingness dawns and they ask: What does it mean for me that my husband has been having an affair?

What is my identity now that this event has been revealed and there is no way for me to avoid my being identifying with this betrayal? What does God think of me now that I'm sick, now that my future is cancer? How can I think of myself now that this event has forced me to identify with it? What is love in the shadow of our son's addiction, when the events of his stealing, lying, and rage give me stabs of hating him, and then shame for doing so?

The pastor enters into time and space where the event of your nothingness happens, meeting you at the site of a crash or in a hospital room. The pastor, present as this event now presses its weight into your being, witnesses to a central chapter in the story you tell, or refuse to. The pastor's just showing up becomes powerful; it witnesses that in nothingness comes arrival. Up against nothingness, the pastor arrives to be present, witnessing with this presence that God too can and will arrive with ministry in just such times and places. The pastor's showing up to share in these events is a powerful testimony to divine action.

Showing up, the pastor might not say anything; it's often better if she doesn't, because her calling is to be present in the event, not leaving you to face the event horizon of nothingness alone. *She witnesses to the presence of God in nothingness through presence.*[38]

A therapist, for good reason, starts with the affect, providing ways of coping with the feelings. But the pastor attends to the event by being present in it. The therapist is not always concerned for the details of the event; *just tell me enough that I can get a sense of how this makes you feel*, often not needing details because she will not be making any moral declarations on the event. And even if the therapist cares for the details, the point, again for good reason, is to discuss strategies to equilibrate. The therapist is not there to share in the event, and particularly not to see how God is identifying with this event that you wish not to identify with. This is why very rarely will your therapist show up to sit with you in your grief. That's not her job. She'll give you an hour to share how your grief is making you feel, sharing how the event of loss is impacting you.

But a pastor is called to join the event, sitting in the grief, not protected by an armchair and an office door from the event horizon of your nothingness. And yet somehow we've lost this or become embarrassed by it, convinced there should be something more, not surprisingly making divine action more opaque. Too often the pastor passes on or diminishes participating in the event, wanting some other more relevant-seeming identity. Yet, if we're to attend to divine action, then it will be in locations of God's arriving. In these

38. Zizioulas highlights the direction of my own argument: "The revelation of God is an event in which man comes to experience, and share in, the life of God and of his fellow-man and the world, and this revelation brings new light and sense to all life." *Lectures in Christian Dogmatics*, 8.

moments of nothingness, the cross-pressure of the immanent frame shifts us open, making us aware that there indeed must be more, some other event that gives the events of my life meaning.

Howard Thurman was one of the greatest pastors in American history. He grew up in the thick racism and poverty of Daytona, Florida, in the early twentieth century. In his autobiography, *With Head and Heart*, he tells the story of what he calls "two events . . . that proved to be momentous."[39] Needing money to continue high school, Thurman took over a friend's shoeshine stand. But it soon became clear that he had neither the skills nor the time to make the funds he needed. It was up against this experience of nothingness that the first event arrived. Thurman explains, "I was seated on the shoeshine stand thinking about my plight when, for some reason, I noticed the gables of a house directly across the river. . . . I knew it was the winter home of Mr. James N. Gamble of the Procter and Gamble soap company. He was well known in our community because of his generosity. . . . On impulse, I decided to write a letter to him asking for a loan."[40]

But there was one big problem; Gamble had already left for Ohio for the season. Dropping the letter at his winter home would get it to him way too late for Thurman to continue in school. Thurman had no way to get Gamble's Ohio address. In this context of mixed decisive impingement—poverty—and impossibility—no way to get the address—a great coincidence occurred, something strangely uncanny.[41] Or maybe it was more than that, for its arrival would change Thurman's history. He explains: "Then, returning to work after lunch, I rode past the home of a very ill-tempered woman who came out of her front door just as I was riding by and yelled, 'Boy! Come here.' . . . She scrutinized me for a moment, then said, 'You look like a boy who can be trusted. Here, mail these letters.'"[42]

Thurman reluctantly agreed. She handed the letters to him, and he headed for the mailbox. Just before placing the letters in the box, "I looked at them, and to my utter amazement, one was addressed to Mr. James N. Gamble, 1430 Union Trust Building, Cincinnati, Ohio."[43] Within a week Thurman received a typewritten letter with a promise to pay for his schooling. Without

39. Thurman, *With Head and Heart: The Autobiography of Howard Thurman* (San Diego: Harcourt Brace & Company, 1979), 25.

40. Thurman, *With Head and Heart*, 25.

41. Nicholas Wolterstorff in his book *Divine Discourse: Philosophical Reflections on the Claim That God Speaks* (Cambridge: Cambridge University Press, 1995) discusses the philosophical conception of God speaking. In a chapter titled "Are We Entitled?" he discusses this coincidence—or uncanny experiences, as he calls them—in relation to divine discourse.

42. Thurman, *With Head and Heart*, 26.

43. Thurman, *With Head and Heart*, 26.

this event, this odd coincidence, Thurman wouldn't have finished high school and never would've become a pastor.

These history-forming events have a way of shaking us loose from the impositions of the immanent frame and its closed spin. If we can discuss them (giving them narrative shape), they can awaken us to the possibility of divine action. Maybe one of the reasons that miracles and God's speaking seem so improbable to people in the secular age is because we never talk about them when they happen in our lives.

The closed spin of the immanent frame has no answer for why Thurman was given the address just when he needed it. The closed spin heralds that it is just pure coincidence. But tending to the event of coincidence and the impact on our person is likely to give us an open take on the immanent frame (i.e., to have the sense that the world, even the immanent frame, is open to mystery and transcendence), leading even unbelieving people to say things like, "I guess it was meant to be" or "Someone was watching out for you." By attending to events in pastoral ministry, we give people eyes to see divine action even in our secular age. This helps them lean into the open take, pushing beyond idioms by telling the stories of how these events of seeming coincidence shape their identity.

To show further how eventful coincidence pushes us to open takes of divine action in the immanent frame, think of one of the best offbeat movies of the last twenty years. In *I Heart Huckabees*, Jason Schwartzman's character, Albert, has a coincidence he can't make sense of. So he decides to visit Bernard and Vivian Jaffe, existential detectives, played by Dustin Hoffman and Lily Tomlin. The Jaffes try to convince Albert that his coincidences are really not coincidences at all, because everything in life is connected. But the Jaffes also have a rogue former student, the French Caterine Vauban, who has fallen far from her teachers' romantic transcendentalism to become a nihilist. Vauban agrees that Albert's coincidence is nothing—not because everything is connected but because nothing is. All life is chaos; there is no meaning in his coincidence; it is surely and totally random. For Vauban the event horizon has no personal redemptive quality but is just evaporation of all meaning and therefore being.

The movie reveals the cross-pressure of the immanent frame. What are our coincidences? Pushing beyond the movie into real life, what are these events like Thurman's that have the potency to form our identity, providing a new direction to our history? Are these random and chaotic experiences? Or are there forces moving us?

At the end of the movie Albert realizes that neither the Jaffes nor Vauban is right. His coincidences aren't just part of the fabric of interconnection, having no real meaning because everything is the same. Nor can his coincidences just be pure chaos. They seem too directional, too important to be random. After witnessing the house fire of his hated antagonist, Brad, Albert, sharing in this personal event, is moved to compassion. This leads Albert to realize that the Jaffes are right and wrong: there is interconnection, *not* because everything is the same but rather because interconnection is born from sharing in the event of nothingness. Then so too is Vauban right and wrong. There is nothingness and chaos in the world, but Albert is recognizing that when events of nothingness are shared, he finds meaning, even a kind of union, swinging him back to the Jaffes, but this union is forged through sharing in brokenness, swinging him back to Vauban. Albert is experiencing that ministry is an event that leads to an interconnection through sharing in another person's events of nothingness. Ministry gives us the ability to look directly at decisive impingements for divine action, wondering if a coincidence is just a blip in the code of our lives or the movements of the minister God in history.

Nadia Bolz-Weber takes this attention to events back to pastoral practice when telling the story of her clinical pastoral education (CPE). It was the Tuesday of Holy Week; her mind centered in on the events that she most deeply identifies with, and her children reminded her that their Easter baskets needed jelly beans. Just then she was paged to go to the ER. She tells what she found: "When I got to the ER, things felt different. Quiet. On the table was a thirty-one-year-old DOA (dead on arrival). She was killed when she stepped out of her car on the highway. Her two-year-old and five-year-old sons were in the minivan. 'They are unhurt, and we need you to stay with them until other family can arrive,' I was instructed."

But then Bolz-Weber says to herself, repeating the information she was given, "They were unhurt. Right."[44] This is the attention to the event—and why, for some, CPE is so valuable: it forces you to attend to events and dig for coincidence, free from concern for budgets and building to do so. Bolz-Weber became aware that this event will forever be part of the history of these boys. It will be the black hole of nothingness that defines their identities. Unhurt? Sure, no broken bones, but what is that next to the obliteration of being and the annihilation of love? What is the amputation even of a limb next to the event of soul-scraping loss? (What actually makes the amputation so painful is the event horizon of loss and recast future.) All she could do was be with them. Feeling inadequate to provide anything else but her presence, she played games with them until their family came.

The pastor joins these kinds of events, and in them inhales, anticipating the possibility of divine action, awaiting the arrival of God, even anticipating coincidence of connection through sharing in brokenness. The pastor waits.

44. Nadia Bolz-Weber, *Pastrix: The Cranky, Beautiful Faith of a Sinner and Saint* (New York: Jericho, 2013), 82.

She doesn't bring the arriving of God; she can only know the conditions, like a farmer looking at the sky. She can sense whether event is arriving, leaning into the darkness to see the connections and actions of God's moving.

God arrives not as a wizard with a magic wand, erasing events like the neuralyzer on *Men in Black*. Rather, this God of Israel is a minister arriving with actions that identify God's own being with an individual event of nothingness. What a pastor does, most particularly in a secular age, is join events of nothingness, witnessing to nothingness in the world. She calls the congregation to confess their events of nothingness, because in these events the God who is the event of ministry comes. The pastor is present in her people's events of nothingness not as a benign charm but as a storyteller. The pastor, standing knee-deep in these events, invites those going through them to narrate them with the pastor's help. But this help that invites narration is most often done not with words but just by being present. We can make sense of the events of our lives only by telling of them, and when we do, we see more interactions and odd coincidences that invite us into open takes. The pastor is able to be present because of the stories of the event she embodies—the testimonies of the community, the story of the exodus and resurrection she's preached.

So the pastor's job is not to conjure up the presence of God (this is impossible both in a secular age and in a theology of God's becoming). From her own talent or skill she can never make light to cast into the darkness, revealing divine action. This doesn't minimize the importance of the pastor; it heightens it. The pastor's job is to bear the darkness, to join the pull of the event horizon of nothingness. And in this pull she prepares—with practices and prayers—for the arriving of a speaking God, ready to even lean into odd events like Thurman's. Even more, these practices (like communion and preaching and prayer) not only give us dispositions to hear the speaking God, but because they do, we claim that it is through these actions that God speaks. But we must remember that in the immanent frame there is no release from cross-pressure. Just when divine action seems its most impossible, when prayer and practices feel weakest, we find ourselves open to God's arrival. The pastor's job in a secular age is to join the cross-pressure, welcoming the cross-pressure as the very location of ministry.

It was when King confessed the nothingness and let his being drift into its impossibility that a new possibility broke forth. The pastor joined his people's events of nothingness, and from within them God arrived, *speaking*, saying, "Stand up for righteousness, stand up for truth; and I will be at your side forever."[45] The call of ministry comes from the event of nothingness. From

45. Burrow, *God and Human Dignity*, 106.

this event God speaks, promising the presence of God's being through acts of ministry that identify God's very being with your events of nothingness. From no way, God makes a way.

Bolz-Weber reflects on her first call on CPE. Entering the emergency room, she was told it was trauma 1; the crisis of the event couldn't be higher. Everyone was rushing to make sure this event didn't end in the morgue. They were all fighting to keep the event horizon of death at bay, to free the man from its quickening pull. All tools of the immanent frame were needed, and all hands were on deck. And like realizing you're underdressed at a fancy dinner party, the young pastor, now standing in the room, became uncomfortably aware that she had nothing to do.

Bolz-Weber says, "A nurse stepped back to where I was standing, and I leaned over to her. 'Everyone seems to have a job, but what am I doing here?'" This question may best encompass the pastoral malaise we wrestled with in part 1. Wanting to help but feeling powerless, everyone else with a job, the pastor asks, "What am I doing here?" Our secular age has led too many pastors to concede that they have nothing really to do with events of people's lives. They don't really need us, until we convince them that our church has some commodity or resource for them.

"She looked at my badge," Bolz-Weber continues, "and said, 'Your job is to be aware of God's presence in the room while we do our jobs.'"

The nurse knew that it was in this event where God seemed absent and circumstances seemed decisively impinged that the God of exodus and resurrection may arrive. In this cross-pressure where all the tools of the immanent frame are pushed to their limit and the event of the crisis shows them feeble, it is now time to breathe and expect an arrival. So the young pastor stepped back, inhaled, opened her eyes, leaned in—not for something to do but into the nothingness itself—and awaited the event of God's arrival. This is what pastors do: they lean into nothingness and expectantly wait, showing up as an invitation for people to lean into the coincidences and uncanny experiences. The pastor holds a space, preparing for a future when God arrives speaking.

Bolz-Weber concludes, giving us a beautiful picture of a pastor in a secular age: "For the rest of those two-and-a-half months I often found myself in the ER trauma room watching life going in and out of the patients on the table—the doctors and nurses violently attempting to resuscitate them. And in that messy chaos, my job was to just stand there and be aware of God's presence in the room. Kind of a weird job description, but there it was, and in those moments, I felt strangely qualified."[46]

46. Bolz-Weber, *Pastrix*, 80–81.

# 12

## a run into the wild

### *meeting the ministering God who sees*

Maybe we shouldn't be surprised. The biblical text is never shy in dealing with the depth of divine and human events. But if you were to list the topics that most clearly reveal God's being as minister, I doubt an event of slut shaming would be on it. But this is Hagar's experience, and it reveals that not only does this God arrive when people are caught in the event horizon of a death experience, but when this God arrives, he comes as minister.

All the key figures in the biblical text are flawed. Abraham is no different. His faith has been reckoned unto him as righteousness. Yet we must remember that his faith is not his accomplishment but his openness and expectation that the future that God speaks will come to be. There is, no doubt, a deep fidelity to the word of God in Abraham, but also a sense of naïveté.

When reading about Abraham, if you're not careful, Forrest Gump starts to emerge. Like Tom Hanks's epic character, Abraham seems a little arrested in his development for a seventy-five-year-old. And he seems to just fall into history-shaping circumstances. Abraham appears unable to make a clear decision, seeking to avoid conflict, which just leads him into more of it.[1] And

---

1. I'm sure that I've overdrawn the line between Abraham and Hanks's character. I do so mainly for dramatic effect, but there is something to it. Terence Fretheim explains, showing both the personality flaw and faithfulness of Abraham: "This characteristic of Abraham has been recurrent in the narrative (cf. [Gen.] 16:6; 17:18). He has difficulty taking decisive action; yet, he shows deep levels of concern for the plight of the human beings involved, and he does not

213

yet he does decide to take a bold step, a history-making move. Leaving his father's house in Ur for a new land, he follows the voice of a God that neither he nor his father has known. It's a little like Forrest unknowingly running himself onto the Alabama football team and then to the all-American team.

As the story unfolds, we learn that Abraham has baby-momma drama, and like Forrest's, it comes more from his frozen inaction than his sly skills. As a matter of fact, whenever Abraham tries to be skilled, things get painfully awkward. Abraham is no player's player; he's mostly a man with a cringe, ducking around corners, a little confused about what he should do next. So when Sarai, his wife—whom Abram has already stupidly told an Egyptian monarch was his sister, only to have her married off and then given back after the truth was discovered (Gen. 20)—tells him that she has a plan of action to give him the heir he needs, he's all ears. Sarai tells Abram that he should sleep with her slave girl, who, not coincidentally, is from Egypt.

The reader knows that this is a little hint of a coming reversal, like an Easter egg on *Game of Thrones*. This whole story of Abraham is only the prehistory to the exodus, which is the event of Yahweh's great identification. An Egyptian is in slavery to the founding father of Israel, and she will be treated harshly, just as Israel is by their Egyptian slave masters. And it all starts when Sarai says to Abram, "You see that the Lord has prevented me from bearing children; go in to my slave-girl; it may be that I shall obtain children by her" (Gen. 16:2).

It's hard to know what's happening here. Maybe Sarai and her slave girl have their wires crossed. Sarai imagines that this is a surrogate situation, a little pay-to-provide and then disappear. After all, Sarai doesn't even use her name but calls her only "my slave girl." Maybe the thought is that the baby, when it arrives, will be given to Sarai as her own. Sure, the slave girl can send a letter on his birthday, but no trips to Disney World, no Mother's Day brunch. Or at the very least, her status as a slave girl won't change, even if she births the heir. But that's not the case, and it's clear even before this baby is born.

As Sarai stands in the shadow of her own impossibility, the event horizon sucking her into nothingness, the event of the slave girl's pregnancy makes Sarai's identity circle around the pit of nothingness. Forced to identify further with this painful event of barrenness, Sarai lashes out. Contempt is what she feels—not *for* the slave girl but *from* her. The event of the slave girl's conception of the heir feels like a cruel reminder of the event of Sarai's barrenness. It is painful because it solidifies both of their identities, and in two opposed

---

finally stand in the way of God's directive." *Abraham: Trails of Family and Faith* (Columbia: University of South Carolina Press, 2007), 100.

directions. The meaningless slave girl now has a new identity as mother of the heir, and Sarai is totalized as barren. She's been barren for decades, but now there is an heir, and he came from someone else. Sarai is now surely cursed to die childless.

She won't stand for these feelings of contempt; she hates the story she assumes everyone is telling about her. The slave girl's pregnant glow is a mocking accusation that Sarai can't stand. Abram's joy and tenderness to the girl are a slap to Sarai's face. After all, this was her idea—that duff! Abram was clueless, and Sarai found a way! And what does she get for her supposed selfless ingenuity? Mockery, derision, and shame—made to feel small by the very girl whose eyes never before left the ground in Sarai's presence.

Sarai's had enough, so she goes to that Forrest Gump of a man Abram and accuses him, saying, "May the wrong done to me be on you! I gave my slave-girl to your embrace, and when she saw that she had conceived, she looked on me with contempt. May the LORD judge between you and me!" (Gen. 16:5).

You can almost see the red running up Abram's neck, the sweat beading on his forehead. He hates conflict and is now confused about what to do next. He feels like this was a trap; this wasn't his plan! As usual, he doesn't have a plan at all but just waits around for something to come about. That's how this all started in the first place; God showed up speaking.

So, unwisely, he says to his irate wife, "Your slave-girl [not even naming her] is in your power; do to her as you please" (Gen. 16:6a). Essentially he is saying, "This wasn't my idea, woman! Do what you want with that girl! She means nothing to me!" There are no questions here that would invite the confession of a death experience, setting the stage for an encounter of personhood in a spirit of ministry. There is no story that reveals the events, that makes a person. There is only self-justification wrapped in the play of power and its rights. This is the perfect climate for dehumanization, because it evacuates the condition for ministry.

And so the slut shaming begins. "Then Sarai dealt harshly with her, and she ran away from her" (Gen. 16:6b). We are left to imagine what mocking words and terrible actions are summed up in the phrase "dealt harshly." Barefoot and pregnant—OK, at least pregnant—the slave girl ran into the *wild* to escape Sarai's harshness.

## Into the Wild

It's become a big thing in our secular age to return to the wilderness. In 1996, Jon Krakauer wrote a nonfiction book called *Into the Wild*. In 2007 Sean

Penn made it into a movie of the same title, starring Emile Hirsch, who plays Christopher McCandless. McCandless graduated from Emory University and left everything behind, traveling the West, eventually making it into the Alaskan wild. McCandless was haunted by the events of his childhood and the distortions of life imposed by a consumeristic society. So with an early 1990s cultural critique that echoed David Foster Wallace, and yearning to encounter something more, McCandless left it all behind. He walked *alone* into the wild, looking for something bigger than strip malls.

In 2012, Cheryl Strayed released her memoir called *Wild: From Lost to Found on the Pacific Crest Trail*. It's Strayed's story of events of loss and self-destruction that could only be healed by her too walking *alone* into the wild, this time on the Pacific Crest Trail. In 2014, Jean-Marc Vallee made Strayed's book into a movie called *Wild*, starring Reese Witherspoon as Strayed. The movie depicts in beautiful detail the dangerous solitary walk into the wild that delivered the healing, perspective, and grounding Strayed needed.

In the summer of 2015 my friend Nancy Lee, the same person who gave me Paul Kalanithi's book, walked part of the Superior Hiking Trail with her husband, Paul. Along the journey, they ran into a half dozen young women, all alone, looking for themselves and something more by following Strayed's lead into the wild.

Charles Taylor explains why this move into the wildness has become big in our secular age. In a chapter called "The Dark Abyss of Time," he says, "The praise of wilderness didn't imply that it offered an alternative site for a better life. Its importance was that it put us in touch with something greater, which we could easily lose sight of [in our secular age]. The wilds being 'desolate' and 'lonesome,' fearful and forbidding, was essential to their having this effect."[2]

With no clear transcendent referent, and divine action hard to spot in our private lives of consumer goods and technological advances, a lonely walk into the wild brings some of us closer to spotting meaning. It puts us at risk, allowing the notes of death and finitude to be heard above the Muzak of malls, YouTube videos, and satellite radio. It is odd that in our secular age some of us must walk into the wild, placing ourselves at great risk, to find ourselves again. But we can do this—young women everywhere have followed Strayed—because we assume disenchantment and yet still sense the weak signal of enchantment.

The wilderness has always been assumed to be a godforsaken place. John the Baptist comes with a word from the wilderness, revealing that he is a prophet (Matt. 3). For most, the wilderness is the place one goes when the

2. Taylor, *A Secular Age* (Cambridge, MA: Belknap Press, 2007), 341.

pull of God's apparent absence throbs with pain. Jesus is tempted in the wilderness (Luke 4), and Israel wanders (Num. 10) in the wilderness due to its disobedience. It is in the wilderness that Israel is taught to trust that, particularly in these godforsaken locales, God acts. McCandless and Strayed enter the wild because they've experienced acute events of nothingness. The nothingness is too strong. Though they both assume no divine action in the world, they nevertheless enter the location of nothingness—the wild—looking for some kind of meaning. They rightly sense that meaning comes through nothingness, and the wilderness is a nothingness of vast beauty that delivers an existential strike. That's why their stories inspire. They heroically enter the nothingness of the wild, without the creature comforts we depend on, to discover if the wild might be a counterintuitive salve to the nothingness that presses into their identities by the events of loss.

For the slave girl in Genesis 16, things are a little different. She isn't hero-ically looking for herself. Rather, she runs into the wild because she feels the sure absence of God. Slut shamed, she is godforsaken; the father of her baby has turned on her. She is alone and disgraced; the wilderness is her destiny. The gods of the area are bound to places and peoples; they do not move, as Michel Foucault has taught us.[3] For the slave girl, to enter the wilderness, particularly alone, is to enter godforsakenness. It is to die, succumbing to a massive black hole of nothingness.

The slave girl enters the wild for the same reason as McCandless and Strayed, because the death experience has become too much. They all run to places where they cannot be found. But unlike Strayed, the slave girl assumes there is no return. Once she is in the wild and godforsaken, her demise is sure. She may make it eventually to a city, but she is just as inclined to let the wild take her. Once you pass the event horizon, there is no coming back, so Abram and his household are gone. When she runs into the wild, she is lost.

## GPS Coordinates in Wilderness

And yet, as an echo that the event of God's arriving is coming, we're told exactly where the slave girl is, almost given her GPS coordinates. We're di-rectly told her location—not her subjective feelings or what ideas were in her head, but where she is. This reveals that what's about to happen is an event of encounter, coming in time and space; it will be a happening in history. *This is where ministry always occurs and why the pastor has to show up.* Ministry happens in concrete locations in time and space, in the wilderness of a death

---

3. See chapter 9, particularly under the section "The Pastor in Motion."

experience, where we worry we're lost and can't be found. That's why we need to know her location.

This is how all stories that are events of encounter begin. I say, "I was driving down Highway 10 at 9:30 or so on a Tuesday, when the deer came from the woods." Stories of encounter demand the details of historical location in time and space. I can't tell a story of encounter without it, and ministry is the event of encounter. I can't say, "Yeah, I hit a deer with my car. It happened at no particular time—it was kind of both night and morning. And where was I? Nowhere really. It was part Minnesota woods, part New South Wales beach, and it was just then that, bang!, the deer ran out."

If you heard this story, you'd imagine, and for good reason, that this wasn't an actual encounter with a real deer, because it couldn't be located in time and space and therefore couldn't be historical. You'd assume that I had an interesting psychic experience, or a dream, but not an encounter with an event that had direct impact on my own being in time and space. The event itself, then, because it happens outside of time and space, couldn't be ministry. To be ministered to, I need another to share in my location—to be there, to show up at a particular time and space. I need someone to share in the depths of the event that I'm experiencing by arriving and being an event who shares in this event that presses in on my identity. And that's exactly what God does here with Hagar.

We're told right where the girl can be found: sitting by the spring on the way to Shur (Gen. 16:7). In this place and at this time, God arrives, speaking. But God arrives because the angel has been seeking her. This God is a minister because this God seeks for us, and in places where any ordinary (non-ministering) deity has no business being found, like the wild. This searching God reflects the eagerness of the shepherd who goes seeking the lost sheep in Jesus's parable in Luke 15; he goes looking for us. God enters time and space to find us. God is the event of arrival, but this arriving isn't random; it isn't just chance, like my encounter with a deer on Highway 10. Rather, when this God arrives, it is because this God has been seeking. The slave girl is not only in a specific location but is found there by the seeking God. The minister who joins the ministering God is concerned to find people where they're at.

When God finds her, he calls her what Abram and Sarai don't: her name, Hagar. This pre-story that will lead to the central story of God's identification in the exodus reveals, again like an Easter egg, that this God operates in names. Names are important to God because God is an arrival who comes to those lost in a black hole of nothingness. This God must operate in names because this God goes looking, calling out (speaking) in the wild. We call out people's names when we look for them.

The addressing by and giving of names reveals what kind of arriving this is. God is a personal event seeking a personal encounter. God comes into a location looking for someone with a name. This is the eventful arrival of personhood—we know because we have a personal name, someone centrally lodged in a specific address. God arrives as an event that is personal—that is the disclosing of God's person to the personhood of another, and as we'll see, always for the sake of ministry. These actions of finding persons and speaking their names, giving them a new future in God's own person, reveal God's being as a minister. God comes speaking in a particular place and time to a particular person with a name. God finds Hagar and speaks to Hagar—first with a question, then with a command, and finally, most lengthily, with a promise.

### The Question

God, through an angel, asks, "Hagar, slave-girl of Sarai, where have you come from and where are you going?" (Gen. 16:8a). We, the hearers of this story, appear to know more than God. We know the facts (as should God): She's coming from Abram's dwelling. She's a pregnant teenage runaway who's gone into the wild. She's a wildling, facing the cold facts that she is shamed, discarded, and unlovable. If she survives the wild, somehow finding a way through its godforsakenness, she's headed to Vegas or Los Angeles (or maybe in this case back to Egypt). The answers are obvious. Why would God ask this question?

God asks not because God doesn't know. God knows enough to rehearse Hagar's story to her, saying, *I know the events that seem to define you. I know your history. You are the slave girl of Sarai. I know you so personally that I know the events that press in and form your identity.*

God isn't looking for information with his question. Much like many of Jesus's questions in the Gospels (e.g., asking the father of the demon-possessed boy, "How long has this been happening to him?" Mark 9:21), this question is the invitation for Hagar to confess her death experience, to testify that she is in the pull of the event horizon of nothingness. *Hagar, where have you come from and where are you going?* She answers, "I am running away from my mistress Sarai" (Gen. 16:8b).

Hagar is telling her story, narrating her experience, confessing the events that press in on her being and form her identity. These events must be confessed, because God's arriving is a new event of God's action for her. This event of God's arriving will press itself on top of the events of her death experience, reshaping her with a new story. God asks a question because God's plan in arriving to Hagar is not to simply fix or scold her. God is there to minister to her. And therefore she must recount the events that painfully press into her being. That's why the encounter begins with a question. The God of Israel is no aloof deity; God is a personal force who addresses us by name, asking us questions and desiring to hear us tell our story. Because our story reveals the events we identify with, they are core to our being in time.

## The Command

From this place of confession, from the narrative of Hagar's death experience, and *only after it* comes the command: "Return to your mistress, and submit to her" (Gen. 16:9). Lost in the wild and confronting eye-to-eye her death experience, Hagar is found by God, who speaks her name and invites her to share her story. Her story is a prayer, a direct way of sharing *in* God's being through God's act of arriving. It is only after this moment of shared personhood that God's speaking turns from a question to a command—*return to Sarai*. It is not a cold, distant deity who gives her this command. It is the one who has heard her story, shared in it, and encountered her as a person.

McCandless and Strayed unknowingly were following the script of Hagar. They entered the wild to come eye-to-eye with their own death experience, hoping that from within the stare-off they'd hear a new calling, an all-new direction for their bruised lives. McCandless wanted to be called *away* from vapid suburbia, and Strayed wanted to get *away* from the burden of her loss. Yet for Hagar something different happens, revealing that it is the God of Israel who finds her. After sharing in Hagar's person by hearing her story, God calls her not *away from something* but *back to someone*, telling her to return to where she started. She's called to return not just to the house of Abram but to the side of Sarai. She's called back to share in Sarai's nothingness, as God has shared in Hagar's. Hagar is called to return to Sarai not as a shamed puppy but as her minister, as God is Hagar's. Hagar is to return empowered with a new identity as minister.

Sarai is in need of ministry; her context of decisive impingement is heavy. Sarai too is in a kind of wilderness, certain she is godforsaken. This all started the day Hagar was celebrated as being with child. The event of Sarai's barrenness pressed down on her being, locking her in with a painful identity she didn't want, leading her to interpret all her interactions contemptuously. Unable to bear the nothingness, she thrust Hagar into it.

Sarai is in need of a minister, and God is sending one. In beautiful irony, the ministering God is sending the very one who has every right to seek revenge. But through his own ministering being, God has called Hagar to put that aside, and with a kenotic[4] disposition (as we discussed in volume 1) to humbly submit. But it must be said again: God is calling Hagar, not to *know her place*, but to *be a minister*. She is called (ordained) to take on the very shape of God's own being and to minister to Sarai in mercy, forgiveness, and care. Now that God has arrived and ministered to Hagar, God has called her to return and minister to Sarai, to stand with her in her nothingness. Just as Moses is in the wild seeking a lost sheep when he stumbles upon the speaking God and then is called to some specific someones (the Israelites in Egypt), so too Hagar is called from an encounter with God in the wild to take on the kenotic form and minister to Sarai.[5]

Interestingly, both McCandless and Strayed enter the wild hoping to hear a call *away from something*, but instead both are called out of the wild when they hear the call *to someone*. Having stared down nothingness, they both hear the beckoning of personhood. A clear inner call arrives, summoning them to return from the wild for the sake of sharing in the life of *someone*. Even in a secular age, the immanent frame can be opened to divine action by the encounters with persons, and we most powerfully experience this openness when we hear the call to give and receive ministry.

In Penn's version of McCandless's story, he has been alone for months, staring into the abyss and beauty of the Alaskan wild, when he reads the prose of Leo Tolstoy's *Family Happiness and Other Stories* and its words of love, encounter, and connection with others. The call comes: *Return to them.* Seeing a vision of his sister, parents, and friends in his mind, he's beckoned from the wild to these specific someones. He has chosen a lonely exile, but now an overwhelming call to join his person with these particular others reaches out for him. Yet tragically the river is swollen, and he is now prisoner to his self-imposed exile. Soon enough, the hunger, aloneness, and finally death end his story.

Strayed's story has a different ending. She realizes that it wasn't the wild at all that saved her but the ministering encounters with other persons along the way. Like Hagar, having her person ministered to, she is called to share in the personhood of others. Vallee's version of her story ends with particular someones—a new husband and children—to which this experience in the wild called her. McCandless's and Strayed's stories witness that, even in a secular age, this calling to a *someone* through the narrating of our death experiences can be a viable path to encounter divine action.

4. *Kenotic* means "self-emptying": out of freedom you choose to humbly be with the other.
5. My use of "kenotic" here is not to impose something on the Old Testament text but to make a connection to the shape of faith formation I articulated in volume 1.

The question, and then the command, come to Hagar, but God is not done speaking. After God's call to Hagar to go and submit (in kenotic form that is God's own being) to the very one who shamed Hagar, before even a beat can pass God speaks a promise. Because God is the event of arrival in the death experience, God meets the actuality of our nothingness with the promise of a new possibility.[6] The arriving God comes questioning (to find us in our nothingness), calling (us to a someone), and promising (us a new future in which we share in God's being by joining God's action).

### The Promise

Promise reveals that this God who acts in history to embrace our death experiences is no soft helicopter parent; God doesn't enter our difficult situations so we're free from bearing them. God comes as a minister filled with compassion and love. That's why God goes looking for Hagar, speaking her name, asking her to speak of the painful events that press in on her being. God is not a pacifier but a pastor, so from the compassion of encounter comes a stiff call to follow. Hagar is directed to follow by emptying herself and being sent by the ministering God to minister to someone else. This isn't simply God giving over God's work to us, as if we were his minions, freeing up more time for God to enjoy some bocce ball. Rather, this calling is the working out of God's future. It is the bringing forth of salvation. God fulfills his promise through acts of ministry. Soteriology (salvation) is bound in the ontology of God's ministerial being. Promise is God's gift of a future, brought forth through God identifying with events of nothingness, ministering new possibilities in them.

God not only shares in Hagar's death experience but also delivers to her a new future. She goes back to Sarai not with her tail between her legs, submitting to her bully, but as an ordained minister blessed with a promise, given an event that delivers a future leagues deeper than her shaming. This new future comes with the weight to recast her death experience. The promise now usurps her death experience as the event of her identity. God does this not by going around the death experience but by going through it, subsuming it. That's why Israel will rehearse again and again the story of God's action by saying, "When in the future your child asks you, 'What does this mean?' you shall answer, 'By strength of hand the LORD brought us out of Egypt, from the house of slavery'" (Exod. 13:14). The death experience of slavery is recast as the concrete encounter with the God who enters history to give us a promise of a new history, saving us from slavery, shaming, and the wilderness. The

---

6. This is a central thrust of Eberhard Jüngel's theology.

God who ministers is the God who saves, because God joins our death experience, calling us through God's presence *in* our death experience to minister to others' death experience. And all this ministry is for the sake of birthing a new future, in which the history of time and space is taken into the history of God's own being—which is enacted in the naming and ministering of the Father to the Son to the Spirit.

God says to Hagar, right in the godforsaken wild, just as the call to return and minister to Sarai is still ringing in her ears, "I will [I promise to] so greatly multiply your offspring that they cannot be counted for multitude" (Gen. 16:10). The one who hears the call out of nothingness is invited to participate in the coming of God's future. Salvation is to participate in the life of God (theosis), and we enter this promised participation by taking on the being of God, by joining God's action of ministry. Hagar is saved because Hagar has not only experienced and therefore knows God but she has also been taken into God's own being by receiving God's acts and going and acting as minister herself. Salvation is to receive and give God's ministry.

Of course, the direct route of salvation history will go through not Hagar's child but Sarai's. The stark impossibility of Sarai's inhabitable womb is just the context for the ministering God to come and birth salvation for the world. Though Hagar's child will not be the direct route, Hagar will play an essential part. She'll minister to Sarai, helping prepare her to see that from the deepest impossibility comes the promise of God's new possibility.[7] She'll tell again and again the story of God's arriving in her impossibility, coming to her in the wild, bringing a call and a promise. Hagar's story won't be enough to keep Sarai from laughing when God tells her at ninety that she will bear a child (Gen. 18:12)—though her response is better than her Forrest Gump of a husband's, who throws himself on the ground overtaken with the giggles (Gen. 17:17)—but it is enough for her to trust that when things are dead, the God who found Hagar and speaks to Abraham can act. Even in the midst of obscurity, Sarai will know because of Hagar that this God fulfills his promises, that what God speaks God will bring to be. The God who ministers to us saves us; the God who saves us does so as minister.[8]

7. Terence Fretheim, commenting on Exodus, echoes the ministerial sovereignty that I'm presenting here: "Any definition of divine sovereignty must take into account the fact that God does not act alone in these events. . . . God works in and through five lowly women to carry out the divine purpose. Ironically, they prove to be highly effective against ruthless forms of power, but choosing such human vehicles means that God works in unobtrusive, unlikely, and vulnerable ways." *Exodus*, Interpretation (Louisville: John Knox, 1991), 17.

8. David Congdon puts together this focus on salvation and the historical acts of God to minister: "If a person's nature is historical—that is, if there is no human essence behind one's concrete actions and decisions—then the question of salvation cannot be decided apart from

## God Has Named the Minister

After giving the promise, God continues to speak, telling Hagar what she is to name this child, whom God promises to multiply. Now that this child is wrapped in promise like a blanket, he can have no identity outside of it. For his whole life the event of God's spoken promise will be the event that he'll identify with. This child is ever claimed by the promise, and this is shown no more clearly than by the personal God who speaks, naming the child: "You shall call him Ishmael, for the Lord has given heed to your affliction [sharing as minister in your nothingness]" (Gen. 16:11). "Ishmael" is Hebrew for "God listens"; this child's identity begins in the God who encounters Hagar as pastor, listening to her story. Because the Lord has come to her in the wild, sharing in her death experience, giving her a calling and a promise, she must name her son Ishmael as a testimony to the event of God's ministry. It won't be the last time that the speaking God names a baby. These names are signs that God has arrived in history, promising through persons (the persons God names) that God brings forth a new history of salvation.

It is a remarkable reality, often missed, that though Hagar is not included directly in the historical unfolding of God's salvation history, her child, who has been abandoned and excluded, has received a promise. God's compassion is too deep to leave this girl to die meaninglessly in the wild. God has seen her affliction, making a promise to her unborn son, testified to by God naming him God Listens.

If this isn't audacious enough, in response to God's naming of an unborn, unwanted baby, Hagar names God. A name in this context reveals purpose: the central action and direction of a being. To give a name is to claim that this is the being of the one named. It is a bold move for a pregnant, runaway slave, disheveled and used up by the world, to have the audacity to name the Holy God. But she has shared in this God's being by experiencing God's ministerial action. This God came looking for her. So she names this God, proclaiming the very nature of God's being, saying, "Thou art a God of seeing" (Gen. 16:13 RSV). The Message says, "You're the God who sees me! Yes! He saw me; and then I saw him!" No one sees God and lives (Exod. 33:20)—unless they see God through his acts of ministry, as the shepherd who comes finding, naming,

---

the particular moment in which a person realizes her historical existence. Salvation is meaningless if it ignores or bypasses a person's historicity, since that would mean ignoring or bypassing the person altogether. Unfortunately, many doctrines of salvation are guilty of doing precisely that, and perhaps none more so than the doctrine of universalism. Indeed, universalism—particularly its theoactualized instantiation—almost by definition trades on an abstract and ahistorical conception of salvation." *The God Who Saves: A Dogmatic Sketch* (Eugene, OR: Cascade, 2016), 18.

and promising. God found Hagar in the wild of her death experience, seeing her nothingness and arriving to minister to her, and then she too saw God—for God's being, as the act of ministry, was revealed. Terence Fretheim adds to this: "At times the community of faith can so center on the speaking God that the theme of the seeing God is left aside. Not so with Hagar, and not so with Israel either. Central to Israel's confession is that its God sees the human situation and responds to it ([Gen.] 29:31–32; 31:12, 42; Exod. 2:25; 3:7; 4:31). God's seeing (and hearing) is crucial, because it means that God's speaking will be directed to the human need in a precise way." Indeed God is a minister. Fretheim continues: "The reason why God's word can bring a future and a hope is that it is grounded in God's having seen the situation for what it is and hence being able to address actual needs in a specific way. God's saving acts directly respond to creaturely need."[9] Salvation comes on the tails of ministry.

It is Hagar who proclaims that God's own being is constituted as the one who ministers.[10] Robert W. Jenson echoes this point of God's ministerial being constituted through God's acts, saying, "God's story is committed as a story with creatures. And so [God] too, as it is, can have no identity except as he meets the temporal end toward which creatures live."[11]

It will be from such experiences that Israel will know that indeed it is the God of Abraham, Isaac, and Jacob who arrives in Egypt with a word: Let *my* people go! It was the ministry of God to a pregnant Egyptian runaway who was slut shamed that reveals God's being as the act of ministry.[12] Yet, before we can turn to the exodus event, we must confront again our secular age and our pastoral practice.

## Back to Divine Action in a Secular Age

Disenchantment, a buffered self, the affirmation of ordinary life, the separation of the private from the public, and a nova explosion in a post-Durkheimian dispensation have led divine action to be opaque. This leaves the pastor to

9. Fretheim, *Abraham*, 98.

10. Eberhard Jüngel gives philosophical and theological language for Hagar's experience: "God wills certainly to be God and He does not will that we should be God. But He does not will to be God for Himself nor as God to be alone with Himself. He wills as God to be for us and with us, who are not God." *God's Being Is in Becoming: The Trinitarian Being of God in the Theology of Karl Barth* (Grand Rapids: Eerdmans, 2001), 81.

11. Jenson, *Systematic Theology: The Triune God* (Oxford: Oxford University Press, 1997), 1:65.

12. Douglas Knight echoes this: "God is a worker. . . . He works a people to become participants in his work. Israel's liturgical task is the labor of imagining, modeling, and preparing for the new creation, and so participating in its arrival." *The Eschatological Economy: Time and Hospitality of God* (Grand Rapids: Eerdmans, 2006), 96.

wonder how his people could ever perceive of God's action in the world. Yet there is a way. As we saw at the end of the previous chapter, if we refuse to succumb to the temptation to flatten divine action into religious experience or ideology, and tend instead to events, most particularly the events of nothingness, we are pulled into a positive cross-pressure, which Taylor calls an open take in the immanent frame. We are moved to recognize that there is more mystery in our encounters than the immanent frame likes to assume.

The secular age—particularly its attention to exclusively human flourishing, authenticity, and mutual regard—makes identity paramount. By turning to the confession of events, we affirm this attention to identity, but we drive it deeper than consumer taste, subjective choice, expressed desire, or identity politics, which often deliver a closed spin to the immanent frame (leading to all sorts of ideological battles).

By attending to events, we can drive identity deeper, seeing it as more directly our interpretation of personal events with which we identify. We need not new ideologies but a minister to share with us in these events. As we tell of these events, speaking about the day our daughter was born or the day her diagnosis was given, we offer our open take on the immanent frame, exploring every coincidence for meaning and divine action. It is nearly impossible to retell and remember the events with which we identify and not use words of encounter, mystery, possibility, hope, fullness, and despair, saying, "Only God knows why I said that," or "I'm not sure why I was there," or "I felt overwhelmed, almost outside myself."

It's no surprise that a core part of Alcoholics Anonymous is believing in a higher power, and almost all addicts in the program are willing, even happy, to claim the presence of divine action. The recovering addict—or sober drunk—becomes our sage in a secular age. They are a heralding witness, if we will listen, to the open take of the immanent frame. They testify that indeed there is divine action in our world. Divine action seems almost a reflex when you retell over and again the events of your addiction, finding transformation when these events are confessed and shared in by others who minister to you by hearing you confess the events that press in on your being. They even forgive you for your part in thrusting negative events onto others.

The depth of Nadia Bolz-Weber's ministry as a pastor (and her writing to other pastors) comes from her experience of divine action through being a recovering addict. It is the heavy-smoking, hard-living women at recovery meetings who are as much her core theologians as Martin Luther; they show her the way of attending to divine action. Luther gives her language for grace and forgiveness, but the sober drunks give her visions of divine action in our cynical secular age.

Like God's encounter with Hagar and our sober-drunk, secular-age sages, the pastor helps her people perceive divine action by creating a space for them to be addressed with questions, asking them to tell the community, "Where have you come from?" and "Where are you going?" This is what new members' classes should be all about. The sharing of these events, however, is not to project our wishes but is to tell the stories of the deep events with which we identify. The pastor helps people perceive divine action in a secular age when the questions invite people to reflect on the arc of their lives. This is why spiritual direction has become so central in our secular age. It is the examination of events, peering into them for the presence of God, which so often comes from God's seeming absence in the wild.

God seeks and finds us. To be seeker sensitive is not to shape your building like a movie theater or using huge screens, but instead it is to create space to answer questions about the events of our lives so that we might recognize that it is God who seeks us. Ministry in a secular age is "seeker sensitive," but the kind of seeker sensitive that perceives divine action. *It proclaims God, not us, as the seeker.* It sees seeking as the shape of divine action, not as a marketing strategy to go after those who haven't yet "found" God.

This pushes us into another lesson for pastoral ministry learned from Hagar. She receives the call to go and minister to *someone*.[13] To move people into open takes in the immanent frame is to also send them as ministers into the events of people around them, out in the world. This is something that Rick Warren and others have sensed as essential in our secular age. Yet too often this calling into ministry has not had the willingness to find people in the wilderness, and therefore has flattened out this call of ministry to adding new members to the church. This hasn't always happened, and at least some of the draw of churches like Saddleback has been to affirm its attention to the centrality of divine encounter through ministry.

Paul Kalanithi gives us a more direct example that links the event of wilderness with ministry, echoing Hagar's story. From within the lost-in-the-wilderness event of Kalanithi's cancer, he is found when he hears the call to minister to *someone* else. He is called to return to the patients he meets in this same wilderness and is called to see them not under the harsh titles of their illnesses and diagnoses but as persons whose names represent events of love,

---

13. Here I'm pushing for transcendence in a secular age that is bound in relational, personal interconnection. Eileen Cantin explains how Mounier's position was similar: "The second level of transcendence is that which is achieved through interpersonal relations. The person is called to surpass himself by sharing himself with another person. The basic paradox of the Gospel is here affirmed. One finds himself only by losing himself—by giving himself away in response to the appeal of another person or persons." *Mounier: A Personalist View of History* (New York: Paulist Press, 1973), 77.

mercy, and blessing. In being called to someone else in ministry, Kalanithi is taken deeply into divine action. Divine action is unveiled through ministry because this action is a true participation in the divine being. It is most often the events of ministry that deliver the direct event of God's arriving in our secular age. It's when we move our bodies into ministry, sharing in the personhood of another, that the thick clouds of immanence break. Sending our people out to recognize events of ministry, to hear God calling them not to *something* but to *someone*—at work, in their neighborhood, and so on—moves them into an open take in the immanent frame. In other words, it helps them see God.

## A Hagar in Our Secular Age

Enuma Okoro in her memoir *Reluctant Pilgrim* tells her story of searching for divine action, yearning for a church that can bear the events of the wild. It is a story marked in almost every way by our secular age. She mixes a deep sense of disenchantment with moments of longing for enchantment, a welcomed and regretted disengagement, an overall search for authenticity, and a cranky sense that almost every church she enters can't provide what she's looking for. Throughout the book, belief and unbelief hang together by a precarious thread. Okoro's only way forward is to live inside the tension and agree to believe while unbelieving, riding the currents of cross-pressure.

Yet, as much as the story is about her search for a spiritual community, it is more about two events of death and the wilderness they send her running into. These events frame her book because they frame her being. They are the events that produce her identity. As a young girl, Enuma was her father's daughter, her love for him vast even as he moved the family back to his native Nigeria. The move led to tension in her parents' marriage, and a painful divorce ensued. Living back in the United States, just before her thirtieth birthday she received news of her father's death. She now needed to return to Nigeria for the funeral. Yet it wasn't so much a return as a run into the wilderness. For months Enuma had refused to talk to this man she loved, angry because of the fallout from the divorce. Even after he reached out, she refused to take his call. Now that she's in Nigeria, the nuclear shock of his death seems to bend time. Walking into the village, seeing his car, touching his things, she feels him, though it only sends her running deeper into the wild.

"When I got back from the funeral," she says, "I couldn't find my prayers for months, but I still ached for God. It just got even harder to access God."[14]

14. Enuma Okoro, *Reluctant Pilgrim: A Moody, Somewhat Self-Indulgent Introvert's Search for Spiritual Community* (Nashville: Fresh Air, 2010), 55.

She is deep in the wild now, like Hagar in a dissolute land of godforsaken-ness. In this place, divine action is feared. In these wild places, we assume a God we can't access, we even fear God's arrival, knowing he'll come with a command we are sure we can't bear.

Enuma starts the next chapter by telling us a secret she has told her friend: "I think God wants me to be a nun."[15] She fears a God who arrives with a command. This, after all, is how God acts. If we can't hear God's ministering questions, recognizing God's ministering being, this command can only feel like harsh condemnation. She has not heard God speak, but she can imagine what God will say, certain God will condemn her to a life she wishes not to live. When one is lost in the wilderness, the thought of divine action can be a terror. It's better to board up skylights to divine action in the immanent frame than risk God's arrival.

But this terror is broken when the questions come. We know that it's the arrival of the living God, because most often God comes with a question: "Hagar, slave-girl of Sarai, where have you come from and where are you going?" (Gen. 16:8); "Saul, Saul, why do you persecute me?" (Acts 9:4). This question is the invitation to share death experiences as prayer, giving them to God. Enuma's friend Anna receives her secret as the GPS coordinates of her location in the wilderness. Enuma is locked in this idea that God will force her to become a nun, when Anna becomes the voice of God, asking, "Where did that come from?"[16]

Now Enuma can pray, pouring out the events that press into her being, particularly those she wishes to deny. She confesses that she is still grieving the loss of her dad and is altogether lonely. Anna and then a spiritual director named Sister Catherine become Enuma's ministers by seeing her and listening to her. They share in these events and help her reidentify with them. They prepare Enuma for the calling that follows.

It is the ministry of Anna and Sister Catherine that finds Enuma in the wild, equipping her for an encounter with Michael. An addict in recovery, with truth and honesty Michael has encountered God in nothingness. Through his confessed brokenness he becomes a sage of divine action to Enuma, reveal-ing again and again how God seeks us. The two of them fall in love, but it isn't meant to be. Over the years their friendship remains strong but is never again romantic.

The last thing Enuma expects is what she hears on the other end of the line, a frightening echo of the phone call that informed her years earlier that

---

15. Okoro, *Reluctant Pilgrim*, 61.
16. Okoro, *Reluctant Pilgrim*, 62.

her father was gone. The words don't register at first. When repeated they sink in like a stone. Michael is dead. The grief stabs to the bone.

But this time, because of the ministry of those like Anna and Sister Catherine and even Michael himself, Enuma doesn't race deeper and deeper into the wild to hide. In the wilderness, she sits like Hagar and waits. And sure enough, it comes: the speaking God states a command that delivers the presence of divine action. God calls Enuma, like a modern-day Hagar, *to someone*, to go and minister to her own Sarah, Michael's new girlfriend. As with the odd threesome of Abraham, Sarah, and Hagar, Enuma ministers to the young woman who has replaced her at Michael's side. Enuma shares with her in the event of Michael's death, which has pressed deeply into both their beings. Enuma becomes Sarah's minister, and as she does, both Enuma and Sarah experience the presence of God.

This is a paradigm for experiencing divine action in a secular age. To give and receive ministry is the shape of God's very being, felt concretely, even in the immanent frame. Both Hagar and Enuma are called from their own wilderness to minister to a Sarah, assured of the promised presence of the God who sees.

# 13

## say my name, say my name

### *the God of exodus*

In college my wife, Kara, had a friend named Mortem. I assumed he must be from Scandinavia, Africa, or some other far-off land, with a name unusual to me but typical in his own country. But I soon learned this wasn't the case. He was from just twenty minutes away. Yet Mortem he was; everyone called him by this unusual name—fellow students, administrators, professors. Mortem was his proper name on campus.

So it shocked me when I learned that on his university ID, under his picture, were the letters S-T-E-V-E. Steve? That wasn't a *Steve* who was pictured; that was *Mortem*, a specific person we all knew. It was disorientating; he looked nothing like a Steve to me. He was, from head to toe, Mortem. To access his being and to most specifically state his actions was to use his name: Mortem.

But my confusion was soon cleared up. His name was indeed Steve; that's what everyone in the world, except on this campus, called him. Steve was his name since birth. Mortem, I learned, was short for Postmortem, a name given to him days into his freshman year by the guys on his dorm floor. In an epic maneuver while playing the throwback Atari video game *Space Invaders*, he had lost his last life right after shooting his final bullet. Although he was dead and about to be out of the game, his last bullet hit the final remaining alien, destroying him. In a postmortem act, Steve had won the level. The maneuver in room 3-H was so epic that Steve disappeared, and born in his place was Postmortem. From that epic act—college boys have a low bar for profundity—he was Mortem forevermore, or at least until he graduated.

## Curious Pyrotechnics

Names are powerful things; just ask Hagar. Once pregnant, she was slut named—named a thing that ate away at her humanity. But when God arrives to minister to her in the wild, the one named "slave girl" names God "the God who sees"—the one who ministers. As we said above, Eugene Peterson argues that one of the core pastoral tasks is to name things properly.[1] Pastoral work can't be done without proper names, helping people see beyond the names painted on them by society and hearing God name them "loved" and "forgiven." To make this point, Peterson draws from the story in Genesis 2 and the *'adam*'s vocation of naming animals. Hagar's naming of God in Genesis 16 echoes the naming in Genesis 2. But all this naming, in the end, reverberates back to its source in the profound naming that sits at the center of the biblical witness, the giving of God's own name in Exodus 3. Hagar names God, but Moses receives God's name directly from God.[2]

Robert W. Jenson has already taught us that God's identity is bound in the events of exodus and resurrection. God is an event who arrives, because not only does God reveal himself in concrete places, but he also moves things in new directions. God is a personal force in history. But, as I've added to Jenson, the force of God's action is bound in ministry. It is ministry to a concrete someone in her death experience that opens up to divine action an assumed impersonal universe in a secular age. Ministry reveals a God who comes speaking and seeing, finding and promising. God arrives and speaks to Abraham, forging a new future, promising a nation of priests (ministers) after God's own heart (Exod. 19:6). Israel doesn't exist until God arrives speaking.

1. "And so pastoral work is a concentration on names. After the Bible, the church roll is the most important book in a pastor's study. We work in communities that are composed of names. The pastor (like Adam in the garden) gives names—presents a person by name at the baptismal font, invokes the name of God at the table, proclaims the name of God from the pulpit, and combines those names in every pastoral conversation and prayer. To become familiar with the name of the other and to find that the other is familiar with one's name is the stuff of intimacy. Without names there can be no pastoral work." Peterson, *Five Smooth Stones for Pastoral Work* (Grand Rapids: Eerdmans, 1992), 48.

2. The story of Hagar and Abraham and the creation story remain oral history, not written down until after the exodus. The exodus story is framing how they will write down and retell all the stories, all of the previous oral history, leading up to it. It remains an open debate in Old Testament scholarship whether the Pentateuch was written after the exodus or much later— after the exile. Even though it was written by different sources at different times, it is read and held as the words of Moses in Jewish and Christian tradition.

But never is Abraham given God's name. God does not disclose the fullness
of his being until Moses stumbles on a bush in the wild.

## A Curious Assassin

This time it is God, not a slave girl, who is found in the wilderness. God's
location is just as specific as Hagar's, the GPS coordinates just as precise.
We're told that Moses "led his flock beyond the wilderness, and came to
Horeb, the mountain of God" (Exod. 3:1).

There, content to minister to sheep, Moses sees something strange: a bush
burning but not consumed. Albert Einstein's deep curiosity about light led
him to many of his amazing 1905 breakthroughs, revealing a whole new way
of perceiving the universe. Curiosity about coincidences led Albert from *I
Heart Huckabees* to discover meaning in the immanent frame.

Moses, like these Alberts, is deeply curious. The NRSV has Moses saying, "I must turn aside"; essentially, he is saying, "My curiosity has gotten
the better of me; I've got to check this out." Peterson, in *The Message*, has
Moses sounding even more like Einstein; delighted in this odd wonder, he
says, "What's going on here? I can't believe this! Amazing! Why doesn't the
bush burn up?" (Exod. 3:3).

This scene reveals two core events that shape Moses's identity, preparing
him to encounter the speaking God. First, he is a shepherd, who as shepherd
is an event. Moses knows what it is like to lead as a minister, as a good, caring
shepherd. Moses meets Jethro and is given his flock to tend only because at the
Midian well Moses chases away, not coincidentally, bad shepherds who are tor-
menting Jethro's daughters. These bad shepherds should know how to minister,
caring for the weak and lost, leading them to safety. Ironically, Moses is here
at this well only because he, too, has tried to lead, but like the bad shepherds,
not as a true minister. Mirroring Hagar, Moses has run into the wilderness to
get lost. And both of their destinies change at a well in the wilderness. Moses
is there because he tried to avenge the Israelites out of his own strength, killing
an Egyptian slave master and hiding the body, Tony Soprano style, in the sand.

The pre-wilderness Moses sees himself as a murdering Robin Hood, a
vigilante Batman, fighting in the shadows for freedom. Moses decides to become a secret assassin not for his own revenge, but to free his people. He sees
his murdering as noble. But Moses has to run into the wild when his secret
identity is revealed. When he rebukes two Israelites for fighting, one says to
him, "Who made you a ruler and judge over us?[3] Do you mean to kill me as

3. This is exactly what Moses will become after the exodus (Exod. 18).

you killed the Egyptian?" Then Moses is afraid and thinks, "Surely the thing is known" (Exod. 2:14). The secret is out, his Clark Kent glasses hiding nothing, his Bruce Wayne mansion clearly the Batcave. Moses races into the wild; the wilderness, again, is the place of godforsakenness. It is a place to get lost.

In this lost place Moses learns new practices. In a significant way this too reveals something of the nature of God. There is no montage of murders in Moses's story. We don't watch Moses hone his skill one body at a time, growing more powerful with each quick-cut scene, the weapons and outfit getting cooler as he goes. Rather, we see a scared man on the run, burying his clumsy assassin ways in the hot sand where he buried the body that now is his shame.

The practices he picks up are supposedly weak, far below the station of a man raised in Pharaoh's court. There is no bow mastery or skillful face-paint disguise, no Jedi mind tricks, no ninja stars or backflips from one shadowy corner to the next. Rather, Moses picks up a shepherd's staff and acquires a slow walk with a contemplative mindset. Ultimately, he learns to care for and love sheep; he learns to be a minister. The ways of the shepherd, not the assassin, ready him to lead. He is to follow in the way of God, the shepherd who ministers, leading his people out of the danger of Egypt.[4]

The second event is the burning bush, which takes us back to curiosity. "I must turn aside" (essentially, "I've got to see this"). Moses's curiosity shows a desire to encounter an event, to "have personal knowledge," as Hungarian chemist and philosopher Michael Polanyi called it. Polanyi shows that there is no such thing as purely empirical work in science. Every great scientific breakthrough starts where Moses does: with a deep personal curiosity. All knowledge is bound in personal encounter with a phenomenon; that's how one discerns reality. The best scientists, like Einstein, are aware of this—ever open to their deepest personal curiosities as the doorway into the reality of the universe.

Moses is an Einstein, or, maybe better, Einstein is a Moses. Einstein, in one of those famous 1905 papers, shows that time and space are actually one whole fabric. Time is not a purely metaphysical reality but is part of creation. It's woven together with space. Moses will soon discover that the God who creates enters creation to minister to creatures. God is not standing outside of space in timeless form; rather, he enters specific locales to minister. For both Moses and Einstein, *personal* curiosity is the engine into breakthrough. Moses's openness to encounter something other draws him into the event of God's arriving.

---

4. This is where Friedrich Nietzsche's genealogy of morality—which is brilliant but cynical—comes in. This shift is the lifting of the slave morality.

There is a debate between biblical scholars. Some assume that Moses, and Moses alone, was chosen to encounter the living God and given his name. They see this choosing happening long before the western walk in the wild. This seems to make sense; Moses's life is dramatically saved when he is put in the basket on the Nile as a baby. Others, however, see the pyrotechnic bush as a calling out. Anyone curious and brave enough to draw their own person to this event of God's arrival could be chosen to shepherd God's people for the shepherd God. Moses's birth only makes sense after the bellows of history compress, when Moses walks his person within reach of the arriving God.

Whatever the case, it appears that the curiosity matters. Exodus 3:4 says, "When the LORD saw that [Moses] had turned aside to see, God called to him out of the bush, 'Moses, Moses!'" This is a challenge in our secular age, but it nevertheless gives direction to pastoral practice. Through reflection on life story we can help our people be curious and brave enough—or foolish enough—to *come see*. The closed spin of the immanent frame can only work to keep divine action opaque if we concede that reality is so flat and impersonal that there is no need to be curious. The pastor's job is not to prove divine action but to invite her people to be curious, to embrace the uncanny, as Nicholas Wolterstorff says.[5] The pastor helps her people step inside these curious events as an open take in the immanent frame, to be willing to look around the wild for curious events. For example, the Sunday after Easter, Kara invites three people from the congregation to tell their own six-minute story of resurrection. It is the invitation for the community to turn aside and be curious together, opening ourselves to the possibility of divine action in the wild.

### The Boundary of Personal Address

Like Hagar's encounter in the wild, God speaks with Moses, addressing him by his name, personally finding him in the wild. It is personal address that takes Moses into an event that will forge an all-new identity. It is so personal that Moses responds, "Here I am." In other words, "*Here* is my being, in this place, open to this encounter. You have called my name, now you have access to my being, Yes, it is me, right here, that you've found."

God responds, "Come no closer!" God calls by name, revealing that God is personal. But being personal doesn't wipe away distinction, otherness; it safeguards it. God's words "Come no closer! Remove the sandals from your feet" (Exod. 3:5) make it clear that this personal God is nevertheless differentiated.

5. See Wolterstorff, *Divine Discourse: Philosophical Reflections on the Claim That God Speaks* (Cambridge: Cambridge University Press, 1995), chap. 15.

God seeks to identify with us, speaking to us, knowing us through a specific event of ministry in time, but never without remaining always the wholly-other God. Moses must take off his shoes, for he is on holy ground. He is encountering the arrival of the wholly-other God. The "no closer" is the boundary that allows for grace. Like the tree at the center of the garden (Gen. 2),[6] it reminds the creature, encountered even by name, that he is but a creature spoken to by the Creator.

All true personal encounter demands this boundary of differentiation. Divine action is encountered in our secular age through personal encounter. But the pastor's job is to create the environment for such personal encounters, not to have deep personal relationships with everyone. And even where she does, for these relationships to echo the personal nature of God, they must be constructed through boundaries of differentiation.

If curious personal encounters are to open us to divine action, even at the human-to-human level, then upholding the boundary of otherness between us is essential. There can be no such thing as ministry without this boundary. Ministry isn't enmeshment. It is never forced on another and is not being swallowed by another. It is always an encounter with another with a name, who calls us by name, and also, rightly, says, "no closer." This "no closer" reminds us that the other's being, which I'm given access to through her name, remains an infinite mystery.[7] The pastor, as Peterson says, operates with proper names. But because she does, she also respects and asserts her own "no closer."

This focus on proper names is not to say that they can't be misused. The liar uses names as well as the minister. The difference is that the liar never respects the "no closer." The liar assumes that having your name gives him the keys to violate your boundary and use your person for his own gain. Pastoral boundary violations are, essentially, possessing the relational power of having people's names while ignoring the "no closer." So though we address each other name-to-name, it is the boundary between us that leads to encounters that can open us to divine action. Ministering to a *someone* within the wild can be the concrete way of encountering divine action in our secular age, but only if we hold in tension the "naming" and the "no closer."

Moses is not invited to possess God. He is invited to encounter God through the personal boundary between them. God is personal but remains transcendent in his personhood. There is an infinite boundary between them, though

6. Dietrich Bonhoeffer, in *Creation and Fall: A Theological Exposition on Genesis 1–3* (Minneapolis: Fortress, 1997), interprets the tree as the boundary of grace.

7. This refers to Emmanuel Levinas, *Totality and Infinity* (Pittsburgh: Duquesne University Press, 1961). Levinas is clear about the need for ethical relationships to uphold this differentiation and to honor the infinity between us.

through personal address there is a true encounter. As the rest of Exodus will show, God is impacted by Moses's speaking and Moses by God's (Exod. 32).

Moses freezes when God says, "no closer," but we get no clue whether he hustles to take off his shoes like commanded. Rather, we're told that God continues speaking, clearing up any confusion regarding who Moses is encountering in this curious personal event. Without as much as a beat, like Hagar receiving the command and then immediately the promise, Moses receives his own command followed immediately with some context. God says, "I am the God of your father, the God of Abraham, the God of Isaac, and the God of Jacob" (Exod. 3:6a). This is code; it is no other than the living God who arrives who is now speaking to Moses. This is no desert spirit, no hallucination brought on by dehydration. This is the living God who speaks—the very God who births a new future out of nothingness.

It's interesting that the text repeats "the God of" for each person named. This signals that each of these particular people has encountered this same arriving God. Naming the three patriarchs reveals continuity, but adding "the God of" communicates that this God arrives, speaking to these particular persons. This God arrives in each person's wilderness (long-childless Abraham with a knife about to be plunged into Isaac's chest, and Jacob alone to wrestle with God). This arrival directs each to a new future, transforming them through the event of God's arrival. It presses in so deeply on their being that it births a new identity, even new names—Abram changed to Abraham, Jacob to Israel. For Moses to hear, "I am the God of your father," means that a new future is about to dawn. The arriving God has come again. History is about to be shaken in a new direction. It's then that Moses knows what he's up against.

## "So Come"

We're never informed whether Moses removes his shoes, but we are told that Moses hides his face after hearing, "I am the God of your father." "He was afraid to look at God" (Exod. 3:6b). Moses hides his face because he knows he's in the event of God's arrival.

With Moses's face hidden, God keeps talking. He reveals to Moses what he revealed to Hagar, that he indeed is the seeing God. God tells Moses that he is preparing to act, disclosing in stark view that God is a minister who saves. God will save the Israelites from the hand of the Egyptians, but only because God sees their suffering—as God did Hagar's. God will save them by ministering freedom to them. The cry of nothingness comes to God, so

God will enter it and minister to his people (Exod. 3:9). God's ministry that saves will birth a new future. This future is not some metaphysical space or ideological shift but a concrete place in the world, because this God arrives and speaks in time. God tells Moses specifically where God will lead them, giving Moses the coordinates to the promise (3:8).

The God who sees continues, "I have also seen how the Egyptians oppress them" (Exod. 3:9). *Yeah, no doubt*, Moses must be thinking. *I saw it too, so I tried to save them myself, becoming a shadow-jumping assassin. But it didn't work; it just led me running into the wild to hide. Now I'm an old man left to care for these little sheep.* God's coming and speaking to Moses reveals that God's saving comes not through the force of the warrior but through the care of the minister, so God continues, saying, "So come."

Just as Hagar was ordained for ministry and sent, now Moses is. God's "so come" calls Moses into participation. This participation is the invitation to share in God's acts as a way into God's being. Joining God's ministry takes us into God's being. Even in a secular age, following the "so come" opens us up to divine encounter. Kalanithi is himself a weak Moses in the wilderness of cancer. Yet when he begins calling his patients by their personal names, he encounters the presence of the living God. Moses shares in the being of this coming God by sharing in God's act and following God into ministry. Just as Hagar is sent back to minister to the very one who bullied her, so too Moses is sent to the ones who sent him running into the wild—the elders of Israel and the pharaoh. Frightened that death would be next when the pharaoh learned of Moses's murder of the slave master from the elders of Israel, Moses ran. But in the wild he's directed back to the pharaoh and these elders with a word of ministry.

Moses goes to the pharaoh as God has come to him, calling the pharaoh to participate in God's ministry. God sees the plight of the Israelites and commands the pharaoh to participate in their liberation, "Let my people go" (Exod. 9:1). Every plague is a reminder that God will minister, that God will save. God gives the pharaoh every merciful opportunity to hear the call of ministry and set the people free. Eventually things will get messy, with blood wiped on doorways and the cries of Egyptian mothers filling the night. And yet the pharaoh refuses Moses's call to join him in ministry as Moses has joined God. Maybe it is better that the pharaoh refuses; maybe it's what God wanted, hardening his heart (Exod. 4:21; 7:3–4; 9:12), so that the Israelites will know that it is no earthly power but God alone who saves by ministering freedom out of nothingness. Just as Isaac is twice born from nothingness—saved from the barren woman of Sarah and the wielded knife of Abraham—so Israel is born again out of death, out of a passover.

## An Annoying Conversation

Back in the wild with shoes off and face covered, Moses is just as obdurate as the pharaoh. Lacking the bravery of Hagar, Moses says no to God's call. Moses isn't interested in following God into ministry; his no is born from a deep, broken sense of inadequacy. Like Martin Luther King Jr., Moses has already tried to lead others to freedom by the power of his own talent. King has his own burning bush experience. As coffee cools at his kitchen table he discovers that this God uses weakness—the "no way"—as the very location for God to make a new way. Moses can only respond to God with, "No way! It's not me," not yet knowing that God revels in calling the weak and broken, for God is a minister. God's power is made perfect out of the sharing of personhood in weakness (2 Cor. 12:9). From impossibility comes new life. But Moses misses this because he identifies too much with the negative events he wishes to forget. They forge his identity too strongly for him to imagine himself as anything but worthless.

Moses responds, "Who am I . . . ?" (Exod. 3:11). This is the direct question of identity. Moses interprets these past events as defining him. He is too weak; the ridicule and mocking of the Israelites still stings; his jagged stuttering is still a deep embarrassment. These events shape his identity. He's a lonely loser, made for the solitary wandering of the shepherd, not for fighting city hall. But this is exactly why God has called him.

And so the discussion begins. Because God arrives speaking a personal name, "Moses, Moses," God must join Moses in dialogue. The negotiations go back and forth; God promises Moses his unwavering presence. God even offers a few tricks, like a staff that turns into a snake and a cloak that makes a hand white and then not. But it's not enough for Moses; he can't free himself from his weakness. His impediments are too much for him to join God in ministry. It's all good to have these Harry Potter tricks, but ministry is something much more. It is a personal act of participation; it is to join in the personhood of God by sharing in the personhood of others. The events that press in on Moses, forging his identity, keep him from believing he can meet these personal demands. "O my Lord, I have never been eloquent, neither in the past nor even now that you have spoken to your servant; but I am slow of speech and slow of tongue" (Exod. 4:10). It appears God has come to another Forrest Gump of a man.

God's response is simple, saying essentially, "Am I not God? I use impediments; I love impediments! Your impediments are a reason for my calling you. I work out of 'no way' to make 'a way,' and your impediment is a witness to the way I act.[8] I am a minister because I arrive to people caught in 'no way' to give them 'a way.' My servants witness to my ministering nature in and through their impediments, disabilities, and thorns in the flesh. My power is perfected in weakness" (cf. 2 Cor. 12:9). The actual text of Exodus 4:12 says, "Now go, and I will be with your mouth and teach you what you are to speak."

But Moses is one tough nut to crack. He can only respond to God's eloquent speech with, "O my Lord, please send someone else" (Exod. 4:13). God's patience is over, and we're told that God's temper goes hot. "Fine!" God as much as says. "I'll make an accommodation for you. I love your impediment; it is out of this impediment that I'll work my saving ministry. But if you can't get past it, then here, your brother Aaron is a good speaker; he'll help. OK?! Now get yourself to Egypt!"

This whole back-and-forth began because, after hearing God's initial call, Moses asked the "Who am I?" question. God answers in one simple way: "You are the one that I'm with" (the NRSV wording of Exod. 3:12 is "I will be with you").

Yet this personal union demands something more. It needs to stretch nearer to the ontological level. It needs to witness to such a deep connection that it becomes a kind of hypostatic union. As we've learned from what follows, Moses—a self-proclaimed clunky speaker—has no problem telling God what he feels and needs. So Moses essentially says, "If I'm to go to the Israelites and say that the God of your ancestors is *with* me, then they're going to say, 'Prove it.' The elders of Israel are going to say, 'This is a deep personal union of which you speak, so prove it by telling us God's personal name. If you know God's personal name, then we will believe that your person shares in God's through a fellowship of action. We will trust that what you intend to do is God's action to save us.'"

God responds without hesitation, giving Moses his personal name, "I am Yahweh."

8. Terence Fretheim explains God's love for impediments: "Rather than using power as it is usually exercised in the world, God works through persons who have no obvious power; indeed, they are unlikely candidates for the exercise of power. The choice of the five women in chapters 1–2 entails much risk and vulnerability for God; that risk is real, for these persons could fail and God would have to begin again. . . . Even more, God's plan for the future of the children of Israel rests squarely on the shoulders of one of its helpless sons, a baby in a fragile basket. Who would have believed that the arm of the Lord could be revealed in such a one (cf. Isa. 53:1)? God moves throughout this section in unobtrusive, unlikely, and vulnerable ways." *Exodus*, Interpretation (Louisville: John Knox, 1991) 38.

## What's in a Name?

I suppose these crazy celebrity names are a sign of those who are the high priests of the age of authenticity. If the ethic of the age of authenticity is that each person has a right to define for oneself what it means to be human, then the "good" or to live a "good life" is to be singularly unique. This sense of "good" makes it necessary to broadcast that uniqueness for all others to recognize and "like" (thanks, Instagram!). You know you're unique, and not just weird, when others like it.

It is no wonder, then, that the high priests of the age of authenticity—celebrities—do what privileged people always do: they give their children an upper hand in the "good life" as defined by their age. In the age of authenticity, money in the bank helps, as does proximity to parents' fame, but in the end the most concrete gift celebrities can give their child to win the game of authenticity is a singularly unique name. And so we get celebrities with baby names (and these are all real) like Pilot Inspektor, Audio Science, Ocean, Blue Angel, Apple, Sage Moonblood, and Tu Morrow.

Names are powerful things. But for Moses to receive God's name—Yahweh—functions much differently than a name does in the age of authenticity. And this gets us all the way back to Mortem and my college campus. My bet is that Mortem was happy to embrace the name because it gave him a unique handle to broadcast his authenticity in the new environment of a college campus. But he wasn't given the name for the sake of authenticity. While Mortem would work great as a celebrity baby name, it became his name only because it described a core event of action that now marked his being (at least on his dorm floor). His name was his identity born from the eventfulness of action.

To call him Mortem was to name his being as one who acts to kill pixelated aliens after death. His name was wrapped tightly around his identity because his name witnessed to his action in the events that pressed into his being. Likely no one in the college dorm thought this, but the Israelites surely would have.

They knew that to have someone's name is to have their being. God is calling Moses into something risky in going to Egypt, but not without God too being vulnerable. Ministry is always a vulnerable risk. To stand before people and proclaim the Word, or enter their moment of nothingness, makes us vulnerable. We risk that our act of ministry will miscommunicate or misrepresent. Because ministry is always an event—a happening in a time and place—and not simply ideas or subjective affiliations, it can be entered only by a vulnerable personal act that joins these eventful moments by giving and knowing names.

For the Israelite to know someone's name is to encounter, unveiled, some-one's identity (who one is). For Moses to have God's name is to have a union with God's being through the events of God's action (a *kind* of hypostatic union). So to call someone by name is to enter into a depth of intimacy.[9] This intimacy—as with all intimacy—is lived out in mutual vulnerability. Moses is vulnerable—hiding his face—for he's encountered God's being through the speaking of God's name. But God is now vulnerable too, because God has disclosed not a title, nor even a formal description, but the availability of God's very being.[10] As Terence Fretheim says, "In becoming so available to the world, God is to some degree at the disposal of those who can name the name. God's name may be misused and abused as well as honored. For God to give the name is to open himself up to hurt. Naming entails the likelihood of divine suffering, and so this act of name-giving is decisively continuous with [Exod.] 3:7: 'I know their sufferings.'"[11] This reveals that God indeed is a minister. The giving of his name is the movement of God into Israel's event of suffering. God gives his name, opening himself to suffering, so he can be the minister who brings a "new way" out of "no way." God is a minister because in vulnerability he gives to Israel, through Moses, his personal intimate name.

It's become old-fashioned now—the bohemianism of the age of authenticity rules it stilted and hierarchical—but when I was a kid we still called our friends' parents by Mr. and Mrs. and their last names. My friends' parents were Mr. Sergot, Mrs. Heyer, and Mr. Robinson. Kara and I, with our neighbors, have worked hard to keep to this Mr. and Mrs., but not without slippage. The last name is gone; now it is just the Mr. and Mrs. in front of the first name. My

9. Christopher Seitz gives us more sense of the importance of name: "The notion that God has a proper name and can be differentiated from other deities with proper names is absolutely clear in the Old Testament. Other gods (elohim) lay claims on humanity, but Israel is to have no god (elohim) before or beside YHWH (Exodus 20:3). Moreover, the character of the name is itself a matter of reverence, since the name really coheres with the God it names (20:7). One cannot therefore malign the name or substitute for the name another name, and somehow leave untouched the deity with whom this name is attached. The very fact that a generic term, elohim, was not deemed satisfactory for describing God or naming Israel's God, is an indication that the proper name YHWH is the name God himself will respond to." *Word without End* (Waco: Baylor University Press, 2004), 253–54.

10. Robert W. Jenson adds to this: "A person's name is not for old Israel a mere designator, it bears the personhood of its bearer. It communicates the 'soul' itself, with its particular *kabod*, and it can do this precisely because it lacks content of its own. To know someone's personal name is therefore to enjoy a mutual commitment with the person—even a kind of hold on him. For Israel to know the name of the God who suddenly intruded in her life was to be provided with access to him, even with a claim: the high priest could go into the most holy place of the temple and implore God by name for the people." *Ezekiel*, Brazos Theological Commentary on the Bible (Grand Rapids: Brazos, 2009), 67.

11. Fretheim, *Exodus*, 65.

kids call our neighbors Mr. Josh and Ms. Sonia, and Maisy's godparents are Dr. Rolf and Ms. Amy. The reason it was once essential to call your teacher or neighbor by Mr. or Mrs. and their last name was because it not only affirmed respect for the adult but also safeguarded the child. It kept intimate names for those closer to the child. For a child to call you Mr. Green was a reminder (to the adult, not the child) of what kind of relationship this was. It defined it as boundaried from direct intimacy. When you were called Mr. Wood, the practice kept the line between adult and child from blurring.

When Moses comes with the name of God, it signals that Moses knows this God's identity, encountering an event of God's arriving presence. But it does something deeper as well. To know God's name is to testify to an intimate experience of personal union. Because the name is not simply a label of authenticity or a formal title but a single word that marks a whole narrative of events that disclose being, to know the name is to know the being as he relates intimately to your own being. To know the name Yahweh is more like using a nickname for one you love—like a romantic partner or a child—than it is like knowing an official name on a passport. To know the name is to be an intimate friend; it is to have a place in that person's being through personal encounter.

A pet name or nickname is allowed to be spoken only by those who share intimately in the other's being. They share in that other person's being by sharing in events. There is a shared history that allows us to use that single name. And using it becomes a way—with just that single word—of saying a whole narrative of love and encounter. There are no intimate names without deep events that have been laced into a narrative. (It works the opposite way as well. To call someone a slut is to pull down on top of a person events, happenings in time and space, that are used for shaming.) To address someone by their nickname is to presume, even know them through, these deep events that pressed into their being. Often these names are secrets, not just because the depth of intimacy makes them embarrassing but more so because they are sacred. Only the one who truly shares in the other's being by being present in the most important of events can say the name. Only a wife who has shared in the event of marrying this man, loving and laughing with him over that weekend at the lake, crying with him as his mother died, and ministering to him through so many disappointments, can call him Sweet Thighs.

To get a little more reverent, even with my example we can now understand more clearly why Orthodox Jews will not say the name Yahweh. To say the name is to have God's being. The risk is too high that it will be misused or watered down. Those who do not know the intimate acts of God's saving love—not respecting the events of God's arriving—haphazardly call him by name. So to safeguard the intimate name, they speak it without speaking it, by rehearsing the narratives of the events of God's arriving. Whenever the name Yahweh appears in Scripture they say, "Adonai," which means "Lord" (translated as small caps "LORD" in our texts).

Ted Chiang and his novella about Banks and the heptapods was right about language after all. We too, like the heptapods, have words that possess within them whole narratives of events, fusing past, present, and future into one word.[12] We have a way, like the heptapods, with this one word to speak across time. It remembers past events while bending toward, even producing, a future. This one word is an intimate name. For the wife to use the intimate name in saying she loves her husband is to bear direct witness to her past acts, her present commitment, and her future destiny. To call him that intimate name is to claim she has no future but with him.

For Moses to speak God's name, then, is to say a whole narrative. The whole narrative of events of God's past and coming arrivals is revealed in the speaking of the single name. Banks says a heptapod word and sees the advent of her daughter's birth, the word unveiling a future. Moses says God's name, compressing the bellows of history and bestowing God's future. That name reveals that on this very mountain a free Israel will worship the God named Yahweh, who sees and ministers.[13]

Mortem is a name that reveals an event. Because of the centrality of the event, to have the name is to have access to his being. Mortem is short, as we said, for Postmortem. Without the event in that particular dorm, in that specific room, at that moment in time, the word Mortem/Postmortem would make no sense. God's intimate name, Yahweh, is the repeating of the Hebrew verb *hayah* (*'ehyeh 'asher 'ehyeh*). Clearly, to have this name is to have some kind of encounter with God's being. It is an ontological event, a kind of hypostatic union, as we mentioned.[14]

---

12. "To name God YHWH is not to call him something else, and it is also to distinguish him from other deities with other proper names, other peoples, and other narratives." Seitz, *Word without End*, 254.

13. Robert W. Jenson points to the future direction of God's speaking: "Thus the revelatory content of the Exodus was not mere escape from the Egyptian past but the future that the escape opened: 'You have seen . . . how I . . . brought you to myself. Now therefore, if you obey my voice and keep my covenant, you shall be.' And this was a true, that is, risky, future: in Israel's memory, Exodus was inseparable from forty years' wandering in the desert, in which the Lord figures as the dangerous leader of a journey whose final end was geographically chancy and temporally unknown, and whose possibility depended every morning on the Lord's new mercy." *Systematic Theology: The Works of God* (Oxford: Oxford University Press, 1999), 1:67.

14. Jenson points to how this Moses event of naming can connect to a hypostatic union as I'm developing it:

The Cappadocians had worked out a system of thought as sophisticated as Origen's. They said the Christian God is one being in three "hypostases," the best English equivalent

But this push into being makes it hard for us to clearly decipher what Yahweh means. "The most common translation is . . . given in the NRSV, 'I AM WHO I AM.' Other translations include: 'I will be what (who) I will be'; 'I will cause to be what I will cause to be'; 'I will be who I am / I am who I will be.'"[15] Fretheim contends that the last, "I will be who I am / I am who I will be," seems the best, saying, "The force is not simply that God is or that God is present but that God will be faithfully God for them."[16]

In other words, echoing one of our esoteric phrases from above, God's being is in becoming. God's being is given to Israel in and through God's faithfulness to minister to Israel. God's name is the event of ministry. God *is* the act that saves through ministry. God is the faithfulness that joins personhood up against nothingness for the sake of ministering a new possibility. To know this God's being—to use the intimate name that possesses a whole narrative—is to encounter God's act of ministry.[17] Moses shares in God's being by encountering God's being through the fellowship of action, through Moses himself becoming a minister. Moses's own being is changed (theosis), not just when God's name is disclosed but also when Moses follows that name into ministry himself. Moses is changed by joining his own being to the events of God's ministering a new way out of no way.

When Moses too acts as minister, he is taken into the being of God. This event, within which God acts through Moses, mutually presses into both of their beings, forging their identities. Moses is the one who leads Israel out of Egypt. God is the one who sets Israel free. This singular event mutually

---

for which is "identities." There is in God, said the Cappadocians, just one being, which is why there is just one God. The is-ness of God is single, but there are three hypostases. A hypostasis is something that can be identified, or even you might say a hypostasis simply is an identity. . . . Now there are three identities of the one being of God. Who is this God? Well, he is God the author of the story with his people. Who is this God? He is God settled into that story and an actor in it. Who is God? He is the wind of God that moves history. Or in the language that came to be standard, Father, Son, and Holy Spirit. And any one of them is a perfect and complete identification of the one God. (*A Theology in Outline: Can These Bones Live?* [Oxford: Oxford University Press, 2016], 48)

15. Fretheim, *Exodus*, 63. Seitz adds, "God's name is the most personal revelation of God's own character, and as such is not a proper name in the strict sense (like Jim or Sally), but a name appropriate to God's character as God. In this case, God's 'name' consists of a disclosure of purpose; it 'means' something approaching 'In the manner that I am, or will be, I am who I am.'" *Word without End*, 239.

16. Fretheim, *Exodus*, 63.

17. Walther Zimmerli explains how the name reveals the action of ministry: "In the only passage where the Old Testament itself attempts to provide an explanation of the name 'Yahweh,' it refuses to 'explain' the name in a way that would confine it within the cage of a definition. It seeks to express the fact that we can speak of Yahweh only in attentive acknowledgment of the way he demonstrates his nature (in his acts and his commandments)." *Old Testament Theology in Outline* (Edinburgh: T&T Clark, 1978), 21.

forms both God's and Moses's identities. To know who they are is to speak
of this ministering event. "I will be who I am / I am who I will be." This intimate name asserts that God's own being is constituted in events of God's
ministry to the world. It is only through the encounter of God's coming acts
of ministry that we can know God and be made into God's children who go
into the world bearing God's name as our own. We bear his name not as a
title but as the very form of our own being through act. We show the world
that we are God's children, not by flashing a privileged religion card, but by
feeding the poor, embracing the brokenhearted, and welcoming the stranger
through a ministry of love (Matt. 25; John 13:35). It is in this fellowship of
action that God's name becomes our own. Our being is inseparable from the
events that deliver God's own being—the events of ministry.

To encounter transcendence or divine action in a secular age, and therefore
be swept into transformation, is to participate in ministry. To hear God's call,
even in our secular age, is to participate in ministry. Sara Miles in her beautiful
memoir *Take This Bread* shows how this occurs in a secular age.[18] Growing
up in a fully, even militantly, secular home with parents who directly walked
away from the church (doubling down on the closed spin of the immanent
frame), Miles followed suit. But in San Francisco, on a lark while wandering in her own wilderness, she meandered into an Episcopalian church. Like
Moses, she was mostly there out of curiosity. The curiosity kept her coming
back. The more she looked into the curious bread that was said to be the
being of Jesus, she heard a call, essentially saying, *Sara, Sara, I'm about to
feed my people. Go and start a food shelf. Join me in this ministry, and this
bread that comes to you as Jesus will take you into my being. For to feed my
hungry people is to feed me. I have so identified with them that they are me,
so as you feed on this bread, feed me, be my minister, be in Christ as Christ is
in you through this bread.* Through participation in the ministry of feeding
real people with specific names in the hungry wilderness, Miles encountered
divine action—even, or most radically, in a secular age.

18. Miles, *Take This Bread* (New York: Ballantine, 2007).

# 14

## when dry bones live again

### *the God of resurrection*

He'd stood before distinguished judges, arguing cases for some of the largest corporations in America, and even rubbed shoulders with leading politicians in Washington; he was counsel for the 1984 Democratic National Convention. As a founder and the managing partner of his law firm, Skip Masback had arrived, reaching a summit few without his drive and talent even dreamed of. But now, sitting at the top of the heap, he found himself each morning draped in an expensive suit, slumped in the corner of a commuter train, sobbing. This wasn't normal, but he couldn't stop it. Without the finely tailored suit and handcrafted English trial case, people would have assumed he was crazy. The fact was, Skip wondered if that was the case; every morning the crying just came without control. The more he tried to shove it down, the more it awkwardly burst to the surface like a beach ball pressed under the water and released. The immanent frame had spun so closed that it was suffocating him. But that's not really what bothered him. It was the crying. He just wanted it to stop. He couldn't control it, and Skip was accustomed to control.

One day, while fighting like hell, and failing, to keep back the tears, he was given a New Testament by some rogue weirdo proselytizer. Opening it, he read the nativity story. The angel's words "Fear not" felt like they were for him. When he read them, the crying stopped. It was a welcome surprise.

Nothing else had worked—not exercise, meditation, or self-help books. Nothing stopped the crying like these tiny words on tissue-thin paper. So the next day, when the crying came again, he reached for the words of the angel, reading them again: "Fear not." And again, peace.

A few days later, things got stranger. As Skip returned to the angel's words, reading them over and over, he lifted his head, and across from him sat the resurrected Jesus. As in the appearance to Thomas, Jesus, dressed in a robe with sandals, sat before him as real as the man reading the *Washington Post* six seats up. Jesus spoke directly to him, saying, "Skip, do not be anxious— I'll take care of everything."[1]

This event bore the same marks as Hagar's and Moses's encounters with God. A personal address—"Skip" ("Hagar"; "Moses")—followed by the naming of a decisive impingement of nothingness: "Do not be anxious" ("Why are you here?"; "I've heard the suffering of my people in Egypt"), leading to a promise of saving through participation in God's being through the act of ministry: "I'll take care of everything" ("Your child will be father of a great nation, for I see you"; "I will set my people free").

Jesus called Skip by his personal name—interestingly not saying the more formal "Harold," which is on his birth certificate, but using the more intimate name of friendship: Skip. Then Jesus named his wilderness and promised to minister to him in and through it. The event of God's speaking led Skip not only to testify to God's acts of ministry but also to name the wilderness that he was saved from. (He actually uses the word "wilderness" when he writes about this experience later.)

Skip experienced the event of God's arrival as nothing other than an encounter with a personal reality of ministry. The Jesus who came to him is the God who is the event of ministry. This encounter healed, loved, and gave life. Skip says, "Maybe all humans had had access to these healing, life-giving, inexplicable encounters except for my little demographic fragment of skeptical yuppies who had decided we were too smart for it all and had managed to maroon ourselves in the *wilderness*, cut off from God."[2]

It is in a wilderness, as with Hagar and Moses, that Jesus encountered Skip. Yet, unlike with Hagar and Moses, Skip's encounter happened in the wild of a secular age. So as much as it seemed real, it appeared foolish; as much as he believed it, he doubted it. He says, "Look, I was still a cynical trial lawyer, so I struggled for an explanation of what had just happened. Jesus son of the most high had suddenly showed up on the Washington Metro to 'save'

1. Ray Waddle, "Gospel Epiphany: A Shared Adventure," Yale Divinity School, December 2, 2013, http://divinity.yale.edu/news/gospel-epiphany-shared-adventure.

2. Waddle, "Gospel Epiphany" (emphasis added).

me? Sure, it certainly seemed like he had." But then came the cross-pressure of doubt: "Or maybe I was just imagining it all."[3]

Showing how bumpy the rapids of cross-pressure can be in the secular age, he immediately doubted his doubts, crossed up again, saying, "All I knew for sure was that I felt grounded, healed, and that no attempted reconstruction of the event was going to clarify the ambiguity or even begin to 'explain' what had just happened."[4]

Regardless of how it can or can't be explained, for Skip God arrived speaking. And this speaking somehow delivered God's being through the act of Jesus's ministry. Skip was invited to share in God's own being. And as we've seen, this happens by both receiving and giving ministry. The only way Skip could make sense of this experience of being ministered to was to enter ministry himself. Only participation in ministry can verify an event as the encounter with the living God who is the event of ministry. For pastors to help people make sense of these uncanny experiences is not to take them into intellectual doctrinal conversations— the cross-pressure of the secular age is too strong to allow any experience of divine action to stand under cold rationalization. The only way for verification of divine action is to enter the form of divine action itself and participate in ministry. Becoming a minister is the gift, or effect, of God's calling you by name. This fellowship of action takes us into the being of God. So where Sara Miles started a food shelf, Skip became a pastor. He found his way of participating in the ministering being that came to him on a train, just as Miles feeds the hungry as a direct way of making sense of the Jesus who met her in bread.

### From Exodus to Exile, from Bondage to Annihilation

Throughout part 2 we've followed Robert W. Jenson and claimed that God is the one who frees Israel from Egypt and resurrects Jesus from the dead. I've added my own contribution to this by claiming that God's action in these events reveals that God is a minister who saves. It is not through God's unadulterated power that God saves. God saves us through God's willingness to identify with us, participate in our events of wilderness by being personally near us, address us by name, and act to give us a "new way" out of the "no way."

In the chapters above we've focused mostly on the exodus and its pre-events of God's ministering arrival to Abraham, Sarah, and Hagar. But how is the revealing of God's ministering being in the act of exodus connected with resurrection? Why does Jenson choose these two events to articulate who God

3. Waddle, "Gospel Epiphany."
4. Waddle, "Gospel Epiphany."

is? Or, to say it through Skip's story, why is it Jesus who appears to him as the event of ministry? Skip's experience is different from Moses's and Hagar's not only by being lodged in the secular age but also by the appearance of the resurrected Christ. So how does resurrection reveal further God's being as the event of ministry? And does focusing in on the resurrection sharpen our ability to spot divine action in our secular age, freeing us from the wilderness of the closed spin of the immanent frame that Skip describes?

To understand the significance of the resurrection, we have to return to the radical claim that God arrives, encountering Abram in his father's house (Gen. 12:1). We've already shown that this claim is unique. Israel is only a people because its beginning happens somewhere in the middle. As we've said, the sun was rising and setting, the tides going in and out, and the earth spinning on its axis, and yet Israel was not. God's arrival to Abram reveals starkly that Israel has a distinct beginning. And if Israel has a beginning—a very point in time when God arrives, electing to minister to Israel—then it is possible that Israel can have an end.[5]

God has shown favor on Israel, promising to be its minister, to save it as a mother does for her child (through loving acts of ministry). But because this God is the one who arrives speaking words of election, choosing to enter wildernesses to minister, this God can freely choose not to act, leaving Israel in its decisive impingement, ministering no "new way out of no way." Israel is a strange people, for unlike its neighbors, it is viscerally aware that because it has a bold beginning point, it too can come to a stark end.[6] If God chooses not to be Israel's minister, and the event horizon of nothingness is no longer the stage for God's ministering action, then it will be lost. If decisive impingement is no longer a locale of God's arriving action, then Israel will disappear.[7] Without the act of ministry reaching into nothingness to create something out of its chaos, nothingness is only demonic annihilation—ultimate death.[8]

---

5. Jenson says, "For Israel knew that creation in its regular course might not have included her, even though her God is the Creator, so that the established order of events in general could not assure her being. Israel knew she existed sheerly by the Lord's act of will: 'it is because the Lord love[s] you.'" *Systematic Theology: The Works of God* (Oxford: Oxford University Press, 1999), 1:67.

6. Jenson, *A Theology in Outline: Can These Bones Live?* (Oxford: Oxford University Press, 2016), 32.

7. Jenson shows how unique this is to Israel. It also reveals that God demands that the Israelites participate in ministry, and if they don't then they lose the essential lifeblood of their identity: "Through the time of exile and for a time after the exile, movement among the prophets arose proclaiming something religiously unprecedented: Israel's own God, they proclaimed, was responsible for their exile! Marduk could not have been responsible for undoing Babylon because if he was, there would not have been anything left of him!" *Theology in Outline*, 22.

8. This is what Karl Barth means when he speaks of nothingness. See section 50 of *Church Dogmatics III/3* (Edinburgh: T&T Clark, 1960).

Some eight hundred years after the exodus, when both kingdoms of Israel—particularly the Southern—fall, exile becomes the new defining event of Israel's identity. It appears that Israel will indeed disappear. The prophets wonder if the king's refusal to minister to the poor as God has ministered to Israel has led to Israel's demise (see Isa. 53 as an example). Did its unwillingness to be ministers send the minister Yahweh to turn his face from it (Isa. 53)? Israel has abandoned God by abandoning ministry. It has disobeyed the law that makes it a nation of ministers. Israel knows God only through the events of ministry. Israel *is* because God arrived as minister, making it a nation of ministers. To refuse the acts of ministry—no longer seeking justice and loving mercy (Mic. 6:8)[9]—is to refuse the being of God. It is to contradict the very action that saves Israel, making and reinstating it as a people.

## Ezekiel

No one sees this more than the prophet Ezekiel. Ezekiel's vision is as haunting as it is simple, as much horror movie as mystery. Israel, now in exile and the temple just rubble, is a field of dry bones. It is over; it is dead; Israel is finished. In exile Israel is nothing more than an army of bones, animated to serve not the living God but death. Israel is like the army of the dead in *Game of Thrones*; their Babylonian captors are the White Walkers. Their bones are for participation in death instead of the ministry that brings life. They are never again to worship in the temple.

Yet now that Israel is dead, Ezekiel sees a new dimension to God's action. It isn't crystal clear, but in the shadow of this pile of dry bones, God is asking a new question. This is so new and profound that Jeremiah even heralds that a new covenant is being birthed (Jer. 31:31). Here in exile it becomes clear that the threat is no longer other nations and the fear of returning to Egypt. That nightmare has happened. Now what's to be feared, and revealed as the true enemy that haunts—as Paul would see centuries later (1 Cor. 15:26)—is death itself. After all, Israel is dead, nothing but a pile of dry bones. God essentially points out to Ezekiel that Israel is just bones; God says he has no use for dead bones. It is just as the prophets feared: God is done with Israel.

For a personal God who arrives speaking, calling us by our intimate names and promising us a new future, what seems to place us beyond the reach of God's ministry is death. In death we are ripped from history, or as we popularly say, we "become history." We are no longer beings who have a becoming in time, encountering events in time in which we identify. Rather, we're over;

9. Many other texts point to this as well (e.g., Ps. 82:3; Isa. 1:16–17; Jer. 7:5–7).

our being is finished and lost. No longer do we have being in time; we can't experience the arriving God who breaks into time as minister. Ministry comes only to the living. Now that Israel is dead, having denied God's ministry, it is lost, dead, and therefore separated from the ministry of God. What use does God have for dry, dead bones? Dry bones cannot enter into ministry, cannot receive or give ministry. God is the God of the living, not of the dead. Ministry happens in encounters that arrive in time.[10] For Abraham, Sarah, Hagar, and Moses, God arrives in events of decisive impingement. But if you die, made a pile of dry bones, you can no longer experience God's arrival. God will remember the faithful, but they are done receiving God's act of ministry. When God arrives, he comes speaking. Dry bones cannot hear; therefore dry bones cannot receive and give ministry, making death a cage that keeps us from participating in the being of God. Death is the great enemy, because in death there can be no personal encounter of speaking and seeing, no ministry, and therefore no access to God's being.

Now that Israel is dead, God asks Ezekiel a question. (This God who is a minister, we've seen, is full of questions.) Seeing these dead bones, God asks Ezekiel, "Mortal, can these bones live [again]?" (Ezek. 37:3).

This is a shocking question. God is asking, in other words, "Can death be reversed? Can these dry, dead bones be resurrected, so they might again receive the ministry of God?" This is a question not of resuscitation but of the impossible possibility of the dead being made alive, saved from death so that they might receive the act of God again. The God who is an arriving event lives, ministering only to the living—no séances or Ouija board needed. Some metaphysical netherworld of shadows won't be enough. If Israel is to receive again the ministry of God, and even be redeemed to be God's ministers once more, then the dead will need to live. God is asking Ezekiel if he believes that God can do the ultimate act of bringing "a new way out of no way"—reversing death itself.

10. Jenson beautifully summarizes but adds profound questions:
As Babylon moved on toward the total destruction of Jerusalem, Ezekiel had a prophetic vision, recorded in chapter 37 of his book, of the Jewish nation as a people of dried out bones. The Lord showed him a valley full of bones so well and truly dead that they no longer made skeletons. And the Lord asked him a question, "Son of a Man, what do you think? Can these bones live again?" There is a way in which the whole story of Israel—everything that had happened to it from the call of Abraham—had led up to that question. The people of God were dead. The nation was finished. And the question was, "can death be reversed?" And that is indeed the question. Does death win? Has it already won? Is death not the champion of our own time? Is not the killing of six million Jews and a few less million Cambodians and the continuing slaughter that is going on right now—does that not more or less prove that death has indeed won? (*Theology in Outline*, 11)

At one level Ezekiel knows that God can do whatever God wishes. God will not abandon God's ministers. Those who have shared in God's being by participating in God's action will not fear death. In their faithfulness they know that the God who arrives will remember them, even if they are no more. Their participation in events of God's ministry in time secures them in the story. But making dry bones live? Ezekiel is not sure. And more, Ezekiel knows that these bones of which God speaks are dry because they are not only surely and completely dead but also disobedient. These elect ministers are dry bones because they have sinned. Can dry bones live if they are dead because they are unfaithful? They were not unfaithful at the periphery but at the center, opposing God's ministering nature by being like all the other nations.[11] What if they have denied their ontological state as ministers, by taking on actions in opposition to ministry? Can God resurrect, reversing death and bringing new life to those who have sinned against ministry and turned their back on the God who arrives to save?

God's answer is the empty tomb.[12]

## The Question at the End the Old Testament

The Old Testament ends with two questions, Jenson believes. One question is explicit, the other implicit. The explicit question—which we've already wrestled with—is "Mortal, can these bones live?" (Ezek. 37:3). The explicit, Jenson believes, is intertwined with the implicit: "Will a true shoot yet somehow spring from the vine stock of Jesse and establish eternal righteousness and peace?"[13]

The explicit anticipates the reversal of death; the implicit anticipates that death will be reserved through a (or better *the*) minister coming from the house

11. "The accusation against the monarchy ([Ezek.] 34:2–6) is made with a rhetorically rich development of the flock and shepherd image, but is materially very simple. Shepherds necessarily live at least in part from the products of the flock, but calling for which they receive these privileges is to live *for* the flock, which the princes of Israel have not done. They have instead done exactly what the Lord predicted when Israel begged Samuel to replace divine rule through charismatics with kings like those of 'all the nations': they have exploited the people for their own indulgence and ambition (1 Sam. 8:5–18). In consequence, the sheep are scattered, the prey of predators (Ezek. 34:5–6). Since these are the Lord's sheep (34:6), the princes must expect the Lord's intervention. A specially announced messenger-word introduces the sentence: termination of the monarchy (34:10)." Jenson, *Ezekiel*, Brazos Theological Commentary on the Bible (Grand Rapids: Brazos, 2009), 265.

12. Jenson says, "For 'the house of Israel' as a nation, Ezekiel himself already receives the hint of resurrection: 'I am going to open your graves . . . O my people; and I will bring you back to the land of Israel.'" *Systematic Theology*, 2:329.

13. Jenson, *Ezekiel*, 153.

of David, the one after God's own ministering heart (1 Sam. 13). If Israel is dead because it has refused to be ministers, then Israel will be saved—as in Egypt—by a minister who enters death as a servant (the suffering servant as Isaiah says in chapter 53). If death is to be reversed, through a radical event of ministry, the minister will need to enter death to reverse it by dying. And in dying, he receives the fullness of ministry, a resurrected, and therefore glorified, body. This minister, being made alive again through an act of ministry, delivers the fullness of God's being.

This minister from the stock of Jesse will empower the people to again be ministers. He will minister so deeply to them that he will give them his Spirit, which ministered new life to him in death, saving him from the grave. It will be his going into the grave that will reverse the pull of death. It is this pull of death that produces the fear to flee from ministry and into sin.[14] This minister will establish a new ministry at the center of death, so that God's ministers will never again be outside God's ministry. Even when they die, they will bear the marks of the resurrection in their humanity, through the humanity of the *one* minister who conquered death. Therefore, though we die we'll anticipate God's direct ministry to resurrect us, as God has this one from the house of Jesse. Jenson says, "Christianity is faith that Mary's child is God's personal answer to both questions."[15]

## Jesus of Nazareth

The identification of God with humanity is complete in Jesus of Nazareth, so much so that there is no separation in being. God has so fully identified (through the hypostatic union) with Jesus that they share the same *ousia* (being)—as the church fathers have said.[16] To see Jesus is to see the Father (John 14:9). To see Jesus is to see *the* minister who saves.

Ezekiel understood that for death to be truly reversed would necessitate a new covenant, a new unveiling of God's being, a new vision of glorification.

---

14. T. F. Torrance explains how resurrection and atonement are connected: "Atonement without resurrection would not be reconciliation, and without reconciliation atonement would not have reached its proper end in union with the Father, in peace. It is thus the resurrection of our human nature in Christ into communion with the life of God that is the end and goal of atonement." *Atonement: The Person and Work of Christ* (Downers Grove, IL: InterVarsity, 2009), 228. He continues and, like Jenson, notes the importance of this historical reality: "The resurrecting of Jesus is to be thought of as the recreating and restoring of man into the same sphere of real being as that to which we human creatures belong, and as such is a historical happening in continuity with the whole historical happening of Jesus, the incarnate Son." Ibid., 244.

15. Jenson, *Ezekiel*, 153.

16. This is the heart of Nicene Christianity and the revolution of the Cappadocians.

Because God is a minister, this reversal will happen only if God not only identifies with events of decisive impediment—like Israel in Egypt—but also identifies God's very being with death itself. The only way to reverse death is for God to enter death. Israel's dry bones must live again to receive the ministry of God. And this will take a new event of ministry in which God identifies completely and fully with Jesus and his crucifixion.

God is so deeply a minister that he's willing to make death part of his identity, part of God's own being, so that death can never separate us from his love (Rom. 8:38).[17] God will not simply throw a rope into death, freeing the lucky from its clutches, heaving a few to heaven. Rather, in Ezekiel's vision and Jesus's ministry, God will make death part of God's identity. Now all who die must come face-to-face with God's loving, ministering being, for death itself is an event that God so identifies with that it is part of God's identity, inseparable from God's story. God will allow death to be an essential event that presses in on God's own being.[18] Just as God so identifies with Israel in Egypt that the event of their exodus reveals God's being, so too will God so fully identify with death that it will be transformed and overcome.[19]

God so deeply identifies with death so that God can decisively act within it, reversing its pull and bringing us back from its clutches. Rescued from death— better said, made alive out of death—we are freed from sin, reconciled to return to God's being by being ministers in the world (by being Christ [1 Cor. 3:23], ministers to our neighbor as Martin Luther says).[20] Free from death's clutches, we can eternally participate in the being of God by eternally experiencing God's acts of ministry (in the realm of the glorification of the resurrection,

17. Eberhard Jüngel shows the depth of claiming that God is love. Following Jüngel, I think it shows God's being as ministry. Jüngel says, "God's placing of himself in relation (being as event) qualifies God's act of revelation as love. God acts as the loving one in that he wills to be ours. But since in his being as Father, Son and Holy Spirit God is also already ours in advance, then in analogy to God's relationship ad extra, it must also follow from the relation of God's three modes of being to one another that God acts as the loving one." *God's Being Is in Becoming: The Trinitarian Being of God in the Theology of Karl Barth* (Grand Rapids: Eerdmans, 2001), 82.

18. Jürgen Moltmann, *The Crucified God* (Minneapolis: Fortress, 1974); and Moltmann, *Trinity in the Kingdom* (Minneapolis: Fortress, 1993).

19. N. T. Wright points to connections between Jesus's resurrection and the shepherd-minister theme I've been arguing. He also connects resurrection and exodus, as Jenson does: "The idea of Jesus, the shepherd, being 'brought up' from the dead echoes Isaiah 63.11–14, where YHWH 'brings up' the shepherd, Moses, from Egypt. Moses 'was "led forth," not as an isolated individual, but as the shepherd of the flock'; this is true of Jesus as well, the first to rise, anticipating the resurrection of all at the end." *The Resurrection of the Son of God* (Minneapolis: Fortress, 2003), 461.

20. Returning to God's being by being ministers in the world (i.e., by being Christ) points to a deep transformational dynamic we called *theosis* in volume 1, *Faith Formation in a Secular Age*. This is the larger point of Luther's *Freedom of a Christian* (Minneapolis: Fortress, 2016).

and the full *eschaton*, where "death will be no more"; Revelation 21:4 says, "he will wipe every tear from their eyes," an undeniable ethos of ministry).

God's ministry is so profound that it not only can find persons in the wild, freeing them from pharaohs, but even more so, when bones are dry and removed from the living, God can bring us back to life to again receive his ministry. In this new covenant, God so identifies with death that, though we die, we are no longer beyond the reach of God's action. Death becomes locked within God's being, never again outside the reach of God's ministry. Though we die, we are promised new life, not because our own life is so grand, for we all have sinned and denied ministry, refusing and opposing God's being by treating our neighbor as nothing but dry bones. We have denied God, opposing his very being by disobeying his commands and refusing to be our brother's keeper, leaving him for a bone pile where all ministry is lost.[21] Yet we are promised new life because God has elected to be a minister. God is so faithful in this action (that unveils his being) that God will resurrect us to eternally minister to us. God will free us from death by giving us a new identity through God's own identity, which overcomes death. This new identity is called Christ (Gal. 2:20), for we wear the marks of receiving and giving ministry and being taken from death into new life.

Then, like the exodus, this event of God's identification with death that unveils God's being will need to arrive not in a dream state or metaphysical netherworld but at a distinct point in time and space. And this will happen on a tree outside Jerusalem, right on a pile of dry bones called Calvary, during the fifteenth year of Tiberius Caesar's rule. Right then, God will so identify with the event of the crucified Jesus that the cross will be inseparable from God's being.[22] This Jesus will reveal that though he is fully flesh and blood, made of bones bound to die and dry, he unwaveringly acts as minister. Jesus's action finds complete fellowship with the ministerial action of the Father through the Spirit. So fully does Jesus share in God's action that there is a complete fusion of being, seen radically when Jesus, after three days dead (another distinct historical point in time), unquestionably on his way to being dry bones, is gloriously resurrected. God arrives on the third day, ministering so deeply to the dead Jesus that his dry bones live. And through his living bones we are saved, made alive in body and spirit to receive and give ministry.

21. In Luke 10 the Samaritan is good because he is willing to risk even his own life and own religious standing to minister to another. My view of sin and hamartiology overall is in line with this particular reading of the parable.

22. In different ways both Jüngel and Moltmann hold to a point very similar to this. In *Death: The Riddle and the Mystery* (Philadelphia: Westminster, 1974), Jüngel asserts that God identifies with the perishing of Jesus, so that perishing is transformed. Moltmann (*Crucified God*) contends that the event of the cross impacts God's being so deeply that death is now surrounded by the love of the Father to the Son.

But isn't it incoherent to say that the dead Jesus receives ministry? Hasn't Ezekiel taught us that dry bones cannot receive ministry? And yet the dead Jesus is ministered to. This is possible only because this Jesus is the very logos of God (John 1), true God of true God, begotten and sent by the Father, but not made. Jesus is the resurrection (this statement from John 11 shows the compression of the bellows of history and Jesus's singular uniqueness to receive ministry in death),[23] because it is only through his body that our dry bones too can live, receiving the ministry of God in death. The Father can minister to the dead Jesus because their union stretches to the level of shared *ousia* (being); though Jesus dies, his being is bound to the Father through the Spirit, for they are but one being. To raise Jesus from the dead is for God to minister to Godself, and this union is so deep that even death cannot impose on it. Because the Father and Son share the same *ousia*, though the Son has died, the being of the Father is able to minister to the Son through the Spirit, for in being they are one.

Yet while this Jesus is true God of true God, one *ousia* with the Father, he is flesh of our flesh, bone of our bone. When God ministers to Jesus's dry bones, resurrecting his body, Jesus is made the resurrection. Now through his body of bones, our dry, sinful bones can live too.[24] God has so identified with the death and humanity of Jesus that when we die, we die in Christ (Rom. 6:8). And in Christ, who is the resurrection (John 11:25), our being is held and taken into Jesus's own, making it able to receive the continuing ministry of God. Though we are dead, we are alive in Christ, taken into the eternal fellowship of the action of ministry. And this destiny of being in Christ means that even before we are dry bones, we are free from the fear of death to share in God's being by being ministers in the world. We are given the Spirit as the sure promise that our acts of ministry find such fellowship with Jesus's own acts that we are in Christ, sharing in the being of God as Jesus does. Being in Christ means we receive and are sent to give others acts of ministry that take us together into the being of God (into participation in God's glorification, as Athanasius says).[25]

In a secular age it is in sharing in the death experience of others as minister that we encounter divine action. Jesus is so fully in a fellowship of action with the Father that there is a complete union ("The Father and I are one," John

---

23. N. T. Wright adds, "'Resurrection' is never, for John, simply a metaphor for present spiritual life, though its wider levels of meaning certainly include that. When Jesus says 'I am the resurrection and the life' he opens up several layers of redefinition: a new life through which new possibilities are available in the present." *Resurrection of the Son of God*, 447.

24. This echoes the words of Irenaeus (*Against Heresies* 1) and Gregory of Nazianzus (*Epistle* 101.32): what is not assumed is not healed.

25. Athanasius, *On the Incarnation* (New York: St. Vladimir's Seminary Press, 2012), 33–73.

10:30). The distinct hypostases of the Father and Son are united through actions of shared ministry, so much so that to experience the actions of Jesus—healing, proclamations of forgiveness, mercy, and more (Matt. 9:1–8)—given to us by our ministering brother or sister is to directly encounter the being of God through the Spirit. To receive the ministry of Jesus from our brother or sister (Matt. 25) is to have Jesus. The pastor in the secular age needs to receive ministry as much as give it. The pastor is able to give ministry only by receiving ministry, for it is as much in receiving as giving that we encounter divine action. It is here, in this dynamic of giving and receiving, that we are given Jesus. And to receive Jesus is to be taken into the being of God, who acts as the minister who makes dry bones live. For us to minister to others in the name and Spirit of this Jesus is to participate *in* the God who saves by ministering resurrection. Ministry is an eventful encounter with personhood, even on a Washington commuter train. And God is a minister because God's being is persons in the event of encounter. Jesus and his resurrection reveal that God is a roomy minister.

### Roomy Jealousy

Jenson makes the strange claim that God is roomy. To understand this esoteric claim, we first have to come to grips with a more straightforward assertion about God's nature found throughout the biblical text: God is jealous. Israel has fallen, dead in exile, in good part because God is jealous. God has identified with certain events. His identity is bound in acts of ministry. For Israel to forget, ignore, or become indifferent to these events of God's action is to oppose God's identity. God is jealous because God demands faithfulness, not to God's fragile ego but to the events of ministry that God has identified with—again, to the stranger, widow, and orphan. To say who God is, is to name these events—like exodus and resurrection. And to forget or misappropriate these events is to oppose God's identity.

When we hear "jealous" we often think of a personality flaw, our minds racing to contestants on *The Bachelor*, for example. To be jealous in a reality TV sense is to be possessive. Corinne is jealous of Nick and Vanessa's relationship because she wants Nick for herself.[26] Yet the vapidity of reality TV, where contestants have just met (and realistically, don't really want to be engaged), reveals that there is another dimension to jealousy than just pure possession.

Corinne is so jealous not only because she wants to possess Nick as her own but more so because her not getting Nick puts her identity at risk. Coming

26. I'm not a faithful *Bachelor* viewer, so I'm thankful to Abigail Russert for her help with these names.

on this show, she's claimed that she identifies with the event of being Nick's choice. The event of dating Nick—or more so, being rejected by him—reveals something about her identity that she doesn't like and therefore feels justified in acting badly to oppose.

Jenson explains that, in a way much different from *The Bachelor* contestants, but nevertheless bound to identity, God too is jealous because God cares about events. God's identity is bound in his identification with events. Therefore God cares how these events are remembered, participated in, and continued. Unlike Greco-Roman deities, God chooses to identify with historical events, revealing his being in the act of ministry in time. Because God's being is bound in the events of God's identifying action, God is jealous.[27]

But this jealousy isn't a personality flaw, because while God is jealous, he is also roomy. Corinne wants Nick for herself, sanctioning who he can interact with, making her jealousy revolting. But as we saw above, "God . . . accommodates other persons in his life without distorting that life." As Jenson says, "God, to state it as boldly as possible, is roomy. Indeed, if we were to list divine attributes, roominess would have to come next after jealousy. He can, if he chooses, distinguish himself from others not by excluding them but by including them."[28] God is a minister because his actions create events of deep inclusion (again, participation in God's being, as Athanasius asserts), seen no more clearly than in the resurrection.

The resurrection reveals that God is so roomy that though he is one—a single acting minister identifying with events of ministry—God is three. God is the eternal relationship of Father, Son, and Holy Spirit. God's being as Trinity reveals the depth of God's ministerial being. God is so deeply a minister that God is the communion of persons ministering to one another in eternity as well as time. And from within this fellowship of ministry, God's trinitarian life reaches out to others, inviting us to also share in God's being by joining in the fellowship of ministerial action. God is jealous because he encounters us, but in this encounter God is roomy, desiring for us to find our life in him. And yet to be in him, because he is jealous, is to reach out into the world in ministry, participating in the events that God identifies with—like the humanity of the hungry, lonely, broken, sick, and imprisoned (Matt. 25).

We know that God is roomy not from some philosophical theorem. The doctrine of the Trinity is not born from some academic philosophical problem. Rather, we come to recognize God as Trinity through encountering the

---

27. See Jenson, *Systematic Theology*, 1:47–60, for a further discussion on this point.
28. Jenson, *Systematic Theology*, 1:226.

events of God's saving ministry.[29] It is the event of resurrection (the Father's ministry to the Son through the Spirit in death) that necessitates, and therefore unveils, that God is Trinity.[30] God's nature as Trinity is revealed by God's arriving to minister to the dead Jesus on the third day. We know that God is Trinity because Jesus was dead and is now alive.

Arius (d. 336) believed that Jesus is special but not true God of true God—he is important but nonetheless a created creature. This seems like a logical academic argument. But the God of Israel does not make himself known in academic arguments. He is made known in events of ministry. The pastors and ministers who opposed Arius, like Alexander the bishop of Alexandria (d. 326/328) and the others who crafted the Nicene Creed, did so because they witnessed people healed, the dead raised, and the broken made whole. They experienced a glorification that overcame death when ministering in the name of Jesus.[31] Ministry in the name of Jesus brought dead bones back to life. Only true God of true God, as Ezekiel witnessed, begotten but not made, could do such ministry. Only one who is fully God could open a direct space for us to share in the being of God, and Jesus does this through incarnation, crucifixion, and, in consummation, resurrection. Athanasius sees salvation through participation because of his experience with the roominess of God through the ministry of Jesus, who overcame death with life, allowing the created to participate in the Creator.[32] In the Father's house there are many rooms (John 14:2), and through Jesus's resurrected humanity we are given residence, made God's roomies.[33]

---

29. Jenson, *Triune Identity: God according to the Gospel* (Eugene, OR: Wipf & Stock, 2002), 39.

30. Colin Gunton echoes this: "The doctrine of the Trinity is what must be true if the biblical witness to revelation is indeed witness to the event that is God. As Jüngel has put it with great precision, the doctrine of the Trinity is our interpretation of God's self-interpretation of himself to us." *Becoming and Being* (Eugene, OR: Wipf & Stock, 2011), 130.

31. I'm referring to how the use of Jesus's name brought the works that only God could do, meaning to name Jesus was to use a proper name for God—true being of God's being. Jenson explains: "However various groups in the primal church may have conceived Jesus' relation to God, 'Jesus' was the way they all invoked God." *Triune Identity*, 9.

32. "Athanasius showed that the heart of the problem was not obedience or disobedience, because this was not a moral but an ontological problem. What was required was for the Logos to come to man, and indeed to become man, so that all that has been created can be united to the uncreated. For death to be overcome, the created has to come into relationship with the uncreated, and source its life from it." John Zizioulas, *Lectures in Christian Dogmatics* (Edinburgh: T&T Clark, 2008), 102.

33. In volume 1, I pushed the conversation on faith in the direction of theosis; Jenson's own theology has done something very similar, a connection that is captured briefly in the following quotes. "You will find an exemplary instance of the first theme, deification, in Athanasius of Alexandria's *On the Incarnation*. So, when he tells us that 'God became man in order that man should become God,' he means the lost unity of God and humanity has been restored in the personal constitution of this one person, Jesus, and that his death and resurrection opened this

## Roomies Are Persons

Ultimately, what it means for God to be jealous and roomy is that God is personal, coming to us fully and completely in the ministry of the person of Jesus Christ. The Cappadocians—ministers and pastors too, like Alexander and Athanasius—showed the depth of this participation, giving further logic to these experiences of ministry, by redefining "hypostasis."

Aristotle used the word synonymously with *ousia*, both having a static sense of being.[34] A stone has being; it has, according to Aristotle, either *ousia* or *hypostasis*. But the Cappadocians realized something revolutionary: being could have more than just a static form. There was also a distinct sense of being that was bound in events of encounter—in other words, being out of relationship, out of arrivals.

The Cappadocians called this kind of being hypostatic—it is a being bound in encounter (I'd add) of ministry, because it is a being that brings something new out of what was not. This sense of being—as interconnection that brings the new—would be confirmed even in the natural sciences some fifteen hundred years after the brilliant Cappadocians proposed it. The physicist Rovelli, as we saw above, asserted that the universe is constructed more like kisses—relational events of encounter—than like stones, or static beings.

The Cappadocians showed that being (*ousia*) could share in other beings as hypostasis. God was one *ousia* in three hypostases. As Jenson explains, God is three relational events of identification or, as I'd say, the ministry of three persons so deeply that they are one. Jesus was true God of true God, begotten but not made, one being (*ousia*) with the Father and Spirit, because of a union of hypostasis.[35]

Personhood (*persona*) is a unique—primary—kind of hypostatic being. Human beings are persons; we have being as biological material (this is a kind of *ousia*), but to really be human is to be a person (a radical kind of hypostatic being). It is to be an encounter of sharing. Particles, we've discovered, are hypostatic; they exist through a union. But they're not persons; they may echo a

---

restoration to others." *Theology in Outline*, 82. "Justification is thus 'a mode of deification.' For Luther's strongest language, we again turn to the *Commentary on Galatians*: 'By faith the human person becomes God.'" *Systematic Theology*, 2:296–97.

34. See Aristotle, *Categories*, in *Organon*.

35. "We cannot maintain that hypostasis, as used by the Cappadocian Fathers, simply unfolds into everything that Zizioulas (and others in the twentieth and twenty-first centuries) understands by the notion of person." Andrew Louth, *Modern Orthodox Thinkers: From Philokalia to the Present* (Downers Grove, IL: InterVarsity, 2015), 225. I'm willing to concede this point to Louth, but I think it is fair to build off the Cappadocians for a constructive theology that addresses our secular age.

personal reality but are not personal in themselves. We, however, are. At a core ontological level we need personal forms of sharing (ministry) to be. All children need a caregiver to embrace them in order to exist.[36] We're hypostatic at the deep personal levels of speaking, seeing, and sharing.[37] God too is personal,[38] having God's own hypostatic being as persons in relation—in ministering one to another as Trinity.[39] The God of Israel is personal because he speaks to Moses and Abraham, sees Hagar, and shares in the life and death of Jesus, who is his full incarnation.

God is jealous because God is a personal being of encounter, identifying personally with events of ministry. But while jealous, God is roomy because God is also personal. God is a unique hypostatic being that encounters us

36. Zizioulas explains: "Every person is unique, unprecedented and irreplaceable, even though he exists only through relation with others. The person is the identity born of a relationship, and exists only in communion with other persons. There cannot be a person without relationship to other persons, so if all the relationships which constitute a person disappear, so does that person. We cannot refer to a person without relating them to something else. Therefore, 'Father', 'Son' and 'Spirit' denote unique persons. Yet, if the Father was without relationship to the Son, there would be no Father, and if the Son was without relationship to the Father, there would be no Son." *Lectures in Christian Dogmatics*, 57.

37. I'm following Zizioulas's anthropology here. Louth explains its important ramification for ontology. This kind of ontology bound in personhood is the best way to get to a participatory ontology in specifically a secular age. Louth explains, "In insisting on personhood as an ontological question, [Zizioulas] is making a valid point. There has been a historical tendency to see ontology in terms of the general and the universal—and therefore the impersonal. Metropolitan John's iterated insistence that personhood is also concerned with being, with ontology—that ontology is primarily personal—is important. . . . It is not just what we are that raises ontological concerns, but also the question of who we are." *Modern Orthodox Thinkers*, 224.

38. Here Zizioulas sounds a lot like Jenson, both asserting God's personal nature, through encounter with personhood. Zizioulas says,

> For Israel God is personal. We could say that God was personal in ancient Greek thought, of course, in that the gods are forces given personal characters. However, when we say that God is personal in the Old Testament we mean that he is acknowledged within relationships between persons. He is the God of Abraham, Isaac and Jacob. God can only be understood in relationship with these particular persons whose encounters with God make up the history of Israel and are recounted in Israel's Scripture. He is never a faceless, supreme power, and he cannot be understood in terms of a mind, or a physical force or a rational origin of existence. This does not tell us anything about the nature of God, but it does tell us that God is always related to specific persons. Israel's God is in a constant relationship of persons and he summons man to enter a relationship that is person to person. (*Lectures in Christian Dogmatics*, 42)

39. "God's being is essentially relational; God's being is 'pure relation.' . . . Pure relation thus means relation as becoming itself, but not from itself. But whence does it become? God's self-relatedness is grounded in God's Yes to himself. In this Yes of God to himself God sets himself in relation to himself, in this way to be who he is. In this sense God's being is in becoming. 'Pure relation' can therefore only be the predicate, but never the subject of a statement concerning God." Jüngel, *God's Being Is in Becoming*, 116–17.

through our own hypostasis—our own personhood.[40] Ministry can bring a union of being (returning us, even in a secular age, to a participatory ontology) because it occurs person-to-person, bringing a hypostatic union. Our personal being, which is distinct from God's, is nevertheless hypostatic like God's. (Our hypostasis imagines God's own. We are the creatures who speak and hear—praying animals, as we'll explore in the next chapter.)

It is our hypostasis that allows us access, through God's invitation, into God's being by sharing in God's personal acts of ministry for other persons. God is roomy because God is a distinct hypostatic being that reaches out to our own hypostatic being, inviting us into God's unique hypostasis through ministry. God is roomy because God is happy to allow others into God's being through God's servants' actions of ministry.[41] To receive the gift of ministry is to be saved through person-to-person encounter, a hypostatic union bound in the body of Jesus, who is the event of all dry bones living again.

Anyone who's had a roommate knows the feeling of annoyance that leads you to no longer see your roommate as a person worth sharing in events of speaking. When jealousy has no hypostatic quality and one roommate becomes overly concerned for things like the TV or the security deposit, personhood is lost, making jealousy dark and roominess impossible. But when we share in personhood, a union of transformation is possible. These communions of personhood bring an encounter of being through ministry that bears witness to, even participates in, resurrection. In these unions of ministry, we experience the arriving of God who ministers so deeply to the personhood of Jesus that even death cannot overcome the union. Jesus is eternally and finally the minister who is loose in the world. He ministers to persons up against death.

40. Alasdair McIntyre similarly claims that humanity is fundamentally humanity in relationship, because we are always, ontologically, coming in and out of disability. We are called through the finitude of our bodies to always minister to the disabilities of others or be ministered to in our disabilities—or better yet, in a christological sense be ministered to by those with disabilities. "We need others to help us avoid encountering and falling victim to disabling conditions, but when, often inescapably, we do fall victim, either temporarily or permanently, to such conditions as those of blindness, deafness, crippling injury, debilitating disease, or psychological disorder, we need others to sustain us, to help us in obtaining needed, often scarce, resources, to help us discover what new ways forward there may be, and to stand in our place from time to time, doing on our behalf what we cannot do for ourselves." *Dependent Rational Animals: Why Human Beings Need the Virtues* (Chicago: Open Court, 1999), 73.

41. Jens Zimmerman, drawing from Emmanuel Levinas, says, "For Levinas, God is revealed in the ethical relationship to another human being because 'the very movement that leads to another leads to God.' . . . Levinas himself sees a convergence of Christianity and Judaism in the idea of divine *kenōsis*." *Incarnational Humanism: A Philosophy of Culture for the Church in the World* (Downers Grove, IL: InterVarsity, 2012), 216–17.

Jesus reaches out to Skip's person, calling him by name and sharing in his anxiety. Jesus is present as living action. The old man experiences a song of resurrection coming to his being through the ministry of a young woman giving her person to his as a baby. This hypostatic union brings forth the glory of the resurrection. The living Jesus meets the man on a hill of death, singing him back to life. This is a true manifestation of resurrection.

For the pastor to help her people encounter divine action in a secular age is to invite them to reflect on these encounters of shared personhood. But it is to do more than just reflect. It is to give them the language and imagination to see and claim that Jesus lives and continues to act in these encounters. God is whoever raised Jesus from the dead, because God is the one who fully and completely identifies with Jesus. But for God to fully and completely identify with Jesus—for God to have his identity in and through the events of Jesus's life and death—Jesus must truly live (this is Christopraxis, as I've described in other places). He must continue to act as minister in the world—even on a commuter train in DC.[42] Jenson beautifully makes this point, showing the importance of Jesus's living action in the world: "Socrates, although he remains dead, is still powerful. But if I am surprised by him, this is because of previously inadequate knowledge. Whereas if Jesus lives, he is an agent in my life, and one whom I must expect to act freely, whom I could know perfectly and yet not always anticipate."[43]

The pastor encourages his people to go into the world, not to do good things, but to find this ministering Jesus. Jesus is doing much more than just "good things." Because this Jesus is the resurrection, he turns death into life, making a new way out of no ways, by ministering to persons, calling those in the church to join him. It then is no wonder that it is Jesus who arrives speaking and ministering to Skip. Jesus is alive, loose in the world, as the fullness of God's ministering in the events of our life.

A core focus of pastoral ministry in a secular age is to help people spot in their encounter with persons the concrete presence of the living Jesus. They join Jesus in sharing in personhood as the way of participating in resurrection. This event of shared personhood (of hypostatic unions) draws us deeply into the life of Christ. It makes our very presence in ministry an embodiment of the eschatological promise of resurrection.[44] Because God is whoever raised

---

42. This is to give further unpacking to my position of Christopraxis. See Root, *Christopraxis: A Practical Theology of the Cross* (Minneapolis: Fortress, 2014).

43. Jenson, *Systematic Theology*, 1:198.

44. "Jesus is risen into the future that God has for his creatures. What certain persons saw after his death was a reality of that future. We are now in position to ask the central question: When we assert Jesus' Resurrection, what do we claim about him?" Jenson, *Systematic Theology*, 1:198.

Jesus from the dead, transcendence is *not* something above but something to come in this world.[45] Transcendence breaks into our world. We experience transcendence when we share in personhood through the act of ministry. The encounter with transcendence, seen through the lens of Jesus, is never outside the world but is more deeply within it. God's transcendence ministers to the world as true manifestation, a real taste of coming resurrection. Ministry, most particularly in a secular age, can lead us back to transcendence. Ministry drives us deeper into the world to find divine action, not outside or above the world, but as the promise *within* the world that death itself will be overcome by the ministry of the Father to the Son in the Spirit. It is the living Jesus who meets us in and through our acts of ministry to persons. Our ministry to our neighbor is a promise of, even an encounter with, the fulfillment of the coming resurrection. The event of encountering and sharing in personhood is the unveiling of—and ontological participation in—Jesus's being through the action of his ministry. Through ministry to persons we encounter divine action.

An example: Sharon is an elementary schoolteacher. At her last Bible study she shared this story:

> I had a powerful experience this week, and I'm not sure what to make of it. Tuesday, as I was lining my class up to return from recess, I noticed that Janny wasn't in line. So I went looking for her. I found her curled up on the slide, crying. I knew her dad had just moved out of the family house and her parents were thinking that the marriage was coming to a fast end. So I waved to my student teacher to take the class inside, and I sat at the bottom of the slide and invited Janny to come out. I asked her, "What are you doing hiding?" And she just started to cry. When I saw her tears, my heart broke. I felt called to her, in some way like Jesus was calling to me. But it was weird, because as much as I felt Jesus calling me to share in her sadness, I knew Jesus to be with me. Jesus was joining me, even—and this sounds crazy—acting through me. All of the sudden I felt calm. It was like in the smallest way, but a real way, I was born for this little flitting moment. So I just sat with her and assured her that I wouldn't leave her. I told her that anytime she wanted, we could talk, and that I understood how hard this was but she wasn't alone. Her eyes said more than I could understand, but I had this powerful sense that my words, my presence, mattered. I took her by the hand and we walked back to the classroom. And I know somehow that this was the most important day of my teaching career. Of course, I've accomplished things that may seem more important when it comes to education or whatever, but I couldn't shake how significant this moment felt. And I don't want to. I felt taken into something

45. I was originally pointed to this idea by stellar Norwegian theologian Bard Norheim, whom I've benefitted greatly from knowing and dialoguing with.

bigger. I feel like this little moment mattered, that what I did in the world did something big, even though it was truly so small and so quick. It had to be a God thing. After school, I found myself thinking about it again, and I started crying. That moment of caring for that little girl made my life—my little job in the dog days of flu season—full. Full of God's presence. I guess that's how I'd describe it.

And indeed we can confess that God was present as the divine action of persons encountering persons for the sake of ministry. Even on a recess slide, this moment witnesses to a God who acts to raise Jesus from the dead and promises life out of death.[46]

## But What Form?

Sharon's encounter with Janny gives flesh to Jenson's assertion that God is jealous and roomy by helping us see that jealousy and roominess are bound in person-to-person encounters that produce a hypostatic union. These person-to-person encounters allow the divine to encounter the human through a fellowship of action. This is an encounter with the event of resurrection, for it is through God's hypostatic union with Jesus that dry bones are made to live and death bears the marks of new possibility through union of personhood.

But to help people like Sharon see divine action in a secular age and make sense of such events, we must push a tad deeper and return to Jesus's own ministry. We must ask, What form does this action take? We know it takes the form of ministry, but to get a firmer handle on the kind of action that allows for those ministered to to share in the being of God, we must look at Jesus's ministry.

In Mark 10:45 Jesus claims that he "came not to be served but to serve, and to give his life a ransom for many." Many will enter the roomy being of God, not by bending knee to Jesus, like Jon Snow to Danny Targaryen (*Game of Thrones*, season 7), but by receiving the service of Jesus, by allowing Jesus to wash their feet (John 13:1–17). Peter cannot join in the being of God through Jesus unless he humbles himself to receive the kenotic ministering service

---

46. Nancy Ammerman found this in her empirical study: "Some work is, however, more susceptible to such understandings. What makes it so is not so much the presence or absence of an individual's power to bring spirituality in as the nature and social definition of the work itself. Work that involves service to others lends itself to spiritual enactment even when the individual worker is not exceptionally religious or spiritual." *Sacred Stories, Spiritual Tribes: Finding Religion in Everyday Life* (New York: Oxford University, 2014), 210.

Jesus gives to his person (John 13:8–9).[47] Jesus reveals that ministry constitutes God's being by *being-in-the-world* as servant, *diakonos*.[48]

*Diakonia* and its family of words is hard to translate, with debatable meanings. It clearly has this kenotic sense of lowliness. Many point out its usage around table fellowship. The *diakonos* is a kind of waiter. But John N. Collins has shown that while *diakonia* has this sense, it also has other first-century uses.[49] Collins explains that the word family can also, and probably more primarily, have a sense of responsibility for going between. A *diakonos* is a servant go-between.[50] Collins is brash and polemical in making this point. He argues that the way *diakonia* has been used to frame a form of church ministry focused on charity led by deacons is not biblical. Collins argues vigorously that deacons as charity givers, with no sense of divine action, has been a concession to the immanent frame.

Rather, *diakonia* and its sense of go-between means a form of service—ministry—that seeks to embrace personhood. It enters personhood not through power or forced persuasion but through loving service. This is to be taken into the being of God. *Diakonia* is a form of action taken by Jesus

47. I'm asserting something very similar to Scott Swain, who in explaining Jenson, says, "Jenson's Trinitarian historicism thus takes a specifically Servant form. God participates in Israel's plight as the Servant who undergoes a sin-bearing death and as the Lord who accepts that death as an offering for sin. Israel participates in the divine life by participating in the Servant, the one who dies on Israel's behalf as a member *of* Israel and who is yet distinct *from* Israel as 'one of the Trinity' and therefore as the one who opens filial space *for* Israel in the triune life. Or so, Jenson insists, Israel was taught to hope." *God of the Gospel: Robert Jenson's Trinitarian Theology* (Downers Grove, IL: IVP Academic, 2013), 94.

48. "Those whom we designate as 'ministers' are, in the New Testament, *diakonoi*, Paul's favorite title for Christian leaders, derived from the Greek word for 'service' (1 Cor. 12:4–30). Significantly, it is the root word for 'butler' and 'waiter.' How odd of the church to designate its leaders by so mundane and lowly a term. No pastor rises much higher than being a butler. Yet, in the topsy-turvy ethics of the kingdom, this is as high as anyone rises—a servant of the servants at the Lord's Table (cf. John 13)." William Willimon, *Pastor: The Theology and Practice of Ordained Ministry* (Nashville: Abingdon, 2016), 35.

49. See John N. Collins, *Diakonia Studies: Critical Issues in Ministry* (London: Oxford University Press, 2014); Collins, *Deacons and the Church: Making Connections between Old and New* (Harrisburg, PA: Morehouse, 2002); and Collins, *Diakonia: Re-Interpreting the Ancient Sources* (London: Oxford, 1990).

50. "The *diakonos*-waiter, as much as the *diakonos*-messenger, is a runner, an in-between person or a go-between. A striking reminder of the capacity of contexts to project this connotation is provided in the list of meanings prepared by B. Justus for Rengstorf's concordance of Josephus; these include 'middleman, go-between, messenger.' Also recall, from earlier in this paper, Schweizer's word, 'mediator.' . . . In other words, his role as minister/*diakonos* placed him in an immediate connection with the sphere of the divine and required him to extend the influence of that sphere among as many as might be open to the grace of its illumination. Those who believed had entered into it. His task thereafter, and the believers' own task within this new phase of existence, was to maintain the vital connection and to nurture the new vitality arising out of it." Collins, *Diakonia Studies*, 109, 149.

that allows for the divine to encounter the human and the human to share in the divine. God's ministers are servants, kenotically entering the world to minister to it.[51] Through their mutual service, they participate in the presence of the living God.

Jesus comes into the world as *the minister*, as we said above, because he has come to serve. He is uniquely the suffering servant, who saves not with weapons and dragons but with acts of ministry, with openness to serve the stranger. We encounter this service of Jesus by ministering to one another as servant. Divine action is experienced within our concrete experiences, such as sitting with a fourth grader on a slide.

It is *diakonia* as the shape of ministry that makes encounters like Skip's on the commuter train and Sara Miles's at the communion table coherent. It is only when both enter *diakonia* by feeding the hungry and caring for the broken that their uncanny encounters are given buoyancy in the choppy waters of the cross-pressure of the immanent frame. Their experience only makes sense when they take subsequent (ministerial) action. Through *diakonia*, they are called to go between and experience divine action by sharing in and giving *diakonia*. The pastor in our secular age invites people to tell their tales of person-to-person encounter, showing how they are encounters of ministry, encouraging the community through these stories to act in the world as ministers. The pastor invites people to directly join ministry—to serve others—as the way to spot and understand the movements of divine action in their lives.

---

51. Hans Urs von Balthasar says, "What [kenosis] does mean . . . is that the divine 'power' is so ordered that it can make room for a possible exteriorization, like that found in the Incarnation and the Cross, and can maintain this exteriorization even to the utmost point." *Mysterium Paschale: The Mystery of Easter* (San Francisco: Ignatius, 1970), 29.

# 15

## invisible gorillas
## and the practice of prayer

It seems like a prank, set up like a reboot of MTV's *Punked* or the CW's *The Jamie Kennedy Project*—one of those shows back in the dark days of TV before we entered our golden age. But it isn't. It's actually empirical science. It's rare that a cutting-edge scientific research project needs a gorilla suit, but so it is for Daniel Simons's inattentional blindness experiment. Simons, who teaches at the University of Illinois, researches in a psychological field called visual cognition. You might have seen on YouTube his most well-known experiment; it is popularly called the invisible gorilla.

The idea is simple but reveals consistently profound results. People tend to believe, particularly in our secular age of the immanent frame, that seeing is believing. But Simons shows that we consistently overemphasize what we are able to see. For instance, you'd assume that if you were watching a scene of people walking in a circle passing a basketball, you'd notice if some dude in a gorilla suit randomly walked through the game waving his arms and jumping up and down. That can't be missed. Yet half the participants in Simons's experiment do. People assume at rates over 90 percent that they are *not* the kind of people to miss obvious, right-in-front-of-your-face events. And yet 50 percent do.

The truth is, of course, that if people are looking for the gorilla, anticipating a gorilla arrival, they see the gorilla dancing into the scene every time. But if your attention is somewhere else—for instance, on counting the passes of the basketball—at least half will miss the odd, obvious interloper. That's just how Simons's experiment is set up. Two groups of people, some in white shirts and others in black, pass a basketball between them as they move. The observer is asked to count how many times people in the white shirts touch the ball. Seconds into their counting the gorilla comes walking through. Half the observers are shocked when asked if they saw a gorilla. Most assume there was no such thing and those that saw a gorilla are liars or crazy.

Simons's point is clear: attention is a powerful thing. Our perceptions of reality are contingent on our attention. What we put our focus on is what we see. But this isn't necessarily a defeatist, anti-realist assertion that says that all there is is what our minds make up. In the end, it wasn't that some people were seeing a gorilla, others a unicorn, a few a purple dragon, and the rest nothing at all. But it does mean that the parts of reality that we do see, as fallible human beings, are contingent on our attention. Our societal imaginaries inform what we give our attention to, often framing what we see. Simons's point is that we can and do miss hugely obvious structures within reality when our attention is on something else.

All of part 1 has shown how our shared societal attention has been drawn away from what our ancestors thought was obvious—that a personal God acted and moved in the world. Either this is a liberation from an antiquated belief or we've entered into a unique observation blindness. It is the latter, with some nuance, that Charles Taylor believes. And we've gotten here, he contends, not through the subtracting of outdated modes of belief. We haven't shed superstition like layers on a hot day, moving us into a secular age. Rather, it's been new, additional imaginations that have drawn our attention away from divine action to something else. New, additional attentions in the modern world have led many to simply not see what was once obvious.

In part 1, we saw that the new observations that move our attention away from the obviousness of divine action are disenchantment, a buffered self, a modern moral order of mutual regard, affirmation of ordinary life as market economy, an ethic of authenticity, and a post-Durkheimianism. These realities give us new imaginaries for what is obvious, encouraging our attention to be on immanent things over transcendent realities.

One of the reasons that Simons's experiment works is that people focus so intently on the white shirts that they block out the black. When the gorilla arrives in his black gorilla suit, for many he's missed as just another part of the background. Taylor's point is that these new realities actually have their birth from within societies that once gave complete and pious attention to God. Now attention to God has not so much been eliminated as made into ignorable background content. As Michael Buckley has argued, atheism is like a bacteria that grows off only the organism of theism and the societies of belief. So it isn't that God has been erased from our society (societies that have tried haven't fared very well). God is simply pushed into the background of our attention, leading some to assume that God was never there at all.[1]

This cultural observation blindness Taylor has called "the immanent frame." We all live inside this constructed frame that imposes levels of attention that make divine action questionable, even for those of us who would *never* define ourselves as atheists. We all are happy with God in the background. Taylor's point is that we *all* live in the immanent frame. There is really no way out of it if you live in the West.

This means that we have a shared presumed attention on immanent things. We are encouraged to keep God as background, rarely seeing him move, arrive, and act, because our attention is drawn to the immanent. We presume, unless otherwise convinced, that our day-to-day, moment-to-moment attention should be on natural, material, and rational things. Living in this de facto state of the immanent frame, some of us spin it closed, and yet others, even within its reductions, embrace open takes and find new possibility for spirituality. This freedom for an open take means that older forms of organized religion, for which pastors are responsible at some level, hold no de facto prominence over hiking, sex, mindfulness, money making, and Coachella. They are, for the most part, all equal—as long as they work for you.

In part 1, we showed why being a pastor in the immanent frame is so challenging. Pastors are easily frustrated by their people's observation blindness. A pastor's job is much harder when even well-meaning people's attention is on all sorts of material and natural happenings, leaving God in the background. Most people are not even willing to stop counting the basketball passes—aka their bank accounts, Twitter followers, promotions, or new shoes—to look again at the scene of life to attend to something different or more.

And the pastor's job is made harder because the pastor too lives in the immanent frame. In frustration or confusion—the source of this frustration and confusion often unable to be clearly named—the pastor too has felt the pull to turn her own attention to immanent realities like church budgets, membership rolls, catalogues of programs, and denominational decline. The pastor has observation blindness too, often feeling either shameful or punk rock in admitting it. The more she or her denomination focuses on counting, the more being a pastor has less and less to do with divine action.

1. Buckley, *At the Origins of Modern Atheism* (New Haven: Yale University Press, 1987).

And yet events of God's arriving and speaking, real experiences of divine action, occur, even to surgeons and suicidal boys. Part 2, up to this final chapter, has sought to show that indeed, even in the immanent frame, God arrives. It is just (to push the analogy maybe too far) that God is the gorilla, arriving in acts of ministry that we experience but are blind to see as the arrival of God's being. Therefore, throughout part 2 I've sought to show that God is a minister. We can share in divine action, even in God's speaking, through a fellowship of action, by giving and receiving ministry by sharing in the lives of one another. The focus of part 2 has been to lift up the importance of ministry as the shape of divine action itself. I've tried to help pull our perception of God from the background to the foreground by exploring God's being as the act of ministry in the world. I've sought to return the pastor from being a religious institutional curate to one who leads us into experiences of the ministering God (if there is a hint on what I think the new form of the pastor after Rick Warren might be, it is here).

## Summary List of Insights about Pastoring in the Secular Age

### The Temptation

Now as we come to this book's close, the temptation is to ask for a program, a bullet-pointed to-do list, a new model, or a direct script for how to operationalize this reality in your church. The temptation is to again push divine action to the background and attend to only immanent realities of a profession, wanting the pragmatic—what works!—over encounters with divine being itself.

Yet a major thread of this book is that to give in to such temptation will only lead to more frustration. It will only move us further into an unintended closed spin on pastoral ministry itself, as divine action is lost to our immanent attention. Of course, big questions remain around what kind of church can attend to divine action as the arriving of God as the event of ministry, speaking new life out of death. I've already given some direction for this kind of church in the final chapter of volume 1. And all of volume 3 will focus on a full-blown ecclesiology, which attends to a God who comes to us as the event of ministry through the body of his Son, who is *the* minister. So to end this book, we must avoid the temptation to make a list of "what works," which will only push us further into observation blindness in the immanent frame. Instead, we will conclude by exploring, to echo Hagar, how we can see that our God is a minister who sees.

## The Way of Prayer

There seems to be one clear way to avoid observation blindness, a way even to encounter the event of God's speaking as the direct movement of receiving and giving ministry. This is the way of prayer.[2]

Prayer is something few people in the immanent frame have been taught. To be a pastor is *not* to be an entrepreneur, community organizer, or budding podcast celebrity. To assume this, as we've said, is to concede to the immanent frame and perpetuate observation blindness, conceding that divine action is too opaque to concern ourselves with. Rather, the pastor's vocation, particularly living in a secular age, is to teach people to pray, and to do so *not just* individually but, more primarily, together.[3] It is even the task of the pastor to form her own life around the practice of prayer.

The core pastoral task in the secular age, then, is *not* to build a big enough church that every immanent attention is lodged inside a one-stop shop—that is one strategy that Rick Warren and other megachurch pastors have used. The idea is that if people are passionately attentive, giving all their observation to their child's sports, brewing beer, yoga, or building their portfolio, then if you can capture that attention inside the church, having it as part of the church, you have their attention. And you may, but only by meeting their wants without freeing their attention to see divine action.

2. William Desmond responds to Taylor by also turning to prayer: "In response to Charles Taylor's idea of the immanent frame, Desmond proposes *porosity of prayer* as a symmetric manifestation of the *porosity of being* central to the elaboration of his autonomous thought. William Desmond writes: 'Prayer at heart is not something that we do, prayer is something that we find ourselves in, something that comes to us as finding ourselves already opened to the divine as other to us and yet as in intimate communication with us. The porosity of prayer is the original site of communication between the divine and the human. The moments of grace happen to us in the most intimate and exposed porosity.'" In João J. Vila-Chã, "Towards an Enlargement of the Horizon: Researching the Dialectic of Church and Society," in *Renewing the Church in a Secular Age: Holistic Dialogue and Kenotic Vision*, ed. Charles Taylor, José Casanova, George McLean, and João Vila-Chã (Washington, DC: Council for Research in Values and Philosophy, 2016), 40–41; for the Desmond quote, see "The Porosity of Being: Towards a Catholic Agapeics. In Response to Charles Taylor," in *Renewing the Church*, 291.

3. "Nothing is more fundamental to religion than prayer. . . . Martin Luther declared that religion is 'prayer and nothing but prayer.' The nineteenth-century German theologian Friedrich Schleiermacher wrote that 'to be religious and to pray—that is really one and the same thing.' And Schleiermacher's contemporary, the German poet Novalis, called prayer 'religion in the making.' Richard Rothe, a famous evangelist, added that 'the religious impulse is essentially the impulse to pray' and that nonpraying people are 'religiously dead.' To his disciples Jesus said to 'pray always without becoming weary' (Luke 18:1)." John F. Haught, *The New Cosmic Story: Inside Our Awakening Universe* (New Haven: Yale University Press, 2017), 189; the citations are from Friedrich Heiler, *Prayer: A Study in the History and Psychology of Religion*, trans. and ed. Samuel McComb (New York: Oxford University Press, 1932), iv–v.

A more faithful—and realistic—option is to simply, but profoundly, teach people to pray, so that instead of buying up their immanent attentions, we can together as a community take on a broader purview that is open to see the movements of divine action coming in and through the encounter of persons in ministry.

To be a pastor, then, is simply to be one who prays and teaches others to do the same. For all the tension we feel in the secular age, and its making of divine action opaque, prayer simply but profoundly directs the pastor's attention back to divine action. It might seem simple, too stripped down, we assume, for the complications of our secular age; we feel the temptation to find some model or strategy outside divine action. But while it is true that prayer may be simple at the level of human action, it is anything but when viewed from the level of divine action. To say that the pastor is the one who prays and teaches others to pray is to say that the pastor leads her people into addressing and being addressed by a speaking God, sharing in the person of Jesus, who prays for the world and teaches his disciples to do the same through the Spirit (Luke 11:1–13). Jesus invites these disciples to pray using the intimate name for God: Abba (Mark 14). In prayer, we come to see that this God is a minister who shares in our lives by caring for us.

The fact that God invites us to pray using his intimate name reveals that God is personal, wanting to share in us by entering into discourse with us.[4] Personal beings share in one another through discourse, through events of communication. These events of communication—telling someone you love them, hate them, pick them, miss them—are some of the deepest events that press in on our being and form our identity. There are events that impact us without words, like car crashes or earthquakes, but it is rare that even these events can be remembered without language. The events that we identify with and that make our identity are usually events bound in discourse, in communication.[5] It is an amazing fact—and one that stands in opposition to the closed spin of the immanent frame—that the most central events that make us are immaterial words. Your life is transformed when someone looks in your eyes and says, "I love you." Even a written note that says, "Yes, I feel the same," can transform your life. The note encompasses a reality much larger than the simple material form of paper and lines. These words constitute a reality that transforms being.

4. Robert W. Jenson makes prayer so central he builds his theological anthropology around it, claiming we are the unique animals who pray. See *Systematic Theology: The Triune God* (Oxford: Oxford University Press, 1997), 2:59–80.

5. This is to draw on Charles Taylor's latest work, *The Language Animal: The Full Shape of the Human Linguistic Capacity* (Cambridge, MA: Harvard University Press, 2016).

Because God is a speaking God, we are invited to pray. Prayer is central only because God speaks, sees, and hears. As a matter of fact, it is often, even in our secular age, those who pray who hear God speak.[6] This of course could be proof that believers are deluded. Or, following Simons, it could be that reality is larger than our perceptions, and so taking on practices that broaden our attention can disclose new dimensions to reality itself. Prayer is the broadening of our attention on the world around us, looking again for the arriving of God, who announces himself by speaking to us, calling us to pray for others in and through our actions of ministry for them. Jesus is *the* minister because he prays for us. God is so fully a speaking God of ministry that he is the never-ending discourse of the Father and Son through the Spirit in prayer.[7]

Prayer disconnects our attention from false gods, not with a ruler to the hand or mocking condemnation, but in and through the ethos of ministry itself. Jesus prays for us because he is our minister who loves us. It is prayer in the immanent frame that leads us to again hear God's speaking. It is prayer that is the direct, embodied action of ministry that sends us to our neighbor to share in their personhood. It is in praying with and for our neighbor, especially our enemy (Matt. 5:44), that we encounter the arriving God "who brings a new way out of no way" through ministry.

Prayer not only reveals God as personal but also shows God to be ontologically a minister. God invites our prayers to impact his being by addressing and directing God's action. When we pray for another, we ask God, who is a minister, to come and minister to this other person in need. God is so deeply a minister that he is willing to leave his action open, responding to our own petitionary prayers for ministry.[8] God is such a deep movement of ministry

6. T. M. Luhrmann's research seems to back this up. See *When God Talks Back: Understanding the American Evangelical Relationship with God* (New York: Vintage, 2012).

7. "Prayer is the actuality of faith; therefore the pattern of this address to God is a defining structure of the specific faith of Jesus' disciples: we approach God as maturing children approach a loving and just father, daring to do so because we come together with one who is native to such sonship. The church is the community that, because the Father has raised Jesus to confirm his sonship, accepts Jesus' invitation as she finds it in the Gospels to pray to the Father with the Son—and just so in their Spirit—and indeed shapes all her life to that pattern. That the church 'finds its model, its origin and its end in the mystery of the one God in three persons' is historically founded in Jesus' affiliation of his disciples with his personal address to God." Jenson, *Systematic Theology*, 2:184–85, citing Joint Roman Catholic–Orthodox Commission, *The Mystery of the Church and the Eucharist in the Light of the Mystery of the Holy Trinity* (Munich report, 1982), ii.2.

8. Jenson explains, "The criterion of the triune God's self-identity is Jesus, just in his openness to his fellow human beings. Therefore, that God listens to us and responds to us, far from being a condescension, is the very way he is faithful to himself. God is not God in spite of changing his mind, in spite of answering prayer or failing to do so; he is God because he does

that when our own prayers for ministry are heaped on another in love, God cannot help but arrive and minister to the one receiving prayer as the event of ministry. Pray constitutes a space in and through our bodies and minds to receive the being of God through his action of ministry.

Because God is a minister, God answers prayers, for prayer is the personal encounter of speaking bound as an event of ministry. God is present when we pray because God is a minister who speaks and sees. Our petitionary prayers free us from observation blindness because they direct us to see by participating in ministry. We stop counting and start tending to personhood as we together as a community pray for the world and one another.

When we pray for and with others we open ourselves to divine action that is ministry. Prayer for and with others is the most central way to encounter the being of God, for it most directly wears the marks of ministry.[9] And inside ministry we come up against the being of the God who is a minister. To prepare our people to encounter the being of God, in and through encounters of ministry in their death experiences, is to teach people to pray together in community as the way to narrate events that press and form their identity. The church is the house of ministry because it is a place of prayer. The pastor prepares his people for ministry by teaching them to pray, by creating space for his people to pray for others and be prayed for. We receive the being of God through giving and receiving ministry. Prayer is the most directed, embodied way to live out of the disposition of giving and receiving. As we together receive communion and the Word preached, we pray, knitting together the events that make up each of our individual stories into our shared story and bringing them before God.

### The Dangers

To say that God is a minister who is present as the event of ministry, and therefore to assert that God is freely open to come ministering to the persons we pray for, doesn't mean that prayer is a magical incantation or instrument that guarantees that if we have the right words and body position God will arrive. God is free to arrive, speaking when and to whom God wishes. Being a pastor, particularly in a secular age, will always be hard, for never can the

---

and can do such things wholeheartedly. Operatively unabashed petitionary prayer is the one decisively appropriate creaturely act over against the true God." *Systematic Theology*, 1:222.

9. Andrew Louth echoes this: "This suggests several things. First of all, this is the language of prayer in the Christian tradition: prayer understood not just as petition, asking God for things, but prayer as engagement with God, an engagement that takes place through the 'three ways' of purification, illumination, and perfection or deification." *Modern Orthodox Thinkers: From Philokalia to the Present* (Downers Grove, IL: IVP Academic, 2015), 3.

pastor control God, releasing him like a gated puppy. Rather, the pastor teaches her people to pray because God's arriving, while sure, is uncontrollable. Prayer is our most trusted way to step back, turning attention away from other observations to seek the action of God in and through ministry. And this in itself is the challenge: to connect prayer with the giving and receiving of ministry. When prayer becomes disconnected from ministry—the eternal praying of Jesus to the Father through the Spirit for us[10]—it oddly can become disconnected from divine action, because it is absent the seeking for participation in the very being of God.

Inside the immanent frame, some pastors have used a focus on prayer as a way to double down on observation blindness and seek an odd superstition in achieving success (or rescue) in the immanent frame. From *The Prayer of Jabez* to the prosperity gospel, prayer has been wrongly seen as a way to continue to focus on the immanent acts of counting dollars, possessions, and followers while insuring yourself against bad luck. This is not really prayer but wishful thinking cased in religious language. Even if not pushed this far, prayer disconnected from ministry becomes a self-serving positivity strategy without God—a true waste of time. This is particularly true for those who believe that prayer is just yearning for luck and who consider themselves brave enough to face the world without this childish charm. In other words, this kind of flat prayer makes atheism seem the logical, grown-up position.

To teach people to pray is to call them into ministry; it is to pray together in and through the acts of ministry. Prayers of thanksgiving and praise are for the arriving of God as minister. Prayer is never abstract, even in the form of praise. We praise God not as a metaphysical force, heralding attributes disconnected from God's arriving action in the world—from encounter with

---

10. There is not room to do justice to the trinitarian element of prayer and particularly to articulate the work of the Spirit in praying. So T. F. Torrance's words will have to do: "It is that Spirit who continues to echo in our stammering prayers on earth the compassionate intercession, the sympathetic intervention of Christ when he came to shoulder the whole burden of our sin, and bear it upon his own heart before God that we might be forgiven and healed. Therefore we are also justified in looking back to this ministry of Christ before the cross to provide us with our understanding of how even now (*mutatis mutandis*) he ever lives to intercede for us, bearing upon his own heart before God all our needs and burdens." *Incarnation: The Person and Life of Christ* (Downers Grove, IL: IVP Academic, 2008), 137. John V. Taylor adds, "That is why prayer addressed to the Holy Spirit is unknown in the Bible and rare in the prayers of the early church. Prayer *in* the Spirit, not *to* the Spirit, is the pattern of the New Testament. He is 'a Spirit that makes us sons, enabling us to cry "Abba! Father!" In that cry the Spirit of God joins with our spirit in testifying that we are God's children' (Rom. 8.15, 16). So, however close I feel God to be—nearer to me, as Luther said, than I am to myself—the Spirit is closer still. I am not, of course, speaking of space but of relation." *The Go-Between God: The Holy Spirit and the Christian Mission* (London: SCM, 1972), 43–44.

events.[11] Rather, in prayer we praise God for his faithfulness as minister, for the ways he's acted for us by ministering to us. In prayer we praise God not as a disconnected deity but as the God who freed Israel from Egypt and resurrected Jesus from the dead.

Praise is remembering and speaking again events of God's arriving to minister to the world (this is why it is impossible to take communion or receive the preached Word without prayer). The pastor's job is to invite the community, through both Scripture and testimony, to pray by praising God for events of his arrival, for the concrete ways God has ministered to us. The pastor must preach the story of the exodus, for instance, as the prayer of our remembering God's ministry. But the pastor must also give opportunity to retell, and therefore remember, the event of God's action for actual congregation members who encounter God's arriving in events of forgiveness, healing, and peace.

A church that worships isn't just a community that repeats a liturgy; but as liturgy it rehearses, remembers, and retells the ancient and present arrival of God to minister. Our praise is for the events of God's action. Our praise, then, is ever close to, essentially fused with, our thanksgiving. We praise God for calling Sharon into ministry to Janny. In prayer we thank God that Jesus arrived on a commuter train to free Skip from the wilderness of his anxiety. We remember, in prayer, that God called Hagar to minister to Sarah, and that God arrived in the wild, calling Moses into ministry through his anxiety and doubt.

This means that prayer and storytelling are connected. The pastor who prays and teaches people to pray does so by creating space for storytelling. But this isn't *The Moth* brought to church—though we might learn a lot from the cultural genre. Rather, this storytelling is prayer; it is the rehearsing of events of ministry.[12] Storytelling as prayer is necessary because the temptation is always there to assume that prayer is insurance from bad luck—that prayer is just for *me*.

There is actually no such thing as solitary, individual prayers completely disconnected from others. Because prayer is ministry in and through the discourse

---

11. "What differentiates the worship of God from a religious relation to impersonal deity is that God must be spoken to. It is therefore decisively characteristic of Israel's faith that her prayers are lavishly documented in her scripture, and that the dominating content of that prayer is recitative reply to the Lord's historical and this verbal agency." Jenson, *Systematic Theology*, 1:80.

12. Eugene Peterson says this about storytelling: "The storytelling pastor differs from the moralizing pastor in the same way that a responsible physician differs from a clerk in a drugstore. . . . The pastor begins this work, then, not so much as a storyteller, but as one who believes that there is a story to be told, the curiosity to be attentive to the life of another, and the determination to listen through the apparently rambling digressions until a plot begins to emerge. . . . The purpose of the pastor is to assist in assembling all the relevant reality, which includes God, and then to encourage the telling of the story coherently." *Five Smooth Stones for Pastoral Work* (Grand Rapids: Eerdmans, 1992), 85, 88, 92.

of the speaking of persons, it is always a relational reality. Individuals cannot pray—and when we try, our prayers become for prosperity and protection for the things we count.

But when we tell our stories of wilderness, those experiences that assure us that we are but dry bones, we confess that we are persons needing the personhood of others and of God to come minister to us by praying for us.[13] It is persons who pray. The pastor should encourage people to pray alone, in moments of mediation and silence. But what is more important, particularly in our secular age, is to pray together. We need to be prayed for and to pray for others. We need to tell our stories of God's seeming absence and coming presence as minister.

The church service is often assumed to be boring because we've forgotten that we are only there to pray for one another and the world. And because of this, the pastor has exhortation to do. She must remind her people over and over again that to pray, particularly through their stories, is to come before God. It will always be easy in an immanent frame, where we are free from the fear of demons and devils, to allow prayer to slide into observation blindness. The pastor's job as the one who teaches people to pray is to exhort them, *not* to fear demons and darkness, but to really seek. She encourages them to step back and pray their stories as a way to see God arriving. And prayer prepares them to go into the world to enter ministry and encounter this living God. The pastor who prays and teaches others to pray is seeker sensitive.[14] But the seeker sensitivity that she attends to is divine action through ministry. She prepares her people to see, and to continue to seek, by receiving and giving prayer.

### Tuesdays, as an End

Throughout part 1, we looked at detailed examples of pastors who fit and participated in the dimension of the secular age I was describing. As we come to the end of this project, it is only fair for me to provide an example of a pastor who has sought divine action in our secular age as the one who prays and teaches others to pray. This pastor is Eugene Peterson.

13. Nancy Ammerman found this in her own study, saying, "When there are shared narratives about the availability of divine power to change the world, human action is often changed accordingly. Far from suppressing agency in deference to otherworldly solutions, as social movement research makes clear, shared spiritual stories have this-worldly power." *Sacred Stories, Spiritual Tribes: Finding Religion in Everyday Life* (New York: Oxford University Press, 2014), 293.

14. Charles Taylor also thinks that seeking is key in our secular age; see "The Church Speaks—To Whom?," in *Church and People: Disjunctions in a Secular Age*, ed. Charles Taylor, Jose Casanova, George McLean, and Joao Vila-Cha (Washington, DC: The Council for Research in Values and Philosophy, 2012).

In his memoir, *The Pastor*, Peterson explains that he was a few years into planting and pastoring his church when he was invited to spend his Tuesdays at the county's Department of Health Services. As the county was growing, it was becoming more and more common for social and mental health issues to arise. Taking initiative, the county gathered the local clergy, offering to train them in dealing with all sorts of issues like passive-aggressive neuroses, alcoholism, depression, and more. All the clergy agreed that this would be helpful. And for the next two years they gathered on Tuesdays for training.

Yet in the middle of this, Peterson had a sinking feeling. While this training promised to help his pastoral ministry take on the growing edge of professional skill and scientific know-how, it also changed his perception of his people. Learning all of these diagnoses led him to see them more as problems needing the cure of medical intervention than as persons receiving and giving ministry.

The immanent frame, while seeming to provide helpful new skills, was dissolving his pastoral identity. He remained thankful for Tuesday meetings; they gave him perspective and networks to which to refer people in need. But the paradigm alone couldn't anchor and support the calling of a pastor. Peterson says, "Tuesdays, besides helping me be a better good Samaritan in my community (a good thing), also introduced me to ways I could be useful to my congregation that would satisfy them without having to deal seriously with God or with themselves as children of God (a bad thing)."[15]

The need for a deeper pastoral identity became clear when, a year later, Peterson visited Marilyn in the hospital. Marilyn was in her mid-twenties, was married, had a new job as a lawyer, and hadn't been at Peterson's church long. She was now getting tests for some ailment they couldn't pinpoint. As Peterson sat with her, she explained that the doctor couldn't find any physical source of her symptoms and was wondering if they might be psychological. Peterson knew what he was to do next. His training on Tuesdays told him that this was the opening to launch into the mode of professional healer. But he was stuck. He'd become aware that this service-providing focus had made the pastoral task coldly immanent. He said nothing. He beat himself up for weeks for being struck mute.

A month later, Peterson visited Marilyn again, this time in her home. She explained that she thought her doctor might be right, so she'd made an appointment with a psychiatrist. Now having the opening for doctor-savior filled, Peterson felt an odd freedom, so he asked, "Is there anything you want me to do?"

15. Peterson, *The Pastor: A Memoir* (San Francisco: HarperOne, 2011), 137.

This question is a profound one. Being near Marilyn's death experience, just showing up and anticipating the arrival of God, Peterson became most fully her pastor. Taking the form of a servant (*diakonos*) and hearing her story, he asked, "Is there anything you want me to do?" *Is there any way I can minister to you?*

To his surprise, Marilyn responded, shyly. "Yes. I've been thinking a lot about it. Would you teach me to pray?" Would you teach me, she was asking, to see divine action? Would you be my pastor and help me to see that indeed God sees me?

This was a breakthrough. Peterson says, "I had been a pastor . . . for three years. It was the first time anyone had asked me to teach them to pray. Marilyn's shy request gave . . . a focus that I had come to believe was at the very center of my pastoral vocation."[16]

Peterson continues: "Up until then I had concluded that prayer was not something for which there was much of a market. Wanting to serve my congregation on their terms, I kept my prayers to myself and did what I was asked. Marilyn's 'Would you teach me to pray?' was a breakthrough."[17]

And so Peterson taught not only Marilyn but many more in his congregation to pray. He no longer kept his prayers to himself, and he found a new sense within him of what it meant to be a pastor. Being a pastor who prayed and taught others to pray formed and directed his life. Never did it lead to a private jet, huge network, or one-hundred-acre property with a massive church building filled with suburbanites. Yet it did lead to a joyous resolve to face the secular age and encounter, again and again, the presence of the living God.

Peterson says, "An inner resolve began forming within me: I was not going to wait to be asked anymore. In the secularizing times in which I am living, God is not taken seriously. God is peripheral. God is nice (or maybe not so nice) but not at the center." Peterson sees clearly the challenge the pastor faces as the secular age makes divine action opaque. But Marilyn's question led him to recognize that even in our secular age, or perhaps *because of it*, we must turn our attention to divine action. Prayer is the most concrete way to do so. He continues, "But if I am going to stay true to my vocation as a pastor, I can't let the 'market' determine what I do. I will find ways to pray with and for people and teach them to pray. . . . I'm not going to wait to be asked. I am a pastor."[18]

May God bless all pastors who seek this living God who freed Israel from Egypt and Jesus from the grave. May God meet you in this secular age.

16. Peterson, *The Pastor*, 142.
17. Peterson, *The Pastor*, 142.
18. Peterson, *The Pastor*, 142.

# index